*f*P

Also by Ian Kelly

Cooking for Kings:
The Life of Antonin Carême, the First Celebrity Chef

BEAU BRUMMELL

The Ultimate Man of Style

IAN KELLY

FREE PRESS

New York   London   Toronto   Sydney

FREE PRESS
A Division of Simon & Schuster, Inc.
1230 Avenue of the Americas
New York, NY 10020

For information about special discounts for bulk purchases,
please contact Simon & Schuster Special Sales:
1-800-456-6798 or business@simonandschuster.com

Manufactured in the United States of America

1   3   5   7   9   10   8   6   4   2

Library of Congress Cataloging-in-Publication Data
is available.

ISBN-13: 978-0-7432-7089-2
ISBN-10:   0-7432-7089-4

For Oscar

Much more than the cult of the individual, Romanticism inaugurated the cult of the personality.

Albert Camus

Contents

CONTENTS

Author's Note

The name Brummell exists with two widely recognized spellings: with one l and two. Because Brummell's first French biographer in the 1840s used a single l, this has been the form most often used in America as in France. George Brummell himself, however, signed his name with two ls, and it is also the spelling in his baptismal record and is used therefore throughout this book.

Money conversions over time are notoriously unreliable. It is traditional to gain a working equivalent of an 1800 sum in the early twenty-first century by multiplying by between sixty and eighty. Brummell's £30,000 fortune on coming of age in 1799 may thus be calculated as equivalent to between £1.8 million and £2.4 million or nearly $5 million today. This calculation bears no relation—as instances—to house prices, staff wages or common foodstuffs, but can hold for some luxury goods. Brummell's house in London recently went on the market at nearly $4 million, which would have eaten all Brummell's money by the usual calculation, but he *was* paying about a sixtieth of the current value of a Savile Row suit for his bespoke outfits. Meanwhile, Brummell's wealth is set against a period of European boom-and-bust, periods of inflation and fluctuating exchange rates. An important undertow of Brummell's story is the effect of the French Revolution and the Napoleonic Wars on Anglo-French exchange rates, and the economic self-confidence of the burgeoning British Empire, which found a visual expression in one exportable art form: men's fashion. At the same time Brummell's ability to support himself in France on a fraction of his London capital was predicated on the strength of the pound against a French currency shaken by the Revolution and the Napoleonic Wars.

Prologue

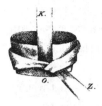

Nothing was lacking. Lustres, candelabra, candles, masses of flowers; and he himself, in the blaze of all the lights, stood in the centre, expectant.

Count d'Aurevilly at Brummell's last soiree

When the Allies took Caen after the D-day Normandy landings in June 1944 they entered a city of rubble. The ancient capital of Lower Normandy and the stronghold of the Twelfth and Twenty-first German Panzer Divisions had suffered a month of bombardment by British and Canadian heavy artillery and 2,500 tons of RAF bombs. The eighteenth-century heart of the Île St. Jean—the area leading up to the German HQ in the château—was destroyed. Canadian tanks plowed straight from the pontoon bridge over the River Orne and right through the ruins of the old town. "Andy's Alley"—as the tank road to the château became known—flattened whatever had been left standing in its path: houses, shops, cafés and hotels.

Caen had been the jewel of the Normandy coast, a city built on a river island, with two royal abbeys and a wealth of bourgeois townhouses in honey-colored stone. Its many English visitors said the city reminded them of Oxford. Andy's Alley cut through Caen's destroyed center, across the place Dauphine, and the rue des Carmes. The tanks plowed on past the ruins of the Salon Littéraire and straight through the dining room of the bombed-out Hôtel d'Angleterre on the rue St. Jean. An American soldier later took a photograph of the hotel, blown open to the winds, which was sold as a postcard souvenir to the GIs. Here, a hundred years before, George Brummell—once the most fashionable foreigner in France—had held soirees for passing English aristocrats. As the tanks rolled by under three stories of flayed hotel rooms, the wallpaper of Brummell's room flapped in the breeze.

~

The year 1839. Room 29 was at the top of the Hôtel d'Angleterre, overlooking the slate roof tiles of Caen. Georgiana, Duchess of Devonshire, en route to Paris with her daughter, was the first guest to admire the view, and within minutes room 29 was pressed with Monsieur Brummell's other friends: the poet Byron, the old playwright Sheridan, the Duke of Wellington and Prince Frederick, Duke of York with Princess Frederica of Prussia.

Fichet, the hotel owner's son, was used to the metropolitan glamour that still clung to the hotel's most famous resident: it fell to Fichet to attend Monsieur Brummell when he was holding one of his soirees. Brummell had taught him how to announce royalty and how much obeisance was expected by the victor of Waterloo, and Monsieur Brummell had taught Fichet about clothes. It was Fichet, also, who acted as valet to the hotel's celebrated dandy and wit, helping him into his evening coat and handing him the whitest of cravats with the reverence of a sacristan.

Yet these soirees would end suddenly and in the same way. One moment, Brummell would hold out his arm to escort the Duchess of Devonshire across the room; the next, his eyes were opened to the reality around him. The room was empty. There was nothing in front of him but the candles, the flowers and the young Frenchman with pity in his eyes. Fichet eventually became inured, he said, to the dark pantomime of announcing Brummell's ghosts: the long-dead duchesses and courtesans, the Regency celebrities who had been Monsieur's friends. But he dreaded the moment when Brummell woke from his masquerade and saw the reality around him: the ruination of his fame and fortune and of his mind. "Babylon in all its desolation," as one friend of Brummell's said, "was a sight less awful." The Frenchman would then blow out the candles, shut the windows and leave Beau Brummell—the most sociable man in London—to the complete privacy, and the utter silence, of his ruined mind.

~

The Canadian soldiers were met with silence as they entered Caen in 1944. The German garrison had fled by cover of night and most of the French population, who had left weeks before when news had reached them of the landings on the Normandy beaches, were sheltering on the outskirts of the city in an eighteenth-century asylum. The nuns, the orphans, the blind, deaf and confused who lived in the Hôpital du Bon Sauveur joined the city refugees in digging up the asylum's flower beds as mass graves for Caen's dead. Stray bombs fell as they worked, destroying some of the garden pavilions where insane gentlefolk had been incarcerated a century before. But the asylum, and its detailed archives of the mentally ill, miraculously survived.

BEAU BRUMMELL

INTRODUCTION

Intimacy with royalty is not for the fainthearted, nor is early fame. Exposure to the false sun of monarchy and publicity have parallel dangers, the light source being in the hands of the capricious and ungoverned. George "Beau" Brummell was chosen as *chevalier d'honneur* (best man) at the royal wedding of the Prince and Princess of Wales in 1795 when still in his teens and was described as the most famous and influential man in London while only in his early twenties, at the center of what amounted to a personality cult. Yet he was to suffer the withdrawal of royal patronage and also, in later life, the withdrawal of what was, to him, the oxygen of publicity and public adoration. He would lose his fortune, and his mind. As a result, though his name is linked to the invention of the suit, the collar and tie and modern trousers, history's foremost social climber could also be seen as the first public figure, the first "celebrity" (a term he knew and used almost in its current sense) to set the now familiar celebrity pattern of a dramatic fall from grace. Meanwhile his acute consciousness of fashion combined with his particular brand of sexual elusiveness—his public persona was rakishly heterosexual although his love life was the subject of intrigued speculation—has led to him being dubbed, more recently, "the first metrosexual."

He might have been remembered simply as the first commoner ever to play a central role in a royal circle in England without being bedfellow to the monarch. He might have been remembered as a witty, well-dressed upstart, one model for his friend Lord Byron's *Don Juan* and later for Pushkin's *Onegin*—a man who made his reputation first in the barrack rooms of the Prince of Wales's own cavalry regiment and who might have gone on to fortune in government or commerce with the advantage of a title bestowed by his boon companion, the later King George IV. Several of Britain's leading aristocractic families can trace their titles in similar manner to that dubious distinction of being the king's, queen's or regent's "favourite," like Brummell. But nothing so familiar to historians awaited George Bryan Brummell. His fame eclipsed even that of his royal master, and his personal cult was described as so bizarre and alarming by his contemporaries it is reasonable to posit him not only as a key personality in the first anonymous metropolis, Regency London, but as the first truly modern celebrity. Moreover he used this fame and influence in a manner that has secured his unique place in the history of Western culture: he taught modern men how to dress. People copied what he wore, how he spoke, even how he shaved. Tobacconists sold out of his favored ranges of snuff, and clubs and dances were judged on his attendance or participation. Tailors gave him their goods simply for the honor, or publicity, of his wearing them, in a manner immediately familiar in our own celebrity- and fashion-obsessed age. The decimation of the beaver population of North America in the nineteenth century was set in motion by his sudden taste for beaver-skin top hats, and the style of dress for modern men—and women—has never been the same since he created and made fashionable the sculptured, urban look that became the suit. But fortune did not shine on him for long, for all that his name has carried on as a byword for style, elegance and excess. By his late thirties he had gambled away his fortune, publicly insulted the powerful prince regent and was set on a downward trajectory of depression and self-delusion that would lead to the ultimate horror of the age: an asylum.

How was it possible for a boy born in a servants' attic in Downing Street, the grandson of a valet and the son of a courtesan, to find himself the most envied man in London and the begetter of a fashion revolution, the consequences of which dictate the way we dress and, to an extent, behave to this day? Was his dramatic downfall the necessary second act to his early fame? Is it true, as later French philosophers claimed, that the independently self-fashioned Brummell and his followers, known as the dandies, signaled a revolutionary age and the death of kings just as surely as the guillotine or the Declaration of Independence? Who was George Bryan Brummell, the man known to his contemporaries simply as "the Beau"?

Brummell's life spans a transformation in fashion, but also in Anglo-Saxon culture and in the history of London, a crucial period in the making of modern manners and masculinity. He came to symbolize a new attitude in response to the novel urban landscape. He was indifferent to politics, above the vagaries of fashion, sought only to be envied and to make people laugh and accrued around his person a cult based on his perceived personality. He was a celebrity in the first age when such a term was used. Brummell refused to take anything very seriously, including, enormously to his credit, himself. As he admitted to Lady Hester Stanhope, the chatelaine of 10 Downing Street, "If the world is so silly as to admire my absurdities, you and I may know better, but what does that signify?" But if he was willing to dismiss his absurdities, a roll call of writers and artists, as well as Lady Hester, line up to insist we should not. Lord Byron, William Thackeray, Thomas Carlyle, Benjamin Disraeli, Charles Baudelaire, Honoré de Balzac, Albert Camus, Edith Sitwell, Max Beerbohm, Oscar Wilde and Virginia Woolf have all felt drawn to reference Brummell in their understanding of the modern mind and manners. As one more recent essayist insists:

If three things sum up our age, they are science and technology, neoliberal economics, and an infatuation with fashion and style. To understand the science [and economics] you must know . . . Darwin and . . . Adam Smith. To understand fully the importance of style and fashion and the instincts on which they rest, [an understanding of] Brummell is essential. . . . The cult of celebrity, preoccupation with appearance, the new dandyism amongst men, the importance of "attitude," the studied ironies of the post-modern era—all have their fore-echo in the astonishing [man].

But long before our time, indeed within a few years of Brummell's death, an amateur French philosopher, Count Jules Amédée Barbey d'Aurevilly, was arguing that Brummell was instructive *not* in his achievements—as if fashion, manners and style were not in the realm of achievement—but rather he was instructive *"in his person."*

The person of Brummell presents several paradoxes. Centrally intriguing is his sexuality. Even were it true—and it turns out it is very much *untrue*—that he was a sexless aesthete, "cold, heartless and satirical," as one famous courtesan said—his image and legacy are intensely sexualized. They exist in the mirror of male sexual vanity: how we dress, act, present ourselves and interact with women and other men. Brummell was the central figure, and the term is apposite, in a new London "look" that drew on some of the more obviously sexual aspects of Augustan art but developed into the suit for modern city life. The way men began to dress because of Brummell was an arresting corollary to the sea change in attitudes toward masculinity, and the debate over gentlemanly behavior that reverberates in the novels of Jane Austen as much as the politics of the Enlightenment. It was a challenging time for men, a time when manners and codes of conduct were changing, as they are today. For some, especially in London, it was also a sexually licentious age, and the fashions for both women and men reflected this. Women flaunted their bodies and so did men. Brummell was intensely scrutinized by men and by women—"the most admired man of all the belles and beaux of Society"—and his fame was closely allied with a reimagining of masculinity. So it is hardly surprising that his love life was a subject for prurient conjecture at the time and subsequently—as, indeed, would be the case for a modern celebrity.

4

Even within his own lifetime, Brummell's name attracted stories and ideas that related more to his fame or notoriety than to the truth. It was commonly believed that he had brought the censure of the prince regent on his head by lounging on an ottoman in Carlton House and demanding of his royal host, "Wales! Ring the bell!" This incident never happened, but Brummell's attempts to deny the story were in vain. Like a modern celebrity, his image—of an insouciant, audacious, stylish brat—had a power of its own that overcame truth. His elegant profligacy was at such a scale that it promoted exaggerations and fictions. He did take hours to dress. He did change his shirt linens with a regularity that shocked contemporaries, though it might not us. He did squander more money in a single night than most of his countrymen would earn in a lifetime. He did ask the prince regent's companion, "Who's your fat friend?" and did declaim languorously when asked if he ate vegetables that he believed he "may once have eaten a pea." Like Oscar Wilde, whose fame secured him an American tour even before his West End successes, Brummell was renowned as a metropolitan wit long before his personal style was copied by Londoners, Parisians and then by urbane men the world over.

One aspect of Brummell's story is the style he made famous. Though George Brummell was known as a dandy, he would not have been pleased to be recognized as such in the sense the word is used today. For Brummell the aphorism that "less is more" might have been invented. He once said "If John Bull [Everyman] turns around to look at you, you are not well dressed; but either too stiff, too tight, or too fashionable." Once he created his style, he stuck to it. This in itself could be said to have been a stance against fashion as currently understood. To the modern mind he was an antidandy. Nevertheless, Brummell was a catalyst and a role model in a fashion revolution, in which men turned their backs on highly decorative dress and took to nuances of cut, fit and proportion—in keeping with a revolutionary, neoclassical age—to express status, strength and sensitivity. His rules of dress have dominated male power dressing ever since. Without Brummell there would be no suit, for men or women, or tailoring in the Savile Row, Wall Street or Chanel sense. He was unorthodox in the way he created the tailored look that has developed out of his style. However, he was that recognizable type: the maverick who created rules. From where those rules, colors and ideas came is one theme in Brummell's life: the collage of Eton colors, military cloth, Hussar trousers, neoclassical aesthetics and the influence of the sexually flamboyant West End. It is a public story but also a very personal one. Brummell became a symbol for a new mode of urbane masculinity, even though his masculinity was possibly the most complex, troubled and compelling aspect of his personality.

The first legacy of Brummell's unusual life is therefore simply fashion. Many details have changed over the years and the classic men's fashion of today, or even of Edwardian England, might seem a world away from Brummell's Mr. Darcy look, yet in principle things remained the same. Through the nineteenth century a structured, sculptural style for men developed out of Brummell's look, in monochrome and military fabrics, that became the uniform for modern man: the urban style of men in black. The governing shape of men's attire remained the classical body, and the reputation of London's tailors grew in accordance with their abilities to remold a figure into the more idealized form made fashionable by Brummell. This style had universal appeal. Men looked powerful, serious and of singular, unified intent, in marked contrast to the fashions for Victorian women. There had been seriousness and sobriety of color in men's fashions before, but the Brummell aesthetic, as it related to clothes, matched well the nineteenth-century male concerns: respectability, homogeneity and Mammon. Like Georgian architecture, neoclassical tailoring has achieved longevity in its fusion of function, form and fashion, of simple craft principles and antique ideals.

The real power of Brummell's genius—or the genius of the style he made famous—is the ubiquity of its elements beyond the close confines of the Savile Row suit. They are resilient constants in every supposed revolution, from the New Look of the 1950s to the New Romantics of the 1980s to the New Men of the 1990s and the recurrent patrician styles of American menswear, as created by Ralph Lauren, Tommy Hilfiger and Tom Ford, among others. In New York or Hong Kong, at every gathering of world leaders, businessmen, lawyers or doctors, even of actors on red carpets, the basic forms of Brummell's look are delineated. As fashion historian Anne Hollander has written, "It is possible to make the case that masculine formal dress of today is directly [Brummell's] responsibility." The colors of Eton's parade polemen, which happened also to be quasimilitaristic—blue, black, white—the cloths and trouser lines of early-nineteenth-century Hussar regiments, the tailoring skills of a nascent West End shopping economy and an artistic cult that drew on ancient ideals with distinctly corporeal attractions all met in Brummell's look and endured.

The second legacy of Brummell's unique career is less clear and less physical but may be more pervasive. "Nothing succeeds in London like insolence," wrote Chateaubriand, a little after Brummell's heyday, and it seems the pose of supposedly effortless superiority, elegance or "cool" was admired and copied in Brummell's wake, a style and manner that have also endured. The dandy-gent was a trope in fiction even before Brummell's death. The manner—the poise, deft wit and an air of languorous indifference—became a signifier of the gentleman, just as clearly as his clothes.

Brummell was not an aristocrat, yet he lorded it over the richest and most class-bound capital in the world: it was a stage trick in part based on his performed masculinity. His masquerade of superiority was noted by contemporaries and admired. The role had obvious uses and appeal: anyone could do it. Thus Brummell, the snob and social climber, is also the son of the French Revolution: a man whose style made it possible for Everyman to act like a prince, and for a regent to relish the title First Gentleman of Europe. For some, therefore, dandyism marked the death of kings, and the dawn of modern concepts of self.

Benjamin Disraeli also wrote a novel inspired by Brummell's dandyism. It was called *Vivian Grey* and presented a subtly different dandy form: the dandy scoundrel. He was a male Becky Sharp: a manipulator and adventurer, able and willing to use the carapace of dandyism to climb in society. Brummell found that his visitors in his exile in Calais and Caen had read about dandyism in novels like *Vivian Grey* and others that made much of the dandy as (misunderstood) hero. But as the century progressed, elements of Brummell's style—a slightly more austere and masculine affectation—were subsumed into the mainstream. From Sydney Carton in *A Tale of Two Cities* to Sherlock Holmes or Richard Hannay, the dandy pose and elements of Brummell's sartorial style became signifiers of complex, intriguing and heroic modern masculinity. In this regard, the emotionally reticent, self-created heroes of the American West, in fact and fiction, have also been described as dandies: men in the tradition of Brummell.

The third strand to be explored in the legacy of Brummell takes us exclusively to the land of his death. The intellectual and artistic aspects of dandies were argued first and most strongly in France. Count d'Aurevilly's 1844 essay, *"On Dandyism and George Brummel"* (*sic*), had a profound, lasting impact on French intellectual life and was taken up by various artists and writers in nineteenth-century Paris. Honoré de Balzac read it, and felt it confirmed his own ideas about Brummell and dandyism. Balzac was one of the first to take up the theme of Brummell as another fallen emperor, as important in his way as the exiled Napoleon on St. Helena. "We owe to Brummell the demonstration [of] how much elegant life is tied to the perfection of all human society," Balzac wrote. Brummell's life as an icon of French philosophy had begun. Then in 1863, Charles Baudelaire's *Le Peintre de la vie moderne* argued that dandies spoke of a society on the point of huge change and appeared "in all periods of transition." Baudelaire was the first writer to recognize the prescience of the dandy: holding the dying culture and a new one in congruence, not just enjoying the liminal but defining it. It was quite a philosophical proposition to base on a man like Brummell, whose dandy set, Byron claimed, were avowedly anti-intellectual. Yes, this aesthetic philosophy of dandyism inspired Whistler, Wilde and later Max Beerbohm, who even titled one of his key essays "In Defence of Cosmetics," in imitation of Baudelaire.

"Dandy of dress, dandy of speech, dandy of manner, dandy of wit, dandy even of ideas and intellect," as Micheál mac Liammóir described him, Oscar Wilde reestablished the unified completeness of the dandy: person and lifestyle as one construct, missing since Beau Brummell. Unsurprisingly, therefore, Brummell and Wilde have almost become fused in the popular imagination, their lives reflected also in the parallel, tragic third acts: in penury and in France.

Wilde's most personal testament to the style created by Brummell is in *The Picture of Dorian Gray,* understood almost from the start as a discourse on dandyism. His cankerous appearance in his attic picture has been discussed in relation to Wilde's own syphilitic condition, and although Wilde cannot have known that Brummell too suffered many years of syphilitic decline, as the medical records have only in recent years come to light, it is tempting to speculate that Wilde re-created in Gray's story a paradigm that he knew from tales of the Beau. In 1929 Virginia Woolf also turned to Beau Brummell as an unexpected subject in a discussion on modernism. "Some curious combination of wit, of taste, of insolence, of independence," she wrote, had propelled Brummell to the forefront of his era, but had also caught her imagination as speaking to her own across a century. Nor was dandyism restricted to the countries in which Brummell had lived. In St. Petersburg, Pushkin read d'Aurevilly's essay and used the hero as the model for his own behavior and dress and in his most famous creation, Eugene Onegin. And it was through translating *Onegin* that Vladimir Nabokov also found inspiration in dandyism and Brummell.

In the twentieth century Brummell's style moved on in unexpected ways: into women's clothing. One fashion historian notes that "what Brummell's aesthetic claimed for men in the nineteenth century won over [in Coco Chanel] the feminine universe. . . . Flamboyant display was eclipsed in favour of the democratic aesthetic of purity, restraint, and comfort." Another asserts that Chanel's "image was founded on the Beau Brummell principle that clothes while they are being worn must seem not to matter at all." Brummell's story meanwhile has had a constant afterlife as drama. There have been numerous plays, in London, America and Paris, an operetta *Brummell*, two Brummell musicals in the 1930s and seven films. In 1954 Stewart Granger, Elizabeth Taylor and Peter Ustinov starred in *Beau Brummell*, and Ron Hutchinson's play *The Beau* was in the West End in 2000 and premiers in New York in 2006.

The name Beau Brummell is bandied about frequently and internationally, in the lyrics of Billy Joel and in *Annie*, the musical, from Beau Brummel American leatherwear, specializing in wallets, to British Beau Brummell school blazers, from a French aftershave to a downtown Manhattan menswear store. The currency of Brummell's name and the ability of dandyism to inspire debate and creativity begs the inevitable question: Who are the modern-day Brummells? For many, the spirit of dandyism has moved away from clothing and fashion, now that we all have access to an unlimited dressing-up box. Rather, dandies are to be found in other media. D'Aurevilly translator George Walden in his book *Who's a Dandy?* suggested Brummell's tradition was flourishing in the modern art scene, and posited Damian Hirst and Tracey Emin as dandified modern icons, while describing Brummell as "a cross between Versace and the late MP Alan Clark." Once you start looking, dandies seem to be everywhere; in fashion, of course, but as much in the Brummellian understated chic of Paul Smith as in the theatricality of Vivienne Westwood or John Galliano. In the cultural landscape outside fashion, the dandy philosophy has been used to describe the works of artists and writers as wide-ranging as Diaghilev, Valentino, the Sitwells, Tom Wolfe, Martin Amis, Andy Warhol, John Malkovich and Madonna.

If the above names have anything in common, it is as star personalities that they relate most obviously to Brummell. He was an icon of the Regency period not just because of the projections upon his person by subsequent writers or even by the many who knew only the public construct of his persona. George Brummell's was a fractured personality, rebuilt in masquerade in the mirror of other people's expectations of him.

Though his end must not define his life, the Dorian Gray disintegration of his physical and sartorial self, understood through the nineteenth century as *emblematic* of a syphilitic decay, and acknowledged and proven only now and in this book as precisely that, gave immense symbolic power to the image of the Beau. Dandyism as masquerade, as performed personality and constructed and commodified persona, is the clear antecedent to the modern celebrity: the movie star and pop icon. Both the early British social dandyism that had its greatest star in Beau Brummell, and the later French philosophical dandyism that used him as its martyr, announced and promulgated the self-created modern man who made an effect, brought about a "happening." Once he departs the eighteenth and early nineteenth century, George Bryan Brummell's dandyism moves inevitably into our understanding of the modern media star and the star's ability to reflect ourselves.

~

The sources for this book have included memoirs and diaries, letters, tailors' accounts, royal and country house archives, as well as school and medical records. Brummell's was a voluble, literary age. His contemporaries wrote voluminously and also recorded lengthy conversations in their diaries and memoirs in the form of dramatic dialogues. People spoke in long, complex sentences, on- and offstage, as is evident from the plays and novels, as well as the diaries and memoirs of contemporaries. It is only fitting, then, to use sources in their original form to give the flavor of Brummell's world and the context within which he spoke and acted. He made impact through his presence, some mixture of insolence, charm and half-expressed sexuality, but he was also a man of words. He chose to write them down himself only in later life, from which period many of his letters survive. Fortunately, although he had neither time nor inclination at the height of his fame to write, many of his contemporaries recorded what he said, where and when. Brummell appears in the memoirs of the courtesans Harriette Wilson and Julia Johnstone, in the works of the diarists Thomas Raikes, Tom Moore, Lord William Pitt Lennox, Charles Macfarlane and Captain Gronow, and in the letters of Lord Byron; Harriet, Lady Granville; Princess Frederica, Duchess of York; Scrope Davies; Mrs. Fitzherbert and the prince regent to name but a few.

Moreover, because the dandy in general and Brummell in person became a trope and type in fiction as well as in memoirs, his world of masculine manners and the man himself are recorded or referenced widely in fiction. He was re-created, in barely concealed fictionalized form, in novels that appeared within his lifetime and were considered by him—more or less reluctantly—to be true likenesses: *Pelham* by Lord Edward Bulwer-Lytton, himself a dandy, and *Granby* by T. H. Lister. Brummell's world of London high society was also the backdrop for a whole school of fiction that used the clubs, gaming houses and ballrooms of the fashionable West End as the setting for tales of love, triumph and ruin. These have all proved invaluable sources.

First among the fresh, vivid lights to be shed on Brummell must be from the courtesans, whose lives have been brilliantly researched and resurrected by recent scholars. Brummell's close association throughout his adult life with these women has been insufficiently acknowledged. They provide a unique perspective on London and the men of the West End whom they entertained, including Brummell. The London demimonde presided over by the Three Graces—the three famous courtesans Harriette Wilson, her sister Amy Dubochet and Julia Johnstone—was also Brummell's world. His participation is hardly surprising as the demimonde of courtesans overlapped the fashion-conscious, aristocratic and royal circles in which Brummell moved. Or, at least, it overlapped the male members of those circles. But he must have been surprised in later life to find himself vividly depicted—gossiping in opera boxes or gorging on late-night buffet suppers—by women whose existence had traditionally depended on discretion. Two whom he had known intimately went on to write detailed memoirs of their lives and loves.

The courtesans—variously known as demireps (representatives of the demimonde) or Cyprians (votaries of the cult of Cypria or Venus)—were most descriptively titled "the Fashionable Impures." They were a key feature of the lives of rich London men at the beginning of the nineteenth century. Within a generation they were gone, as the blanket of Victorian hypocrisy created a different economy of prostitution and more covert adultery—but an elegant veneer had existed over the West End sex trade through the later eighteenth century, one to which Brummell's family and Brummell himself were quite closely allied. Although the courtesans shared the same privileged world of theater, opera, masquerade balls and racing carriages with high society, they were outside respectable society and the company of respectable women. (The popularity of masquerade balls was predicated on the understanding that they allowed all to mix freely: society ladies and gentlemen, and women deemed unrespectable or "impure.") As a result, the courtesans had a privileged access to society, but also a sardonic perspective on its foibles that matched Brummell's own take on the world. One who was particularly well placed to understand this was the courtesan Harriette Wilson, who provides a major source of detail and speculation on the subject of Beau Brummell.

The memoirs of Thomas Raikes are another key source in this biography. He had known Brummell since their first days at Eton and they remained friends throughout their lives. "Amongst the dandies, no one was held in greater estimation, at least by himself, than Thomas Raikes," wrote Lord William Pitt Lennox archly. He thought Raikes "a gossip, flâneur and servile tuft-hunter . . . a Boswell never stumbling upon his Johnson" until, that is, he decided he would be "satellite to the great [Brummell] and chronicler of [his] sayings and doings." Captain Rees-Howell Gronow was less sympathetic to Brummell, but again left a wealth of anecdotes and period detail on Brummell's life and times in his book *Reminiscences and Recollections,* published between 1861 and 1866. He wrote with nostalgia for a London that was fast disappearing. The captain's sartorial aspirations to dandyism, however, had been mocked by the dandy clique around Brummell, as was his diminutive stature. They called him "Captain No-grow." His *Recollections,* though fascinating and detailed, are often tinged, perhaps as a result, with a twist of bitterness.

Brummell himself was an accomplished writer and his own letters are also quoted at length. He wrote in the style of comic whimsy he had learned as an Eton schoolboy and from the boxes of Drury Lane, but this does nothing to reduce the letters' impact. Comedy, as they say, is harder work, and he labored to amuse his correspondents, which is as endearing as it is sometimes obscuring. Even as his world crumbled around him, Brummell's instinct as a writer was to hone sentences of elegant and lengthy density and to crack a joke. For all these reasons I make no apology for quoting from his and others' letters and poems and for letting George and the rest tell their story in their own words.

The voice that can never be ignored on Brummell is that of his first biographer, or more precisely chronicler, Captain William Jesse. He also collated and published nearly all the letters of Brummell that form the core primary source for any biographer. His was an adventuresome and wandering mind, and both qualities are amply on show in the seven-hundred-page *Life of George Brummell Esq. Commonly known as Beau Brummell,* which he wrote and published within a few years of Brummell's death. Jesse was a professional translator before he began to write his own works, and some of this background as a self-effacing reporter served him well as Brummell's chronicler. More than a third of the 1844 publication is taken up with Brummell's own writings, or those of his familiars. Every subsequent writer on Brummell owes Jesse an immense debt of gratitude. His *Life of Brummell* was a truly monumental achievement, but also, in parts, arrestingly modern in its approach to reportage and celebrity. Jesse recorded verbatim conversations as recounted by Brummell's friends, and his mixture of prescience and prurience led him to "interview"—by letter or in person—anyone and everyone he could think of whom he knew to have known Brummell and who might be willing to cooperate. He was indefatigable in searching for the sort of arcane detail that would doubtless have been lost without his efforts. Dozens of otherwise unavailable sources were collated while Brummell was still a living memory and as a result the thoughts of Brummell's schoolfriends are accessible to us, as are those of the asylum nurse and Anglican priest who attended his deathbed.

Also down to Jesse is the survival of Brummell's extensive collection of poems (his own and others') in a collection dubbed by him "the album." Captain Jesse appears to have acquired it in France after Brummell's death. This not only provides the sources for Brummell's own verses, but works especially composed for him, or in his company, by Sheridan, Byron, Lord Erskine and Georgiana, Duchess of Devonshire, among many others. They provide richly atmospheric detail on what filled Brummell's heart and mind as well as what made him laugh. More recently discovered is Brummell's own *Male and Female Costume,* a treatise on fashion. This, like Brummell's memoirs, he intended for publication, but, unlike his memoirs, he did not destroy. Jesse alludes to this treatise, but it turned up in its entirety only in the twentieth century in New York. It forms an invaluable foundation to our understanding of Brummell's own philosophies on fashion.

At the same time that Jesse brought out his hefty *Life of Brummell* in 1844, on the other side of the channel, Count Jules Amédée Barbey d'Aurevilly, a Norman man of letters in the French philosophical tradition, had also become obsessed with Brummell and dandyism and had embarked on a biography. The English Dandy of Caen had become as famous in France as he was in Britain, and dandyism achieved a life of its own in France in the mid-nineteenth century, inspiring Frenchmen from Count d'Orsay to Napoleon III to, later, Marcel Proust. Count d'Aurevilly decided after hearing of Jesse's monumental work, however, not to compete directly but to write as counterpoint his own book, which became so well received. First circulated in Caen among those who had known Brummell, later it was published in Paris. D'Aurevilly had had access to many residents of Caen and Calais who knew Brummell—he had been a student there himself from 1829 to 1833—and his description of Brummell's final descent into madness makes compelling, distressing reading.

Thus were laid down the twin tracks of Brummell scholarship: the biographers following Jesse's lead and those dandy-philosophical essayists following in the spirit of d'Aurevilly. Because Brummell was never heard to express a philosophical position on anything more challenging than his shirt linen ("plenty of it, and country washing"), the biographers have scoffed at the attempts to endow him and dandyism with portent. Conversely, because his achievements were unheroic, his style light comedic and his love life assumed to be bland, essayists have not considered him a subject for serious biography. I hope to disprove both.

Beau Brummell has a story as both symbol and man. His position as arbiter in the Age of Elegance and as preeminent figure in the culture of the first modern city and in the first Age of Surfaces (as his "friend Sherry [Sheridan] had it), and his role as fashion plate at the birth of modern male fashion ought to secure his fame. His statue on Jermyn Street stands as testament to his position as founding father of London's tailoring reputation. His life also unlocks the turbulent, venal, fashion-and-celebrity–obsessed Regency age, but naturally turns a mirror on our own at the same time, with its familiar fascination with "attitude," with fashion and with projections of sexual personae and celebrity. Dandyism is a quintessentially modernist pose, so to look anew at the ultimate and first dandy with fresh eyes and new evidence is timely. George Brummell, the man behind the Beau façade, tells his own story with little need for argument or embellishment: he was a man who claimed many hearts in his lifetime, made unique and original impact and died more alone than is common. In the midst of the elegance and excess of his life and times is an utterly human story, with both high comedy and low tragedy, and the ever-changing panorama of London as its theater. The "eruption of caprice," as d'Aurevilly has it, that lends Brummell's life its singularity and dandyism its dazzle, was something the Frenchman thought peculiarly British. This may be so, but d'Aurevilly hovered more apparently to me when I read his admonition that only those who have never learned to smile disdain the dandy. Brummell can amuse and intrigue across the centuries, as he perhaps intended. "So it was," wrote d'Aurevilly, "that Frivolity could show its head amongst a people with strict codes of behaviour and crude militaristic tendencies, as Imagination demanded its rights in the face of a morality too prescriptive to be true. Together they were translated into a science of manners and attitudes impossible elsewhere, of which Brummell was the finished expression and which will never be equalled again. We will now see why."

PART ONE

ASCENDANCY
1778–1799

The DANDY was got by *Vanity* out of *Affectation*—his dam . . .
Macaroni—his grandma, *Fribble*—his great-grandam, *Bronze*—
his great-great-grandam, *Coxcomb*—and his earliest ancestor,
FOP.

Pierce Egan, Life in London, 1820

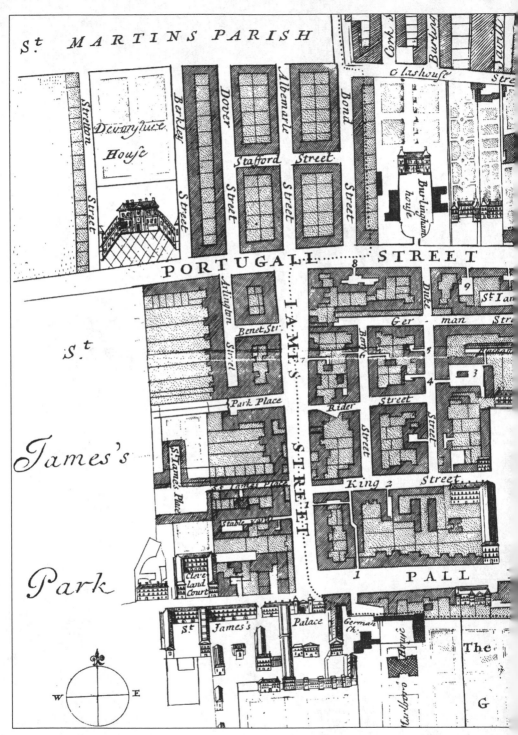

Part of the Parish of St. James's, Westminster

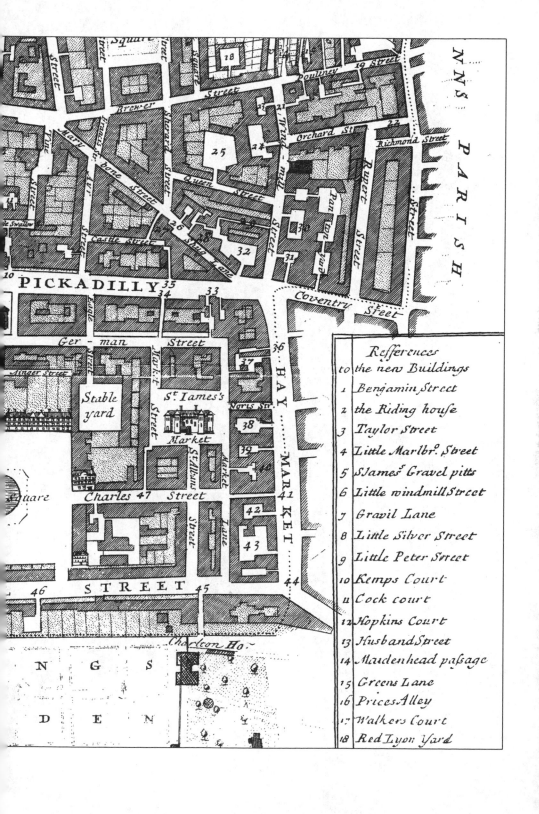

NN's PARISH

Square Street

18

Boulney 19 Street

Brewer Street 21

Orchard Str. 22

Richmond Street

25 24

Queen Street

Tyndmill Street

Panton yard

Rupert Street

26 Slug Lane

32 31

Castle Street

10

PICKADILLY 35
34 33

Coventry Street

Ger - man Street 36

Ainger Street

Market Street 37

Stable yard

St. Iames's

Norrs Str.

38

Market

St. Albans Street

39

Square

Charles 47 Street 41

Market Lane

42

43

44

STREET 45

46

Charlton Ho.

N G S

D E N

I

BLESSED ARE
THE PLACEMAKERS

1778–1786

Walk in gentlemen, walk in; here they are—the family of the
Surfaces . . . Gad, I never knew till now that ancestors were
such valuable acquaintance.

Charles Surface in *The School for Scandal,* 1777

On June 7, 1778 a fair-haired boy was born in Downing Street,
London. He was given the name George Bryan and his birth completed the family of three children born to Mr. and Mrs. Billy
Brummell in quick succession. George's mother was a strikingly
beautiful and stridently unconventional woman, who had lived
openly as mistress to the man she later married. Billy Brummell had
been a valet of sorts, like his own father, until he rose through the
ranks of the Treasury with his playwright friend Richard Brinsley
Sheridan, and found himself private secretary to Lord North,
Britain's prime minister during the American War of Independence,
and living in or near North's official residence at 10 Downing
Street. The Brummell family ascendancy through eighteenth-
century London had been fast and signal to the age.

They came from the wrong side of town: Billy's parents owned a
boardinghouse on Bury Street in an area notorious for its high-class
brothels. But Billy had found a way out through politics, or rather
by recourse to using his political contacts to feather his own nest.
Billy Brummell grew up helping to run a boardinghouse that may

well also have been a bawdy house, but he died worth £60,000 (over $15 million), in possession of a country estate, the approbation of Britain's political elite and even private apartments in the former royal palace at Hampton Court.

George Bryan Brummell's mother almost certainly endured her confinements at the apartments above what is now number 10 or number 11 Downing Street. George was baptized on July 2 at St. Margaret's, Westminster, the parish church of the House of Commons, and the Brummells were still living in Downing Street two years later. They had moved into the official residence of Britain's prime minister (a post which did not then exist in constitutional terms) around 1770 when the house was quite new. Billy's employer, the "prime minister" and First Lord of the Treasury Lord North, kept Billy always close by, and the Brummell children, George, William and Maria, grew up playing with Lord North's own children of similar ages.

George Bryan's earliest childhood was spent mainly at his parents' apartments in Downing Street and at his grandmother and Aunt Mary's in Bury Street. He was taken to the collective bosom of a close-knit circle of women. His mother had three sisters living in London. His father's sister and mother lived and worked on Bury Street, and as the youngest grandchild on both sides, it can be assumed he was petted and adored.

George, happily, was a large and robust baby, whose appetite bordered on greedy—a trait upon which his aunts felt compelled to comment. His aunt Brawne later said her main memory of George in early childhood was of a boy so determined to eat damson tart that he screamed with frustration when he was too full to continue—a recognizable, healthy toddler.

Brummell's childhood was set to be a safe and privileged city upbringing. This was interrupted, however, by the political unrest that surrounded his father's employer. On June 7, 1780, George Bryan's second birthday, the family home was besieged by a violent mob. London was quite precisely alight with antipopery, fueled by

Lord North's attempts at making concessions to Roman Catholics in Britain, and "mad" Lord Gordon's hysterical anti-Catholic rhetoric in response. Seven major fires were visible from the roof of Downing Street, mainly the houses of prominent Catholics and the Catholic chapels of foreign embassies. Fifty thousand people marched on Westminster and, late in the day, a mob moved on the prime minister's residence. Lord North was having dinner with friends, including Brummell and Sir John Macpherson, later governor general of India, who left this account:

We sat down at table, and dinner had scarcely been removed, when Downing Square [now Street], through which there is no outlet, became thronged with people, who manifested a disposition, or rather a determination, to proceed to acts of outrage . . . Mr. Brummell, Lord North's private secretary, who lived likewise [there] was in attendance, but did not make the company. With his habitual good humour, the Prime Minister asked what was being done to defend No. 10. There were, he was told, "twenty more grenadiers, well armed, stationed above stairs . . . ready on the first order to fire on the mob." He gave instructions that "two or three persons" should be sent out to the mob to warn them there were troops in the house ready to fire if there was "any outrage." The populace continued to fill the little square, and became very noisy, but they never attempted to force the street door . . . By degrees, as the evening advanced, the people . . . began to cool. We then sat down again quietly at the table and finished our wine.

Night was coming on . . . and the capital presenting a scene of tumult and conflagration in many quarters, Lord North, accompanied by us all, mounted to the top of the house, where we beheld London blazing in seven places, and could hear the platoons firing regularly in several directions.

George Bryan's father, interrupted from family birthday celebrations to attend a political dinner below, would have been understandably alarmed to have troops stationed in the family apartment, and mob violence overwhelming Westminster. After this the boys and their sister spent more and more time out at Hampton with their mother.

On September 28, 1782 the Brummells were granted a suite of apartments in Hampton Court Palace, once the royal home of Henry VIII but by the late eighteenth century out of favor and out of fashion and used to house civil servants and retired members of the court. The Brummells moved into a suite of rooms on the top floor on the north side of Fountain Court and commissioned their friend Joshua Reynolds to paint their sons as if in the grounds of the palace; the result was exhibited to great acclaim at the Royal Academy Exhibition in 1783. Both George and his brother William wear dresses in the picture, as was customary for young boys at the time, and frolic in the manner that was so admired of Reynolds's child portraits: at ease with nature and their innocent place in it. The artist spent hours playing with his young sitters to catch this fluid, easy and apparently unaffected moment. Then he sent the children away and dressed wooden dolls in their clothes in his London studio in Leicester Fields, now Leicester Square, where he could more easily work at re-creating the "moment" without the distraction of being in it. Reynolds's pupil, James Northcote, recalled the "grand rackets there used to be at Sir Joshua's when the children were with him! He used to romp, and play with them, and talk to them in their own way; and whilst all this was going on, he actually snatched these exquisite touches of expression which make his portraits of children so captivating." George and William had thirteen appointments with their father's artist friend, for sittings always at 11:00 A.M. while they were still playful and awake, all between December 27, 1781 and February 26, 1782. Their mother visited the studio on March 22, 1782 to see the completed portrait. The Brummells also commissioned a picture from Thomas Gainsborough of their daughter Maria, sitting alone, again as if in the grounds of Hampton Court.

These two paintings were, in a sense, the first entrance into society of the Brummell heirs. The Reynolds studio was in itself an entree into society, a place where the great and the good—and the up-and-coming—all met. One visitor to Reynolds's studio never forgot meeting the precocious youngest Brummell boy. She too was sitting for a portrait, a more studied occupation for her, as she was the actress and writer Mary Robinson, known to history and to her lover the Prince of Wales as "Perdita." Her day at Reynolds's studio proved the inspiration for her first major poem. It marks the first literary appearance of Beau Brummell, age four, as Perdita Robinson's "infant cherub."

The slightly androgynous quality of Reynolds's portraits of children, so admired at the time, was precisely reiterated by the wearing of dresses, irrespective of the sitter's sex. Boys did not get into "long trousers" until as late as their seventh birthday, though in practice it often made sense to put them into soft leather trousers as young as four. These were worn by boys only, and not by men: a sort of inversion of later practice, as it was knee breeches and stockings that young men adopted once they entered adolescence. George Brummell is shown in this first portrait quite typical of a boy of his time and class; it is not, as has been suggested, some harbinger of later sartorial unorthodoxy. The wide-set, playful, pale eyes of the grown man are recognizable in this first portrait, as well as the slightly petulant turn of the mouth that helped so much, later writers claimed, with his comic delivery. George's coloring, like his siblings, favored his mother. His hair went darker in adulthood—it is variously described as red, dark brown or sandy—but as a small child he was almost strawberry blond.

In late 1783 the North administration collapsed and the prime minister resigned his office. So disheartened was he with politics that when Billy Brummell informed him that officers had arrived to collect the ancient seals of office, North opted to stay in bed, Lady North with him, as they were collected from his bedside table. He was not to vacate Downing Street with the alacrity that has typified later changes of government. The new prime minister, William Pitt the Younger, was only twenty-four, and showed no immediate desire to move into a house he later described as "vast and awkward." The Norths loitered at number 10, but the Brummells moved out faster. They bought a house in Abingdon Street, Westminster, which they used as a London address until at least 1786.

Billy Brummell had profited enormously from his time in Downing Street. Though still only in his fifties, he decided to quit the civil service and, in large part, London. In the style of many other *nouveaux riches* of the age, he decided to put his money into property and land and duly bought a country estate that came onto the market that year, sixty miles west of London.

The country house William Brummell bought on his retirement from politics in 1783 was at the very height of architectural fashion, and the perfect family home for his young family. Donnington Grove in Berkshire was a new house, built only twenty years before in pink-gray grizzle brick in the radically modish style that came to be known as "Strawberry Hill Gothic." Its architect, John Chute of the Vyne, had been a member of Horace Walpole's Committee of Taste, men who had sought to fuse with neoclassicism a whimsical and imagined style of olde England they called "Gothick." Consequently Donnington Grove had imitation battlements and mullioned windows, Gothic arches supporting high Georgian doorframes and a medieval style "cloister" that led off to the children's bedrooms, suspended below a glass skylight thirty feet above the hall. The house was and is exquisitely pretty—a remarkable early example of Georgian Gothic, designed for urbane owners expecting the most modern comfort and decorated in a style that felt romantically ancient. Of course it was all fake.

As soon as the Brummells had acquired the property they set about making additions and improvements. The previous owner and the man who built Donnington Grove, Sir Joseph Pettit Andrews, an antiquarian and lawyer, had been forced to sell. He had overspent on his Gothick pile, and, as his fortune declined still further, found himself obliged also to sell to the Brummells the neighboring manors of Church Speen and Chieveley. With this extra land—nearly eight hundred acres in total—Billy Brummell set about major landscaping of the gardens, realigning the old Bagnor and Lambourn roads and diverting the river to form that most necessary of eighteenth-century garden features: a reflecting lake. Next the Brummells began to worry about the style of entertainment possible at their new country seat.

Donnington Grove still bears the marks of the Brummells' social ambitions. Like all fashion-conscious Georgian landowners, they wanted to create an Arcadia without visible signs of the economy that supported their luxury. They had a paper mill demolished—it spoiled the view—and replaced it with a medieval-style fishing pavilion. The lower Gothic windows were replaced with modern sashes such that the view of nature so artfully arranged might not be interrupted, and guests could step straight from the lower-floor rooms into Arcadia. The entrance of the house was remodeled, with the importation of a "Chippendale Gothic" porch, and finally the original symmetry of the house was destroyed by the addition of two dining rooms. One, later a drawing room, was built in perfect classical proportions, but sticking out to the side of the Gothic house. The second was a dining pavilion, quite near the house but commanding sunset views of the park and designed for summer entertaining, for the withdrawal of ladies or for the most private political soirees. In their two new dining rooms—the one attached to the house also doubling on occasion as a ballroom—the Brummells set about playing host to their London friends and to the local gentry.

Sheridan also introduced the Brummell boys to his own son, Tom. Tom Sheridan was older than George and William, and as bad an example as any parent might fear for their sons. Tom's schoolmaster described him as having "wit and humour, but not a particle of knowledge." The wit doubtless impressed young George as it did all of Tom's schoolfellows. When his father later told Tom to take a wife, Tom replied, "Yes, sir, but whose?" When his father, in an interchange worthy of Captain and Jack Absolute in *The Rivals*, told Tom that he would cut him off with just a penny to his name, Tom asked if he might have the penny straightaway. It was through Tom Sheridan that George Brummell would later be introduced to London's most famous courtesan, Harriette Wilson, who once said she could not trust herself alone in a hackney coach with the playwright's playboy son.

There was shooting and riding for visitors like Sheridan and his son Tom, and evidence that the Brummells employed liveried servants to help with shoots and serving guests in the park. George learned to ride, from the stable block his father had built, as well as to hunt, shoot and swim—a useful skill, as it turned out, at school—in the inviting, clear, slow waters of the Lambourn. There were some local playmates as the other large house of the neighborhood, confusingly called Donnington Priory, had children of the same age as George, and the Brummells entertained families from the wider area, once George's father sought to inveigle himself in local politics (he was made high sheriff of Berkshire in 1788).

Yet the house, for all its extensions and pretensions, was not a large country seat. There were only eight principal bedrooms, so that, with the children in residence, house parties were necessarily intimate. It is easy to imagine George, William and Maria at the low iron railings of the upper cloister, watching the comings and goings of their parents' glamorous friends from their vantage point high above the hall: three pairs of dazzled eyes. The house and its guests affected the children in different ways.

George's sister Maria never really left Donnington. Typical of her class and sex, she was not sent away to school, met, very young, a Captain George Blackshaw of a local family and married him. She settled on the captain her generous inheritance and with it he bought a nearby cottage in which they lived, off her money, bringing up two daughters who in their turn married well. She and her young brother George were never close, but they were brought up, in effect, separately. George and William were soon to be sent away to school. Maria's move from London to landed gentility came to define her life as though she were a Jane Austen heroine and accordingly her marriage brought her obscurity. George chose the city.

It has become part of the legend of the house that the two boys, unlike Maria, were occasionally invited to join the adult party, and that George's early introductions to the Devonshire House set in London, presided over by the ageless Georgiana, Duchess of Devonshire, came as a result of his easy relationship with the avuncular figures of Sheridan and Fox. The scale of Donnington Grove makes this plausible. There is even a revealing story of how George Brummell, back from school, first heard of the French Revolution in the flint hermitage by the weir at Donnington and from none other than Charles James Fox. An image more appropriate to the age and characters could not easily be invented: the boy who would eschew politics in favor of fashion was told of the French Revolution in the setting of an artificial hermitage, itself a sort of foppery of English landscape design. That he should be delivered the news straight from a key player in the world of London politics, a former Macaroni but by 1789 a dress-down Whig, links so many strands of Brummell's early life that one is tempted to assume the story apocryphal.

But undoubtedly Donnington Grove made its impression upon young George Brummell. It could not fail to engage the imagination, and was built to appeal to those whose image of the countryside and of English history is formed more by literature than by reality. George learned the essential country skills of a gentleman at Donnington: hunting, shooting, fishing, swimming, perhaps also the landscape architecture and drawing he used in later life. But unlike his sister he never chose to live in the country again. Donnington had allowed him to mix easily and comfortably with some of the greatest, and wittiest, minds in England and to be groomed in the skills of what it was to be a gentleman in a manner his father, whose adolescence was shaped on Bury Street, must have envied.

Likewise it is tempting to see the louche metropolitan figure of Charles James Fox as a model by which George would begin to define and redefine what it was to be a gentleman. Fox, a former poseur, instinctively political, romantically and sexually dissolute, was also a great wit, the foremost epigrammatist of his day. And it was broadly these qualities that brought young George Brummell to the attention of his schoolfellows at Eton College, where Fox himself had been a schoolboy twenty-five years earlier.

2

THESE ARE NOT
CHILDISH THINGS

ETON, 1786–1793

Would you your son be sot or dunce?
Lascivious, headstrong, or all at once?
Train him in Public with a mob of boys
Childish in mischief only, and in noise,
Else of mannish growth, and five in ten
In infidelity and lewdness, men.
There shall he learn, ere sixteen winters old,
That authors are most useful pawned or sold,
That pedantry is all that schools impart,
But taverns teach the knowledge of the heart.
There waiter Dick with Bacchanalian lays
Shall win his heart, and have his drunken praise,
His counsellor and bosom-friend shall prove
And some street-pacing harlot his first love.
                    Thomas Cowper, 1731–1800

In 1786 Eton College already spilled across both sides of the small street that extends from Windsor Old Bridge, twenty-five miles upriver from London. The chapel roof and the Tudor school buildings—newly extended—dominated the skyline of the little town and were visible from Windsor Castle and from the water meadows for miles around. The high street that linked the royal castle to the college was lined with the shops that supported the school community: Pote's the bookseller, Miller's the tailor, Egelstone's the hatter and Atkins's the shoemaker. There were three coffeehouses: Jones's, Ramlet's and Layton's, which sold, among other provisions, large quantities of oysters—the cheap fast food of eighteenth-century youth. There was a haberdasher's too, Charter's, that sold, as a sideline, toothbrushes, "Spence's tooth powder" and soap to those adolescent boys who had advanced ideas of personal hygiene.

There was an inn, too, the Christopher, of somewhat ill repute, where older boys drank. It was just opposite the school's main gate. The masters had it shut down a little after Brummell's time at Eton, as soon as they could acquire the land from the Crown, and suspiciously soon after a bastardy writ was issued from a barmaid there, against one Lord Hinchingbrooke, an Eton sixth-former. He was given ten strokes of the cane for his misdemeanor—fewer than the punishment for a missed "absence" call at school.

The chapel and ancient buildings of the school were on the right as one crosses the river, the boardinghouses, largely, on the left. The lives of the Eton boys, then as now, straddled two worlds: Eton itself—insular, gossipy as any academic institution, constipated with arcane traditions—and the real world of provincial England. They studied classics in the mornings and bet on horses and brawled with bargemen in the afternoons; their education would encompass Greek tragedy in the original, but also the bawdy low comedy of the Christopher Inn and its rumored brothel. They would grow from small, unworldly boys into classical scholars and seasoned drinkers. It was an education well suited to the age.

Like Fox and Lord North before him, and George Canning his contemporary, Brummell learned at Eton to be a confident public speaker, in Latin, Greek and later English, and his physical poise and confidence on the stage of London life also owed much to an Eton fascination with classical drama and amateur theatricals.

The style of humor for which Brummell later became famous also dates from his time at Eton. The monastic erudition of the

Eton boys was put to more unexpected use than just performance of Greek plays. A late-eighteenth-century Etonian was expected to be a poet, an actor—but also a wit. Etonians were schooled, from the late eighteenth century onward, to emulate a manner of witty adumbration, the style of the classical Roman epigrammatists, and to excel in the reduction of an argument or idea into a pithy closing comment. George Brummell, who carried on writing classically scanned verse into old age, was clearly inspired to polish the sheen of his classical education by relishing wit and brevity more than grandiose rhetoric or even verse writing. This trait, which sometimes played out as the incisive "put-down," but just as often figured as the casually warm and witty aside, was one of the signal traits of his personality, one remarked upon, copied and admired. It was a style, it should be noted, that typified the high comedy of the period, also classically inspired: the apparently frothy comedies of Sheridan and Garrick, of Colley Cibber, George Coleman or Fanny Burney that allowed the language of the Augustan age a comic life. It was a style that stayed with Brummell into old age, and even beyond the departure of his reason.

It was an age that saw only good in the beating of children— especially schoolboys. Their social class was no deterrent. One of George III's daughters, Princess Sophia, recalled the Prince of Wales and Duke of York as children at Windsor being "held by their arms and flogged like dogs with a long whip." The violent lifestyle of a later generation of "Regency bucks" (and their apparent interest in *le vice anglais* as catered to by the brothel madams of St. James's) may perhaps be attributed to the late-eighteenth-century reliance on the whip as the fundamental tool of schooling.

The Etonians were constantly at loggerheads with the "cads": the Eton town youths of similar age who sought to fleece them of their pocket money by fairish means or foul. The "cads" were eventually banned from the college precincts. George himself only narrowly avoided getting involved in one violent escapade on the river, and then only with recourse to the age-old armor of comedy. A boatman cad who had found himself in some altercation with the schoolboys was on the point of being thrown over the bridge into the low waters of the Thames by a mob of over a hundred Etonians. Buck Brummell—perhaps fourteen at the time—caught the attention and laughter of the Etonian and cad hooligans alike by shouting: "My dear fellows, don't send him into the river. The man is evidently in a state of perspiration, and it almost amounts to a certainty that he will catch cold." Brummell was rewarded with guffaws, perhaps some bemusement in the face of such paradoxical whimsy—typical of his later style—and the boatman was released. Another contemporary left a vivid portrait of the young Brummell at school:

All these three most happy years George was my fag.[1] He was a far livelier lad than his . . . brother, William: indeed no one at the school was so full of animation, fun and wit. He was a general favourite. Our dame [Mrs Yonge] his tutor [Hawtrey] and my tutor . . . and Dr Goodall, all petted him. You ask me whether he was pugnacious; I do not remember that he ever fought or quarrelled with anyone; indeed it was impossible for anyone to be more good-natured than he was. With . . . all his . . . intimate companions, I never heard of his having a single disagreement. Like them he was not in the least studious, but a very *clever* and a very *idle* boy, and very *frank*; and then, whatever he became afterwards, not in the least conceited, though Nature seemed to have supplied him with a quadruple portion of amusing repartee . . . I really believe that no Etonian was ever more popular with all his companions than George Brummell.

He played cricket for Eton in the first eleven in the summer of 1793, scoring zero out and twelve runs, and making three catches in his opponents' second innings in a match against Oldfield Club of Berkshire. He swam, and was on the river in the summer more than the playing fields. He also played football. Old Etonian Cap-

[1] A student who is obligated to perform errands or other small, tedious tasks for an older boy in the school.

tain Gronow later insisted that Brummell "distinguished himself at Eton as the best scholar, the best boatman and the best cricketer; and, more than all, he [possessed] the comprehensive excellences that are represented by the familiar term 'good fellow.' "

This was the Eton his father had intended for him, the one, as envisaged in a contemporary novel, where a son might be "roughed about among boys, [and thereby] learn to be a man." Billy Brummell was closely allied to a government that saw the most humiliating defeat in British military history: the American War of Independence. It had a direct effect on schooling at the time, especially at Eton. Many had queried the competence of the British military and ruling elite and "whether some miscarriages on the naval and military departments have not been indirectly caused by the selection of fine gentlemen, of men of levity of appearance . . . to command armaments." George's education was designed to make him seem, and ideally be, a paragon of English gentle*manliness*. Eton rose to the challenge in Brummell's time, such that, by the beginning of the new century, a professor of modern history could happily assert that Britain's greatness came "from hardy sports [and] from manly schools" like Eton.

~

Key elements of Brummell's dress sense were honed at Eton. As Eton boys progressed through the school, they became regulars at the local drapery and tailor's, ordering their own bespoke clothes— even trousers—in some of the latest fabrics. This facet of the Eton education was almost unique: the boys were far enough from home to be obliged to clothe themselves according to their own taste but near enough to the fashionable world and the court for the boys to be encouraged in a competitive dandyism as the new fabric economy allowed. They also formed, courtesy of Eton, the ruinous habit of shopping on account—at their parents' expense.

Although there was no uniform as such, one Eton ritual closely informed Brummell's thoughts on clothing, and in turn therefore holds its own place in the history of fashion. Montem was a holiday of misrule and fancy dress at Eton. The origins of this ritual called Montem, or Ad Montem ("To the hill!"), are lost in time but clearly predate the college. The fancy-dress festival was described as an "ancient tradition" in 1561. It involved a procession of the entire school to nearby Salt Hill on the first Tuesday after Whitsun. Every boy was involved, all assigned titles, duties and ranks in a military-style parade. The "Captain of Montem," a "blooming youth" called Harris in Brummell's last Montem in 1793, had flowers thrown at him by Windsor shopgirls and odes composed in his honor by local songwriters. Harris found himself the Lord of Misrule for a day, which could also earn him substantial sums. The rest of the school was ranked as mareschals, ensigns, colonels, lieutenants, stewards, sergeants, corporals and saltbearers, with the youngest boys titled "polemen." Each rank tried to outdo the ones below in the flamboyance of their dress, which by Brummell's time was hired from theaters as far away as London and included costumes of "Turks, Albanians, courtiers of Charles II and George I, Highlanders and hidalgos." Coaches came out from London filled with the boys' families, and locals gathered to watch the spectacle in the manner of the celebrations at Eton today of June Fourth (which marks King George III's birthday and is the festival that has taken over as the high point of the Eton year). The boys would leave school early in the morning, and the march was both musical and high-spirited. The violence that became associated with Montem was a result partly of drinking, but mainly of the "trick-or-treat" extortion that also defined the day. Eton boys in bizarre fancy dress were posted on the main highways and waterways near Eton and Windsor, and demanded a toll on Montem day, shouting, "Salt, salt," or "Mos Pro Lege" ("Custom before law"). All the monies went to the captain, to help him with his university career, though to him also fell the expenses of the day, which could be great. Young "Captain" Dyson spent £205 on his Montem in 1784 against a taking of £451. Even royal spectators were not exempt from this schoolboy toll. It is said that William III's Dutch guards were so alarmed by a direct demand for money on the way to

Windsor that they came near to killing several schoolboys, who were saved only by the ridiculousness of their garb. Brummell's schoolfellows found themselves handed fifty guineas each by King George and Queen Charlotte in 1793 and "blooming" Captain Harris netted £1,000 from his Montem.

Some years things got out of hand. Salt festivals generally have ancient lineage, and are often associated with springtime, fertility rituals and children, but also with an element of enacted violence. Eton College seems to have colonized this local salt rite in the late Middle Ages, and assigned to it its own brand of colorful militarism and more than a dash of sadism. Eventually Queen Charlotte put an end to the whipping of the "dirtiest boy" all the way down Salt Hill by the entire school, but as a result of the chaos caused by the attendant toll extortions, Montem became, by Brummell's time, a triennial event and the festival was eventually banned by Prince Albert in the 1840s.

According to the college archives, Brummell took part in three Montems. They are worth noting, with regard to an event involving a local girl in 1793, but also as Montem relates to an understanding of Eton costume, Brummell and fashion. Montem provided an occasion for the renewal of Eton garb, just as it did for a restocking of crockery in the lower hall—one of the captain's expenses. The boys were expected to dress up for Montem, even if they were not appointed officers in the parade. In portraits of George and William Brummell from this period, owned by descendants of the family, the boys have been wrongly described as wearing "Eton uniform": in fact they are in the dress of the Montem "polemen" or "musician polemen," the positions they held in the Montem parades in 1787 and 1790. Indeed, this was the look of the majority of the school at Montem: a dark blue jacket with two rows of brass buttons, allowing a view of a white stock at the neck and paired with paler breeches. In contrast, the older boys dressed in a parody of courtiers and looked, deliberately, overdressed and ridiculous.

The Montem polemen's garb is a fascinating precursor to what became, twenty years later, part of the London dress style that Brummell made famous. It was in effect a uniform: quasimilitaristic, flattering to the chest and shoulders but softened around the neck, featuring a palette of dark blue, buff and white. If, as seems possible, Brummell first saw the Prince of Wales—the most overdressed man in Europe—at the Montem of 1790 or 1793, he might well have been struck even then by the parallels between what then passed for high male fashion and the ridiculousness of the Montem officers' fancy dress. He, in contrast, spent most of his Montems, and much of his time at Eton, in a sober uniform that counterpointed outré excess.

The 1793 Montem was the occasion of Brummell's first recorded attempt at seduction—fueled to what degree by alcohol, schoolboy bravado or hormonal high spirits we cannot know. He was spotted, later in the day after Eton had descended into a sort of good-humored anarchy, using his Montem musical instrument to unorthodox ends: serenading the headmaster's daughter.

This first time I saw him is thoroughly impressed upon my recollection. I was returning at night . . . along the lane [and] I heard music, and on clearing the end of the house, which was then Harrington's, since then Holt's, I saw three boys dressed in fantastic dress, making a mock serenade under the window of Miss Susan Heath, the eldest daughter of the headmaster. The instruments which thus interpreted their feelings for his lady were a hurdy-gurdy, a triangle, and a French horn—the last being played by Brummell mi[nor]. Who held the other two, I do not remember, but the scene was so infinitely amusing, that I could never forget it. I did not know his name, but I soon learned it; afterwards I was often fagged by him, and his gaiety and good nature to lower boys were felt and acknowledged.

Key elements of the Brummell legend are already in place: details of his dress, his humor and a sort of playacted sexuality, a sexuality enacted within the arena of other men, which in modern terms would be seen as typical teenage behavior.

"Buck" Brummell, as he was known at school, would have been remembered from his school days even if he had not gone on to be the most famous man in England. His fag master, his fag and other contemporaries write lovingly of him from the far side of fifty years and the Victorian cultural revolution. He used his formidable wit and good looks to become the most popular boy at school, never succeeding too conspicuously in his schoolwork to threaten such a position and avoiding through eight years of a potentially brutalizing establishment a flogging at the hands of either schoolmasters or fellow pupils. In all of this he was, before he even left Eton in late 1793 or 1794, recognizably the later man and well en route to being the very mold of fashion. But his poise and repartee hid a profound sense of personal unworthiness that was more than a reflection of his lowly background. For one thing, he was already developing traits of fastidiousness that would in time become legendary and may speak partly of an uncomfortable relationship with his body. This may be attributed to his position in the male gaze at Eton, a supremely homosexualized environment. It may also be related to growing up in a highly sexualized society that was at the same time violently antipathetic to the direct outlet of adolescent male sexual energy. Worse still, as this final anecdote suggests, though George Brummell was in every point the Man of Feeling of his age and the idol of his schoolfellows, in his father's eyes he remained a failure, a wastrel and a second-best second son:

About [this time] his father, having been informed of some peccadillo he [George] had committed [possibly the incident with the headmaster's daughter], sent his butler from Donnington with a paternal letter to his eldest son, which began, "My dear William," and another to the Beau, commencing "George." George's letter was in other respects a most disagreeable one intimating as it did the order for his immediate return, with all his clothes, his father having determined not to allow him to return again to Eton. Hearing of his trouble I went to his room and found him with the two letters before him: they were wet with tears:—such a stream of tears I never saw, and have never seen since.

"George," said I, "what's the matter?" He could not speak: but, sobbing, pointed first to—"My dear William," and then to the monosyllable "George." I give you this anecdote as a trait of his being possessed . . . of a warm heart. His father relented also, for after the next holidays George reappeared amongst his companions, the most manly boy of them all.

The last phrase was pointed. Jesse's anonymous contributor to the collection of Brummell-at-school sources recalled not just George's warm heart, but his return to Eton "the most manly boy of them all." Had his father's antipathy hardened him in some recognizable way? Was this purely a physical description, one of several that sketch an object of schoolboy hero worship? Or did Brummell boast, or did his school friend merely sense, that something momentous had happened that holiday from Eton back at the family apartments in Hampton Court Palace? For where Susan Heath, the headmaster's daughter, had merely laughed at his musical wooing, at home "Buck" Brummell had experienced both the romance, and trauma, of the adult sexual world. Next door to his father's apartments he had found a kindred spirit, a girl destined to be one of the most famous courtesans of their age, but then only sixteen, not yet "fallen" and quite possibly for the first time in love. Her name was Julia Johnstone.

3

THE WORLD IS
VERY UNCHARITABLE

1793–1794

[A young man] may commit an hundred deviations from the path of rectitude, yet he can still return, every one invites him; in sober truth he gains an *éclat* by his failings, that establish him in *The Ton,* and make him envied, instead of pitied or despised. But woman, when she makes one false step . . . becomes a mark for the slow moving finger of scorn . . . The world is very uncharitable.

Julia Johnstone, née Storer

Julia Storer was a year older than George Brummell, a year that makes an appreciable difference between a fifteen-year-old boy and a sixteen-year-old girl. Her parents had apartments in Hampton Court Palace that overlooked the Brummells' from the opposite side of Fountain Court. The families shared privileged access to the palace grounds but had little else in common. George's parents came from a line of hard-working servants and civil servants, their wealth founded on officially sanctioned peculation and rental property in the West End. Julia's antecedents, on the other hand, were aristocrats. Her mother was the Honourable Elizabeth Proby, daughter of Lord Carysfort, and maid of honor to Queen Charlotte. It was because of her mother's court appointment that the family had grace-and-favor apartments in the palace, used by the

Hon. Mrs. Proby when the queen did not require her attendance in London. Julia's father was Thomas Storer of Belle Isle, Jamaica, and Golden Square, London. He had married well with his money—based on the West Indian slave trade—acquiring a whole set of aristocratic in-laws. Julia started her seventeenth year as a well-connected debutante, but ended it a "fallen woman," pregnant and disgraced. She was never accepted back into society and barely spoke again to any female members of her family. Harriette Wilson—who lived with Julia in adult life when they were both professional courtesans—later claimed Julia's "fall" began uncomfortably on a stone staircase, next door to the Brummell family apartments at Hampton Court Palace. She further claimed that Julia and George had been in love.

Julia's father died in 1792. That year she was presented at court. She had been expensively educated abroad to the most polished standard. But Julia quickly decided on a more independent course than the one her widowed mother or old Queen Charlotte had in mind for her. "What a fortune is my mother's!—said I, such a one will never do for me; I am for freedom and independence." She gave up on her German lessons—the queen had said she would help her make a solid German match—and decided to take a more adventurous path. Julia was free-spirited from the first, her heart "so very, very mad," according to Tom Sheridan, "a woman of very violent passions," according to Harriette, but "combined with an extremely shy and reserved disposition." She was also unusual in her looks: not a classic beauty of her age or any other, she had great strength of features. She was dark with large, piercing eyes and hair that fell in long ringlets, after natural or artificial means. She was a tomboy of sorts, like her friend Harriette Wilson, with a certain masculinity of manner—as it was described at the time—that allowed her to hold her own in a world dominated by men. George Brummell's first love was from a mold that would cast many to come: an unconventional beauty, a strong, independent-minded woman. And somewhat older than he was.

The story of Julia, and of George, was described by Harriette Wilson and Julia. Their versions differ wildly.

It was much later in life that Julia came to write her *Confessions* just as her former friend Harriette Wilson had done. But Julia wrote "in contradiction to the fables of Harriette Wilson." Their memoirs often contradict directly, and if they do not, they offer very different slants on actions and consequences. This much both memoirs had in common: George Brummell, and a desire to paint as sympathetically as possible their own initial "fall from grace" that prefigures the whole of the rest of the story. The thread of George's role—at exactly this point in Julia's narrative—can be woven only by splicing together these two conflicting strands.

Julia's own account of her "fall," a scene set in her own record and all others at Hampton Court Palace, is at odds with Harriette's in key respects. Julia insists she ran away from home, taking an unpaid position as a companion to one Mrs. Cotton, whose husband, a dragoon captain, happened to have apartments at Hampton Court Palace where he duly seduced her. "At the early age of sixteen I fell victim to my own inexperience," she wrote. "I was handed out of the carriage [at Hampton Court] by a military officer: the sight inspired me with unusual pleasure." In truth this was not quite how it happened, and Julia was not quite the ingenue she paints herself to be.

Colonel Cotton cut something of a dash around Hampton Court Palace. He was in the Tenth Light Dragoons, the country's most fashionable regiment. Julia, like George, first saw the modish uniform around the formal gardens of Hampton Court and its ancient barracks. But Julia is lying in saying she first saw the uniform or the man when she was an unguarded female at large in the world. Julia started an affair with Cotton, and, it has been suggested, with her young neighbor George Brummell, some time around her sixteenth birthday when her whole family was at Hampton Court. It suited her later purposes to draw herself as a friendless, orphaned lady's companion, "abandoned to the care of strangers at the most critical period of a young girl's existence" and undone by her master and her own "inexperience." The truth was a little more complicated.

Harriette Wilson, meanwhile, insisted Brummell was in love with Julia Storer at Hampton Court in 1792 and 1793 when they were fifteen and sixteen respectively. The Brummell family had moved from suite 17 in the Gold Staff Gallery on the South Front to the even more prestigious set of connected suites in Fountain Court, Numbers 29 and 30 in the Silver Staff Gallery. The Cottons were near neighbors, in suite 21, a floor above. The Storers were just opposite, almost underneath the Cottons. The picture Harriette Wilson draws of the Hampton Court Julia and George knew was entirely accurate in key physical details. A Hampton Court Palace address sounded gracious; the reality was often less so. The palace apartments ranged from palatial to single rooms in the former galleries. Some were made by jerry-building extra floors in the great Tudor kitchens, and others had been created by completely restructuring the early Georgian kitchen buildings as a private house. Each grace-and-favor apartment found a way to improvise a cooking space out of fireplaces or former closets after the royal kitchens had ceased to exist. The Storers, for instance, cooked in what had previously been the royal Chocolate Room on the "Coffee Room Staircase." Practically and architecturally the palace was being turned into a rabbit warren. Some addresses referred to apartments so tiny that they had been created from former galleries simply by curtaining off "cubicles" from the immediate neighbors. The division walls that were put in—a very few remain—were thin. Harriette Wilson's version takes this into account and, though partisan, has a clearer ring of truth to it than Julia's own.

This is Harriette's version of Julia's story, the one she swore Julia had told her. Sixteen-year-old Julia Storer was overcome with boredom at the "starchied and stately . . . old Anglo-Germanic" court, and alarmed at the prospect of an arranged marriage into the German nobility. Yet the palace suited her imaginative nature, and she found there two alternative prospects of adventure and romance. One, a cocky Eton schoolboy, her neighbor George Brummell, "violently in love with her"; the other, a thirty-year-old married man, Colonel Cotton.

The colonel was described by both Julia and Harriette as one of the handsomest men in England. His wife had recently given birth to their ninth child and was suffering from some malaise—possibly postpartum depression—and for this reason, or simply as a means of birth control, she had made her intention clear never to share a bed with the colonel again. Who seduced whom then is unclear: the priapic dragoon or the rebellious schoolgirl. Their first sexual encounter took place "on a stone staircase" probably off Fountain Court, or the unused kitchen staircase to the Great Hall. Later trysts took place in Julia's own bedroom, with only a curtain partition between the lovers and the sixteen-year-old girl's mother, the Hon. Mrs. Storer. The palace was fulfilling its potential for Julia, for romance, intrigue and adventure, and living up to its subsequent reputation as a hotbed of sexual intrigue in confined spaces. Once she hid the colonel under her bed. The lovers' joke backfired on Julia, to her eternal embarrassment, as the naked soldier was treated not only to the sight of her sister undressing (Julia's room was also the family dressing room), but to a private conversation between teenage sisters about their pimples. George, meanwhile, was left out in the cold. "He is an old flame of mine," Julia was later heard to remark, "who was violently in love with me, when I was a girl, at Hampton Court." After she started sleeping with Cotton, she said, she never saw him again, till they bumped into each other years later at the opera. Brummell, ever the gentleman, greeted her "with surprise, joy and astonishment at meeting with her." They later rekindled their affair. With Cotton, George was less sanguine. "No man in England stinks like Cotton," he later averred, making him the one exception for his general rule against perfumes: Cotton, he spat, could do with "a little Eau de Portugal."

In choosing Cotton and not Brummell, Julia changed her life forever. Where a teenage romance, even consummated, might have been hushed up and forgiven, an affair with an older married man put Julia on the path to her later notoriety. Within a few months of losing her virginity on a back staircase of Fountain Court, Julia realized she was pregnant. Like many an unwanted teenage pregnancy, its very fact was denied by those most immediately associated with it—even Julia—until the last possible moment. The hidden pregnancy was eventually revealed when Julia's waters broke in the middle of one of Queen Charlotte's interminable standing audiences. The consequent scandal nearly ruined the family. Julia's brother challenged Cotton to a duel, Julia was thrown out of both the Storer and Cotton apartments and, alone and unattended, suffered five hours of labor in an unused room at Hampton Court Palace before delivering her baby boy herself. George was sent back to school, both shaken and moved by Julia's plight and that of her baby son.

As Julia well knew, the punishment for her was to be much harsher than anything a man might suffer for a similar "indiscretion." She was never received in respectable society again. She and the colonel went on to have five children together, and a marriage of sorts based in a little cottage in Primrose Hill. This was only possible because Julia had some financial means independent of her family or lover—a highly unusual situation for a Georgian woman. She called herself "Mrs. Johnstone" and the colonel kept up a double, quasibigamous life, known as "Mr. Johnstone" in Primrose Hill with his children and "wife" and Colonel Cotton by his regiment and in town. But by the time Brummell met Julia again, sometime in 1804 or 1805, she had been deserted by Cotton and was living with Harriette, leading members both of the "Cyprians," who had such wealth and fame as courtesans that they could throw balls attended by all the greatest figures of the day, many of them their lovers. Julia was comprehensively "fallen" and a seasoned, professional mistress.

> For never handsome gypsy drew in
> A man so soon to shame and ruin . . .

wrote Henry Luttrell of the professional love life of his fictionalized Julia. George and she resumed their affair, however halfheartedly, and George went on to introduce her to a number of her later "protectors."

"I never had the honour to refuse his hand in marriage," Julia wrote of Brummell, "because he never offered it to me." She counterclaimed that it was Harriette who was in love with George. "I verily believe . . . Harriette would most gladly have taken him," but this is typical of her step-by-step contradiction of everything Harriette wrote. George himself was evasive on the subject: "Julia and I," said Brummell, "are very old friends you know." If he held Julia's affair with Cotton against her—in terms of sexual morality or pure sexual jealousy—it didn't prevent him making "strong love" to her later in life, perhaps in the manner of an affair born of a school reunion. But for a first affair, his tryst with Julia certainly had a dramatic and sobering conclusion. If there was anything more to what went on at Hampton Court, any sexual content to their teenage romance, he did not follow the example of Harriette and Julia in publishing. But it is intriguing to note that Julia is insistent she lost her virginity to "the impassioned solicitations of . . . one of the handsomest and most accomplished [men] of the age." Brummell is a hovering presence in both courtesans' memoirs: not rich enough to warrant their threat of scandal mongering, still famous enough to be worth mentioning. Perhaps Julia did indeed have two lovers, both Cotton and the schoolboy "violently in love with her." Such would be typical of her later behavior. Certainly Colonel Cotton himself is never described elsewhere as either "accomplished" or "passionate," so she might have been alluding to a truth that she could not admit as it contradicted her position as an ingenue fallen prey to an older man: namely that she had been Brummell's lover. This poem he wrote for and about Julia and her "love-child":

> Unhappy child of indiscretion,
> Poor slumberer on a breast forlorn!

Pledge and reproof of past transgression,
Dear, though unwelcome to be born.
. . . .
And lest the injurious world upbraid thee
For mine, or for thy mother's ill,
A nameless father still shall aid thee
A Hand unseen protect thee still.
Meanwhile, in these sequester'd valleys
Still shalt thou rest in calm content;
For innocence may smile at malice,
And thou—oh! Thou art innocent!

The second and fourth stanzas give the impression that George felt himself implicated in the birth, but they were written many years later and may even allude to another affair entirely. Almost certainly the child was Cotton's. George's love was more akin to the hopeless crush many teenage boys experience for the more sexually mature girls of their own age, but as a first lesson in adult love it was certainly harsh and scarring. It rang chords with him throughout his adult life, surrounded as he was by unwanted pregnancies and inconstant love affairs and adulterous liaisons, and later still when he was living with the reminder of "past transgression": his own degenerative venereal disease.

Cotton, as Julia wrote, came out of the affair neither "pitied" nor "despised," but only "envied." This did not go unnoticed by his rival in love. George Bryan Brummell, rejected by Julia in favor of an older man in uniform, set his heart on winning a commission with the colonel's own regiment, the Tenth Light Dragoons. As Julia said, "A hussar's cap and feather gives such a fillip to the spirits of a young miss, you don't know."

In early March 1793, George's mother died. She was buried on March 16 in a new family vault in the crypt of St. Martin-in-the-Fields. The boys came back to London for the funeral, but were at Eton through the following summer term, their last but one.

Though George clearly resembled his mother in his looks, he makes no mention ever of an affinity of character or a particular closeness. His world had become almost entirely masculine in his time at Eton, and quite possibly the death of Mary Brummell, following fast on his bruising affair with Julia Johnstone, pushed him further into a world in which the feminine was, essentially, foreign. Like his later friend, the Prince of Wales, George Brummell had a series of relationships with rather older women. This may articulate some of the loss he felt when his mother, a virtual stranger to him through his later childhood, was taken from him completely.

George, William and Maria were about to face a still harsher test, which had far more dramatic repercussions on their young lives. In early March 1794 news came from Donnington Grove that their father had also died. The siblings again gathered in London to see their father taken down the steps to the crypt of St. Martin's, a year and a day exactly after their mother. None of the three teenage Brummells could take control of the finances, as stated in the terms of their father's will, due to their legal minority. The estate, valued at around £60,000, nearly £5 million in today's money, was to be administered by the executors—first among them the former MP Charles Jenkinson, by then Lord Liverpool—and Donnington Grove sold.

Old Mr. Billy Brummell had stayed in London after his wife's funeral in 1793 and instructed the completion of a new will. Possibly he had been ill for some time, and certainly the death of his wife had alerted him, just in time as it happened, to his own mortality. The will's unusual stipulation that the family estate be sold and the proceeds split equally between the children was in the new fashion of land tenure pioneered in France. It was also the same principle followed by Billy's own father, William. Charles James Fox would have approved of this undermining of primogeniture. The thoughts of George's elder brother, William, on the matter are not recorded. George therefore, although a "younger son," faced none of the usual social impediments of that position. He would be as rich, on coming of age, as his brother or, for that matter, as his sister's husband. But as minors, the three bereaved Brummells had no say in what immediately happened.

George was still only fifteen, and he had lost the glamorous but distant figure of his mother and his disapproving father. Shortly after their father's death, he and William were both removed from the world they knew best, Eton, neither of them yet in the sixth form, and sent to Oxford. Sir John Macpherson and the lawyer Mr. White of Lincolns Inn, the old family friend who had so often been a visitor at Donnington, stood as guardians. They might have been acting in accordance with the last wishes of Billy Brummell, an understandably anxious father. He seems to have felt that the boys' best interests after his death would be served away from school in the less exalted, more hardworking crowd at Oriel. Oxford was the next rung on the ladder of political success, should either boy be inspired to follow in their father's profession. (Cambridge tended to serve better for aspiring churchmen and lawyers.) Doubtless old Billy Brummell had tired of George's school reports that came thick, fast and complaining during his final illness, and had necessitated sending his butler from Donnington with letters of such severity that George was reduced to tears. The bitter loneliness of this period of his life when he lost both parents fast on the trauma of his abortive first love affair began to shape, out of the cocky Eton schoolboy, the emotionally reticent adult man.

In May 1794, after the Easter holidays during which they had buried their father, William and George Brummell arrived as commoner undergraduates at Oriel College, Oxford. There is little record of George's involvement in college or university life. Some buttery receipts are all that attest to his undergraduate career. A later fellow of the college, writing in the 1880s, fails to make any mention of either Brummell in the alumni of the late eighteenth century. In 1794 Oriel contrasted little with Eton in terms of dull religious routine, glorious architecture and bad food. But as an Oxford undergraduate, for the few months George could count himself such, Oxford offered a much freer lifestyle than Eton had. "I spent fourteen months at Magdalen College," wrote the historian Gibbon, of Oxford in Brummell's day. "They proved to be the fourteen months the most idle and unprofitable of my whole life." Lord Malmesbury, similarly, who had been at Oxford before George, wrote that "the discipline of the university happened to be so lax that a gentleman commoner was under no restraint and never called upon to attend either lectures or chapel or hall . . . The set of men with whom I lived were very pleasant but very idle fellows. Our life was an imitation of high life in London." Nor should it be assumed that George Brummell was unusually young in going up to Oxford before his sixteenth birthday. The lifestyle, as hard-drinking as has been the case for more modern undergraduates, was enjoyed by students as young as fourteen.

In any event, Brummell's life as a student was short-lived. His Oxford career lasted only a few months. He was expected back after the summer vacation of 1794, but only William showed up. Instead, George had approached Sir John Macpherson, the chief executor of his father's will, with a proposition. He suggested a small part of his inheritance be used to buy an army commission.

In the years when all boys disassociate themselves from their parents, with greater or lesser animosity but with necessary effect for their later psychosexual health, George Brummell lost both of his to the crypt of St. Martin's. Studies on any childhood bereavement make for dark reading, but the loss of parents during adolescence can be particularly damaging, often more so than loss at an earlier age. It can leave an adolescent confused, angry and self-doubting—unable to enact the subtle distancing of leaving home because home ceases to exist. The bereaved themselves later talk of the concomitant feelings of anxiety and of guilt—as if the parent's death is the adolescent's fault. At the same time that George Brummell, lost his parents he lost also his first "violent" love, Julia Storer (Johnstone) to an older man. These were trying times for Brummell for all that his contemporaries described him as on the brink of manhood and a picture, even in Trebeck's fiction, of insouciant breeziness. It was an act. Brummell was, and remained, a lonely figure and a bleakly misanthropic comic. The "much admired drawing" he hung over his mantelpiece in adult life was titled *The Angry Child*.

George ran away from Oxford to join the army—an artificial family of men. The regiment was the same in which his one-time rival Colonel Cotton served. It was the most fashionable in the country, and the Prince of Wales had recently been appointed its colonel-in-chief. Quite how a sixteen-year-old came to take up a commission in the glamorous Tenth Light Dragoons is the next question in the unprecedented ascendancy of Beau Brummell.

4

THE PRINCE'S OWN

1794–1799

You all no doubt have heard
What has lately occurred
In the celebrated Troop of the Hussars
Where if you like to pay
A Cornetcy you may
Now purchase and avoid those ugly scars!
                    Song, "The 10th Hussars"

George Bryan Brummell met George Augustus Frederick, Prince of Wales, in 1793 or 1794. The heir to the throne was in his early thirties but nevertheless a friendship developed between him and the teenage Oxford undergraduate. The passion they shared was for clothes.

As early as 1782 the Duchess of Devonshire, friend to both the prince and later Brummell, described George III's eldest son as "fond of dress even to a tawdry degree" and that "his person, his dress and the admiration he has met . . . from women take up his thoughts chiefly." Although *Gentleman's Magazine* and *Bon Ton Magazine* wrote of the prince as "always the best dressed man at court," he had come of age in the last great epoch of the peacock male and was frequently overly—not to say ridiculously—dressed. Thirty years after George IV's death, William Thackeray recalled that as Prince of Wales he had dressed up in every kind of uniform, and every possible court dress—in long fair hair, with powder, with and without a pigtail—in every conceivable cocked-hat—in dragoon [hussar] uniform—in Windsor uniform—in a field marshal's clothes—in a Scotch kilt and tartans, with dirk and claymore (a stupendous figure)—in a frogged frock-coat with a fur collar and tight breeches and silk stockings—in wigs of every colour, fair, brown, and black.

The Duchess of Devonshire had been of the opinion since the Prince of Wales's youth that he would run to fat early in life and that his large frame and imposing bearing would lose their battle with his expanding weight. She was right. By 1799, Thomas Farington the artist was aware of the added attention to dress his bulk demanded, and that the prince "dresses surrounded by 3 glasses in which he can see his person." His stomach had to be corseted in a "Bastille of Whalebone"—euphemistically titled a "belt" by his tailors—and he had begun, when he met Brummell, to pioneer a fashion for the highest of collars, bound with a stiff "stock" that helped push his ruffle of chins into the semblance of a jawline. The Thomas Lawrence paintings from the turn of the century featuring this high collar, a sort of neck corset, allow an appreciation of how far fashion and art can go in flattering royalty.

Hiding the truth of his corpulence was one sartorial obsession for the prince. The other was military uniforms. George III had not allowed his eldest son any role in the military, despite ever more pressing demands from the prince that he, like his younger brothers, be given something to do. More than doing was the appearance of doing, and the prince was determined to be able to wear a uniform. When his brother, the Duke of York, visited Berlin in 1791, the Prince of Wales demanded of him a catalogue of details on continental uniforms. He wanted his brother to buy for him "the compleat uniforms, accoutrements, saddle, bridle, &c, of one of the Zieten's Hussars . . . as well as one of the Officers compleat uniforms, cloathing, sword, cap, saddle, bridle, chabrack, pistols, in short, everything compleat." He then studied what was brought back, and began designing and ordering his own version. As Caroline, Princess of Wales, observed cattily, "My husband understands how a shoe should be made or a coat cut . . . and would have made an excellent tailor, or shoemaker or hairdresser;—but nothing else."

For a man obsessed with the image of royalty, the military uniform assumed a key significance. The principal icon of monarchy that the age allowed was that of the "soldier-prince" in the mold of Frederick the Great of Prussia, and all the Hanoverian princes were schooled to admire the look and manner of martinet Teutonic royalty. Even without the heroic drama of Bonaparte on the other side of the channel, the prince would have sought for himself the image of a military leader. Such was the issue's importance in his mind that he wrote directly to Sir Henry Dundas, secretary for war, threatening that if he were not granted the rank and uniform of major general "it must lead to a total separation between the King and [myself]." He put it more eloquently to his father: "I have no option but to lead a life which must to the public eye wear the colour of an idleness . . . and which, from the sense of its so appearing, must sit irksomely upon me." A uniform would make him appear properly royal—a soldier-prince leading his people. In letters to his father he likened himself to the Black Prince, and in the portraits he commissioned he posed himself as a man of action, a military prince. Seeking in adult life the approbation he had never received from his parents, he often appeared to be trying to impress with clothes: an actor in search of a role. In the end, the military costume was all he got.

The prince wanted to head a regiment of his own, which he could both command and dress as he pleased. In 1783 his wish was, in part, granted. The young Tenth Regiment of Light Dragoons (a cavalry regiment) was "honoured" by the king with the title "the Prince of Wales's Own." The prince became colonel-in-chief only in 1793, when Britain declared war on revolutionary France and royalty in the military suddenly seemed like a useful rallying call. The prince's new military title was backdated to November 1782 so he would not be deemed a novice colonel in army orders of precedence—most importantly, relative to his brothers. But it was made clear that he would never serve in battle or abroad, and it was therefore unlikely that the Tenth Regiment would see harsh service. Because they were reserved for occasions when looking good was important—when not in Brighton, they acted as royal escorts in Windsor and London—and were treated with delicacy by military command, the regiment became known as the "China Tenth." As a result it began to attract officers intent on a noncombatant military career in close proximity to the courts of the Prince of Wales at Carlton House and the Royal Pavilion at Brighton. In these regards a commission in the Tenth Regiment became at once both a sort of draft dodge and entree to high society. It also furnished its officers and men with an excuse to wear by far the most up-to-date and flattering of uniforms.

How, then, did George Brummell, who had in no sense completed his education at either Eton or Oxford, and was, no matter how mature his demeanor, aged only sixteen, receive such a prize as a commission in the Prince's Own? It was widely assumed he had been selected for his cornetcy—the first rank of commissioned officer in a British cavalry troop—by none other than the new colonel-in-chief himself. Within a few years three stories were in circulation explaining how the Prince of Wales and the schoolboy had come to know each other. In two versions they had met in London; in the other, at Windsor. Conflicting tales were cited in different editions of the *Reminiscences and Recollections* of Captain Gronow. None of these stories reflects very well on George Brummell, as a social climber, or on Prince George, as an abuser of his position.

One version of the story quoted by Gronow, among others, had young George first meeting the commander of his future regiment in Green Park. This picturesque anecdote cast George's aunt Searle—his mother's sister—as leading lady. She worked in Green Park as a milkmaid at the ornamental dairy, just near Clarges Street where there was at that time a small duckpond. Mrs. Searle claimed that she was looking after her nephew there in the summer of 1792 when the dairy was honored by a visit from the Marchioness of Salisbury, accompanied by the Prince of Wales. The prince struck up conversation with the schoolboy and asked him, in the recognizable manner of royals in conversation with schoolchildren, what he intended to do when he left school. George replied that he wanted to be an officer in the prince's own regiment. This combination of cheek and ambition gives this story some credibility. The prince laughed and said George should write to him when he left Eton. Mrs. Searle, in a believable aside in Gronow's version, added that she saw little of Brummell as "soon as he began to mix in society with the Prince, and his visits to me became less and less frequent and now he hardly ever calls to see his old aunt," but that he had, in his youth, had "nice manners." The true story is probably more prosaic.

George, by his own telling, first encountered the Prince of Wales at Eton and Windsor. This was inevitably the case, as members of the royal family were frequent visitors to the school, being both patrons and near neighbors when in residence at Windsor Castle. Whether the prince and schoolboy actually spoke is less clear. Brummell said they did, on the terrace at Windsor Castle, and that even then each recognized in the other a fascination with what they were wearing, and what it was to present oneself in public as a gentleman, and that in this respect Brummell "acquitted himself to the Prince's satisfaction." It seems the prince was struck not so much by Brummell's attire—most likely the blue, buff and white of the Montem polemen—as by his confident self-assurance, always the more arresting in the very young. "He . . . displayed there all that the Prince of Wales most esteemed of human things: a splendid youth enhanced by the aplomb of the man who has judged life and can dominate it, the subtlest and most audacious mingling of impertinence and respect, and finally a genius for dress and deportment protected by a gift for perpetually witty repartee."

A third possibility remains that George was slightly known in the prince's circle even before this as a result of an early introduction at Devonshire House in Mayfair. His father's friends Sheridan and Charles James Fox were on easy terms with the Duchess of Devonshire, who in turn was the sort of hostess who sought out new, glamorous and young additions to her London guest lists. This places Brummell's first introduction to Georgiana, Duchess of Devonshire, in late 1793, fast on the heels of her return from a scandalous exile in which she had given birth to an illegitimate child. This at least was Tom Raikes's later account of the connection that got young Buck Brummell from Eton into the flashest regiment in town.

All this said, the application to the regiment probably went by the usual route. The prince had the opportunity to blackball candidates, and he certainly made Brummell's life regally easy once he was in the regiment, but to begin with Brummell probably had strings pulled for him by one of his guardians. Sir John Macpherson, a close associate of Brummell in the North administration and frequent Donnington guest, was the first named of the several guardians appointed for Maria, William and George by the terms of their father's will. He was also one of several figures at Westminster who regularly placed names on lists of applicants to suitable regiments. It seems that George wrote from Oriel to Sir John Macpherson, bypassing Mr. Joseph White at Lincolns Inn, who was supposedly in charge of the Brummell sons' education, requesting that money be released from the estate to buy a cornetcy in the Tenth Light Dragoons. It would cost him £735. Thence, he knew, he would be in much closer proximity to his friendly acquaintance, the Prince of Wales, and en route to a much more exciting life than Oriel could offer.

The first thing George needed to do, which occupied his interest as much as it had for his colonel-in-chief, was to order a uniform. The Tenth Light Dragoons' uniform was dark blue, with pale yellow facings and silver-thread braiding. It was also alarmingly expensive. There was a blue, sleeveless "upper jacket" or "shell" with braided epaulettes, cut long on the body and worn over a sleeved underjacket. Both items were "frogged and looped" or embroidered with horizontal braidings in white satin, and were further decorated with real silver tassels and "Elliot" balls. The entire body was lined with white silk. The headdress was a large "Tarleton" helmet—named after a hero of the American War of Independence, Colonel Banastre Tarleton: "a perfect model of manly strength and vigour," who loved to gamble, could tame a wild stallion and was a well-known womanizer. The outlandish helmet he made fashionable was formed of a peaked leather skull, bound around with a leopard-skin turban, fastened on the left with a silver clasp; the Tenth Light Dragoons' was in the style of the Prince of Wales's feathers. To cap it all there was a high black fur crest, in antique Roman style, from front to back.

A singular feature of the Tenth Regiment was their riding breeches. They were white, tight, trouser length and worn uncomfortably, considering they were a cavalry regiment, without underwear. They were themselves a sort of fashion item. In part, this was because British riding wear was being adopted in postrevolutionary France, which saw in riding breeches and boots an egalitarian corollary to the politics of the Enlightenment: a look for Everyman. Partly this was an unexpected echo, in the design of military uniforms, of neoclassicism. The cavalry officers doubtless thought of their breeches as a practical solution to controlling a horse in the English manner, which is to say with their legs rather than the horse's bridle, and in this they were right: the design was functional in allowing close contact between horse and rider. Fashion became wedded to functionality, however, in the pale and form-fitting breeches, which echoed classical statuary: the marble-colored wool, woven on stocking looms, gave the rider's legs the appearance of nakedness.

Moreover the Tenth, uniquely, had breeches that in some cases reached their feet—trousers, in effect—held in place with instep stirrups, over which riding boots could be worn, or shoes at night. Brummell first tried on this military hybrid, pantaloons—for all they had the appearance most often of knee-length breeches—in the early summer of 1794. It would eventually be the style he made fashionable for a new generation, one that became, ultimately, modern trousers.

A young officer like Brummell was expected to buy his own uniform. In May 1794 he made his first trip, financed by the trust fund set up for the Brummell children, to Schweitzer and Davidson's at 12 Cork Street. They made all the prince's uniforms, and all the uniforms for his officers at this time. An infantry officer could expect to pay up to forty pounds for his uniform—more than a working man's annual wage. A Light Dragoon or heavy-cavalry officer, meanwhile, was expected to pay around £150. The regiments that came to relish the name "Hussars," however, had uniforms and accoutrements costing up to £300. Records for one officer of the Tenth Light Dragoons show a single uniform bill of £399 7s. 6d., and the prince's uniforms, only slightly more elaborate than the other officers', regularly cost over £344 each. Once cornetcy and uniform were paid for, George had little change out of a thousand pounds from his inheritance.

There was no standard-issue cloak for the Light Dragoons; instead they pioneered a continental fashion for the pelisse, an off-the-shoulder fur throw. It was the most expensive part of their uniform; one belonging to the prince cost a hundred pounds. Another, hardly less expensive, was described as an "Extra superfine blue cloth Polony Peless [pelisse] richly trimmed with silver, the borders and edges of rich silver work, rich silver bullion fringes for the hips, silver tassels on the skirts . . . fur trimming, silk lining and pockets, extra double plated buttons, [with] lambs wool interlining and materials compleat." In wearing fur pelisses the dragoons were signaling their desire—and the prince's—that they should be regarded as "Hussars," a title unknown in the British Army until they were granted this sobriquet in 1811. The term was Hungarian in origin, a corruption of the Magyar *husz ara,* "the price of twenty," alluding to the conscription of every twentieth man, or a man from every twentieth household. Brummell later referred to his time in the "Hussars" and it was to have a profound influence on his sartorial style, and as a result that of Regency London. But in point of fact the regiment he joined in 1794 called themselves Light Dragoons and continued to do so for all his time there. However, they thought of themselves as Hussars, behaved like Hussars and dressed like them accordingly.

The Hussar regiments in continental Europe had grown a reputation in the eighteenth century for wild living, military prowess, and for dazzling, flattering uniforms that veered toward the outlandish. Consequently the Hussar look had been a commonplace masquerade costume in the late eighteenth century in London, and this was how the Prince of Wales first wore it. The pelisse harked back to the original "Hussars" in medieval Hungary, who hunted wolves on horseback and flung the pelts over their shoulders. The fur pelisse as a fashion statement in early nineteenth-century Europe was a distant echo of this wild-man soldiering.

Kitted out in the blue, white and silver of the Tenth, Brummell set off for Brighton. The coaches left from the White Horse cellar at the western end of Piccadilly, with tickets for sale from Davies and Co. in the sanded-floor undercroft waiting room. The coach ran via Lewes and East Grinstead and took twelve hours to get to Brighton. Only four passengers could ride inside.

It was during the course of this first hot Brighton summer that Brummell and the prince got to know each other well. It was an easy atmosphere in which to mingle with royalty and with the well connected—an atmosphere, royalty aside, not unlike the Eton sixth form of the day, but a good deal more raucous. The prince was not above engineering the election of young officers, like Brummell, to maintain the party atmosphere at Brighton. When a vacancy occurred, the prince took an interest. The regiment had already attracted the sons of the Duke of Rutland, Lords Charles and Robert Manners, who became close friends of Brummell. It also boasted among its number Lord Charles Stanhope (later Petersham), who remained friends with Brummell for the next twenty years; Lord Charles Kerr, son of the Duke of Roxburghe; Lord Bligh, son of the Earl of Darnley; Lord Lumley, son of the Earl of Scarborough; and

Lord Edward Somerset, son of the Duke of Beaufort; as well as Frederick Ponsonby, Lord Bessborough's son and the only man Harriette Wilson said she had truly loved.

Jack Slade, who joined the regiment a little before Brummell, recalled the hard drinking in the mess. The officers of the Tenth had wineglasses specially made with no stems, so that they could be replaced on the table only once they had been emptied. The prince, when once asked to sing, replied that all the best songs he knew were "two-bottle songs," and proceeded to down such—and sing. Those who could not keep up with the pace quietly emptied their glasses under the table. But most drank. It was a mixed crowd, insofar as they were not all noblemen, but they were all considered worthy of the prince's company in terms of being, as the prince put it, "men of Fashion and Gentlemen." It was an enclosed world of men in which wit was relished but in the barrack-room manner—a convivial but knockabout atmosphere, recalled by a veteran thirty years later with rueful nostalgia:

The officers of those days [were] . . . thrown headlong into a vicious school . . . where at times they were expected to act as if in reality they were thinking beings, and at others chastised for merely thinking. [The officers] were suffered to get drunk, swear, gamble, seduce, and run into debt at pleasure; that such a school produced many scamps, many incorrigible, bad characters is but little surprising; it is indeed, truly wonderful that it produced anything else.

Life as a dragoon officer in the late eighteenth century was a school for scandalous behavior:

The reputation of being what in slang phraseology of the day was called "a three bottle man," "a devil of a fellow for the ladies," "a wild and extravagant dog" was at this time far from being injurious to [an officer's] professional reputation, and was quite likely to get him an appointment as that of an Aide de Camp, whose principal duty in those days was to fill the decanters and see that they were emptied before they left the table.

Consequently Brummell's particular brand of rhetorical whimsy, honed at Eton and Oxford, was redirected in the army into a darker comic inversion where everything that the outside world deemed bad was good—and funny. Brummell was "the life and soul of the mess with his regiment, for his original wit and collection of good stories were inexhaustible; and at the dinner table he always kept his brother officers in roars of laughter." "Every regiment in those days had a practised and privileged jester . . . whose province it was to put an immediate stop to serious conversation by a pun or joke" and restore "that hilarity which usually pervades military society." Black humor was evidently prized; lewdness and scatology were reserved for occasions exclusive of respectable women, which most, of course, were. Brummell's gift of mimicry was honed in the course of all this barracks badinage, a gift he shared with the prince. The only man whose range of impersonations was acknowledged to be wider than Brummell's was the prince himself, whose "powers of mimicry were so extraordinary," said Brummell, "that if his lot [had] fallen that way, he would have been the best comic actor in Europe."

The raucous regiment became notorious in Brummell's time as "the most expensive, the most impertinent, the best dressed, the worst moralled regiment in the British Army." For a young man without parental guidance in the world, he was running with a wild crowd. "Its officers, many of them titled," were derided as "all more or less distinguished in the trying campaigns of the London season . . . all intimates of the Prince-Colonel." The Tenth responded to the prince's example by drinking heavily, living loosely, riding well and dressing superbly when the occasion demanded. They could certainly put on a good show. On August 10, 1794 they were reviewed on the Sussex Downs with the Royal Horse Artillery by General Bruce and commended on their "soldierly appearance and the exact manner in which they went through their military evolutions."

George Brummell had learned some horsemanship at Donnington Grove, so in this respect he was well suited to life with the

Tenth. They took great pride both in their riding and in their horses—officers were expected to provide their own—and Brummell's preeminent task as a cornet was to look good on horseback while bearing the flag. There was no formal provision of basic training for an officer in the army until 1801, but there were guidebooks that young cavalrymen like Brummell were encouraged to keep always in the pockets of their jackets—the guides of Bland and Simes. These explained how to perform the manual and platoon exercises of the firelock and carbine rifles. Constant study of these and the regimental orderly and records books constituted officer instruction. Training with the lower ranks in the company of more experienced officers was, in theory, meant to allow every newly commissioned man to learn by example "and inform themselves of every article of their Duty . . . by asking Questions of their superiors."

There was a drill sergeant who attacked the ears of the new recruits and officers, memorably recorded by one of the Tenth "girls" woken from her slumbers by the daily 8:00 A.M. harangue:

"Tik nuttis!! The wurd "dror" is oney a carshun. A t'wurd "suards" ye drors um hout, tekin a farm un possitif grip o'th'hilt!

Sem time, throwing th'shith smartly backords, thus! "DROR SUARDS!!' "

Senior officers, in turn, were "to teach their Subalterns their duty and see they do it by fair means, and tell them their faults and omissions . . . and let them know they are not to have their Pay to be Idle." For the officers it was a clubby atmosphere of enthusiastic amateurism, quite at odds with the brutal realities of the war raging across the channel.

Brummell addressed the regimen with an air he was developing even as a teenager: amused indifference. Quite soon after his gazetting in the summer of 1794, a loose charger was seen galloping down the ranks of the regiment as it stood in formation on parade. This exchange was considered worthy of record by a military memoirist:

"WHOSE HORSE IS THAT?" bawled the Colonel. "Mr Brummell's sir!" came the reply. "Send him here!" Brummell duly came. "What have you to say?" demanded the Colonel (the story is recorded with the note that the colonel used additional military expletives).

"The fact is, Colonel," [dead-panned the young cornet] "my horse is a very fine animal and wanted to show off his paces, so I let him go."

A reply, [noted the old soldier] which merely added fuel to the fire.

Army training had its costs, however, even for a cavalryman like Brummell, set on avoiding all appearance of effort or anxiety. Sometime early in his military career, Brummell took a bad fall from his horse. He met with an uncooperative cobblestone, which smashed his nose to the left. The bridge was set, but crooked to the side. To some, this added character and a rougher edge to a face that had looked soft and somewhat haughty beforehand. To others, Julia Johnstone in particular, Brummell's broken nose forever ruined his looks. He was no longer the perfect boy.

Brummell rode with aplomb, and played his part to the hilt as one of the Falstaffian drinking partners to the Prince of Wales's Prince Hal. But it can have been of no surprise to his family or Eton friends that he turned out not to be a born soldier.

The best-known anecdote in military circles became the story of how Brummell recognized the men under his command. At parade each day, he made it his habit to arrive late and get in line quickly on his mount by the expedient of riding to the front of one particular militiaman foot soldier with a drinker's bloodshot nose. It was the sort of thing Cornet Brummell noticed. The troop, inevitably, was rearranged pending the enrollment of some new recruits, and Brummell's blue-nosed marking point was moved.

Brummell galloped into place.

"How now, Mr. Brummell?" cried the sorely tried colonel. "You are with the wrong troop!"

Brummell swiveled in his saddle to check that he was in front of the bloodshot nose, which, indeed, he was, although not in front of any other of his men. "No, no, sir, you are quite wrong. A pretty thing indeed, if I did not know my own troop!"

The story that evening was added to Brummell's repertoire of self-deprecating mess-room anecdotes at a dinner with the prince, and a small piece of the mosaic of his legend fell into place: Brummell, too insouciant to know or care who his men were. Brummell, the disengaged, witty amateur. Waggish and indifferent. His prince-colonel laughed. The style of gentlemanly behavior Brummell was developing meant never looking as if you cared too much, or worked too hard. Except, perhaps, at play.

For a well-dressed young dragoon officer around Brighton, there was plenty to amuse. Within a few months of his gazetting in 1794, the dragoons were given a central role in Brighton's annual celebrations of the prince's birthday. There was music and fireworks, "a transparent painting of His Royal Highness's coronet and crest adorned with red roses, a garter star decorated with woodbine and lilies and HRH's initials beautifully written in flowers"; the decorations were further embellished with "a wreath of laurel, the whole encircled with the British oak and acorns and the motto 'Brighton's Support' " in honor of the prince who was quite simply that.

The *Public Advertiser* claimed nothing could outshine the prince-colonel's "principal amusement," which was "in manoeuvring his regiment," and so on August 30 a still larger grand field day and sham battle were staged on the downs, with the prince-colonel commanding and charging with his men. "All the beauty and fashion of the neighbourhood attended the field."

According to *The Times* the young blades of the Tenth Regiment kept a schedule that summer in accordance with Brighton high life: "Most of them keep their own blood-horses and their girls. At one o'clock they appear on parade to hear the word of command given to the subaltern guard; afterwards they toss off their *goes* of brandy, dine about five, and come about eight to the theatre." It was a fine life, a metropolitan life. Brighton's population might hover around five thousand out of season, almost a village, but when the prince and the dragoons were in town—seven thousand assorted militiamen and foot soldiers under the command of officers like Brummell—the whole tone of Brighton changed.

In 1794 Brighton was already Mayfair-by-the-Sea. The architecture, even the clotted-cream paint on the stucco, was indistinguishable from the most fashionable parts of London, and the inhabitants in many cases were the same people. Henry Holland had designed an elegant neoclassical "Marine Pavilion" for the prince, which dominated the Steine—Brighton's main promenade route perpendicular to the seafront. The Brighton that Cornet Brummell knew looked like London and was, in style, everything the later Regency period came to epitomize: restrained, elegant, classical. This hid a very different style of living for the coterie around the young Prince of Wales. For them, Brighton was relaxed and indulgent, much freer than London—especially in terms of sexual morality. The young officers of the Tenth were all out of sight of their parents, the moral guardians of the previous generation, and were setting the rules themselves, rules that, come the Regency, would be the orthodoxy of London society, too.

The new wife of Sir John Lade, Letitia, Lady Lade, was typical of Brighton society in Brummell's time. She had previously served the Duke of York, in a nonmilitary position, and also Mr. Rann, a notorious highwayman. She was said to act as procuress for the prince, soliciting on his behalf the virgin daughters of genteel Brighton families. She was also conspicuous around Brighton for driving her own carriages at breakneck speed. There was also the Marquess of Queensberry, an ageing roué nicknamed "Old Tick" by the Tenth Light Dragoons. The prince had spotted him at the Brighton theater with Mrs. Harris, the fruit woman, and asked her if she was not afraid of the consequences of flirting with the rake. "No, Your Highness," she rejoined "for alas, His Grace is like an old clock: he can tick but he can't strike."

Many of the dragoons kept common-law wives in Brighton, their "girls," who were set up in styles strictly in accordance with the rank of their lover. It was unusual for a dragoon officer to be married. When the Marquess of Worcester took a commission in the Tenth, Harriette Wilson came with him; he arrived ahead of her to set up a household for her on Marine Parade as if she were his marchioness.

As colonel-in-chief, the prince occasionally had cause to explain a type of battle fatigue particular to the Tenth on maneuvers in Brighton: "A very serious venereal attack," he wrote to the army commander-in-chief, his brother, the Duke of York, on September 15, 1795, was laying up one Captain Fuller of the Tenth and putting him outside active duty for the immediate future. "Nothing fresh but an old business which has hitherto only been patched up," the worldly prince explained, "but which [the doctor] assures him now with perseverance he will completely get rid of." He enclosed a medical note.

Brummell kept no particular "girl" in Brighton but was exposed for the first time in his adult life to the frequent company of women—most of whom, it should be allowed, were far from respectable. Although Harriette Wilson was in Brighton a little after Brummell, her memoirs are a vivid reminder that the world Elizabeth Bennet dreaded for her sister Lydia in *Pride and Prejudice* was very real, very brazen and based all around the Tenth Light Dragoons' officers' mess. The Tenth took their "girls" to the Brighton theater, and even took them to the Marine Pavilion. They openly cohabited with them, and invited them to wild nights in the barracks dining room. In leaving Oxford and joining the dragoons at Brighton, Brummell conformed to a family pattern his father had tried to break: he was once again in the demimonde, among prostitutes and courtesans just as if he had been back at Bury Street. Sexual license was all around him. He was nineteen. If, as seems most probable, he contracted the venereal disease that eventually killed him from a whore, it would have been at Brighton that he formed the habit, typical of his class and era, of frequenting prostitutes.

"These great [army] depots," wrote one contemporary, "are the fertile hotbeds where syphilitic disease is sown broadcast amongst the young soldiers."

The most highly regarded of the kept women of Brighton was the secret wife of the prince-colonel himself, Mrs. Fitzherbert. Hers was the grandest house on the Steine apart from the prince's own, and she was held in good regard by the people of Brighton and by the Tenth Light Dragoons. She even attended military parades to watch her "husband," the prince, dressed in her own version of the Light Dragoons uniform, Prince of Wales feathers in her hair.

The widowed Maria Fitzherbert had married the Prince of Wales in December 1785. This marriage was illegal in the eyes of the law but not in the eyes of the Roman Catholic Church, to which she claimed devotion, and allowed her to accept the prince's attentions and money. She may have known he would not and could not stay faithful to her, but seemingly, she loved him. At the same time she enjoyed the status and privileges of royalty—especially in Brighton. In Brighton she was "treated as a queen" and when she dined out she was "led out to dinner before princesses."

Mrs. Fitzherbert organized entertainments for the Tenth Light Dragoons officers, perhaps in an attempt to lure them away from drink. There was music, a passion of the prince, but also amateur dramatics, at which George Brummell excelled. There were cricket matches, fencing competitions, dinner parties and dances. She also attended with them the race meetings—and she and the prince even had a run of good luck on the horses.

Mrs. Fitzherbert was thirty-seven when she and Brummell first met in the summer of 1794, and coming to the end of her second reign of influence. She had already lost the Prince of Wales more than once to other mistresses, and the fact of her marriage had been denied twice in the House of Commons, on the direct authority of the prince. But they had reunited in 1791, and maintained a brief period of domestic content and relative financial rectitude until things began to go wrong again in 1793.

One of the least attractive qualities of the man Maria Fitzherbert called her husband was his inconstancy. Few friends, no family members and none of his many lovers remained close to the prince throughout his life: he was always falling out of friendships and falling in love. This trait had disastrous consequences for his young protégé, George Brummell, and in 1794, in a different manner, a grave effect on the prince's relationship with Maria. By the time George Brummell came to know them, the prince's attentions had moved away—again temporarily—from Mrs. Fitzherbert, who found herself in the distressing position of being two-timed by a husband who was being leaned on by Parliament and the king to take a legitimate, royal, Protestant bride. As with all the trials of her long life, she took these latest blows—the prince's intended marriage and his simultaneous affair with an overweight grandmother nine years his senior—with a grace that impressed many, including the new young cornet in her husband's regiment, George Brummell. To complicate matters, Mrs. Fitzherbert may also have been pregnant, although the evidence for this is not conclusive, with the first of three "secret" daughters fathered by the prince. Two of these supposed daughters, Mary Anne Smyth and Minney Seymour, were later "adopted" by Mrs. Fitzherbert as her nieces and referred to by the prince (by then George IV) as his "daughters." Brummell's close association with the prince during the years in which he may have fathered a secret family, as well as a legitimate one, was part of what made the potential of his memoirs in later life so explosive.

The newer, older woman in the prince's life in 1794, however, was the redoubtable Countess of Jersey, a confidante of his mother, Queen Charlotte, and a formidable rival to Mrs. Fitzherbert. Lady Jersey was described as "clever, unprincipled, but a beautiful and fascinating woman, though with scarcely any retrieving really good quality." In a scurrilous rating of the attributes of leading London ladies by the *Morning Post,* she had scored nought out of twenty for both principles and sense. In London society she was known as "Lucretia." Maria Fitzherbert later allowed that her split with the Prince of Wales in 1794 was as a direct result of "the twofold influence of the pressure of his debts on the mind of the Prince, and a wish on the part of Lady Jersey to enlarge the Royal Establishment in which she was to have an important situation." Or, as *Bon Ton Magazine* put it, "the union between this fashionable pair, the prince and Mrs F . . . has at length been resolved. The lady retires to Switzerland . . . and a settlement of £6000 per annum. The gentleman visits Jersey."

Lady Jersey, unlike Mrs. Fitzherbert, had some interest in pushing the prince toward the legal marriage he had long been avoiding. Queen Charlotte may have encouraged her to suggest to him that he could resolve his debts and his unpopularity if he were to take a legal wife and beget an heir. He seems not to have needed too much convincing. William Pitt reluctantly agreed that the country would increase his Civil List income from £60,000 to £100,000 a year, and there was also his income from the Duchy of Cornwall. William Cobbett, writing in 1830, pointed out bitterly that the original sum already represented enough to support "3000 labouring families for a year." Parliament also allowed him more than £20,000 toward a royal wedding. The prince agreed, and immediately spent £54,000 on jewels for his nuptials.

It shows some considerable success on the part of George Brummell, in terms of his social ascendancy and his budding friendship with the prince, that less than a year after joining the regiment and still only in his teens he found himself standing as *chevalier d'honneur* at the ensuing wedding of George, Prince of Wales, to Princess Caroline of Brunswick.

The choice of bride was another effect of Lady Jersey's influence. Of all the many eligible Protestant princesses of Europe, Princess Caroline Amelia Elizabeth of Brunswick-Wolfenbüttel was perhaps the least suited to be sacrificed on the altar of dynastic obligations to a man like the Prince of Wales, sensitive, insecure and fastidious as he was. Lady Jersey knew this: she intended the young bride to be no real rival to her. Princess Caroline had been brought up in a small German court far from the cosmopolitan sophistication of London. She was six years younger than the prince, utterly inexperienced in the world and given to girlish fits of pique (that much they had in common) but also crass and vulgar jokes. She was said to eat raw onions, a German fashion of the day, and wash rarely. Wellington said it was self-evident that Lady Jersey had chosen Caroline to be Princess of Wales for her "indelicate manners, indifferent character, and not very inviting appearance from the hope that disgust for the wife would secure constancy to the mistress." If so, she was to be disappointed, but the marriage nevertheless proved a disaster.

George Brummell fell headlong for the romance of a royal wedding, and blithely described the princess as "a very handsome and desirable looking woman."

Once the marriage settlement had been arranged between the courts of St. James and Brunswick-Wolfenbüttel, with no more than an exchange of portraits between the couple themselves, the princess was readied to be shipped off from Germany in the company of Lord Malmesbury. His round trip to collect her took him nearly five months, partly due to inclement weather during the winter of 1794–1795 and the advance, despite this, of Napoleon in the Netherlands, but also to Malmesbury's deliberate delay as he endeavored to polish Caroline's manners. It was a hopeless task. She lacked, he wrote "character and tact . . . she has no governing powers . . . with a steady man she would do vastly well, but with one of different description there are great risks." Caroline, with Malmesbury, arrived at Greenwich on April 5, 1795.

The escort sent to greet her was from the prince's own Tenth Light Dragoons, and was headed by Lord Edward Somerset and Cornet Brummell. Somerset and Brummell were late. It was a Sunday morning, and they had been carousing on the previous Saturday night in London with a disconsolate prince. They and the carriage for the princess, drawn by six horses, galloped up to the quayside, with an annoyed and flustered Lady Jersey inside. She had been appointed lady of the bedchamber to the new bride, an act of astonishing tactlessness and cruelty even on the part of a prince famous for both—and her first responsibility had been to meet the princess. She greeted her, criticized her dress, then told the princess that she would not sit facing backward, as it made her feel sick. Lord Malmesbury was forced to point out that, were that the case, she should never have accepted the post.

The dragoons thence escorted the bride-to-be and the piqued mistress of the bridegroom to St. James's Palace. Brummell, as his rank befitted, flew the standard of the regiment, along with the princess's.

On meeting Caroline for the first time, the Prince of Wales took one look at her and turned to Lord Malmesbury to mutter ungallantly, "Harris, I am not well; pray get me a glass of brandy." Then he left the room. Brummell, Malmesbury, Lord Edward Somerset and Lord Moira stared at the floor as the benighted princess exclaimed, in French, "Does the prince always behave like this? I think he's very fat, and he's nothing like as handsome as his portrait."

It was an unimpressive insight for seventeen-year-old Brummell not only into the character of his new friend and princely "patron," but also into the unique pressures of palace life.

Brummell, like many of his contemporaries, was broadly sympathetic to the plight of a young woman who, whatever her personal shortcomings, was hopelessly out of her depth in her marriage to the Prince of Wales. The prince's actions continued to reflect extremely badly on him, though Brummell tended to put the best possible gloss on things. For a young man just eighteen months out of school, these were heady days. "Never," wrote *Bon Ton Magazine,* "was public as well as private solicitude wound up to such a high pitch." But public and press were determined that this was to be a fairy-tale wedding and poured compliments on the diminutive German princess, "whose virtues no less than her personal charms give her a lawful claim to love and esteem as to the admiration of the British nation in general."

The royal couple were given no time to reflect on the mistake they might be making, and were due to be married a few days later, on the following Wednesday night. The king did not see that this was fit reason to withdraw the prince's unmarried brothers from their military duties, so Lord Moira and George Brummell stood in as "best men," along with the Dukes of Bedford and Roxburghe. Cornet Brummell was becoming part of the inner royal sanctum, taken to the warm heart of the prince—a place, however, where it was not always comfortable to be.

It must have been exciting and alarming in fairly equal measure, exposed both to the glamour of royalty and the tawdry personal politics of the House of Hanover. On their way to the ceremony the prince confessed to Moira and Brummell his eternal love for Mrs. Fitzherbert. At the wedding—in Inigo Jones's Queen's Chapel by St. James's Palace, acting as Chapel Royal at the time, swagged in crimson velvet and silver tissue—the groom was conspicuously drunk. He, Moira and Brummell had been drinking the prince's favorite brandy, marasquin (or maraschino), in an attempt to improve the prince's mood and his breath. To the strains of Handel's wedding anthem, "he hiccoughed out his vows of fidelity" while making eyes at his mistress, Lady Jersey, placed nearby in the choir pews. When the Archbishop of Canterbury asked if anyone knew of any impediment why the prince might not be married, Brummell and Moira fixed their eyes on the floor and the prince burst into tears. The "happy" couple retired almost immediately to bed (the wedding had been inexpediently timed for 8:00 P.M., precisely when the prince and his cronies would usually be drunk), and the bride said the groom was so inebriated he "passed the greatest part of his bridal night under the [fire] grate, where he fell."

The next day Brummell accompanied the newlyweds to Windsor, and thence to Kempshott. He was one of the party whom Caroline later claimed ruined her honeymoon by partying with the prince and lying about the castle "constantly drunk, sleeping and snoring in boots on the sofas . . . & the whole resembling a bad brothel much more than a palace." Rather than making love to his wife, the prince seems to have decided to act up to his coterie of young male friends, playing partly for sympathy and partly in the traditional spirit of drunken male braggadocio. After his wedding night, Brummell was the first person he saw, and he bragged through his hangover that "nothing could [have gone off] better," and winked that although "her manners were not those of a novice," on seeing him naked she had gasped, like a heroine of erotica, "Mon dieu, qu'il est gros!" [My God, it's huge! Or, alternatively, My God, he's so fat!]. He seems not to have taken this as a double-edged compliment.

Yet at the same time he complained viciously at the simple dynastic imperative of impregnation, claiming that she had eschewed Malmesbury's advice to try washing all over and that she "showed . . . such marks of filth both in the fore and hind part of her . . . that she turned my stomach and from that moment I made a vow never to touch her again." In the three nights they spent together, however, they conceived a child—Princess Charlotte of Wales, born nine months later. But it was an ugly start to an ugly marriage, and one in which Brummell felt ever more torn between his loyalties to the prince and his instinctive kindheartedness toward the princess. His is a lone voice from this period in their marriage, one that puts an unusually positive glow on what was largely reported as a disaster. His singularity in this, as the one close witness who claimed, briefly, there was some good feeling between the royal couple, may be the nostalgia for his own youth and first taste of royal glamour, or equally a small truth remembered by one who had little more to do with the princess beyond her honeymoon. "[They] then appeared very satisfied with each other," he later said, "and it was only when the intrigues of [Lady Jersey] began to take effect that any disagreement between them became apparent." Or so it seemed to Cornet Brummell. The new Prince and Princess of Wales moved to their new, separate apartments at Carlton House, and Brummell returned to his regiment.

Brummell's late teens were spent on the regular progress with the Tenth Light Dragoons, with occasional elevations to the highest society. It must have been a disturbingly schizophrenic existence. Long summers in Brighton with the regiment meant days in the mess tents and on horseback, and evenings at the Marine Pavilion with the Prince of Wales. October generally saw a decamp inland. Next the Tenth went to "Croydon and the places of the neighbourhood," and then on "King's Duty" at Windsor or as ceremonial guards at the empty royal palace at Hampton Court. Brummell found himself each autumn back in his childhood home, but this time staying in the barracks by the palace, not within it, with the ghosts all around of his family and the heartbreak of Julia.

There would often be a return to Brighton around Christmas, and in the spring another round of mock battles and a larger camp. Some years the troops around Brighton numbered over ten thousand. The 1794 and 1795 camps, high above Brighton's Race Hill, served also as lookouts into the channel and the expected French invasion. On a clear day messages could be sent to Shoreham and Seaford or passed to ships off the coast. Panic broke out one morning when troops rallied on Brighton beach after a signal was misread at the camp. Townsfolk heard the rumor of invasion, took to the beach with their own weapons and started a fight with British soldiers, whom they mistook for French.

The Light Dragoons saw action in Brighton only once, against smugglers. In October 1794 they impounded five hundred "tubs" of contraband gin, leaving two of their number to guard them while the others went to Shoreham to alert the customs office there. On returning, they found that the two officers left in charge had decided to open the gin, in the true spirit of the times and of the regiment, and started an impromptu party on the beach.

Brummell rose in the ranks to lieutenant in 1795 and then, in 1796, to captain. This gave him extra duties, which he would not have appreciated, and cost him dear: £997 10s. for the lieutenancy and £2782 10s. to be a captain. But the prize was worth it in one regard: the uniform kept getting better.

As a captain, Brummell had the right to wear yellow facings on his jacket and have a red busby bag and red cloth facing to the *sabretache* that supported his sword. The swords were curved like scimitars with a plain cross bar over the "Mameluke" hilt, which had no knuckle bow or any protection for the fingers. It was designed to terrify the enemy in battle, to cut falling silk—an unlikely necessity in combat—but its delicacy of line and real lack of weight exposed its owner's knuckles to serious injury. It was all about the look: it was, as the Marquess of Worcester put it, "the square thing."

Officers had gray fur for their pelisse and for their busby, real silver lace on the jacket, with three loops of silver at the cuff, as a reference to the Prince of Wales's feathers. All this ate into Brummell's inheritance. He was expected to "keep up [repair] his expensive uniform and horse appointments, to purchase his own chargers and barrack furniture." He was also obliged to "pay 8s. 5d. a day for the forage of each of his horses and to subscribe considerable sums to the mess and band fund, to pay his own groom and servant and to pay [their] income tax." An officer's pay was slightly less than the price of his commission would have gained him if invested as an annuity: officers were meant to lose money in the army. It was argued that this was what guaranteed they were gentlemen, not mercenaries, and "gave them an interest in the country which they defended."

All this was less a point of contention for Brummell and his fellow officers, however, than their hair. In the Tenth they wore it long, in a queue, or tied pigtail, and powdered, which Brummell abhorred. In civilian life all those possessed of a fine head of hair, and with the inclination to show it off, had eschewed the fashion for powder and wigs for several years. William Pitt's tax on hair powder in 1795, levied to help pay for the war with France, proved the death knell to the fashion. By the late 1790s men of fashion wore their hair short and brushed forward in the style that brought to mind marble Roman emperors, and, ironically, Napoleon. In September 1795 there had even been a ritual cropping and washing of hair in the former powder room of the fashion-conscious household of the Duke of Bedford at Woburn Abbey. But in the army the style of queues and powder persisted, the one element of Tenth Light Dragoon dress that was considered less than stylish.

It was unkindly suggested that the reason Brummell decided to quit the army in the late 1790s was due to hair fashion. It was typical of the sort of jibe levied against him, but he had probably initiated it himself as a self-deprecatory aside—making consequence out of inconsequence as was increasingly his style. His real reasons for handing in his commission had to do with timing and his disinclination to face a long-term military career. In 1799 he would come of age and, meanwhile, the Tenth Light Dragoons were about to be sent to the North.

The small 1795 Brighton garrison "mutiny" served as a foretaste for Brummell of the new political realities of wartime Britain. Poor harvests, heavy taxation and the upheavals of the Industrial Revolution conspired to spoil the fun of the Tenth Light Dragoons. Their ability to handle this mutinous Sussex crowd had been noted, and they were due to be sent to the north of England, not for any specific duties so much as to provide a show of strength in troubled times and to help assert the rule of law. In early 1798 they received orders of a transfer to Manchester, and Brummell took this as his signal to act on an idea that had been brewing since the Prince of Wales's wedding. Of the two sides of his army life that he had experienced— the glamour of being an officer escort of the Prince of Wales at his wedding, and the institutionalized mindlessness that typified his military role in Brighton—it was clear which one better suited his personality. Brummell had decided to quit the army some time before he did so, but the prospect of a freer rein with his inheritance, and the prospect of being outside the royal circle, precipitated a decision. It wasn't so much that a tour of duty in the North threatened harsh duties without the excitement of battle—although it did—as it was the inevitability that the Prince of Wales would not accompany them that convinced Brummell Manchester was not for him. The story he told, naturally, put a slightly more glib spin on things: "The fact is, Your Royal Highness," began Captain Brummell, interrupting the prince at his toilette at the Marine Pavilion, Brighton, "I have heard that we are ordered to Manchester. Now you must be aware how disagreeable this would be to me. I could really not go: think, Your Royal Highness, *Manchester*!"

The joke was for a moment lost on the prince, so Brummell was obliged to carry on: "Besides, *you* would not be there. I have, therefore, with Your Royal Highness's permission, determined to sell out."

If he had worried that this might offend his friend and colonel-in-chief, he was mistaken: "Oh, by all means, Brummell," said the prince, "do as you please."

Brummell left the regiment in late 1798. He was followed soon afterward by some of the officers who had made his life and the prince's such fun: Lords Charles and Robert Manners and Lord Edward Somerset. The regiment continued to attract the second sons of the aristocracy and those who imagined Brighton exactly as Lydia Bennet had in *Pride and Prejudice*: a vista of tents, officers and girls chasing men in uniform. But the prince's love for his Tenth Light Dragoons waned, as it was wont to do with all his passions. He kept the uniform, naturally, constantly let out to fit his bulk, for suitable occasions and military portraits. Appropriately enough, therefore, it was the regiment's impact on fashion that was of far greater import than anything it might have effected on the battlefield:

Hussar dress—outlandish, outrageous and foreign—was an ideal vehicle for the expression of [the Prince of Wales's] opposition to his royal father. The "hussar craze" became the military manifestation of the same desire for "exclusivity" that pervaded the upper realms of London society . . . and was responsible for the rise of the "Dandy"; in fact, the two were inextricably bound up, as many of the leading dandies had, at one time or another, been hussar officers.

Prince among them, of course, was Brummell.

In the months before his twenty-first birthday in June 1799, Brummell continued to spend time with the officers of the regiment. His immediate expectations, his portion of the inheritance, which had grown under Macpherson's care, allowed him to set up the lifestyle for which he would become famous. He furnished himself with a racing curricle, horses and staff. None of this was remarkable for a young man in his position, but the style with which he flaunted his wealth was. His friends were amused. As Jesse wrote,

"He drove [back] into the barracks yard in his carriage, with four posters [post-horses]. "Halloo, George!" said a friend from the mess-room window, "when did you take to four horses?" "Only since my valet gave me warning for making him travel with a pair."

The friendship founded in the regiment between the prince and Captain Brummell was singular. "The future George IV," wrote Count d'Aurevilly, "recognised in Brummell a portion of himself, a portion which had remained healthy and luminous; and this is the secret of the favour he showed him."

It cannot be ignored that from the first there was a subtext to the "violent intimacy" between Brummell and the Prince of Wales that bordered on the homoerotic. Indeed, one biographer of the prince regent has gone so far as to suggest that a friendship played out around a mutual fascination with clothes and fashion went some way to suggesting that both men were bisexual. Within a few years, certainly, the prince would be attending Brummell's half-naked toilette, rather than the other way around, as if it were a royal levee and he a loyal valet. But there was no direct sexual content in their relationship: it was more complex and intriguing than that. At the start of the friendship the prince was in the position of power, not only as Brummell's—indeed almost everyone's—social superior, but also as commander of the regiment. Absent from most accounts is the further simple fact that he was twice Brummell's age. The wedding to Caroline of Brunswick, which placed Brummell for the first time at the center of royal life, saw him standing shoulder to shoulder with the Earl Moira and the Dukes of Bedford and Roxburghe—all men in their early middle years, like the prince. Brummell's place in the regiment was that of a joker: it was this that was noted rather than, necessarily, the clothes he had in common with everyone else. It was a world of men in which he had learned to excel, different from Eton only in the added spice of disreputable women, extra freedom, cash and the shared irresponsibility of the mess room, which always mitigates against the formation of separate, romantic bonds. It was part of the prolonged adolescence that was the prince's world, and by extension the world of many over-privileged men of the time.

His school friend Thomas Raikes noted Brummell's ease in the presence of royalty, and the unflappable good humor that characterizes those who can swim in the immediate wake of the famous. "He was liberal, friendly . . . always living with the highest in the land on terms of intimacy but without *bassesse* or truckling . . . it is only justice to say that he was not only good-natured, but thoroughly good tempered. I never remember to have seen him out of humour . . . He also had a peculiar talent for ridicule (not ill-natured) . . . which enabled him to laugh people out of bad habits."

Brummell's place at the royal wedding was assured by neither age nor privilege: quite simply, he must have been enormously liked. His interest in uniforms, the first shared passion with the Prince of Wales, can hardly have accounted for this, any more than a sexual frisson would have done, even had there been one.

Brummell's good looks and assured bearing must have helped his entree into the adult world, but one other key factor, especially on that tense and unpleasant wedding day at St. James's Palace, was the signal trait of Brummell's character, and the most elusive: he made people laugh.

PART TWO

A DAY IN THE HIGH LIFE
1799–1816

I will attempt to sketch the day of a young man of fashion; and of such a one a single day describes his whole life.

He thinks of rising about eleven in the morning and, having taken a slight breakfast, puts on his riding coat and repairs to . . . all the fashionable streets off Hyde Park . . . visits the most noted shops and . . . After bespeaking something there, he . . . drives from one exhibition to the other, stops at the caricature shops and, about three, drives to a fashionable hotel. Here he takes his lunch, reads the papers, arranges his parties for the evening and at five strolls home. His toilet he finds prepared and his valet waiting for him . . . by seven he is dressed and goes to dinner . . . At nine he goes to the play. Not to see it . . . but to flirt from box to box, to look at ladies whom he knows and to show himself to others whom he does not . . . he then proceeds to a rout, a ball, or the faro-bank of some lady of distinction . . . about four in the morning, exhausted with fatigue he returns home; to recommence, the next morning, the follies of the past day.

"A Day in the Life of a Young Man of Fashion,"
The Stranger in England, Christian Goede, 1807

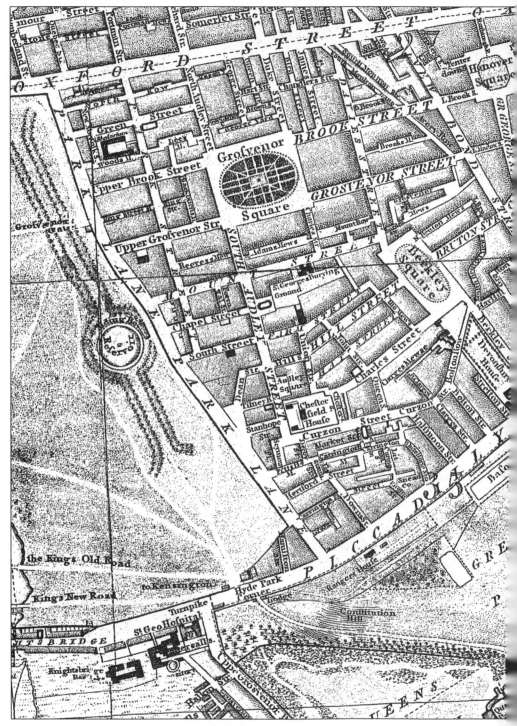

London's West End in 1800 before the construction of Regent's Street.
Bottom left, Rotten Row (The Route du Roi or King's Road).

MORNING

5

DANDIACAL BODY

A Dandy is heroically consecrated in this one object; the wearing of clothes wisely and well, so that as others dress to live, he lives to dress.

Thomas Carlyle, "The Dandiacal Body" in
Sartor Resartus (The Tailor Retailored), 1833

Amongst the curious freaks of fortune there is none more remarkable in my memory than the sudden appearance, in the highest and best society in London, of a young man whose antecedents warranted a much less conspicuous career . . . there are comparatively few examples of men obtaining a similarly elevated position simply from their attractive personal appearance and fascinating manners.

Captain Gronow, *Reminiscences,* 1862

"In London," Casanova said, "everything is easy to him who has money and is not afraid of spending it." It was an aphorism by which twenty-one-year-old George Brummell set about his assault on London society. On his coming of age in 1799, a third of the family estate was released to him. *Gentleman's Magazine* estimated this fortune to be £20,000, Brummell later claimed it was between £40,000 and £50,000 and Thomas Raikes struck at a middle figure of £30,000, or nearly £2.5 million in today's money.

His brother William bought an estate at Wivenhoe near Colchester with his third of the inheritance and lived the life of a country squire. His sister Maria's money was given over by law to her husband, Captain Blackshaw, and eventually it allowed their daughters to marry into continental nobility. George Bryan Brummell, however—the youngest of the three and in the usual run of things the one who should have had no "expectations" and been forced into a career—spent his inheritance rather differently. His first acquisitions were the finest wardrobe the West End could offer, and a suitably fashionable address in which to wear it.

The house he moved into in 1799, 4 Chesterfield Street, still stands. It has barely been altered in the intervening centuries, save for the addition of Victorian bay windows at the back—overlooking the current Saudi Embassy—and the removal of a hidden servants' staircase. It is a tall, thin house with only two rooms, front and back, on each of the three main floors, either side of the central staircase. There is a kitchen basement below and servants' attic above. The fan window above the front door and the wrought-iron lamp arch through which one enters the house could have been designed to replicate those Brummell would have remembered from his childhood home in Downing Street. It was a modish house, but a modest one—at any event, by the standards of Mayfair—yet it was perfectly placed for George Brummell to make his entrance into society. Chesterfield Street was ten minutes' walk from Hyde Park Corner and only yards from the back of Devonshire House (since demolished), the epicenter of the Whig aristocracy. It was at the precise midpoint of that "parallelogram between Oxford Street, Piccadilly, Regent Street and Hyde Park," which Sydney Smith said, at the time, "enclose[d] more intelligence and human ability, to say nothing of wealth and beauty, than the world has ever collected in such a space before." George Selwyn, the wit and politician, had lived on the same street, and the Duke of Clarence, later William IV, took the house at the north end with his mistress, the celebrated comedy actress Mrs. Jordan. The Prince of Wales became a regular visitor to Brummell's bachelor townhouse, and the men who became known as the "Dandiacal Body" crowded into the small front room each morning in the hope of being invited upstairs to see Brummell.

Quite soon after Brummell's acquisition of 4 Chesterfield Street this upper room became, bizarrely, as important a focus of London society for fashionable young men as Ranelagh or Vauxhall Gardens, Drury Lane or the Oxford Street Pantheon had been to their parents. The front dressing room at 4 Chesterfield Street was the inner sanctum where Brummell's levee took place, and this became a sophisticated diversion in its own right. Brummell's coterie, many of them former dragoon officers launching their London careers in politics, the arts or society, was attracted to Chesterfield Street to watch how he dressed. They included the Dukes of Bedford, Argyll and Rutland, Lords Charles and Robert Manners and the Marquess of Worcester. Lord Alvanley was a constant member along with Lord Frederick Bentinck, Henry Pierrepoint, "Poodle" Byng, Thomas Raikes, Tom Sheridan, Scrope Davies and, later, the young Lord Byron. (No respectable woman, of course, could visit an unmarried young man like Brummell, with the possible exception of his sister, who never came to London.)

Brummell's wealth, among such a body of men, was not considered extraordinary. Nor had he displayed any particular talents, except for witty repartee and good humor. But the way he dressed, in an age when the rules of attire were changing, was considered so remarkable that men en route to Tattershall's to see their horses, to Carlton House to see the prince or to Berry Brothers to order port wine and have themselves weighed, first called in on Chesterfield Street to see how they should dress to be considered—from all angles—gentlemen.

Brummell's new household was small. There was a manservant and a cook (also a man) and this "small but *recherché ménage*" was completed by two horses—one of which was a fine Arab stallion named Stiletto, looked after by a groom, James Ell, for Brummell to ride in Hyde Park in the afternoons. He took particular interest in the hiring of valets. His first, Robinson, like his successors, stayed with him for more than a decade. This must attest to reasonable working conditions in the Brummell household, despite the exactitudes of the wardrobe care and dressing routines, although Brummell did not pay his valets particularly well. Perhaps he considered the advantages of the job—a fashionable address and employer, some cast-off clothes and minimal dinner service duties—as sufficient perquisites. He tried to hire one particularly sought-after valet soon after he arrived at Chesterfield Street. The man had found himself out of work when his master, Colonel Kelly, "the vainest man in London," burned to death trying to rescue his favorite boots. The valet asked for two hundred pounds a year. "Make it two hundred guineas," said Brummell, "and I'll work for *you*."

Brummell furnished his home with the latest fashions, Buhl furniture and Sevres porcelain. The small library, at the back on the ground floor, "was stored with . . . works [showing] the same good taste." Brummell became an avid collector of books and poetry so that eventually his library expanded to include "the best works of the best authors of every period and every country." Among the books were "some good historical works, the standard poets, two editions of Shakespeare, his friend Ellis's Specimens of Early English Metrical Romances, bound curiously in raised calf, the Quarterly and Edinburgh [Reviews] the Memoirs of de Grammont, Chesterfield's Letters, Berrington's Abelard and Eloise and a large collection of novels." He spent little on paintings, for fear, perhaps, that they might distract from the main artwork he intended his guests to admire: himself. But he was not considered extravagant in anything he did, even in his clothes. Some of his inheritance he even spent wisely on annuities, which were paid to him until his death. He would have been well advised to put more of his capital into "the funds" and certainly to have done the same with his later substantial gambling wins. But he was not wise with money. The gaming book at White's club, which he joined that year, records that he lost a bet that he would be married before the end of the century. Perhaps he thought he would marry a fortune so did not have to hold on to his own. Or perhaps he did not think about the future—after all, he was twenty-one.

There is limited wine cellar space in the house but an unexpectedly large coal cellar for such a modest house, which extends under Chesterfield Street. Sea coal fueled London and, more specifically, Brummell's addiction to bathing. He was not in the vanguard of fashion in this area: an earlier gentleman's house in Bristol was built with a stone plunge pool and, of course, the Prince of Wales and his set honored the custom of sea bathing in Brighton, if "more on the beach" as one contemporary had it, "than in the observance." But Brummell bathed in hot water, and this was considered remarkable. Almost as remarkable as the fact that he bathed every day "and every part of his body."

Although he kept eau de cologne as part of his "comestibles," his most famous early dictum on personal style was so unusual it was recorded by several diarists: "No perfumes, he used to say, but very fine linen, plenty of it, and country washing." Captain Jesse noted this, and Harriette Wilson used the same words in her *Memoirs,* which predated Jesse's. The fields of Islington were hung with the shirts of men like Brummell, not just to infuse them with the neutral smell of country air, but to avoid the soot spotting that marked city-dried whites. The clothes were to be clean and so, Brummell reasoned, should be the body underneath, rather than masked with perfume. The musk, civet, pomatum and geranium scents with which the previous generation had sought to disguise their lack of personal hygiene were banished, like wigs and lace. Bathing was the foundation of Brummell's Spartan aesthetic: his dandiacal body was to face the world unalloyed with perfumes or powders, "trinkets or gew-gaws," as natural as the classical statues his style would emulate.

Those visitors who were allowed upstairs into Brummell's dressing room were presented with an unexpected sight. Brummell kept the door to his bedroom ajar so that he could carry on a conversation while he washed, shaved and dressed. For some or all of this he was totally or partially naked, "in the buffs, *in naturalibis,*" as he put it, which was part of the reason, no doubt, that his physique was noted in so many memoirs. He exfoliated his body all over with a coarse-hair brush and later in life, as guard against a recurrent skin complaint, he took to bathing in milk first and then water. An attitude to his own body, which was at once both exhibitionist and, in practice, ascetic and self-punishing, may have been a hangover from his Etonian education. He was also quite clever enough to enjoy the ridiculousness and despise the shallowness of his own sudden fame.

Rather than trusting Robinson the valet, Brummell shaved himself. "Kings by birth were shaved by others," as Napoleon said to Talleyrand, "but he who has made himself *Roi,* shaves himself." The Dandiacal Body bought cakes of shaving soap (1*s.* 6*d.*), badger brushes (5*s.* 6*d.*) and razors (sixpence a sharpening) from Renard's of St. James's, along with toothbrushes, nailbrushes, combs and soap. Brummell used a series of miniature cut-throat razors, then applied himself to "stray hairs" with the aid of tweezers and a dentist's magnifying mirror. Such scrupulous attention to detail was revered: his "ablutions," it was said, "would have gained him a reputation for sanctity in a Mahomedan country." He later bought a complete shaving set, including a spitting bowl—spitting being considered a vital morning ablution—made out of best silver, on the soundly Brummellesque principle that "it is impossible to spit into *clay.*"

Brummell, it was said, "was the first who revived and improved the taste for dress [among gentlemen] and his first great innovation was effected upon neckcloths." The "neckcloths . . . were then worn without stiffening of any kind, and bagged out in front, rucking up to the chin in a roll." Either that, or they were so highly starched that men could only "test their fitness for use by raising three parts of their length by one corner without [the neckcloth] bending." Brummell found a discreet compromise that was difficult and time-consuming to effect, but which came to be considered the acme of understated style.

First Robinson handed his master a plain shirt, lightly starched, with a collar attached "so large that, before being folded down it completely hid his head and face," and did up the tiny Dorset buttons at the neck and cuffs. The collars on Brummell's shirts were high, but there was a dart of fabric removed at the back that allowed freer movement. "The first *coup d'archet* was made with the shirt collar which Brummell folded down to its proper size," in other words so that the collar fold almost touched the ears. Next Brummell was presented with a triangle of fine Irish muslin, cut diagonally from a square yard and plainly seamed. This was folded twice over at its widest point and wrapped carefully around the neck. Brummell stood in front of a mirror keeping his chin in the air—before he tied the tail ends in one of several manners that became signifiers themselves of allegiance and taste. An extensive pseudo-political treatise was later published on the subject, *Necklothitania*, stating as a well-understood axiom that "it must be a great desideratum to every gentleman to persuade the rest of the world that he is one: as, however, he cannot employ the same means to prove it to them as he would to his intimates, he necessarily must accomplish it by his dress, for 'The [neckcloth] oft bespeaks the man.' "

The initial tying of the neckcloth was only the first move. The Dandiacal Body who gathered to watch were more interested in Brummell's next move. Slowly he lowered his chin in a series of small "declensions" that rucked down the necktie. Ideally it held the contours of the neck rather than bulging out or folding inward. It was this moment of self-sculpting that men came to study and emulate, because it was this that framed the face as well as dictating the angle of the head. Once the starched cloth was pressed into place, and the whole rubbed with an older shirt to preserve the pleats, it would stand the rigors of the day. "If the cravat was not properly tied at the first effort it was always rejected." Often the shirts, too, would have to come off: perfection cost in laundering as well as in time. Wealth and style was no longer to be flaunted with lace and spangles but in a perfection of line that the cognoscenti would recognize, and cost the wearer in other ways. So the theatricality of understated chic became signal, with Brummell casting himself—even in this first adornment of the day—as both protagonist and *metteur-en-scène*.

Not all of Brummell's morning guests were honored with a personal audience. Many waited downstairs. However, they were not altogether denied an element of the theatrical experience enacted in the dressing room. Robinson the valet made a point of passing the downstairs room with "a quantity of tumbled neckcloths under one arm" and, naturally, this was noted by the gentlemen. On being interrogated, Robinson would solemnly reply, "Oh, these sir? These are our failures." Certainly something of Brummell's deadpan style had rubbed off on the valet. More tellingly, the arrangement of 4 Chesterfield Street makes it apparent that Robinson had to go out of his way to pass the first-floor rooms. The "tumbled neckcloths" were part of Brummell's stagecraft.

Tying a neckcloth in the Brummell manner was the first of Brummell's sartorial gifts to a small coterie of young but influential men. It became the badge of dandyism and evolved slowly into the starched collar and tie that descended to the modern day. It was, for Brummell, the beginnings of his antistyle style: a simple perfection of line that took attention and know-how (and Brummell to set the fashion), but did not, per se, require wealth. As one dandy wrote,

> *My neckcloth, of course, forms my principal care,*
> *For by that we criterions of elegance swear*
> *And cost me each morning some hours of flurry*
> *To make it appear to be tied in a hurry.*

Lord Byron was an assiduous disciple of the style, adding, later, a twist of Romantic dishabille and leaving his collar and neckcloth a little undone. Several of his early portraits were later overpainted to replace a Brummell neckcloth with a Byronic open shirt. In his dandy youth, Byron followed Brummell's style to the letter.

Linen, like all other items of clothing, was not bought ready to use in Brummell's day. Bedsheets, towels and tablecloths, as well as shirts and undergarments, were bought as fabric lengths and made up, often within the household, as required. Because they needed most frequent washing or repair, they fell outside the usual realms of interest for the fashionable: a valet would shop for linen for his employer and it fell to Robinson, initially, to keep up a constant supply of white linen at Chesterfield Street.

One early effect of Brummell and his followers was to make neckties, shirts and their scrupulous whiteness desiderata of gentlemanly fashion. So tailors began to take a specialist interest in linen for their clients, and some of their bills survive. There is a fascinating document in the collection kept by John Murray of Lord Byron's complex financial arrangements showing just how wide-ranging the linen requirements of a young follower of Brummell were becoming. In April and May 1805 the young Lord Byron required over seventy-five yards of fine Irish linen for shirts and bedsheets, costing more than fifteen pounds, and four and three-eighths yards and half a nail of expensive French cambric, at eighteen shillings a yard for shirt fronts, which were often of separate material from the rest of the garment (finest Irish muslin or cambric). Russia toweling was ordered for bath towels, and diaper toweling (damask linen) for nightshirts. Lord Byron also required six nightcaps, considered so essential to good health that they remained on the lists of requirements at some Oxbridge colleges and at Eton into the late nineteenth century.

Like Brummell, and all young men of fashion, it appears that Byron wore underwear rarely or not at all. A study of Scrope Davies's accounts reveals a similar absence, and Prince Pückler-Muskau's mention of the number of "summer trousers" a gentleman needed refers to the same issue. The older generation kept with older ways; some of the very rare examples of male undergarments surviving from the period belonged to Thomas Jefferson and Thomas Coutts, the banker, but in their dotage. The younger set aspired to a different aesthetic, and the line of the trouser was not to be interrupted by rucked shirttails or underwear. It was a style inspired by neoclassicism, revolutionary ideals, cavalry chic and cockiness. But the young followers of Brummell were flaunting, primarily, their wealth.

The fashion for the whitest clothes—trousers and waistcoats, as well as shirts and neckties—that was pioneered by Brummell gave subtle expression to a disinterest in the cost of linen and laundering. The accounts of Brummell's dandy friend Scrope Davies allude to frequent and expensive repairs and replacements of pale pantaloons and breeches, and shirts are reordered (and monogrammed) with expensive regularity. Small triangles of fabric, gores or gussets, were sewn into underarms for ease of movement, but also to be replaced, in an age before antiperspirant, once irredeemably sweat-stained. Even so, it was an expensive business. Shirt cuffs, likewise, were worn long, more than an inch beyond the arm of the jacket, in order to establish the unacceptability of getting one's hands dirty. The semiotics of peacockery were changing. Instead of flamboyance, Brummell and his followers chose a style that discreetly asserted their wealth. Pure, clean lines and fabrics appeared classically egalitarian, but to the trained eye the new classical wardrobe also signified wealth, status and style. Less, for the first time, was more. For this same reason the fashion for trouser stirrups Brummell imported into London from the military came to have a dual meaning. Leather straps that did up under the instep kept the line of the trouser in place—stretched from braces to feet. This was entirely within a neoclassical precept: "The character of the classical body is established . . . through an emphasis on continuity of surface, line, form and contour . . . the qualities to be demanded of . . . figures are those of unity, simplicity and a continuously flowing movement from one part of the body to the next." At the same time, trouser stirrups could only be done up with the aid of servants. Brummell's wardrobe might hint at idealized lines and statuelike simplicity, but it took staff and money to maintain, and at every occasion of dressing and undressing throughout the day, Robinson was indispensable.

It was a singular facet of his sudden fame that one element of it was explained in very physical terms. "He was tall, well made, and

a very good figure," wrote Thomas Raikes of Brummell's own dandiacal body. "Nature had indeed been most liberal to him," wrote
Jesse, adding more specifically:

He was about the same height as Apollo [the Apollo Belvedere was
newly exhibited in London] and the just proportions of his form were remarkable . . . and, had he been inclined to earn his livelihood . . . he
would readily have found an engagement as a life sitter to an artist, or
got paid to perambulate . . . from fair to fair, to personate the statues of
the ancients.

This arrestingly allusive description was in keeping with Jesse's
own hero worship of Brummell, but also with a new fascination for
the physical form of man. Not unlike our own age, Brummell's had
seen a reappraisal of male physicality that alarmed the older generation as much as it defined the younger. The pugilist clubs that
opened in the West End could even be understood as forerunners of
modern gyms insofar as fashionable gentlemen were forced to consider their physical well-being from the point of view of how they
looked.

Brummell's early celebrity rested on the role he assumed as
poster boy for a new version of metropolitan masculinity: restrained, muscular, unfoppish, anything but the "dandy" of folk-
lore. His rapidly established status as the leader of fashion, quite
separate from his reputation as a wit, was built on a "look" that
perfectly mirrored the age.

In large part Brummell's place in the history of fashion can be
attributed to some simple facts: he possessed naturally a neoclassical body and was in a position to be noted for it on account of his
celebrated wit and his friendship with the prince. Brummell's
physique was mentioned by contemporaries from his school days
onward. The 1790s, indeed, was probably the first period when
such a thing as "proportion" might be discussed openly as part of a
gentleman's attributes. Modern men might feel restricted by the
clothes of Brummell's period, but the tailored and close-fitting style

Brummell pioneered was in direct response to the fascination he and his contemporaries felt for new ideas of freedom and Greek aesthetics. Men were displaying the lines of their bodies every bit as much as the "nymphs" of Kensington Gardens in their gauze drapes. In a sense, men's fashions were more naked. The Greek and Roman statuary on display in London depicted draped female figures, but the highest ideals of antique art were expressed by men, in the nude. Ladies who aspired to the Empress Josephine look might, according to legend, have dampened their muslin dresses to make them cling to their bodies. Men's fashion, for which Brummell played catalyst, found another route.

Matte fabrics—especially wool, and tailoring that either held the body or sculpted it—replaced draped silk, glitter and swathing. A radical restriction of color to white, skin tones, blue, gray and black no longer signified humility or even sobriety. Instead the sculptural strength of form and line was reiterated, in the manner understood latterly by black-and-white photographers. This may or may not have been a misunderstanding of actual antiquity— many statues originally were brightly colored—but as classical forms were understood and valued in Brummell's day, classical male nudity could be suggested in cloth.

Men's coats were the most sculpted garments—displaying the craft of London's tailors rather more than the torso muscles of the wearer, but both aspiring to the same classical ideal. As one fashion historian has claimed, "Dressed form became an abstraction of nude form, a new ideal naked man expressed not in marble but in natural wool, linen, leather . . . The perfect man, as conceived by English tailors, was part English gentleman, part innocent natural Adam, and part naked Apollo . . . a combination with an enduring appeal in other countries and other centuries."

Many visitors to the statuary depository or the Royal Academy were uncomfortable with any context in which the male body was gazed at, as being both weakening to the male sex or even perverse (the Royal Academy and the British Museum routinely removed male genitals and replaced them with carved fig leaves). Brummell, as a leader of body-conscious fashions, was likewise in danger of censure. He might not exhibit himself naked, even if Jesse suggested he could have made a living in so doing, yet his style drew a mixed response parallel to that of the male nudes at Cheere's statuary yard. As counterpoint, Brummell took inspiration from a quite separate aesthetic: English country horsemanship. This contextualized in a sporty and military milieu the arrestingly body-formed clothing. It also equated masculine corporality with horseflesh (which could be more openly admired than the male body): "I have heard sensible people say that a man has nothing to do with beauty—That a man is handsome enough if he does not frighten his Horse. But is beauty confined to one sex? If you have a handsome mare, does it signify nothing what an awkward clumsey [sic] beast your horse be? Beauty most certainly belongs to both sexes." The equestrian portrait and equestrian statue—sometimes with seminaked rider—lent martial masculinity to Napoleon, the Prince of Wales and Czar Alexander I, among others. The bravura physicality—both equine and human—of the Elgin marbles, exhibited in 1806, gave further authenticity and acceptability to the look; it was the ideal visual corollary of Empire; noble, muscular, self-evidently aspirational, utterly uneffeminate. The clothes that seem so restrictive to us were the casual sportswear of their day—Hessian riding boots, riding breeches and cutaway riding jackets—so that even West End "loungers," who had no intention of riding anywhere, could give the appearance of readiness to mount a horse and gallop toward revolution.

The perfect man—as conceived by English tailors and the hybrid of neoclassical aesthetics and sporty cavalry chic—turned out to be George Brummell. He might have ruined the perfect aquiline symmetry of his face in the Tenth Light Dragoons, but as a clothes-horse he was unrivaled, and his physicality accordingly noted and admired as it might be of a modern celebrity. His ascendancy as a leader of fashion was predicated on creating and modeling a London look that came to dominate men's fashion. The strength, the vitality and some of the self-doubt of the age was expressed in its fashions and their relationship to ideals of manhood and gentle-manliness. The age, similarly, is naked to the eye in its interest in the male body—in fashion and art, and in the case specifically of George Brummell's.

Brummell's physique was considered a more salient feature even than his height, which was telling in itself once it is established that he was, for the age, remarkably tall. Thanks to the descriptions of Brummell, and his known weight, recorded assiduously by his wine merchants, Berry Brothers of St. James's, it is possible to deduce his height with reasonable precision. Brummell was first weighed on Berry Brothers' coffee scales, as was the habit of the loungers of St. James's, on January 23, 1798. The records are still kept at the shop, detailing the fluctuating girths of all Brummell's contemporaries, including the royal dukes and displaced French royalty. After four years of almost constant riding, Brummell weighed twelve stone, nine pounds (179 pounds, or 81 kilograms) in 1799. It was a weight he maintained, with brief fluctuations, until he suddenly gained bulk around his thirtieth birthday—when he was appointed perpetual president of a new club, Watier's, said to serve the best dinners in London. The constant references to his slimness, or the perfection of his proportions in his twenties, however, when taken in conjunction with the currently accepted scale of ideal weight, would put a man of this weight at between six feet and six feet two inches, or 183 and 190 centimeters in height—a full six inches (fifteen centimeters) taller than the average in 1799. Even so, it was the manner in which he bore himself that caused greater interest, as well as his tailors' skills in turning his physique, the "turn of his leg," into a feature of his fame.

The clothing, then, of this perfect dandiacal body forged Brummell's initial fame. The style was in strict accord with the same classical principles of sculptured proportion that were noted in his naked self, applied to his clothes. It is a paradox that discussion of Beau Brummell and dandyism should have become synonymous with each other, when one considers that Brummell's simplicity in dress was inimical to the modern understanding of the word "dandy." It was revolutionary primarily in its simplicity.

"The look" was described by Jesse, Byron, Raikes, Gronow and Harriette Wilson among others; it was that of "having well-fashioned the character of a gentleman." Over his white shirt and perfect neckcloth, Brummell wore a pale or white waistcoat—or "vest" in the parlance of tailors of the period and in modern American usage. The waistcoat hid a small addition to a gentleman's wardrobe that is often forgotten in the annals of fashion history, and Brummell's place in it: braces or suspenders. These are absent from the wardrobes of the previous generation, but make up a regular feature in the surviving tailors' bills of Brummell's friends Scrope Davies and Lord Byron. Without them, the severe line along the thighs and lower legs was impossible, as belts were both inimical to the style and unflattering to the majority. Brummell wore breeches or tight pantaloons in the morning, in soft stocking-woven fabric or often soft leather. All this pale and white palette was thrown into sharp relief with two items in dark colors. A dark jacket—always deep blue—was cut away at the front to form tails, for ease on horseback but also to increase the apparent length of the wearer's legs. Black Hessian boots—from Hesse in Germany—completed the ensemble. These were riding and walking boots with a tassel at the front that served to distinguish them from turn-top riding boots, which briefly had about them the taint of Napoleon. The perfection of the cut and sculptural strength of the style were communicated with even greater clarity and seriousness by the sober palette. The specific colors of white, buff and dark blue owed a good deal to the Montem polemen dress at Eton, which was in itself a version of a military cadet's attire. Brummell's ensemble appeared a little like a military uniform for urban, civilian man.

Descriptions of the items in terms of color, construction and feel can only sketch their meaning to Brummell and his Dandiacal Body. The effect of the limited palette was, and has remained, to underscore the sculptural qualities of the "suit," and to prioritize cut and tailoring. The point of Brummell's clothes was that they fitted him perfectly. It was not a showy or a colorful look. It was exceptionally well modeled on him, but it came to suit, quite literally, everybody. It was a small thing to be famous for, but of unexpected consequence for Brummell and London.

The style made an immediate impact. This was not so much because Brummell had been an innovator, although in small part he had. His impact came because the style required a reeducation of many men—notably Brummell's friend the Prince of Wales. The prince became a devotee of this pared-down style, and is depicted dressed in exact imitation of Brummell as late as 1821. No style could easily flatter the ever-widening prince, but the skill of the tailors Brummell and he shared reshaped him. The austerity and simplicity of the style was at first antithetical to the creator of the Brighton Pavilion, but he, like the rest of London, was by the turn of the century in the thrall of neoclassical tailoring and the rules of dress dictated by a young commoner with an intuitive understanding of restrained elegance and some natural gifts with which to deploy it.

In this revivification of London men's fashion, Brummell was easily cast as priest and prophet. Once his friend the Prince of Wales adopted both the style and the habit of attending the Chesterfield Street levees, Brummell's position in fashion history became assured. He had the required arrogance, poise and connections, but also understood that the rules were intimidating to many. "The Father of Modern Costume," as Max Beerbohm titled Brummell, had a style that was uniquely his, but perfect to the spirit of the age; "quiet . . . reasonable, and beautiful: free from folly or affection, yet susceptible to exquisite ordering; plastic, austere, economical." It appeared postrevolutionary, neoclassical, ordered and Enlightened, and in this it did indeed seem democratic. It did not shout wealth or privilege, it quietly insisted the point. It celebrated, not least in the sheer time it took to achieve the look, wealth, privilege and elegant indolence. Brummell's revolutionary fetishizing of detail was later described by Baudelaire as defining "the man who is rich and idle, and who . . . has no other occupation than the perpetual pursuit of happiness . . . whose solitary vice is elegance."

~

Brummell's rules of dress and manner were spread by the immediate dandy set around him, so that soon the style was seen all over fashion-conscious London. Foreigners noted the increasing homogeneity of men's attire in London, and, largely, this was viewed admiringly. Max Beerbohm later dated the birth of the suit itself to "that bright morning when Mr Brummell, at his mirror, conceived the notion of trousers and simple coats."

The sobriquet "Beau" stuck to Brummell around this time, at the turn of the century. Just as the meaning of "dandy" is skewed to the modern ear when taken in the context of Brummell's Dandiacal Body—men of deliberately understated chic, not outré dress—so the term "Beau" came to be read differently in the light of Beau Brummell. It was universally accepted as his name or title soon after his first season in London in 1799. At its simplest, it was merely a description: Brummell was good-looking, and women as well as men noted this. "He was," said Lady Hester Stanhope, "envied and admired by both beaux and belles of all ranks of society." Brummell was not conspicuously dressed—that was not the meaning of being Beau. Another observer wrote that when he first saw the celebrated young Beau Brummell he was "struck by the misapplication of this title [Beau] . . . he was dressed as plain as any man in the field, and the manly expression of his countenance ill accorded with the implication the sobriquet conveyed."

As it turned out London society granted him a sort of immortality by christening him "Beau," but it was a double-edged compliment. Like "Perdita" Robinson or "Gentleman" Lewis—actors and adventurers also—Beau was admired but also lightly scorned: his fame, like theirs, was fascinating because it spoke of the evanescence of things, of the surfaces, which Sheridan said were the traits of the age.

To some of the Dandiacal Body, Beau Brummell's dressing ritual at Chesterfield Street had the appearance of a knight preparing for battle or a matador for a bullfight. By 1800 he was well on his way to building the carapace that would protect him in the social and sexual warfare waged in the salons and on the streets of London.

His style was intimidating in its precision and austerity, and because his wit was developing the harshness of the professional cynic, few became close with him, for all that he was wildly sociable. For some, the emotional unavailability of "the Beau" added to his attractiveness. But he maintained only a few close friends— notably his former dragoon officer friends the Manners brothers, and Thomas Raikes, whom he had known at Eton. And, of course, he had no family to speak of. But at twenty-one, with wealth, health and London at his feet, it is hardly surprising that he gave little consideration to either past or future and lived for his moment in the high life.

By late morning Brummell was dressed and ready for London: "Hessians [boots] and pantaloons, or top-boots and buckskins, with a blue coat, and a light or buff-coloured waistcoat; of course fitting to admiration on the best figure in England." He donned off-white or pale yellow kid gloves in the hallway and stepped out into Chesterfield Street. He turned left, toward Curzon Street, and faced London with the insouciant confidence of one who knows he is young, envied and perfectly but not overdressed.

6

SIC ITUR AD ASTRA

SHOPPING IN LONDON

> Turning the corner of a lane I came upon a Signpost, whereon
> stood written that such-and-such a one was "Breeches Maker
> to His Majesty," and stood painted effigies of a Pair of
> Leather Breeches, and between the knees, these memorable
> words SIC ITUR AD ASTRA [This is the way to the Stars].
>
> Thomas Carlyle, *Sartor Resartus*
> (The Tailor Retailored), 1833

By the time Brummell left Chesterfield Street each day it was gone twelve. In wet weather it was his habit to have Robinson order a sedan chair—the umbrella being a novelty that never met his approval—but more often he walked. At the turn of the nineteenth century men strolled arm in arm in London as a matter of habit and routine, and it came to be considered a mark of particularly high social standing in the West End to be seen walking with Beau Brummell, and notably to be part of the coterie seen leaving Chesterfield Street with him.

Brummell collected walking sticks, some topped in the fashion of the time with shapes that revealed themselves as caricatures of famous friends only once their shadow was cast across a wall. Accessories were part of the London look. Walking sticks, fob watches, snuff boxes, gloves and hats: these were vital desiderata in the creation of the perfect dandy, and their acquisition was part of Brummell's daily round of London pleasures. As well as the canes (there were many in the later sale of his effects), Brummell allowed a few links of a watch chain to show across his waistcoat, wore occasionally one plain ring and claimed eventually to have a different snuff box for every day of the year. And single-handedly he began the decimation of the beaver population of North America after he was seen out with a glossy, beaver-skin top hat. New gloves, always in the palest leather, had to be bought frequently as they could not easily be cleaned and soon showed dirt. But the choice of accessories was not the primary interest of those who turned to look at Brummell. Harriette Wilson recorded how men in the West End "made it a rule to copy the cut of [Brummell's] coat, the shape of his hat, or the tie of his neckcloth," so that he was pointed out in the street as he walked.

Because his sartorial choices were admired and copied, the character of the emerging West End began to be shaped by his shopping habits. The new tailors and accoutrements shops opening north of Piccadilly, on the redeveloped Burlington Estate, soon realized the potential benefits of young Captain Brummell's custom. Not only might it bring the Prince of Wales to them, and his fashion expenditure was legendary—in 1803 he spent £681 14s. 9d. at one tailor's alone—but also many male customers "made it a rule to copy the cut of his [Brummell's] coat." Those most anxiously on the lookout for young Beau Brummell therefore were the shopkeepers who needed the imprimatur of his custom. And, from the start, they extended their credit to him.

Five streets in particular formed Brummell's shopping constituency, establishing themselves as magnets for male shoppers for decades if not centuries to come: Bond Street, Savile Street (later Row), Jermyn Street, St. James's Street and later parts of the new Regent Street. The all-male preserve of St. James's Street was in effect extended north of Piccadilly as a result of Brummell and his coterie, establishing a whole area of the new West End as the site for satisfying masculine desire. And although there were pugilist clubs and pornographic print shops on Bond Street, and tobacconists and wine merchants on St. James's street, increasingly the desire this part of London met in men was for clothes.

Brummell was a great connoisseur of fabric. He had learned a certain amount on Eton high street, in ordering and having his Eton clothes made up, but in London he developed a passion for cloth and what could be done with it. As he walked farther east from Bond Street he came to the alleys of the redeveloped Burlington Estate, which merged seamlessly into Soho before the construction of Regent Street. Here, between Piccadilly to the south and Berkeley Square and Conduit Street to the north, a new fabric economy was forming on Cork Street, Glasshouse Street and a small cut-through called Savile (sometimes Saville) Row. It was familiar terrain for Brummell even before 1799 as his avuncular family friend Mr. Sheridan had set up home there with his young wife, Hecca.

The range of fabrics, lacings, leathers and buttons available around Savile Row rose with the twin forces of empire and industrialization. Merinos, jersey weaves and doeskins were bought to make day clothes, while evening-dress pantaloons and trousers were made from cashmere, keysermere or cassimir and stretchy silk stockinette imported from India but often worked and woven in Macclesfield. In summer, Brummell also bought drill, a stout linen, and nankeen, a heavy twilled cotton. Velvet and pure silk, so far as men were concerned, were employed only for collar turns and linings respectively. Even in high summer, coats were most often made of wool, always with the smoothest of matte surfaces. Brummell popularized "superfine" broadcloth, keysermere and a mix of the two: "Bath coating." These feltlike fabrics were not the easiest with which to work, as they held their own line unless skilfully cut and "sculpted" with paddings made of layers of linen, cotton, buckram and wool. One tailor, Mr. Schweitzer of Schweitzer and Davidson, was considered the master at working these fabrics, and he began to quote Brummell to other customers as an authority on what would work best: "The Prince wears superfine and Mr Brummell the Bath coating; but it is immaterial which you choose, Sir, you must be right . . . Suppose sir we say the Bath coating—I think Mr Brummell has a trifle the preference."

Tailors stocked their own fabrics also and could take samples to clients less interested in "a-shopping," but the fabric emporia continued to have a grip on the market. Material, tailoring and cut— along with posture and body consciousness—became necessary considerations for the male London elite. For many, the expression of an interest in fabric, like an appreciation of Greek statuary, was simply one more signifier of the cultured gentleman. As so often in commodity culture, however, there was some erotic context to this new arena of expenditure. Tailoring was an exclusively male preserve, but fabric shops, like milliners and hat makers, were staffed by women. They were some of the few young women in this predominantly male part of town who were not sex workers, so naturally enough lines became blurred. By the time the Burlington Arcade opened a few years later the millinery girls were immediately associated with prostitution. The glazed, oil-lit windows provided the perfect shop front for "professional beauties," as well as for fabric and hats.

Nor did the elision of the old West End sex trade into new West End tailoring end there. Some tailors were known to provide the space, facilities and alibis necessary for illicit liaisons. It could be one reason for the numerous fittings: "it was a gentleman's world, a gentleman's club. So they had twenty fittings at their tailors . . . and in the back, round the corner, there would be something else . . ." The West End thereby extended north of Piccadilly its long tradition of sex trade, but Brummell and his coterie grafted on to this something much more respectable, exportable and long-lasting. They added a new, though allied, desire for the finest outfits, and gave a newly sexualized and masculine context to an activity that had been traditionally outside the preserve of establishment men: clothes shopping.

In his early years in London Brummell patronized primarily three tailors. The first, Schweitzer and Davidson on Cork Street, between Bond Street and Savile Row, was also popular with the Prince of Wales. Schweitzer became famous for the cut of his coats. Davidson made a small fortune simply from the trade in alterations on the coats made for the prince. Second, there was John Weston's at 34 Old Bond Street, which made waistcoats, breeches and shirts and became, as the result of Brummell's patronage, a favorite of the prince and later Lord Byron. The third was Jonathan Meyer's on Conduit Street, a little farther north, which had made Brummell's later Hussar uniforms and with whom he pioneered the forerunner of modern trousers. Although Captain Gronow wrote that Brummell favored most frequently "that superior genius Mr Weston, tailor, of Old Bond Street," his was not a singular loyalty. He also shopped at Stultz, Staub, Delacroix, Nugée and others, variously on Savile Row, Glasshouse Street, Bond Street and Jermyn Street. He also shopped independently for fabrics, as the London leisured classes could, on Bond Street, Jermyn Street and, after 1813, Regent Street. He bought his hats on St. James's Street, his boots on Bond Street and Piccadilly and called in frequently, according to their accounts, to buy his snuff tobacco at Fribourg and Treyer, which remained, until quite recently, at the top of the Haymarket.

Toward the end of the eighteenth century London tailors began to assume a reputation throughout Europe and the New World as fashion leaders. It helped that they were at the center of the world's richest city just when male fashions were changing, but specifically they had sought-after skills based on their working knowledge of heavier wool-based fabrics. This in turn was consequent to their long experience in fine cloth—as opposed to silks; a result of climatic need to fashion layers of clothes of varying functions and work with wool. Some of the businesses Brummell frequented, however, were not British. Several of the key names in the birth of Savile Row tailoring were German and Bourbon French, for all they relied on British craftsmen in their cellars and attics: Schweitzer, Meyer, Nugée and Stultz were all refugees who had fled the advance of Napoleon's armies. Their skills had been honed on continental uniforms, themselves often versions of British cavalry-wear in heavy military broadcloths, using water-resistant fabrics to make strong, sculptural impressions.

The Napoleonic Wars had enormously increased demand for uniforms in early nineteenth-century Europe, and, just as medical knowledge advances tenfold on the battlefield, so men's tailoring, it might seem, was advanced by Napoleon's cannon. These continental military tailors had also, necessarily, honed their skills only on men. In Theodore Hook's early-nineteenth-century book *The Man of Many Friends,* when Colonel Arden is setting up home in London he is advised to have clothes made at one of Brummell's tailors, Nugée's. "[This] tailor was of course a foreigner, like the proposed cook; it being an established axiom in this country that its natives are incompetent to the dressing either of dinner or dandies." Nugée later retired to Brighton with "a small fortune invested in some superb houses in Kemp Town." Brummell's tailors may have come to London as refugees, but they could retire on £100,000 or more, if they had been fortunate enough to have their craftsmanship recognized and publicized by the Beau.

In order for this to happen, the new tailors of the West End tended to specialize in particular items of the wardrobe. In one satire on the West End from 1806, the hero is astonished by the range of specialized tailors on Bond Street alone:

When he stopped to be measured for a suit of clothes, what was his surprise to learn that Mr Larolle made only coats, and they had a dozen doors further to drive before they reached "the first hand in the world at waistcoats, braces and inexpressibles." The same "artist" who excelled at fitting a dress shoe, would have been intolerable as the manufacturer of a pair of boots and though Mr Flint the hatter assured us that for round walking hats there was not a superior shop in London; yet he would confess that for an *opera hat* Mr Breach did certainly "cut the trade."

Schweitzer and Davidson on Cork Street specialized in coats. They began experimenting on new cuts and seams both with, and on, Brummell through the first decade of the nineteenth century. The system of "darting" the back of men's coats to shape the cloth to the body was pioneered in London at this time, as well the "fish dart" that added a seam at the side. The three-seam kite back of the previous century worked well on the flat cloths that came into fashion: together they helped mold the coat inward from the widest point at the shoulders, following the line of an idealized torso, which might or might not be represented in reality underneath. Soft domette padding was sewn over form-holding but coarse horsehair cloth called lappet cloth. Wool and buckram layers were oversewn with thousands of individual stitches, in patterns like cornrows. Slowly the layers of the upper torso and shoulders were built up before the cut flat cloth was molded over the top. And always, in hand sewing, Schweitzer and his assistants pulled the cloth in the direction it would eventually hold. A bespoke collar or lapel could only ever turn in the direction the tailor intended; a thousand of his stitches insinuated every contour. A first "baiste" fitting for the baisters or finishers assured Brummell that the garment was progressing as he intended. A second and third fitting was customary. Collar, cuffs and blind buttonholes were achieved last. Pockets were relegated by Brummell to the back of the coat, so as not to spoil the line, hidden in the folds of the tails. So precisely could the new tailors mold the fabric to the body, while subtly flattering or improving where necessary, that Lord Byron was moved to remark of a Schweitzer coat on Brummell that "you might almost say the body thought."

Contemporaries noted the revolutionary new style, and Brummell's preeminence in having it adopted:

The shape of the coat, which had varied [in the 1790s] from a sort of Newmarket cut-away to a short-waisted thing with tails descending to the ankles, à la Robespierre, now received a great deal of attention. A young man of no family pretensions . . . became the oracle of fashion. The dandies of the day regarded him as their king; even the Prince of Wales, who aspired to the character of being the best dressed man in his royal father's dominions, was content to take the pattern of his garments for this influential person: Mr George Brummell.

Brummel also ordered surtouts or greatcoats from Schweitzer and Davidson for winter wear. These were significantly heavier garments, so much so that they were noted in the weighing books at Berry Brothers. Made out of even heavier worsteds and "Norwich stuff"—another feltlike beaten wool—they were still exquisitely cut and molded. An example from 1803 survived unworn and unblemished in a bank vault in the City. Though the cut is fuller, and the coat billows almost into a skirt below the waist, the lines of the upper torso are strongly cut and assume a martial bearing in the wearer. Small references to military chic were also part of the appeal of Schweitzer's coats and surtouts. The shoulder padding was in imitation of epaulettes and also restructured the torso to the V shape of classical statuary. The buttons, meanwhile, as with uniforms of the period, were not all strictly functional. They alluded to the pips of military rank, and have remained on jacket cuffs into modern times with similar disregard for utility. The placing and number of buttons and blind buttonholes developed their own arcane semiotics, as is still the case. The custom then was velvet cuffs and cuff buttons for Tories, none for Whigs; metal stud buttons for daywear, never in the evening, except for staff in livery.

Shapes and styles of men's tailoring that have become almost invisible through their ubiquity can be dated to this time, and in part to Brummell. In order to sculpt the heavy fabrics into the neck and shoulders of demanding clients like Brummell, the collar came eventually to be formed from two pieces. The lapels were turned out as if from the lining of the coat. The collar itself, however, was cut from a different piece of fabric, with the warp and weft of the cloth in line with the vertical muscles of the neck. This separate collar stood around the back of the neck and lifted the fabric up and into the nape and hairline, and was joined to the lapels, which then lay flat across the pectoral muscles. In keeping with the sculptural aesthetic, the face, neck and shoulders would never be draped, but always framed, and the cloth would repeat the structure of the muscles underneath. Between these two parts of the new, sculptural coat collar, a signature of West End tailoring was born: the W cut, which sits either side of all suit and jacket lapels and has endured, in varying dimensions, to this day.

The intimate relationship Brummell developed with his tailors was a product of this attention to detail. Theirs was a partnership of sorts in that they both benefited from each other, but more than that, there was a physical and creative intimacy woven into their joint projects. One such encounter between Brummell and his tailor was immortalized in this extract from the "Brummell" novel *Pelham,* in which Schweitzer also made an appearance as "Mr Schneider," the somewhat sycophantic tailor of Cork Street:

"Good morning Sir; happy to see you returned. Do I disturb you too early? Shall I wait on you [later]?"

"No, you may renew your measure."

"We are a very good figure, sir, very good figure," replied Mr Schneider surveying me from head to foot, while he was preparing his measure. "We want a little assistance though; we must be padded well here, we must have our chest thrown out, and have an additional inch across the shoulder . . . all the Gentlemen in the Life Guards are padded there sir, we must live for effect in this world, sir. A *leetle* tighter round the waist eh?"

The tape measure itself as a tool central to tailoring can also be dated to Brummell's era in London. Measuring came to be standardized, and the tape measure brought into regular use where beforehand tailors had used "strings" and cut on the body and on tailors' dummies. In order to express the homogeneity and classical proportions that Brummell made the central feature of men's dress, individual measurements, ironically, assumed a greater importance. In the absence of color and dazzle, the appearance of perfect proportion would be noticed as never before. Although radical expedients such as corsets (known as belts) and calf-muscle stocking implants were not unknown, the new look was achieved mainly in the subtle remolding of the body achieved by cutters, tailors and effects like the sculpted W-shaped collar. These neoclassical tailors learned to conform to principles long understood in art, but based on Greek mathematical aesthetics. Like Michelangelo and Albrecht Dürer before them, tailors split the man into eight equal parts, or head lengths. According to these classical proportions, the frontal measure from head tip to chin should be equal to one eighth of an adult man's full height, or one quarter of the distance from chin to fingertips. By the same token, the nipple line falls two-eighths of the way down the full height of a man. If it didn't, the tailor could still give the impression that it did. More specifically, the tails of Brummell's coats were cut precisely two-thirds of the way down the seven-eighths of his height that made up his body—this was considered the best-proportioned look. In Brummell's case therefore Schweitzer cut tails forty-two and a half inches from nape to tail tip. Men come in many different shapes, but the eight head lengths of classically proportioned tailoring theorized that more men could be made to appear of perfect Brummellesque proportions if the rules were followed.

One of the next shops to benefit from Brummell's custom and his sudden celebrity was John Meyer's on Conduit Street. Where Schweitzer and Davidson made Brummell's coats, Meyer's made Brummell's breeches and trousers. Before the age of the suit, this was considered a quite separate job. Trousers, breeches and pantaloons made for complicated tailoring. There were darts and corset lacings cut into the lower back, a defining seam on some between the buttocks and a "fall" of between five and eight inches wide, buttoned at the side, instead of flies. Behind this flap were small pockets, usually one on each side, for small change. Some trousers had side pockets, as well. There were matching brace buttons on some and attached stays, strings and internal linings behind the flap—all frequently replaced. The whole was expected to be a figure-perfect fit. Brummell eschewed the wide pantaloon, favored in Brighton perhaps in imitation of sailors, as he did the similarly baggy Cossack fashion that followed Czar Alexander I to London in 1814. He wore slim-cut trousers or "pantaloons" that flattered his famously long-legged frame. For daywear these were made of leather, mercerized cotton or nankeen and plain cotton in summer. Evening wear necessitated black, according to the new aesthetic, and Brummell wore sheer black silk jersey, made up as breeches for Carlton House or the theater, and as pantaloons for the clubs. He defused accusations that he was vain about his legs by typically absurd whimsy: when he was spotted limping on Bond Street with an injured leg, he explained the true tragedy of the circumstance: "I know, it's a deuced bore, but the worst of it is, that it is my *favourite* leg."

In trouser design he had some immediate impact and also long-term effect. The fashion magazine *Le Beau Monde* (1808) described his trousers as "stocking breeches and stockings all in one piece . . . [a] longitudinal pantaloon." They were not always stocking woven, however. Brummell and Jonathan Meyer the tailor pioneered an alternative style that attempted to replicate in fabric or leather the three-dimensional form-fitting style of stockings and silk jersey stockinette. Brummell's pantaloons and trousers therefore had only one seam on each leg, running down the outside. Sometimes it was discreetly embroidered, as was also the case with the "clocks" or embroidered panels that ran up the outer side of men's and women's stockings. This practice is lightly alluded to still in the braiding that runs down dinner jacket and military trousers. Moreover it was at Meyer's, one morning in 1799 or 1800, that Brummell suggested attaching a strap to the bottom cuff of new trousers. The trousers would not wrinkle irrespective of whether boots were worn or not, or in the move from sitting to standing or in and out of carriages. It also lengthened the appearance of the leg. The fashion survived into the early twentieth century in civilian wear and is still a commonplace of formal military uniforms, where they are known as "overalls."

At Meyer's, Brummell's list of requirements grew with each season. Knee breeches were being replaced by (usually wide) trousers or (usually narrow) pantaloons, but not entirely. Brummell retained breeches as part of his summer wardrobe, and for his occasional visits to the country. They were also required formal wear when attending the prince at Carlton House. Brummell had them made of light materials such as nankeen (a hardy cotton fabric, closely woven and often in the Whig buff or white) and knitted silk stockinette. He often wore leather breeches for informal daywear, which suggested sportsmanlike intent among the leisured classes, whether or not they truly intended to ride in Hyde Park. These were more durable than the other materials used, but also highly sensuous garments made of doeskin or chamois leather, which cut well and again suggested the classical nudity that impressed the age. Meyer's presumably employed a specialist leather worker, as they were difficult garments to get right. Harriette Wilson wrote of Brummell's discriminating eye:

I found my very constant and steady admirer Lord Frederick Bentinck waiting for me.

"I have got on a new pair of leather breeches, today, and I want [you] to see how they fit," [said Lord Fred.]

Brummell, at this moment, was announced.

"How very *a propos* you are arrived," I remarked. "Lord Frederick wants your opinion of his new leather breeches."

"Come here, Fred!" said Brummell! "There is only one man on earth [at Meyer's] who can make leather breeches!"

"Mine were made by a man in the Haymarket," Bentinck observed, looking down at them with much pride.

"My dear fellow, take them off directly," said Brummell.

"I beg he may do no such thing," said I, hastily, "else, where would he go to, I wonder, without even his small clothes?"

"They only came home this morning," proceeded Fred, "and I thought they were rather neat."

"Bad knees, my dear fellow, bad knees!" said Brummell, shrugging his shoulders.

Brummell went on to advise his friend both to moderate his passion for the expensive courtesan Miss Wilson and to burn his new leather breeches. Harriette Wilson was exactly the sort of person young men visited to show off their new breeches. The lightness of color, the use of stocking silk and brushed leather, the framing of the thighs with boots and cutaway jackets was not lost on her any more than on other contemporaries. Brummell may have thought of this perfect tailoring and use of pale colors and sensuous materials as the subtlest echoing of classical lines, but others raised eyebrows. Often his style of trouser, copied all over London and by the Prince of Wales himself, courted censure.

Recent fashion theorists Anne Hollander and Aileen Ribiero have pointed out what is apparent from many paintings of the period; that tight pale breeches, such as those pioneered by George Brummell, accented the crotch exactly as do the poses of antique statuary. It was the first time since the codpieces of the Tudor and Jacobean court that fashion had made a central feature of the male sex organs. But if the fashion framed the genital area, it did not lend any support to the occasion—and in polite society, as a result, Brummell's style of trousers was sometimes referred to as "inexpressibles." One Persian ambassador to the Court of St. James's was moved to write that he found the Brummell style of trousers "immodest and unflattering to the figure . . . [they] look just like underdrawers—could they be designed to appeal to the ladies?" A more sympathetic or aroused observer noted that they were "extremely handsome and very fit to expose a muscular Thigh," and society hostesses were later said to regret the passing of the fashion because "one could always tell what a young man was thinking." Some have even suggested that phrase "the turn of the leg," signaling female approval of men in novels and plays of the period, was understood euphemistically. *The Taylor's Complete Guide* suggested the simple expedient of lining tight trousers—especially if made for light summer wear and depending on the wearer's interest in modesty or revealing his thoughts—either with swanskin (flannel) or cotton.

The third of Brummell's favored tailors was "the superior genius" John Weston on Old Bond Street. He was an exception to Brummell's usual choice of tailor in that he was British. He is credited by Captain Gronow with having an overview of Brummell's attire, but specifically he also made his waistcoats. These were either white, black or buff. The front of Brummell's waistcoats was, of course, the most conspicuous part of his clothing and was therefore remarkable for its austerity and simplicity. The back of the waistcoats, meanwhile, though never seen in public, was a testament to Weston's art. Seams in cruciform curved the fabric into the back, and there were lacings down the lower vertebrae—two or three strings—that pulled the diaphragm slightly in and encouraged flat-stomached posture while forcing the chest out. Often, for ease of movement, these back panels were made of silk, which moved more freely against the same material lining the coat. The waistcoats had ten to twelve buttons running down the cotton-twill front, and a repetition at the neckline of the W-cut detail used in the coats. The waistcoats had pockets on either side and, if the surviving examples are to be trusted, were ruthlessly starched. Though Brummell insisted that necks should remain quite stiffly held in starched collar and neckcloths, and arms could not articulate very freely at the shoulder, there was nevertheless a good deal of freedom possible in every other regard. The legs and lower torso were the freest part of the body when fully dressed, for ease of horse riding and dancing. This was one more echo of classical statuary; expressing nobility and strength of purpose in a pose held stiffly above the waist, and freedom, as well as sexuality, in a fluid lower body.

The dandiacal connoisseurs were expected to recognize true quality in the clothes they wore. The tailor who was sure of his work, therefore, needed only his goods on the right back. Indeed, the tradesmen of the area around Savile Row found it expedient, as the dandy craze grew, to eschew advertising altogether and did not even put anything in their shop window or a nameplate on the door. It was a question of exclusivity and the nuances of class: exactly what the English had long excelled at but defined in cloth. Tailors looked instead to the appeal generated by Brummell. This was why they extended their credit to him, and why, over the years, they began to come to Brummell, rather than the other way around. The shaping of the old Burlington Estate into the center of men's tailoring, as it has remained, was achieved through Brummell's corralling of the country's wealthiest men, who all lived or had residences nearby, into the tailors' shops around Savile Row. It could never have been done by advertising, or without key characteristics of the area and of London society that Brummell well understood. The West End had never known such affluence but also had an established history of catering to masculine desire. The same clubbability of the men on the one side, and exclusivity of the institutions on the other, which supported the St. James's Street gaming houses and the King's Place bagnios, granted clientele, prestige and fame to the new tailors of Savile Row—especially those who found their clothes worn publicly by Brummell.

Brummell's promiscuous shopping habits, however, meant that no one tailor could claim he was responsible for the Brummell look. As Jesse said "[it is unclear whether Meyer] or Brummell . . . first invented the trouser foot loop. The Beau at any rate was the first who wore them, and they immediately became quite the fashion." Meyer benefited from the innovation, but presumably not exclusively. Other tailors caught on to the idea via Brummell, such that the tailor could in no way eclipse Brummell's fame. "Give me the man who makes the tailor, not the tailor who makes the man," as the Brummell character in the novel *Pelham* exclaims. "You can tell a Stultz coat anywhere, which is quite enough to damn it; the moment a man's known by an invariable cut [and tailor's name] it ought to be all over with him." Likewise, Brummell's other fictional characterization in *Granby* fulminated that he "scorned to share his fame with his tailor, and was, moreover, seriously disgusted at seeing a well-fancied waistcoat, almost unique, before the expiration of its 'honeymoon' adorning the person of a natty apprentice."

Brummell further guarded his preeminence as *arbiter elegantiarum* by refusing to offer serious advice on the subject. Instead he developed a detached and ironic attitude to fashion, quite as polished as his coat buttons. Whether this was a deliberate ploy, or simply a result of his instinct for comedy, is unclear, but the effect was that he deflected direct inquiry into his style or his shopping choices by deft use of the ridiculous or the barbed. When asked how he kept his boots so brilliantly black, he coolly advised the use of the best champagne froth for polishing. When asked by the Duke of Bedford for a direct opinion on a coat, he replied, "Coat? You call that a coat?" Then there was his positively proto-Wildean instruction that men should never "ride in ladies' gloves, particularly," he said, "with leather breeches."

Like many with an intuitive understanding of a style or art, he was not particularly interested in talking or writing about it, and though he later essayed a treatise on male fashion, his heart was not in it. He was for the wearing of it, not the discussing of it. Being a dandy, more to the point, was never going to be just about clothes for Brummell. It was a pose with which to fascinate and intrigue, and he would have been a good deal less fascinating about style if he had chosen to talk about it more—or more seriously.

He never gave the impression of being bored with clothes or shopping, but it would be unfair to consider him a devotee of fashion. He helped create a style, then stuck with it as if it were an immutable orthodoxy. The higher pedestal to which he aspired was not the high office his creditors must have wished for him. Rather, his clothes were the first signifier of the dandy pose, "the polished ease" that impressed society much more than what he wore and which appeared to some a higher calling in itself.

"Dandyism," wrote Count d'Aurevilly, of his hero Beau Brummell, "plays with the regulations, but at the same time pays them due respect." It is the perfect insider's revolt, and Brummell seems to have known the essential ridiculousness of being radically fashionable. "It is folly that is the making of me," he told one of the few women he felt understood him. When she asked him why he did not devote himself to a higher calling or use his cleverness to greater purpose than fashion, he rejoined that he knew human nature well enough to realize such was his best and fastest route "to separate himself from the ordinary herd of men."

"Eccentricity [is the] fruit of English soil. [It is] the revolt of the individual against the established order," explained d'Aurevilly, from the perspective of a Frenchman, and furthermore, "Dandyism . . . is the force of English originality when applied to human vanity."

Beau Brummell needed the oxygen of society: he was rarely alone from waking to sleeping through all his days in the high life. But he felt himself unique in a way he seems to have found unforgiving. Though his impact on the history of men's tailoring and the West End economy was far reaching, he was no tailor's dummy. His style was aped, but he was increasingly a man apart, dissecting with his own sardonic wit the style to which he gave his name and counterpointing high fashion with an accretion of affectations that began to alienate as much as they fascinated. How else, as d'Aurevilly remarked, but by comic affectation, to establish himself in his highly affected society?

Before the end of his first season in London, Brummell's debts began to mount. Most tailors would not expect to be paid for at least six months, and some submitted only annual accounts. In this it should be allowed that their stock outgoings were covered to some extent by gentlefolk supplying their own fabrics. Even so, many tailors operated almost like banks, with more prestigious clients offered better overdraft terms: Harriette Wilson described Stultz the tailor as a moneylender in exactly this context, and Lord Byron's tailors were still asking for payment for his servant's mourning liveries four years after the death of his mother. Joseph Lock, Brummell's hatter at 6 St. James's Street, gave a shilling reduction on all items for cash payment, but this was a rare incentive. It was quite common for credit to be extended for two or three years at a time, and the gentry took ample advantage of this.

Brummell, however, was encouraged to shop even further beyond his means. The supposition of the tailors was partly commercial—his custom worked for them as ideal advertising, and partly pragmatic: Brummell appeared to be headed for great high office as one of the favorites of the heir to the throne. His ability to maintain a line of credit relied therefore on his maintaining his position in fashion and society, and both, in effect, were reliant on the prince.

AFTERNOON

7

THE LADIES WHO RIDE

Civility, my good fellow, may truly be said to cost nothing: if it does not meet with a due return, it at least leaves you in the most creditable position.

George Bryan Brummell

As for love—I conceive it a mere empty bubble
And the fruits of success never worth half the trouble;
Yet as Fashion decrees it, I bear the fatigue
That the world may suppose me a "man of intrigue."
"The Fine Man or Buck of the First Set,"
The Pursuits of Fashion, 1810

London society operated in Brummell's day like a series of concentric circles. High society was exclusive by its very nature, but what typified Regency society through the glory days of Brummell's reign was the systematic way in which it went about excluding others. Exclusion was one of the key raisons d'être of the gentlemen's clubs, but also of the etiquette of greeting and dressing. The signal peculiarity of Brummell's career was that he came from outside the immediate spheres that had formed society but came to dictate the language of exclusion from an apparently unassailable position at the center.

A whole language was developing for expressing the subtleties of exclusivity. Chateaubriand, the French writer and diplomat, noted that the vocabulary of Brummell's associates seemed to change in London "almost as often as each session of Parliament . . . the fashions for words, the affectations of language and pronunciation in High Society change so often that a man who thought he knew English finds six months later that he does not." In London, this system of exclusivity was nowhere so conspicuously played out as in the West End's premier park: Hyde Park.

In the afternoon, especially in good weather, Brummell took to riding in the park, which extended then as now from Tyburn Lane (Park Lane) to Kensington Palace: three hundred and fifty acres of city parkland. He was an accomplished horseman, but this was not a sport of the physical variety. Rather, Hyde Park—notably the horse-and-carriage avenue called Rotten Row—functioned as a sort of outdoor salon, where the rituals of greeting and not greeting, doffing hats in acknowledgment or "cutting" those out of favor were enacted with the rigor of a military inspection. "Where the fashionable fair," as Lord Byron put it, "can form a slight acquaintance with fresh air."

One fictionalized account from the period describing a Brummell "cut" gives a clear, and unattractive, impression of the man in action on Rotten Row: "In the art of cutting he shone unrivalled: he knew the 'when' the 'where' and the 'how.' Without affecting useless short-sightedness, he could assume that calm but wandering gaze, which veers, as if unconsciously, round the proscribed individual." This was Brummell's world; distance was preserved, anyone could be escaped, all was show and banter. The callous snobbery involved in his self-appointed position as one of the regulators of who was "in" and who was "out" at the park is distinctly unappealing to the modern ear and eye. To Brummell's contemporaries all this was mitigated by his wit. "Have you ever endured so poor a summer?" shouted one friend in passing.

"Yes," he replied, "last winter!"

It was in Hyde Park that he was asked by another dandy where he got his boots blacked and announced to all who might hear, "My blacking positively ruins me; it is made with the finest champagne!" A talent to amuse remained a signal part of his attraction to the wider world: an ability to enliven the inherent tedium of society rituals with well-placed impertinences and pronouncements designed to make people laugh.

Though accessible from Piccadilly and Oxford Street, Hyde Park remained largely rural in Brummell's day, with tethered cows, roaming sheep and wild deer. In this mock-sylvan setting Brummell rode in the company of women as well as men. Men would ride singly or accompanied by a groom—Brummell stabled his horses on the edge of Hyde Park—while women rode in a vis-à-vis for two, furnished with "powdered footmen in smart liveries, and a coachman who assumed all the gaiety and appearance of a wigged archbishop."

Coachmen notwithstanding, it was an easy-going and attractive environment in which to exercise, socialize and flirt.

In the age of the Romantic poets, everyone acknowledged that in Hyde Park the landscape was tame:

> None view it awestruck or surprised
> But still, 'tis smart and civilized.

Brummell saw the comedic possibilities of the false pastoralism of the park and of Romanticism itself. It was the age when the Romantic landscape was being discovered, or created, in art and gardens. Brummell went to elaborate lengths of satire when faced in Hyde Park with a rider extolling the virtues of the rugged lakeland landscape and asking Brummell which lake he most admired (he never ventured so far north).

"Robinson," he said, turning to his valet who sometimes accompanied him in the park.

"Sir?"

"Which of the lakes do I admire?"

"Windermere, sir."

"Ah, yes, Windermere, so it is."

The exchange would be worthy of Jeeves and Wooster or the

plays of Oscar Wilde. It also made a point in a subtly Brummellesque manner: few pretensions are as ridiculous as the urban fashion for the countryside. Hyde Park, for fashion-conscious Londoners like Brummell, was quite rural enough.

Brummell rode in through the Apsley Gate, which led straight to the main axis of social intercourse: Rotten Row. "Is there a more gay and graceful spectacle in the world?" wrote Disraeli of Rotten Row. "Where can one see such beautiful women, such gallant cavaliers, such fine horses, and such brilliant equipages?" It provided more than the opportunity for Brummell to show off his riding, his horses and his ability to quip. It was also one of the few environments in which men and women "of rank and fashion" could mix easily with one another in large numbers. Unlike Vauxhall Gardens, where the fashionable ran the risk of a rather too intimate proximity with those outside their charmed sphere, Rotten Row remained the preserve of the highest echelons of society. "In those days," Captain Gronow pointed out, only the cream of society "would have dared to show themselves . . . nor did you see any of the lower or middle classes of London intruding themselves in the regions [of Hyde Park] which, with a sort of tacit understanding, were given up exclusively to persons of rank and of fashion." Why this should have been so when there was no charge for admission or porter at the gate beggars easy understanding.

The fortunes of Ranelagh, Vauxhall and the Pantheon on Oxford Street had all waned over the precise issue of too easy an access for the "exclusives" to feel comfortable. Prices had gone up accordingly, but the Regency and snobs like Brummell were discovering a more insidious system of social filtration and nowhere was this easier than in the open air, and on horseback. The bon ton self-selected those who were to be included—the fashionable and well connected—and the cost of maintaining a horse, equipage and the related costumes excluded all but the very rich. Anyone on Rotten Row, therefore, was rich and fashionable. Consequently mothers and chaperones were a little less watchful of their daughters and companions: everyone was deemed eligible company. There was more gossip and exchange of news and views between the sexes than was possible at any other time of day except a late-night ball at Almack's. It was in Hyde Park, therefore—and necessarily—that Brummell's acquaintance with women grew exponentially. And his popularity, humor and easy clubbability with men should not be read as an inability to enjoy the company of women, or for women to enjoy his. Quite the contrary:

Never was there such a man [wrote Tom Raikes], who during his career had such unbounded influence and what is seldom the case, such general popularity in society. Without being a man of intrigue . . . he was the idol of the women . . . Not only because he was a host of amusement in himself, with his jokes and his jeers, but because he was such a favourite with the *men,* that *all* were anxious then to join the party [of women] . . . Brummell was as great an oracle among the women of the highest rank in London, and his society much courted and followed, as amongst his male associates.

The attributes that had allowed Brummell an entree into the world of London fashion as a style leader for men were attractive to many women. And it is important to realize that, unlike many men of his class and education, he came to form intimate and affec-tionate relationships with women.

Brummell's dandy pose held the world in satirical contempt just as much as it held tailoring to be the supreme art, while a subver-sive and sardonic manner, then as now, begot a crowd. Beyond this Brummell's personable warmth and his wit—often lost in the retelling of those jokes that closely equate snobbery with humor—brought him many admirers. The women who were drawn to him and whom he chose in friendships or love affairs are especially re-vealing of the man, his mind and manner. He met them first, and most frequently, in Hyde Park.

The women with whom Brummell shared the most enduring and intense relationships over his years in London, and who rode with him on Rotten Row, were often strong, intelligent—and usually titled. Although he had many sexual trysts with women—and possibly with men—and with professional courtesans, they were shallow affairs compared with the profound friendships that structured his days in London and his later letter writing from France. These longer-term friendships remained just that, and the sexual frisson that undoubtedly underpinned them was not acted upon—with one likely exception. Of the women to whom he was most closely linked in London, and for some time afterward, Georgiana, Duchess of Devonshire, and Princess Frederica, Duchess of York, formed with him the most revealing pairings. They were both of high social rank and more than a decade older than Brummell. They were both strong, independent, willful and artistic—women who could offer Brummell support in his social advancement and access to the best that London had to offer, but who also found a complicity of mind and taste with the young dragoon who had had such a sudden impact on London, and who seems to have made them laugh.

Georgiana, Duchess of Devonshire, fast-living doyenne of London society and the most celebrated political hostess of the previous generation, was twenty-one years older than Brummell and had known him since he was a schoolboy. He had been introduced to Devonshire House on Piccadilly by Fox and Sheridan when he was still at Eton and his initial exposure to the circle surrounding the Prince of Wales in the late 1790s was attributable to the rapprochement then between Georgiana and the prince. Georgiana was forty-three in 1800, when she and Brummell first came to see more of each other in the close world of the Whig aristocracy, in Hyde Park and at Georgiana's parties.

The duchess was facing the twin problems of reintroducing herself to London after several years' exile abroad—since the birth of her illegitimate baby, Eliza, by Earl Grey—while simultaneously launching her legitimate daughter, "Little G." (Georgiana), on London society. Devonshire House—the Cavendishes' main Lon-

don residence, a veritable palace on the north side of Green Park—
had been undergoing major renovation, but was ready by June
1799, according to the *Morning Post,* "for the reception of its
noble owners." The balls and parties in honor of Little G. at Devonshire House and Chiswick, where the duchess also entertained,
marked the beginning of the new phase in Georgiana's life also:
reacceptance by society, by the Prince of Wales and even by Mrs.
Fitzherbert, with whom she had clashed violently in the past. The
same parties were also young Brummell's earliest forays into her
world.

Described in her youth by Horace Walpole as a "phenomenon"
and by the *Morning Post* as the "Most Envied Woman of the Day,"
Georgiana was more pitied than envied by 1800. Her unorthodox
but spectacular looks were lost: she had suffered a tumor behind
her right eye, which, after the invasive techniques of eighteenth-
century medicine—leeches, "flushing," blisterings and caustics—
had left her scarred and half blind. She had exhausted her restive
spirits on politics and politicians and was also deep in debt—to the
tune of £200,000.

Georgiana had not only seen her place as a great beauty and
leader of fashion eroded. Before her illness she had been used to a
radical degree of independence, such that her physical disability
(the eye tumor left her with chronic headaches) depressed her even
more than it attacked her vanity. She remained able to write, however, and poured much of her energies into letters and verse, and
encouraging the same in others. She wrote one poem to the woman
who had shared much of her life, and indeed had shared her
husband, in the age's most scandalous ménage à trois, with Lady
Elizabeth (Bess) Foster—who married her lover, the Duke of Devonshire, after Georgiana's death. The poem expresses the softening
heart of a woman who had learned some of the comfort of surren-
dering independence to the arm of another. George Brummell, her
new young friend, also received a copy, slightly extended, its sense
changed in the context of an experienced older woman writing to a
young man. He kept it, in her handwriting, in his album.

I've Known all the Blessings of Sight
By the Duchess of Devonshire

I've known all the blessings of sight
The beauties that nature displays
And traced in the splendour of light
The glories that streamed in the blaze
Yet though darkness its sorrow has spread,
I grudge not the pleasures I've known,
Since, reclining, I thus lay my head
On a breast that I know is my own.

I've valued the charms of the rose,
As I pluck'd it all fresh from the tree;
I have kiss'd it, and bid it disclose
Its sweets, for I meant it for thee.
But memory still has its bliss,
Though no longer I gaze on thee now;
More sweet than the rose is thy kiss
And more fresh and more lovely art thou[.]

The life of roebuck was mine
As I bounded o'er valley and lawn
I watch'd the grey twilight decline
And worshipp'd the day-breaking dawn.
I regret not the freedom of will,
Or sigh as uncertain I tread:
I am freer and happier still
When by thee I am carefully led[.]

Ere my sight I was doom'd to resign
My heart I surrender'd to thee
Not a thought or an action was mine
But I saw as thou bads't me to see
Thy watchful affection I wait,

And hang with delight on thy voice;
And dependence is soften'd by fate
Since dependence on thee was my choice.

The poem's inclusion in the collection Brummell kept of verses written to or for him goes unmentioned in works on Georgiana, but if it was written or extended with him in mind, it makes an impressively moving case for a hopeless infatuation on the duchess's part. The first three stanzas do not appear in the version she wrote to Lady Elizabeth Foster. These additional stanzas in Brummell's version define a breast to lean on as well as regret, on the other's part, that she is no longer seeing or able to see her "lover." Brummell's famously delightful voice is referenced, and he plays the part of the worshiped dawn to the cold twilight of (Lord) grey. Georgiana knew all about the life of the roebuck that was Brummell's, and no longer hers, but there is more than the affectionate counsel of an old family friend on offer: she mentions his tender kiss.

Poems are not evidence, and love poems are more slippery than most. Nevertheless, as related by more than this poem, there grew between Brummell and Georgiana a complicity, as past and present darlings of society. He knew his advancement was aided by her place in the *haut ton,* just as she knew that the success of the Devonshire House balls in launching her gauche daughter on London was heightened by Brummell's presence. The poem, in the context of the anecdotes that surrounded Georgiana and George, and Brummell's later writings after the duchess's untimely death, suggest their friendship had a profoundly felt core and that he had a special place in her affections as her star was fading and his rising.

Brummell's album came to be littered with the poetic effusions of Georgiana and their mutual friends. In this respect theirs was a literary relationship and it may well have been that Georgiana, like Hester Stanhope, felt the need to suggest to Brummell he *do* something with his fame and talents. She had offered protection and encouragement to artists and writers in the past—even accommodating the novelist Charlotte Smith at Devonshire House. Together she and Brummell read in French and Italian, and she translated verses to be inscribed into the album. Though the archive at Chatsworth yields no evidence that Brummell was invited there, he claimed he was and there is little reason to doubt him based on the intimacy on show in their writings. He called her "beautiful and enthusiastic" and cited as a particular family trait the "generous natures" of the Devonshires. Their literary flirtation started off innocently enough, and in keeping with the age's accepted intercourse between the sexes. When Brummell had his hair cut, the aging coquette wrote that she would

> Here in the bower of beauty, newly shorn,
> Let fancy sit and sing how love was born.

Their friends knew of their literary sport and joined in. When the duchess's favorite spaniel, Faddle, died, Charles James Fox penned some verses for Brummell to put into his album: "On the Death of Faddle . . . an early victim to love." When they were all together, at Devonshire House we assume but cannot know, the duchess read a poem she had written about Fox's friend James Hare, "a loved companion and a friend sincere." She next wrote a long mock-heroic saga in verse, "Borino the Brave," almost certainly for performance, and one must imagine them laughing together as she describes a "Bedlamite Duchess" who "with gesture uncouth" aims her arms and her heart "straight at the Youth." How much was meant by any of this is unclear: on the one hand it was a parlor game played by talented amateurs with time and ink on their hands. On the other, it was a literary flirtation between two arch flirts, which may or may not have exhausted itself on the page. Within the playful rules of their poetical soirees almost anything could be said, but Brummell chose to keep a series of poems that are remarkable for their frank depiction of an older woman revivified by the attention of a younger man. The classically inspired heavy breathing of these poems aside, the roles Georgiana and Brummell take on in their writings (mainly hers to him) place their relationship in the long tradition of courtly love. It was the obvious model for a friendship, played out in poetry, of an older, high-status woman and a romantic young man. There is one Jesse anecdote on Brummell that can reasonably be attached to his "affair" with Georgiana and, if correctly so, the implication is inevitable that their literary love affair did get a little too close for comfort. The story is of Brummell's dismissal from a country-seat house party. The style of the scene as it was related around London bears much similarity to the drama of the period, but that in no way under-mines its authenticity. Brummell had learned his manners and his wit from the theater and from theater practitioners. So, too, it might be added, had the "duke." The scene, as relayed by Jesse, took place at Chatsworth, Hardwick or Chiswick, one of the Dev-onshires' country retreats:

It is related of [Brummell] that he came one morning into the library of a noble friend, at whose house he was frequently a visitor, and told him, with much warmth and sincerity of manner, that he was very sorry, very sorry indeed but he must positively leave.

"Why, you were not to go till next month!" said the hospitable peer.

"True, true," replied Brummell anxiously, "but I must be off."

"But what for?"

"Why the fact is—I am in love with your duchess."

"Well, my dear fellow, never mind that, so was I twenty years ago—is she in love with you?"

The Beau hesitated, and after for a few seconds staring at the white sheep-skin rug, said faintly, "I—believe she is."

"Oh! That alters the case entirely," replied the peer, "I will send for your post horse immediately."

Jesse's anecdote, like so many in his collection, is deliberately vague about persons, place and dates, but there is every reason to believe this story was current in London as a minor comic scandal involving the Duchess of Devonshire. If so, it places Brummell in an idealized light as *chevalier d'honneur* in their poetic tale of courtly love: knowing precisely when to bow out once his sentiments, out of keeping with the tradition, are returned in kind by his lady.

In 1806 Georgiana died unexpectedly, and in great pain, from an abscess on the liver. Brummell was as shocked and moved as the many who had found her the most vivacious and exciting woman in London. William Roscoe had recently had some success with a poem meant for children but taken up by many, called "The Butterfly's Ball." In memory of Georgiana, Brummell himself wrote a companion piece, "The Butterfly's Funeral." Such poems, he later wrote, "were in vogue with all the world in London" and because Georgiana Spencer had been the sort of celebrity whose death— like that of her distant kinswoman, Diana Spencer—was treated as an occasion for public mourning, Brummell briefly found an alternative and unexpected fame himself, as the people's poet:

The Butterfly's Funeral

Oh ye! Who so lately were blythesome and gay,
At the Butterfly's banquet carousing away;
Your feasts and your revels of pleasure are fled,
For the soul of the banquet, the Butterfly's dead!

No longer the Flies and the Emmets advance,
To join with the friends in the Grasshopper
  dance;
For see his thin form o'er the favourite bed,
And the Grasshopper mourns for the loss of his
  friend.
. . .
At the solemn spot, where the green rushes wave,
Here sadly we bent o'er the Butterfly's grave;
'Twas here we to beauty our obsequies paid,
And hallow'd the mound which her ashes had
  made.

And here shall the daisy and violet blow,
And the lily discover her bosom of snow;
While under the leaf, in the evenings of spring,
  Still mourning his friend shall the Grasshopper
    sing.

What is one to make of such whimsy? Brummell was right to proscribe the poem in years to come with the explanation that it was the fashion of the time, and it should be read also with the usual allowances for the recently bereaved. "The Butterfly's Funeral," however, was an unexpected commercial success (Brummell's only one and, like most society poets of the period, he did not benefit financially by a single penny). It sold three thousand copies as soon as it came out, and its publisher, John Wallis, went on to sell more. It also set Brummell in the public mind as the Grasshopper, and it described, in a sense accurately, the false, childlike world in which he, Georgiana and their friends lived. To the rest of the world, fascinated though they might be by the scandalous liaisons and gargantuan debts of Georgiana, she, like Brummell, lived an unreal existence, as light as quicksilver and as insubstantial as grass.

More perplexing, however, is what to make of an "affair" conducted over several years by two of the leading celebrities of the age that has left in its wake no letters, no gossip and little evidence beyond sentimental verse. Doubtless, had the infatuation moved toward anything worthy of gossip there would be record, so it is fair to assume that the two social gadflies from different generations held a mutual fascination for each other more thrilling for them than romance. In any event, he was, in the time-honored phrase, young enough to be her son.

A touching coda on the affair is presented by one of Georgiana's daughters, Lady Harriet Cavendish. She also met Brummell in Hyde Park and around London after she was presented to society in 1802, but was unimpressed with many of her mother's more glittering friends. "Mr Brummell," she later wrote, "keeps us waiting rather than wishing for him. I feel it a matter of perfect indifference whether he arrives at any moment or not at all." He was due at a house party she was holding at Tixal Hall in Staffordshire, an event all but buried in the emotional fallout of her mother's generation's sexual roundelays. For one thing, Harriet had been married off to Lord Granville Leveson-Gower, even though he had two illegitimate children with Georgiana's sister Lady Bessborough. Lady Bessborough was also among the guests, as both aunt-in-law and mistress of the host, along with her married daughter, Lady Caroline Lamb, who was deranged with love for Brummell's friend Lord Byron and "alternating in tearing spirits and in tears." Perhaps Brummell was meant to lighten the occasion. He and Harriet took refuge from the emotional dramas around them in memories of her mother. He sketched for her a copy of the famous Joshua Reynolds painting of Harriet's mother and sister at play. She gave him a poem she had written about her mother that she thought he might understand: "The Voice of Praise." It concludes:

> The lover lulls his rankling wound
> By hanging on his fair one's name!
> The mother listens for the sound
> Of her young warrior's growing fame.
> Thy voice can soothe the mourning dame
> Of her soul's wedded partner riven,
> Who cherishes the hallow'd flame
> Parted on Earth, to meet in Heaven!
>
> That voice can quiet passion's mood,
> Can humble merit raise on high,
> And from the wise, and from the good
> It breathes of immortality!
> There is a lip, there is an eye
> Where most I love to see it shine,
> To hear it speak, to feel it sigh,
> My Mother! Need I say 'tis thine?

1. *The Brummell Children* by Joshua Reynolds: George Bryan "Beau" Brummell age three and a half (with dog) and his elder brother William, age five. Exhibited at the Royal Academy in 1783, this painting marked the Brummell family's new status in London society.

2. William (Billy) Brummell, Beau Brummell's father. "He is active and intelligent, and has more influence than any man with Lord North."

3. Charles James Fox, politician, gambler and bon viveur. Fox was a close friend and frequent house guest of Brummell's parents.

4. "My friend Sherry." Richard Brinsley Sheridan, playwright and politician, was another avuncular figure in Brummell's childhood.

5. Lord North, Second Earl of Guildford, the "God of Emoluments." Prime minister from 1770 to 1782.

6. Beau Brummell's mother, Mary Richardson, later Mrs. Brummell, was well connected but also unconventional: she lived openly as Billy Brummell's mistress before they were married.

7. Downing Street, where the Brummell family lived until the Gordon Riots of 1780. Beau Brummell was born there, possibly in what is now number 10 or 11.

8. Hampton Court was divided into grace-and-favor residences in the late eighteenth century. The Brummell family was granted apartments overlooking Fountain Court. The mother and boys playing with the dog are thought to be the Brummells.

9. Donnington Grove, Berkshire. The Brummell country residence through Brummell's childhood and adolescence.

10. Eton College, Windsor. "George Brummell was a very clever and a very idle boy, and Nature seemed to have supplied him with a quadruple portion of amusing repartee."

11. and 12. William (*left*) and George (*right*) in 1790 in the uniform of the Eton Montem polemen. At Eton, George was known as "Buck Brummell."

13. Eton Montem, or Ad Montem ("To the hill!"). This ancient festival grew so riotous that Prince Albert eventually banned it.

14. The Montem polemen uniform was remarkably sober. Although Montem involved misrule and fancy dress, the polemen dressed in sober quasi-militaristic "suits." This democratic and pared-down style seems to have struck Brummell as more flattering and more masculine than the prevalent male fashions of the period.

15. Theatricals in Eton's Long Chamber. Though the curriculum at Eton adhered strictly to the classics, it was expected also that boys would excel in oratory, performance and at honing pithy aphorisms (in Greek and Latin).

16. The Christopher Inn, Eton high street, the pub where older Eton boys drank and gambled. It was shut down shortly after Brummell's time at Eton, amid rumors that it catered to other adolescent vices than merely drink.

17. Oxford. "Our life was an imitation of high life in London." Brummell entered Oriel College in 1794 but left to take up his army commission.

18-21. Despite being celebrated for his looks and style, George Bryan (Beau) Brummell never sat for a full-length portrait. In his late teens he broke his nose badly after a fall from his horse, which may account for the different renderings of his features in the four portraits—miniatures and etchings—attributed as him.

22. Brummell was an officer in the 10th Light Dragoons from 1794 to 1798. The Prince of Wales's regiment, "the most expensive, the most impertinent, the best dressed and worst moralled regiment in the British Army," was stationed mainly in Brighton to be near the prince.

23. George, Prince of Wales (prince regent, 1811–1820. King George IV, 1820–1830) in his Hussar uniform as colonel of the 10th Light Dragoons. When only seventeen, Brummell was asked to act as *chevalier d'honneur* ("best man") at the prince's wedding. They remained friends, fitfully, for fifteen years.

24. Brighton seafront. "Most of the officers keep their own blood-horses and their girls. At one o'clock they appear on parade, they dine about five, and come about eight to the theatre." Brighton was known as "Mayfair by the sea."

25. An illustration, finished by Brummell and from Brummell's own *Male and Female Costume* (1822). "A Greek Warrior in His Travelling Dress." Brummell believed men's fashions should follow classical lines and flatter the body.

26. This dandy wears pantaloons that mimic nude Greek statuary, though their tailoring is inspired more directly by Hussar riding breeches. He is also wearing Hessian boots, made fashionable by Brummell.

27. London became renowned for the finest men's tailoring in the world, working on principles of classical proportion. This tailor is taking the key measurement from the scye or "shoulder's eye."

28. Meyer (later Meyer & Mortimer) pioneered with Brummell the modern trouser, often with instep straps in the style of military overalls. They still trade on Sackville Street.

29. "I, Brummell, put the modern man into pants, dark coat, white shirt and clean linen. I dare say that will be sufficient to secure my fame." An early-nineteenth-century coat with gilt metal buttons, velvet collar and plain waistcoat and breeches.

30. and 31. Brummell bought his hats from Lock & Co., hatters on St. James's Street, which is also still in business. Their records include one 1808 order from Brummell for two new hats with the intriguing note that they be delivered to Brummell's steam baths: the "New Hummums" (hammams), "a place where people get themselves cupped."

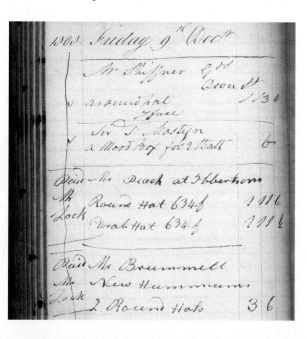

32. William Arden, Lord Alvanley, Brummell's most constant friend. He "combined brilliant wit with the most perfect good nature."

33. Thomas Raikes was known as "Apollo" because, as a City banker, he "rose in the east but set in the West End." He and Brummell were friends from their first days at Eton.

34. Poodle Byng's tightly curling blond hair prompted Brummell to remark when he saw him in a carriage with a real poodle, "Ah, Byng—a family vehicle I see!"

35. Golden Ball Hughes. One of the richest rakes in London, Hughes "looked as if he walked on stilts, and had swallowed the kitchen poker."

36. Brooks's club gaming chips, as used by Brummell. "He was a constant winner at play, and I believe realized [in one season] nearly £30,000." Later he lost everything.

37. Brooks's Great Subscription Room, designed by Henry Holland and considered at the time the finest interior in London. Betting and gambling carried on day and night.

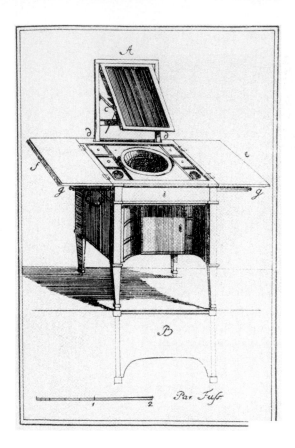

38. "His ablutions would have gained him a reputation for sanctity in a Mahomedan country." A dandy's dressing table, after Chippendale. Brummell took several hours to shave and dress, and an invitation to his levee became highly prized amongst London's fashion-conscious elite.

39. Silver and glass ointment or pill box with Brummell's crest. Similar boxes were inserted into the Chippendale shaving table above.

40. "Brummell's snuff-boxes," from a collection owned by descendants of the Brummell family. Brummell's tobacconists sold out of any snuff brand to which he lent his name.

In losing Georgiana, in 1806, Brummell had not lost a great love, but in its way the removal of the Voice of Praise was as damaging to him as if he had. Not only would the death of this mother figure have reopened the wounds of his own mother's death, but had she lived, Georgiana might have been the ideal voice of admonition: she had known all the beauties of society; she had also known all the dangers of gambling.

The woman whose friendship endured the longest, and who has the strongest claim to have been the love of Brummell's life, was a royal duchess: Princess Frederica Charlotte Ulrica Catherine, Princess Royal of Prussia and Duchess of York and Albany. She was twelve years his senior. Princess Frederica had grown up in the court of King William II of Prussia, spoke English with a strong German accent and corresponded invariably in French, signing herself "Frederique." Brummell wrote back in English. She and Brummell first met in 1800 through her husband, the Prince of Wales's bluff brother Frederick, Duke of York and Albany. The royal couple were already nearly a decade into their childless marriage and nearly as long into an informal though amicable separation. The duke lived in London at his house in Piccadilly, later converted into apartments and named after his second title, Albany, or he lived with his regiments. The duchess occupied Oatlands Park, near Weybridge in Surrey. The Yorks had bought Oatlands on their marriage in 1791 with the impressive allowances of £18,000 from the Civil List, £7,000 from Ireland and a full £45,000 a year from the duke's holdings as Prince-Bishop of Osnabruck. Prince Fred visited "Princess Fred" at weekends, but kept a mistress, Mrs. Clarke, in town.

Thomas Raikes was certain of the issue between Princess Fred and Beau Brummell: to begin with, she was the most useful stepping-stone in his social ascendancy. "The Duchess [of York] was very partial to Brummell, and, as she has great finesse and was a very nice discriminator of good breeding and manner the approbation of such a woman must be highly creditable to the individual himself." She was kind and cultured but possibly rather bored with the Hanoverian court. London's fashion-conscious *Bon Ton Magazine* implied criticism when it wrote that "The Duchess resides entirely at Oatlands and sees no one but the royal family."

She shared with Brummell a love of animals, of sketching and of house party frolics. Brummell's acceptance in society was enormously bolstered by his popularity in the affable alternative "court" at Oatlands. His power base widened from the Prince of Wales and the Duke of York's louche and pseudo-military circle of loud men, to one in which he was equally at home: a house party set only hours from London.

Oatlands, by virtue of having a legitimate regal chatelaine who was also considered a charming hostess, was unique among the royal palaces, and it had a special place in the memories of those who were invited there as a result. "Oatlands might be deemed a court," wrote Raikes, "in which the affability on one side and the respectful attention on the other were equally remarkable . . . [it was] the only existing retreat of correct manners and high breeding." The stamp of character upon the place was Princess Frederica's, and Oatlands came to represent an attractive hybrid of aristocratic respectability and distinct eccentricity. Princess Frederica kept many animals, mainly dogs but also monkeys, parrots, a llama and a kangaroo, and was said to have been distraught when Oatlands had a major fire—not by the damage it caused so much as the upset to her animals. Their elaborate mausoleums are the only legacy at Oatlands of this characterful and popular hostess.

In truth, Frederica was not greatly suited to the Hanoverian British court at the beginning of the nineteenth century. It was not that she was an intellectual, but she was more keenly interested in her immediate domestic sphere and friends and, unfashionably, the welfare of animals, than with the court or high society. *"Mein Gott,"* she was quoted saying, as imitated by Monk Lewis, "dey are so dependent on us for kindness and protection, I t'ink we ought to love dem, if only to wake the better part of our nature; dey are sincere; dey are honest." A Newfoundland dog walked obediently in her funeral cortege some years later, from Oatlands to Weybridge Church. In this somewhat suburban, dog-loving mien she might be seen as the precursor to modern British royal ladies. "The Duchess of York is a pattern for others to emulate," wrote *Bon Ton Magazine,* but could find little more exhilarating to say about her than that "she pays her tradesmen's bills regularly, and writes her own drafts on her banker." These were enclosed with her trademark pink notepaper, heavily embossed with flowers and lyres.

She was somewhat ahead of her time in seeing part of the role of royal consort as charitable, and put her name to innocuous local causes. Barely a year after her marriage her support was solicited in a much more political campaign: slavery abolition in the West Indies. "It has been mentioned," intoned the obsequious writer of "An Address to HRH the Dutchess [*sic*] of York Against the Use of Sugar," "that you were the friend of the poor and that your acts of beneficence were such as required exertion." She did not or could not lend her name to the abolitionist cause, but it was supposed she talked to the duke about it. She was briefly then the focus for that mixture of gallantry, prurience and politicking that surrounded a new member of the royal family, but it did not survive her seclusion at Oatlands. Public attention soon moved on, forgot that she had briefly inspired a fashion for tiny, tight shoes, and she was left in peace.

She was not, however, unattached to the capital. She made dutiful appearances at court and at the opera, but chose to stay twenty miles to the southwest with her pets, and receive weekly gossip and updates on the metropolis from the crowd around Brummell she asked down for weekends.

A chaise was booked every Friday to leave St. James's Street at five o'clock with the Duke of York and any of his party to go to Oatlands. The initial invitation to Brummell was certainly made with the assumption that he would be an entertaining house guest for the duke and would help keep him, to some extent, away from the card tables. But Frederica enjoyed the attentions lavished on her by her husband's young friend. She had "a very superior mind," according to one Oatlands visitor, "highly cultivated by books . . . she was able to take the lead on any subject . . . she had very refined taste and great knowledge." She was a country lady who knew all about the world, but had decided to withdraw from the city in favor of her garden, dogs and—in her case—shell-decked "grottoes." Oatlands was the ideal weekend retreat from the hurly-burly of the West End and Brummell came to treasure it—and Frederica.

Oddly enough, the Yorks' marriage was known as one of "the most unvarying steadfast affection" and she and the duke ended their days on good terms. The early years of their marriage, however, before and during her friendship with Brummell, were typified by structured and consensual separations, despite the intense pressure on them both to provide further heirs (the duke was second in line to the throne when they married). This distance may be explained by some sexual misalliance. The princess was fastidious and sensitive. The duke was "big, burly, loud and cursing." The duke became embroiled in so disastrous a sex scandal—his mistress sold army commissions and was arraigned in front of the House of Lords—and he was forced to resign as commander-in-chief. Some claimed the Yorks had an open marriage, and there was some likelihood of this once it became widely known from her less-than-discreet doctor that medical opinion considered her incapable of producing an heir. If she did take lovers, Brummell was a prime candidate. "Believe me that no one can feel the loss of your society more keenly than I do," she wrote coyly in French. "I will never forget the tender moments that I have had because of you, and the only thing that can compensate me would be the certainty of your welfare." She sent him lavish presents and also tenderly home-wrought items, including hand-sewn cushions. They once bought a lottery ticket together, with what future spending in mind one can only speculate.

He gave her a dog, which they immediately christened "Fidelité." "No one could be more sensible than I to your kind thoughts on my birthday," she wrote to him. "Please accept my most sincere thanks for this handsome little dog, that, I like to flatter myself, can be a symbol of faithfulness in our ongoing friend-ship, to which I can assure you I attach the highest value." He even once essayed that most reckless of gifts from a man to a woman: a dress. It was made entirely of Brussels lace and he thought it would suit her. It cost him 150 guineas.

At least one rather lavish gift is recorded in return: for Christ-mas of 1818, Princess Frederica ordered for Brummell a tortoise-shell and gold-inlay snuff box. It was one of the more expensive items on the shopping list she gave her lady-in-waiting, but, at ten pounds, cost rather less than he had spent on her. Brummell's Christmases and New Year's Eves were almost invariably spent at Oatlands. The princess imported German Christmas traditions to England a full generation before Prince Albert effected a similar change in royal and British yuletide festivities. The first Christmas tree in Britain—loaded with oranges and sweetmeats—was proba-bly displayed at an Oatlands Christmas early in the nineteenth cen-tury, and Princess Frederica converted the whole ballroom at Oatlands into a traditional German Christmas fair, with greenery, gingerbread and candles.

Was there anything more to Brummell's long and close relation-ship with the princess? Almost certainly. For one thing, when Brummell's creditors were pushing him to publish his memoirs, in the style of Harriette Wilson or Julia Johnstone, and secure his re-tirement by selling stories from his day in the high life, he refused because Princess Frederica had made him promise, he said, that as long as any of the royal brothers lived, he would not reveal any-thing from their shared past. This may conceivably have been out of extreme loyalty to her husband, who had heaped scandal on the royal family already after his affair with Mrs. Clarke and forced resignation from the army. Frederica may, as a royal princess, have felt a strong loyalty to the tarnished Crown and the benighted per-son of the regent and simply wanted to preserve him from further revelations about their wilder youth. But these seem insufficient claims on her or Brummell's indulgence. Probably there was some-thing more specific she wanted kept secret . . . an affair to which

Brummell could allude only by mentioning her name whenever he was asked why he would not publish his memoirs. To some this looked like either extreme gallantry or extreme foolishness. Others guessed that his gentlemanly code of honor kept one card close to his heart.

According to one report, the duke once caught the duchess in flagrante delicto when he returned to Oatlands unexpectedly. With whom, it is not known. But when Brummell died, one of the few possessions he had kept from his day in the high life was a miniature of a woman's eye. An odd keepsake—but one that in its day was given as a token between lovers. The prince regent kept a miniature of the eye of Mrs. Fitzherbert and the talisman was buried with him. Brummell's miniature was of the left eye of Princess Frederica.

8

THE DANDY CLUBS

No tender love-suits in their thoughts could he trace,
The suits of the Tailor had taken their place,
For beauty's soft chains that the true lover feels,
They had only brass chains, dangling over their heels,
He could read in the hearts of those dashing young
    Friskers
Only curricles, Overalls, Boots and Large Whiskers.
For love &c
        "Cupid in Bond Street," composed by Mr. Hook,
                written by Mr. Lawler, c. 1806

White's and Brooks's, the St. James's Street gentlemen's clubs, both elected Brummell as a new member when he first moved to London in 1799, and he later became a founding member of Watier's club and its president for life. His late afternoons were spent in the elegant fug of these clubs, from which women were barred, and two of which, White's and Brooks's, remain today much as they were when he knew them.

The most important of the Regency clubs, because of the difficulty of entry, was White's. Founded in 1693, originally as White's Chocolate House on the site that is now Boodle's on St. James's Street, the club was considered practically an alternative House of Lords by the time Brummell was elected at the end of the eighteenth century. "To be admitted a member of that body gave a young man a 'cachet' such as nothing else could give." For Brummell, known initially only to the Prince of Wales's set, these clubs were an entrée to the wider world of establishment men. Though Watier's became briefly a rival in terms of exclusivity, membership at White's was such a supreme form of distinction within London society that Disraeli was moved to compare acceptance as an accolade outranking the monarch's own chivalric Order of the Garter.

White's had been established as a refuge for Tory grandees, but by 1800 its politics were subordinate to its social preeminence to the extent that Brummell, a notional Whig, could become a leading member. He revived the club's reputation among the young and fashionable, rather than simply among the aristocratic and distinguished, thereby helping to blur the lines between the Old Club and the Young Club. As a side effect, White's finances improved steadily during Brummell's time as a member, as young men stayed later and spent more. The rules of the club, dating from 1781, laid down the ten guineas annual membership, procedures for terminating subscriptions and for "blackballing" aspiring candidates. The rules also stipulated that the three-hundred-strong membership was to be renewed every time it fell to two hundred eighty by twenty new members chosen by a committee. The nineteen others who joined with Brummell in 1799 were nearly all in their twenties, and members already of his unofficial Dandiacal Body.

The façade of White's clubhouse—formerly the home of the Countess of Northumberland—was remodeled during the second half of the eighteenth century, and a little later a bay window was added over a former doorway that became a landmark on St. James's Street. Here Brummell held court in the afternoons, in a bow window that became known as the Beau Window. The men of the Dandiacal Body re-formed several hours after they had gone their separate ways from Chesterfield Street, "mustered in force" around Brummell's chair in the Beau Window, watching the world go by and telling jokes. It was said that "an ordinary frequenter of White's would as soon have thought of taking his seat on the throne in the House of Lords as of appropriating one of the chairs in the bow window." Lord William Pitt Lennox was one of their number and described Brummell "holding his own, in [his] quiet manner, above the brilliant sestette," but struggled to define the comic moment: "The conversation upon the topics and the scandal of the day . . . wild humour has its instant, its supreme moment for real enjoyment, and that pleasantry which has kept a company in a roar of laughter at the right time is vapid when revived."

Some of Brummell's uglier bons mots can be placed to the chair in the Beau Window—even when they cannot be dated. When asked if he had seen his brother in town, Brummell replied to his friends that he had ordered his rustic relative "to walk the back-streets" until he had visited a decent tailor. When asked what he had thought of a weekend in the country, he said he had had to return to town, as he had found a cobweb in his chamber pot. Grantley Berkeley, Goldstream Guards officer and son of Earl Berkeley by his mistress Mary Cole, recorded one particularly inane conversation among the dandies, at the expense of one less well dressed:

"My dear fellow," said Brummell, "where did you pick up that extraordinary affair you have put on your back? I protest I have never seen anything so singular."

"Most singular indeed," said Lord Yarmouth.

"Maybe it's an heirloom?" Lord Fife suggested.

"Coeval with Alfred the Great, at least," observed Lord Alvanley.

"Exactly!" said Lord Wilton.

"It is not your fault, mine goot sir," said Prince Esterhazy, "you shall be not to blame because a devoid-of-conscience-influencing tradesman deceived you when you him the honour do to purchase of his delusive fabrics."

"Is there anything the matter with my coat?"

"Coat?" exclaimed Brummell. "Coat?" cried the others in chorus. "For heaven's sake my dear fellow, don't misapply names so abominably! It is no more like a coat than it is to a cauliflower—if it is, I'll be damned!"

Such was the style that passed for repartee among the fashionistas of Whites's Beau Window.

The world of White's was tight, exclusive and, some claimed, bitchy. "Damn the fellows," retorted a notoriously bad-tempered member of the Guards' club opposite, who had been denied membership in White's, "they're upstarts, fit only for the society of tailors." The Beau Window serves as a perfect image for the *haut ton,* the society Brummell conquered: insular, exclusive, indolent, looking out on the world and down on it. It also encouraged men of fashion in an age before mass media to hone their skills as fashion commentators or, given the inability of passers-by to respond, as voyeurs. The members of Brummell's Beau Window set were, in a sense, the first "fashion police." However, the comment, censure and wit of the Beau Window was not all fashion-conscious, fatuous or ill-considered. Sir William Fraser in his *Words on Wellington* wrote later that "within that sacred semi-circle . . . there was more shrewdness, good sense and knowledge of things, to be found than in any other space of the same size on the face of the globe." Brummell passed judgments not just on dress from his chair in White's window, but also on gentlemanly behavior. The Duke of Wellington was not a man to be impressed by clothes, yet Sir William Fraser, who knew him well, claimed he "had a high opinion of that mysterious and terrible tribunal, 'White's Bow Window.' " The duke said that the members of the Guards were the most troublesome people in the army when there was nothing to do, but when active operations began, they were the best soldiers. None of them misbehaved when there was duty to be done. "White's Window would not permit it."

⁓

Slightly less fashionable than White's, but joined by Brummell nonetheless, was Brooks's. This was and is just across the street from White's, slightly nearer St. James's Palace. It had been founded only twenty years before by the former manager of another club, Almack's, called William Brooks, and initially it was the most political of the clubs—"the most famous political club that will ever have existed in London." While the Church of England received the discourtesy title of "the Tory Party at Prayer," Brooks's became known as "the Whig Party at Dinner." Brummell later expressed the opinion that "the Whigs kept the best company" in London.

Brooks's was arguably the most elegant of the London clubs in architectural terms. Henry Holland, son-in-law of Capability Brown and architect to the Prince of Wales, had created in the Great Subscription Room one of the finest interiors in London. Restrained, neoclassical, the style of Brooks's was the style its members exported to their country seats and civic buildings all over Britain and beyond. The walls in Brummell's day were greenish gray and the curtains red damask. There were painted allegories over the doors, appropriately of Bacchus, Venus and Cupid, and one of the largest barrel vaults in the capital, festooned with gilt swags, crowned the famous Subscription Room. The effect, however, was cool and patrician. The Eating Room, just right beyond the Venetian Window, was even painted in the buff colors of the Whig party, the same muted colors Brummell chose for his pantaloons and waistcoat, setting the fashion for all Brooks's members to do the same.

Brummell was invited to join by his father's Westminster drinking partners, Charles James Fox and Richard Sheridan, and Brooks's, by 1800, had acquired a good deal of their louche and high-spending reputation. The club had entered its years as a gambling den, where family fortunes accumulated over generations were lost on the roll of a die or turn of a card. But if fortunes were lost, others were made. One founding member, Mr. Thynne, "having won only £12,000 during the last two months [from fellow members] . . . retired in disgust." On the other hand, Lord Cholmondeley and Mr. Thompson of Grosvenor Square made nearly £400,000 between them at the Brooks's tables from other club members.

When Brummell joined, the club was populated by a slightly more raucous, though older, crowd than White's. Garrick, the aging theater star, was a member. So, too, was the Duke of York, who had once become so intoxicated at the club with some older cronies that he and they wrecked all the furniture and were persuaded off the premises only at the open end of a blunderbuss. Brooks's members had also included the more sedate Sir Joshua Reynolds, the slavery abolitionist William Wilberforce, the historians and philosophers David Hume and Edward Gibbon, the prime minister William Pitt and Thomas Greville, whose book collection was one nexus of the British Museum. It was a mixed crowd. Brummell joined with his friends "Poodle" Byng and Thomas "Apollo" Raikes and encouraged, as at White's, a return to the roaring days of the clubs' and members' youth. The tone at Brook's, therefore, changed somewhat between day and night, as the older men, generally, left the club to the gambling and drinking of a younger, more aristocratic crowd, unencumbered by families, scruples or political careers.

Brooks's was open, in effect, twenty-four hours a day. Over the years a night at Brooks's ended for many with a trip to a usurer or money lender—often in the City—to secure a loan to pay the gambling debts accrued in the club. One of the first rooms Brummell passed, therefore, on entering Brooks's during the afternoon, was the Strangers' Room, which became known as "the Jerusalem Chamber" as it was so often crowded with Jewish moneylenders during the day, attempting to accost members and retrieve their money.

On the whole the serious card and dice gambling of Brooks's and White's was left to the evening. Daytime gambling was of a different hue. Brummell and his friends ended arguments and disputes by entering abstruse bets in the leatherbound betting books that are still owned by Brooks's and White's. Members bet on horses and prizefighters, as one might expect. They also bet on the sex of their own children, or of other people's children or of their mistresses. They bet with macabre frequency on the imminent deaths of friends and enemies and on each other's illnesses, and on the tragic degeneration of the old king's mental state. They bet through the French Revolution on the heads of France's aristocracy, and as battles loomed in the Revolutionary and Napoleonic Wars, they bet on who would win and how. Brummell, however, most often made political and military wagers. "Mr Brummell bets Mr Irby one hundred guineas to ten that Buonaparte returns to Paris (Decr 12th 1812)"; "Mr Brummell bets Mr Methuen 200 gs to 20 g that Buonaparte returns alive to Paris, [from Moscow] Decr 12th 1812." Brummell won. Similarly he entered bets on which of his friends would win by-elections and on the likely majorities in the House of Commons. No one would argue with Brummell on a matter of taste or elegance, but about politics he was forced to defend his corner and bet accordingly. His father's political intentions for his second son in sending him to Eton and Oxford paid off at least in Brummell's ability to wager and win on Westminster by-elections.

Money changed hands daily, often very large sums. No matter how much a man like Brummell might be in debt to his "duns"— the shopkeepers, tailors and servants who supported his lifestyle— it was anathema to renege on a gambling debt for all that it was unenforceable in law. It was a debt of honor between gentlemen, taken with enormous seriousness, even though, or perhaps because, the wagers often expressed the refusal of high society to take life seriously.

White's betting book dates from 1743. At first the bets were recorded by a club servant, but by Brummell's time they were registered by members. When they took over the responsibility one wag scribbled in the margin, "About this time it is supposed the nobility of England began to learn to write." The bets were meant to amuse as well as to end or defuse arguments, but they also provide a simple glance at the rarefied and ridiculous world in which Brummell flourished. For the gentlemen of Brooks's, White's and Watier's, the Napoleonic Wars were treated with the same casual amusement as the sex of the Duke of Clarence's latest illegitimate offspring. But the bets provide a tragicomic footnote to the world of Brummell.

He and his friends described the divinity that shaped their lives with recourse to financially incontinent wagers, some of which, ultimately, provided endings in themselves.

Brummell ate at his clubs. He moved twice in his time in London, from Chesterfield Street to South Audley Street and then to 13 Chapel Street (now Alford Street)—these houses are now demolished—but he stayed within walking distance of his clubs. As well as all the formal meals, when Parliament was in session, food was always laid out for ad hoc dining; "cold meats, oysters etc at 4s malt liquor only included . . . or biscuits, oranges, apples and olives at 10s 6d." Although there was no gaming or betting in the Eating Rooms, there was, conversely, eating at the gaming tables. Pulled chicken (chicken "pulled" into shreds) was a club favorite and also "cold fowl, fruit, bisquits [sic] with to drink, tea, coffee, cyder [sic] and spruce beer [a dark molasses beer flavored with spruce twigs]."

Brummell's clubs, Brooks's and White's, also pioneered the meal that need not interrupt conversation or gaming, the "sandwich," named after the eponymous gambling-addict earl. One of the earliest uses of the word is to be found in the journal of Edward Gibbon, a Brooks's member. The clubs encouraged day-long eating and drinking for those with an appetite for either, but the food, despite White's statutes inviting members to contribute an annual extra guinea "towards having a good cook," was poor. Brummell turned out to be fashion-conscious about more than his clothes, and to have more in common with the gourmet Prince of Wales than an interest in tailoring: he became the leader of a small group of dissenters within clubland who sought to import finer—French—food and cooking styles. Ultimately, this led to the foundation of a new and rival club.

Captain Gronow recalled a dinner at Carlton House in 1814 attended by Brummell and other members of both White's and Brooks's when the prince asked for everyone's opinion of clubland food. Sir Thomas Stepney spoke for all the men present in describing "the eternal joints, or beef-steaks, the boiled fowl with oyster sauce, and an apple tart—this is what we have, sir, at our clubs, and very monotonous fare it is."

Sir Thomas—according to Thomas Raikes an "epicurean Croesus"—was inspired to improve the situation along with Brummell and the prince. There and then the prince suggested that they found a club together aspiring to the higher ideals of the novel French cult of "gastronomy." Brummell was to be appointed perpetual president and the prince summoned his personal chef for advice on the kitchens. Jean Baptiste Watier—until the arrival in 1817 of the French star chef Antonin Carême, the leading authority on food in Regency England—was duly sent for from the cavernous kitchens of Carlton House. The new club, it was decided, would be named in his honor. Watier declined to cook at the club, or the prince declined on his behalf, but the chef suggested another royal cook, Labourie, to run the kitchen in his stead and Madison, a royal page, to manage it. It was soon said that "Labourie's dinners were exquisite; the best Parisian cooks could not beat Labourie." At first the club was billed as a musical society and singing club— there were several in London at the time—but its key selling point was the higher ideals of French gastronomy espoused by Labourie and the achingly fashionable sensibilities of its founding members. As intended, the twin attractions of the finest food in London and the famous wit and dandy Beau Brummell as perpetual president soon attracted "all the young men of fashion and fortune." Thomas Raikes recorded in his journal that "the dinners were so recherché and so much talked of in town that . . . the catches and glees [the singing clubs] were superseded by card and dice and most luxurious dinners were furnished at any price, as the deep play rendered all [meal] charges a matter of indifference." The club, at 81 Piccadilly, on the corner of Bolton Street, was a runaway success— at least, as far as the reputations of its food and its social sophistication were concerned. Unfortunately Brummell made no money from it.

Brummell's taste in food had begun typical of his class and age;

Harriette Wilson described him as a dedicated carnivore. But the occasion of dining provided, for Brummell, another stage on which to shine, and he became more interested in food through his twenties and as a result of his presidency of Watier's. His famously slim and athletic figure, unsurprisingly, suffered as a result and his weight grew steadily, especially after the opening of Watier's, from 177 pounds at the start of his London career to 192 pounds a decade later. Like his young friend Byron—who took to an eccentric diet consisting of vinegar and bread—Brummell suffered from the conflicting fashions of the time: sophisticated gastronomy on the one hand and tight clothes on the other. Neither poet nor dandy maintained the figure that London society and tailors had first admired.

Watier's did not last long by clubland standards. It closed in 1817, a result of the exile of its president, Brummell, and the near ruin of most of its members. However, it set a pattern that has persisted in clubland: great chefs, trained in royal or restaurant kitchens, are headhunted by clubs to attract members. The most food-centered of the London clubs, Crockford's, which arose from the ashes of Watier's in 1828, appointed as chefs first Louis Eustache Ude and then Francatelli, pupil of Antonin Carême. Consequently Brummell played a part in introducing French haute cuisine to clubland. Watier's and Labourie set a pattern followed subsequently by many London clubs in quietly educating English gentlemen about fine French food and wines.

At the clubs, snuff had ousted smoking as the tobacco vice of choice. By 1773, Dr. Johnson had noted that "smoking has quite gone out," but it took Brummell and the dandies to put an end, temporarily as it turned out, to pipes and cigars in fashionable London circles. Snuff—the ground, often moist stems of the tobacco plant—was very expensive. Spanish Stuff, the Prince of Wales's favorite, cost three pounds per pound. Brummell bought snuff for the prince as early as 1799: a pound of Bureau and Canister as a thank-you token for we know not what, priced at seven shillings and sixpence. Between 1810 and 1824, of the ten regimental messes with accounts at the snuff purveyors Fribourg and Treyer, only two bought cigars as well as snuff, and White's accounts concur that snuff was what gentlemen, in Brummell's time, preferred. Brummell bought Martinique, twenty to thirty pounds at a time, as it arrived fresh from the London docks, with an occasional jar or two of Marino or Macouba—the latter scented with attar of roses.

Brummell was the supreme dictator at his clubs, but especially at Watier's, of the manner in which snuff was to be taken. It was a habit defined by its paraphernalia as much as the addictive pleasure of tobacco. The small, hinged boxes were kept in the hidden pockets of tailcoats, or, if they were slim, in the side pockets of waistcoats. Brummell maintained that snuff boxes should be opened and the snuff taken from box to nostril with the use of only one hand. This required dexterity and concentration. Of course, the ideal was to effect the whole operation midsentence without appearing even to glance at the expensive commodity or its more expensive container. Brummell flicked open the lid of the snuff box with the thumb of his right hand, which had the effect of presenting the lid, usually highly decorated or even jeweled, to the onlooker. Then the same thumb was used to convey a small amount of snuff in the indentation by the thumbnail to the nose, the box meanwhile held at the chin. A small nicotine "hit" was thereby delivered via the septum as powdered cocaine was taken in the Jazz Age. The haughty angle of the head that became a feature of dandy caricatures, and is the pose taken by Brummell in one miniature, may have been a tilt adopted by habitual snuff takers to avoid unsightly brown drips. This appears, parenthetically, to be the etymology of the terms "toffee-nosed" and by extension "toff." "Sniff [the snuff] with precision," one 1800 dandy manual advises, "with both nostrils, and without any grimace."

Brummell's collection of elaborate boxes was sold off after his exile, but many from the period survive and the descendants who own the Brummell family portraits have also inherited a large collection of snuff boxes, many of which are likely to have been Beau's. The snuff box lid miniatures express political or amorous affiliations or depict pets, houses, children or classical or erotic scenes. One popular design was in the shape of a woman's lower leg and shoe. One of Brummell's had an invisible hinge, called a "Lawrence Kirk," which caused much amusement at Carlton House when the prince failed to find a way in. Lord Liverpool, the prime minister (son of the Brummell family lodger, Charles Jenkinson), tried to open it with a knife, prompting Brummell to cry out, "My Lord! Allow me to observe that's not an oyster but a snuff-box!"

Brummell's habit of collecting snuff boxes was copied by the Prince of Wales and the Duke of York. The latter did not even like snuff, but was given so many boxes for his collection he decided eventually to have them melted down and made into a silver-gilt salver with the names of all the donors on the side.

Brummell was not above using his influence to his own financial ends—at least to the extent of making a joke of the situation. When the snuff purveyors Fribourg and Treyer had a new consignment or "hogshead" of snuff due to be opened, they invited Brummell to take the first sniff in the hope he would spread the fashion for a new brand as he might a new cut of waistcoat.

The hogshead was duly opened in the presence of the arbiter [Brummell] who, after taking a few pinches, gravely pronounced it a detestable compound and not at all the style of thing that any man, with the slightest pretensions to correct taste could possibly patronize. This . . . petrified the purveyors and the companions of [Brummell] left him to discuss the matter with the proprietors. No sooner had they gone than Brummell said "By some oversight I did not put my name down on your Martinique list . . . since the Hogshead has been condemned you won't object to my having three jars full of it." Messrs Fribourg gladly yielded [according to Jesse at least], for in a few days it having become known [that Brummell was taking the new snuff] not a grain was left.

⁓

It was Byron who dubbed Watier's "the Dandy Club." He cited four dandies as the prime movers in the club: Brummell, Alvanley,

Henry Mildmay and Henry Pierrepoint. They were also members of Brooks's and White's, like most of the members of Watier's. But where White's and Brooks's had other affiliations, as political party headquarters and gambling dens and also had long-established membership, Watier's relied entirely on the dandy set. The evanescence of the club was ordained in its foundation; Brummell was the club's key player and its fate was linked to his.

Brummell initially had "the good sense to eschew [the] deep potations, blade-bones of mutton and the music of the dice box" at Watier's, wrote Captain Jesse. "'Tis true he dropped in occasionally on their orgies . . . to enjoy the jokes, but not to steep his own intellects in wine."

This was all to change after his relationship with the Prince of Wales went into decline. At Watiers, Brummell had sown the seeds of his downfall—or, at least, the financial aspect of it. He developed there what would now be termed a gambling addiction. So long as the gambling was restricted to the inanities of the betting book, he and his fortune were relatively safe: he could return to Chesterfield Street with cash in his pocket or the promise of it, where Robinson awaited with a more formal change of clothes for the evening. Later in the day, however, the gaming got much more serious at the clubs, and at Watier's in particular. As perpetual president of a club that became as notorious for gambling as for gastronomy, Brummell's dangerous addiction was fed and encouraged daily, to the despair of his friends and of his growing number of creditors.

EVENING

9

THEATRE ROYAL

Many a beau turned his head wishfully towards our box, anxiously waiting to observe a vacancy . . . Beau Brummell, Fred Bentinck, Lord Fife, the Duc de Berri and a great many more were visitors [but] when the performance had concluded, we always remained late in the rooms, amusing ourselves with George Brummell, Tom Raikes, and various others. [Brummell's] person, was rather good. Besides this he possessed a sort of quaint, dry humour. It became the fashion to court Brummell's society [at the opera] through fear—for all knew him to be cold, heartless, and satirical.

Harriette Wilson, *Memoirs*

After nightfall the most dazzlingly illuminated spaces in London were the theaters. Just two had royal patents to perform plays—the Theatre Royal, Drury Lane and Covent Garden. The King's Theatre (confusingly, later Her Majesty's) was the primary opera house and there was a fourth drama venue opposite the King's on the Haymarket, called the Little Theatre, though its license to perform plays extended through the summer season only. The Lyceum on the Strand achieved popularity after the Drury Lane company decamped there in 1809 (while the Theatre Royal was being rebuilt). After that it returned to staging musical dramas. There were smaller music venues, but these five West End houses—Drury Lane, Covent Garden, the King's Theatre, the Little Theatre and the Lyceum—were the ones frequented by society. Between them, by the beginning of the nineteenth century, with a London population that numbered nearly a million, they sold twelve thousand seats a week. And for those, like Brummell, who might consider themselves fashionable or cultured, it was unthinkable not to be a regular theatergoer.

The Theatre Royal waxed and waned in popularity. Drury Lane was run by Sheridan—past his most prolific years as a playwright by 1800 but still a successful producer—and Covent Garden by Thomas Harris. Both managers were family friends of Brummell, who referred to Sheridan as "my friend Sherry." The King's Theatre in the Haymarket—larger and grander than La Scala in Milan—achieved preeminence in fashionable circles over both Covent Garden and Drury Lane, once it dedicated itself exclusively to opera.

All five theaters, however, were crowded, noisy and—throughout the evening and on both sides of the footlights—brilliantly lit: so much so that it was suggested that a Persian arriving unschooled in European ways would be hard pressed to distinguish who was onstage and who was watching. One reason for this was that the theaters had no practical means of dimming lights even had they wanted to, so the audience was as illuminated to itself as to the actors onstage. But the audience had no inclination to sit in the dark. Whereas those in the galleries had perhaps more real interest in the play, Brummell and his friends in the boxes and pit—as the stalls were then called—came just as much "to furnish out a part of the entertainment themselves [as if] acting a part in a dumb show." The *haut ton* seemed "to assemble only to see and be seen." The London theaters provided the opening act of Brummell's evening play, but for him, like everyone else on and off the stage, going to the theater was a performance in itself.

The arrival of Brummell and the *haut ton* more than halfway through the evening's entertainment coincided with a separate commotion. After the second interval, theaters sold off all empty upper and lower gallery seats at half price. What with the arrival of Brummell and his crowd in the boxes and the noise of the extra seats being filled, the performers and middle-class theatergoers faced a good deal of disruption. But this was only one of the many distractions of the theater and opera-going experience. The hundreds of candles that lit both the auditorium and the stage were tended assiduously and nervously by candle trimmers and snuffers. If they trimmed too soon they risked knocking lit candles down and starting fires—both Covent Garden and Drury Lane burned to the ground in 1808–1809—but if they trimmed too late, theatergoers complained of hot wax dripping on them from above. Fruit sellers plied their trade throughout the performances, and some plied other trades on the side; business transactions took place between members of the audience and those in the boxes, and theater staff, personal messengers and footmen carried around the theater items of gossip, orders for carriages, money, love notes and bills of exchange. And many more people were packed in than would be considered comfortable or safe in generations to come. Sheridan for one employed a large front-of-house staff at Drury Lane to cope with the melee: there were individual box keepers, box inspectors (against the worst excesses of the upper classes in dark corners), also four lobby keepers, fourteen doorkeepers, four messengers and seven box-office staff.

There was hustle, distraction and excitement. In an age when Londoners were patently self-regarding and referred without irony to their city as "The World," the theater was the one place where everyone was on show together. Passions were high, even before the music struck up or the first lines were spoken, and so were the stakes—for the performers both on- and offstage. Like the society of which it was a perfect cross section, the theater seemed almost ungovernable. As a crowd it felt, like society, always on the point of revolution, which was part of the thrill. It hissed and applauded, shouted, laughed and cried, always in full view of its own image. As a crowd it could be entertained or enthralled, amused, amazed or appalled, but was never predictable. The theater was the place where the demimonde and real world, the factual and the imaginary, the political and the artistic, the sexual and mercenary all met together. Decorous and highly decorated on the surface—the King's Theatre auditorium was even considered worth seeing in its own right—the theaters were also riotous, sexually heightened arenas in which passions of every variety were stirred and the crowd could never be ruled.

When prices rose in 1809 after the theater fires, the Covent Garden audience rioted for sixty-seven nights in a row. When in 1805 the tailors of London found that Brummell's exacting standards—which had brought them such commercial success—were to be parodied in a comedy called *The Tailors, or a Tragedy in Warm Weather,* they organized a boycott, sent death threats to the lead actor and threw scissors and cutting shears at him when he made his first entrance on the opening night. The ensuing riot spilled out into the Haymarket and was only broken up by a platoon of Life Guards called from duty at Carlton House. The play closed.

Brummell arrived almost nightly by sedan chair or carriage. He was reputed to ask his chair carriers to take him several paces into the theater so that he could step straight from the quilted swansdown interior to the plush inside of the opera foyer. This was probably an exaggeration, but evening wear for Brummell and his followers was much lighter than daywear, so some worry over the cold was perhaps understandable. The theater was not ticketed at each entrance, and entry to the boxes and the pit was by token—made of silver in the case of the King's Theatre—or by recognition. The Duke of Bedford, for instance, had granted Brummell himself free entree to his box (number 38), but declined to lend it to him so that he could invite a party. "I make it a rule never to lend my box, but you have the *entrée libre* whenever you wish to go there, as I informed the box keeper last year." After working his way through the crush and the darkness of the corridors and candlelit staircases, Brummell entered the theater itself and his gilded box, awash with light and "all fitted up with crimson velvet." "The lighting [of a theater box] is better adapted for being seen than for seeing," wrote Prince Pückler-Muskau, "in front of every box hangs a chandelier which dazzles one and throws the actors into shade." Brummell's box was, of course, a stage in its own right.

One's appearance in a particular box at the theater signaled the shifting allegiances and relative status within society. It announced one's presence in London and participation in its life. How one was received and acknowledged, whom one invited in, or to which boxes one was invited, all served to illustrate the changing web of alliances: financial, sexual or political. The Princess of Wales was roundly applauded at the theater when her treatment by the prince became public knowledge. The reentry of Georgiana, Duchess of Devonshire, into society was also acknowledged at the opera, as was her rapprochement with Mrs. Fitzherbert. The Marquess of Worcester "ran up three times to the opera" to see if Harriette Wilson was back in London, but lamented to the Duke of Leinster "she did not make her appearance." When Brummell needed his creditors to know he was in London and in confident, rude health, he showed himself at the opera.

As well as presenting a spectacle of aristocratic power play, boxes, like the stage, were the site of more prurient voyeurism. Just as the elision between the skid-alley careers of actresses and prostitutes was well established and understood, so, too, theater boxes offered a stage on which to perform rituals of sexual display and availability. The owners of boxes might want only to strut and fret for the purposes of personal vanity, but the boxes also shop-fronted flirtations with romantic or mercenary intent. And, generally, the nearer the stage, the more exhibitionist the occupants of the boxes were thought to be, like the two rakes Bulwer-Lytton describes "seated in the box nearest the stage [indulging] in debauchery as if it were an attribute of manliness and esteemed it, as long as it were hearty and English, rather a virtue to boast of than a vice to disown." Walter Scott harrumphed against these same front boxes, where "one half come to prosecute their debaucheries so openly that it would degrade a bagnio."

Brummell's friend Harriette Wilson took her regular box in this theatrical and exhibitionist spirit. Like all of the most celebrated courtesans, she rented boxes near the stage for the season. She took a box at the opera every Tuesday and Sunday night, and at the theater from Thursday to Saturday. These boxes were showcases in which she could flaunt her attractions, but also from which she could solicit and meet potential "protectors." "Many a beau," she wrote, "turned his head wishfully towards our box, anxiously waiting to observe a vacancy for one." A young man's reputation could be made, in a certain sense, from being seen next to Harriette, Julia or one of the other "Fashionable Impures." "Beau Brummell, Fred Bentinck, Lord Fife, the Duc de Berri, Berkeley Crave and a great many more were visitors," wrote Harriette. The box at the theater provided Harriette and her later readers with a chance to view Brummell as the theater crowd saw him, making his entrance:

The celebrated beau, George Brummell, who had been presented to Amy [Harriette's sister] by Julia, in the Round Room at the opera [a notorious pickup venue at the King's Theatre], now entered our box . . . He was extremely fair, and the expression of his countenance far from disagreeable. His person, too, was rather good. Besides this, he was neither uneducated nor deficient. He possessed, also, a sort of quaint, dry humour [so] it became the fashion to court Brummell's society, which was enough to make many seek it, who cared not for it.

Harriette later admits that "when the performance had concluded, we always remained late in the rooms, amusing ourselves with George Brummell, Tom Raikes, and various others . . . Tom Raikes . . . is a mimic [as well as Brummell] and he can take off Brummell very tolerably, as well as the manners of the *vielle cour France beaux* [sic] but I never discovered that he could do anything else. Brummell often dined with him." Raikes remembered those times fondly and stated categorically that "happy was she in whose opera box Brummell would pass an hour" while neglecting to mention that in his youth he, too, had been part of the jolly party with

Harriette and the other "Impures." Such was the crush of beaux attempting to spend time with the courtesans, and with Brummell, and be seen in their company, that a row erupted over the numbers allowed entry into boxes. Sheridan and the theater managers eventually set a rule that the main boxes "were meant for no more than six."

By spending so much time at the theater in the company of courtesans, Brummell was expressing the clear double standard of his age. He, as a single man, could move freely from the boxes of the courtesans to those taken by members of high society. No woman could move so easily between the different spheres of demimonde and real world that overlapped at the theater—and a married man was offering a direct insult to his wife if he publicly consorted with courtesans in her presence. Brummell, on the other hand, was always drawn to glamour. Harriette, her sister Amy and his childhood friend Julia allied him with the decadent world of the Cyprians—and allowed him the semipublic performance of a flirtation that was not just sexual but dangerous. These women relied even more on image and on presentation than did Brummell, but he had no need to acknowledge them as publicly as Harriette would have us believe he did. Something in him drew him to Harriette and Julia and to the rituals of sexualized social intercourse. This may have been a performance to vie with the one onstage, yet Harriette positions Brummell as an insider at her court, sufficient for her to lose patience with his "absurdities" or grow jealous of his fame.

The presence of Harriette Wilson, Julia Johnstone and their "Impure" associates at the theater made some society ladies uncomfortable. The managers of the Italian Opera House on the Haymarket saw an opportunity. In 1804 they suggested that the opera employ the same system as the clubs: only those deemed fashionable *and* respectable might be allocated tickets for the pit and boxes. Opera was already more expensive than the theater: prices started at a guinea for a seat in the gallery, as opposed to a shilling in the theater. Opera boxes could cost from a hundred to as much as a thousand guineas for the season. "The opera may be called the exclusive property of the affluent, who take boxes by the year," wrote one German traveler, "the pit [also] has been added to the accommodation of the nobility, and in order to exclude improper company, the admission was raised to half-a-guinea [and] the dress is the same as the boxes."

This new exclusivity was considered absolutely necessary once the King's Theatre extended the entertainment on offer from just an opera to supper and a ball afterward. "Let the theatre be got up upon the same exclusive system [as the clubs]," wrote one critic, "and you shall have . . . the most gorgeous audience." The most gorgeous audience duly arrived, once, after 1805, "no one could obtain a box or a ticket for the pit without a voucher from one of the lady patronesses," namely the Duchesses of Marlborough, Devonshire and Bedford, and Lady Carlisle, the Duchess of Rutland's mother. This was a pivotal moment in the evolution of the modern West End as it stamped opera, as compared to plays, an aristocratic art form. Not only did the men dress, again, according to Brummell's strict dicta, but on evenings following royal "Drawing Rooms" (the official receptions for ambassadors at royal residences, for instance), Brummell and his cronies would attend the opera "in full court dress." The opera might be even more "stamped with aristocratic elegance" than the theater, but the audience still arrived late, and noisily. There were more boxes at the King's Theatre and many bought exclusively for the season. The ruse failed, however, in terms of keeping the likes of Harriette from the opera: she had her lovers book in their names, and so the game continued. At one point she even kept a box, bought in the name of her young lover the Marquess of Worcester, just opposite that taken by his mother, the Duchess of Beaufort. They stared daggers at each other for an entire season. It suited Harriette's purposes to be in more select company and to have her coquettish games and elegant solicitations accompanied by the music of Italian opera.

Between acts and after the final performance, the King's Theatre opera furnished a further luxurious locale for sophisticated flirtation. This was the Round Room. The chamber was a "circular vestibule, almost lined with looking glass, and furnished with sophas [sic] in which female loveliness is not only seen but reflected." So central was this room to the linked love life and career of Harriette Wilson that she intended originally to title her memoirs *Sketches from the Round Room of the Opera House.* For men like Brummell, the life after the opera, or even during intermissions, was both in the Round Room and also the Green Room (dressing room) of the King's Theatre. Here, dancers and actresses were used to entertaining their sponsors and protectors and, in some cases, making extra money by allowing them to watch them undress.

Intriguing to relate, Brummell, often credited as one of the models for Byron's *Don Juan,* was almost certainly in the audience at the London premiere of *Don Giovanni* at the King's Theatre in 1816. Its sexually licentious themes had been considered too shocking for it to be performed in any of the thirty years since its first production in Prague in 1787. When the London premiere finally took place, elements of Giuseppe Gazzaniga's alternative score were interpolated along with new words by the librettist Lorenzo da Ponte, then working in London. But it proved a huge success at the King's, where the audience were well attuned to the nuances of seduction and betrayal. It struck many as having direct parallels with the new men-about-town, with their sardonic, indifferent posturing and the sexually sophisticated mores—and some would have noted, too, the parallels between the heartless Don and the social adventurer in Harriette Wilson's box, whom she described as "cold, heartless and satirical." Three years later, Byron published *Don Juan.*

After the theater, or instead of it, Brummell repaired to the company of the Prince of Wales, later prince regent, at Carlton House. This was the scene of Brummell's anointing as a member of the prince's immediate circle—it was one thing to have been on familiar terms with him in the environments of the dragoons barracks and the Brighton Pavilion, but quite another to have ease of admission to an official royal residence, built, precociously, with its own Throne Room. But Carlton House was also the site both of Brummell's Bacchanalian partying with the prince and of their bitter rows. It was a suitably dramatic backdrop.

Alterations on the house had begun in 1783 under the direction of the prince's favored architect, Henry Holland. From under Holland's Ionic columns (one of the few elements of the palace to survive later demolition), Brummell stepped late at night into a palace unrivaled in England and across the marble flagstones of a forty-four-by-twenty-nine-foot vestibule supporting a domed roof on Siena marble pillars. From this his eye could turn, via a Pompeiian green-and-red octagonal hallway, lit entirely by gaslight, into apartments displaying every style and taste that had titillated the prince. There was a Red Satin Drawing Room, a Blue Velvet Drawing Room and a Golden Drawing Room. There were Doric and Corinthian columns, Grecian busts, Roman mosaics and French Gothic fan vaulting. It was not, it must be safely assumed, the taste that Brummell himself might have enjoyed, but it had been built to impress and it did. The stairway that connected these apartments to the prince's private suites above was lit by a stained-glass dome (illuminated from behind at night, again by gas) painted in imitation of Raphael, and at the foot of this staircase stood guard a monumentally tall hall porter.

The prince liked tall servants—footmen were recruited from the army and from France, and paid on a scale that favored the tall to encourage tall young men to apply. The porter who could "see over the gates," however, was also grossly overweight, and was dubbed as a result, possibly by Brummell, Big Ben. It was a joke he came to regret.

This nickname predates the famous bell and its tower on the new Palace of Westminster, built after the fire of 1834. It also predates the infamous prizefighter Big Ben Caunt, a celebrity at the time, after whom the bell was named. It may just be, then, that the boxer who lent his nickname to the clocktower bell and who came from near Byron's home at Newstead in Nottinghamshire was, in turn, nicknamed Big Ben as a reference to the bulky porter so well known to the dandies of London.

All the visitors to Carlton House passed Big Ben on their way in, and he and his nickname were established long before Brummell made the mistake of using the same name to tease the similarly hefty Prince of Wales. He compounded this misfired joke by applying the name, by extension, to Mrs. Fitzherbert, also caricatured by this period (1810 and onward) as greatly overweight. He called her "Benina." These were the first of a series of Carlton House faux pas that began to strain Brummell's relationship with the prince. Perhaps familiarity at the prince's, even his mistress's, expense might have been acceptable in the Brighton barracks of the Tenth Light Dragoons. Now, though, they were all a good deal older, and perhaps also Brummell was less secure in the prince's affections. Or he cared less about the prince's approbation.

Because Brummell was permitted the Privilege of Entrée—into the royal presence—he was shown by footmen not into the lesser West Ante Room but into the Circular Room. It was at the time the largest circular room in the country after the Chelsea rotunda at Ranelagh Gardens. There was Roman tent drapery around the walls, and a domed ceiling painted in representation of the sky from which hung a chandelier of cut glass representing an inverted fountain. The whole was reflected in giant mirrors between porphyry columns. There were blue silk-covered settees lining the circumference, on which Brummell awaited the prince.

The prince's intimate friends would gather regularly under the new gas chandeliers. Musicians often played in an adjacent room and the wine flowed freely. Unsurprisingly, in this atmosphere of luxury and easy familiarity, the prince was at his most relaxed. His guests, however, forgot at their peril their host's position, and Brummell trod a thin line between behavior that was amusing and that which was considered rude.

During one drinking session at Carlton House, a comment of Brummell's so enraged the prince that he threw a glass of wine into Brummell's face. Brummell, sitting on his right, picked up his own glass and threw its contents into the face of the person on *his* right with the loud instruction, "The Prince's Toast: pass it round!" This much was greeted with laughter.

Brummell did, however, misread the prince's loyalties to his various mistresses and very possibly once ordered "*Mistress* Fitzherbert's carriage"—a double insult as it misapplied both Maria's class and her marital status, as she understood it, vis-à-vis the prince. At the time the prince was in the hands of Lady Jersey, but he returned, repeatedly, to the forgiving Mrs. Fitzherbert, who decided not to forgive Brummell.

The deterioration of the friendship between Brummell and the prince was signaled by small fissures that grew—imperceptibly to many—into a rift. When Brummell put down his snuff box on a sideboard in front of Mrs. Fitzherbert (women had only recently taken to snuff), the prince snapped, "Mr Brummell, the place for your box is in your pocket, not the table."

When the prince saw a snuff box of Brummell's he particularly liked, he asked if he might have it, then said, "Go to Gray's [the jewelers on Bond Street] and order any box you like in lieu of it." Brummell asked diplomatically to be allowed one with the prince's miniature on it, studded with gems, to which the prince agreed. The snuff box was duly commissioned, only for Brummell to find, when he called for it, that the prince had expressly canceled the order. He also refused to return Brummell's original. "It was this more than anything else," according to one who knew them both, "which induced Brummell to bear himself with such unbending hostility towards the Prince of Wales. He felt that he had treated him unworthily and, from this moment, he indulged himself by saying the bitterest of things."

There was, then, no clear falling-out. Brummell had witnessed the prince's inconstancy in friendship and in love, and as he himself grew in status and experience he seems to have considered the prince's behavior merely immature. At first he addressed the issue by making a joke of it. One of his dandy friends, Colonel McMahon, asked him what he thought of the prince's displeasure and Brummell responded, "I made him what he is, and I can un-make him." It was a classic comic inversion of the plain facts, which in its Wildean way stated a small truth: by 1811, Brummell was more fashionable than the prince. This in turn led Tom Moore to pen a short satire of a (forged) letter that had been printed from the prince to the Duke of York in 1812. The author is in theory the prince.

> Neither have I resentments, nor wish there should
>   come ill
> To mortal, except, now I think on't, Beau
>   Brummell;
> Who threatened last year, in a superfine passion,
> To cut me, and bring the old King into fashion.

Nevertheless, Brummell was included on the guest list for those invited to Carlton House in June 1811 for the celebratory ball marking the accession of the Prince of Wales as prince regent. Because of the tragic circumstance that had led to the prince's assumption of monarchical prerogatives—the madness of his father, George III—there were mixed responses to his eager desire to celebrate the occasion. Old Queen Charlotte boycotted the festivity, and insisted her five surviving daughters do the same. Both the Princess of Wales and "the other wife," Mrs. Fitzherbert, stayed at home, the first uninvited, the second invited but refusing to attend unless granted the "Rank given her by yourself [the regent] above that of any other person." Nothing, however, could dampen the spirits of the new regent, who broke all Brummell's codes of elegant dress, returning to the diamonds, the aigrettes and red velvet ensemble of his youth "of not very good taste or very well made." Three thousand guests were invited and two thousand entertained to dinner, most of them in the Gothic Conservatory Dining Room; £2,585 had been spent on the "fittings"—decorations—but this paled in comparison with the £61,340 gold dinner service off which Brummell and the guests ate. "Nothing was ever half so magnificent," wrote Tom Moore, "it was in reality all that they try to imitate in the gorgeous scenery of the theatre; and I really sat for three quarters of an hour in the Prince's room after supper, silently looking at the spectacle, and feeding my eyes with the assemblage of beauty, splendour, and profuse magnificence which it presented."

Three days after the fete the gates of the palace were thrown open to the public and thousands flocked in to see the famous interiors that had been a backdrop for so many years to Brummell and the prince's revels and rows. On June 25, 1811 thirty thousand visitors traipsed through to gawk. The regent vowed never to let it happen again, and his affection for the palace began to wane, just as it had for so many of his lovers and friends. His inconstancy was legend so far as women were concerned, but two betrayals caused a different sort of comment and bewilderment, among friends and in the press, as they seemed so inexplicable. One was his abandonment of his friendship with Brummell and the other was his abandonment of Carlton House, which he ordered pulled down in 1826. For Brummell, the evening of June 19, 1811 at Carlton House was his last view of the inside of that or any other royal palace.

10

SEVENTH HEAVEN OF THE FASHIONABLE WORLD

To that Most Distinguished and Despotic
CONCLAVE
Composed of their High Mightinesses
Of
Almack's

The Rulers of Fashion, the Arbiters of Taste,
The Leaders of Ton, and the Makers of Manners,
Whose sovereign sway over "the world"
of London has
Long been established on the firmest basis,
Whose Decrees are Laws,
and from whose judgment there is no appeal

Miss Hester Stanhope's dedication
in her novel *Almack's,* 1827

On Wednesday nights, the epicenter of the World as understood by Brummell was neither Carlton House nor the theater but Almack's Assembly Rooms on King's Street, St. James's. Unlike the clubs of St. James's Street, Almack's was attended by women as well as men and was open only at night. The club's years of success as *the* assembly rooms for the *haut ton* were precisely contemporary with

Brummell's own glory days, a time when, as Lord William Pitt Lennox said, "happy was the young lady and young gentleman who basked in the sunshine of [Almack's]," a club Captain Gronow described simply as "the Seventh Heaven of the Fashionable World."

The Assembly Rooms had been opened by a Scot called Mac-Call or Macall (who decided some anagram of his name might sound more aristocratic) in 1764 in order to create a "most magnificent suite of rooms" as a safe haven for high society. One prerequisite of entry was the correct attire, and this came to be in Brummell's gift. By 1801 the Brummell look was required uniform for Almack's—which meant his evening costume, consisting of white cravat and waistcoat, dark blue or black tailcoat and black knee breeches and stockings or tight black pantaloons. A "solemn proclamation" went out from the club to the effect that only "silk stockings, thin shoes, and white neckcloths [were to be] invariably worn." Wider trousers, or any addition of color, were unacceptable. Brummell's rules for men's attire at Almack's began to pare down men's evening wear to the formal black and white that has remained, evolving by the end of the nineteenth century into the even more structured "white tie and tails."

Admission itself was by ticket only—called a voucher of admission and made of cardboard—on sale, in theory, on Bond Street. They could only be bought, however, by those on "the list." The list was compiled—in the manner espoused by Wilde's Lady Bracknell—on lines of respectability, genealogy and fashionability: two out of three might suffice. This was "selection with a vengeance," wrote Lady Clementia Davies, "the very quintessence of aristocracy." The arbitrators were known as the lady patronesses. In Brummell's day they were Lady Castlereagh, Lady Jersey, Lady Cowper (later Lady Palmerston), Lady Sefton, Mrs. Drummond Burrell (later Lady Gwydyr and later still Lady Willoughby de Eresby) and the ambassadresses, the Austrian Princess Esterhazy and Russian Countess Lieven. Between them, it was supposed, all European gentry and nobility might be scrutinized and found acceptable . . . or wanting. Wealth would not guarantee entry, of course, but neither, automatically, would birth. "Into this sanctum sanctorum of course the sons of commerce never think of entering on a Wednesday night [but also] three fourths of the nobility knock in vain." Good looks or talent might help, but what the lady patronesses scrutinized was *"ton."* Dandies had a good chance: Tom Moore was admitted and noted proudly in his diary, "Went to Almack's (the regular Assembly) and stayed till three in the morning. Lord Morpeth said to me: You and I *live* at Almack's." Many were refused entry: of the three hundred officers of the prestigious Foot Guards, Captain Gronow reckoned, "not more than half a dozen were honoured with vouchers of admission." Almack's was, he said, "a temple of the *beau monde.*"

Brummell had not the slightest problem getting on to the patronesses' list, but began to wield power himself as one of the arbiters of whom to include and whom to strike off. The lady patronesses looked to him for acknowledgment that the party was as it should be, and it was because of this that the story circulated that a duchess had insisted her daughter court favor with Mr. Brummell before anyone else in the room.

Lady Louisa Lennox, daughter of the Duchess of Richmond, was reminded in no uncertain terms that she must solicit Brummell's good favor, as well as that of the lady patronesses. "Do you see that gentleman near the door?" the duchess was reported by Jesse to have said to her daughter, "whom she had brought for the first time into the arena of Almack's."

"He is now speaking to Lord [Alvanley?]."

"Yes I see him," replied the light-hearted as yet unsophisticated girl; "Who is he?"

"A person, my dear, who will probably come a speak to us; and if he enters into conversation, be careful to give him a favourable impression of you, for," and she sunk her voice to a whisper, "he is the celebrated Mr Brummell."

At the time this story was considered remarkable. Possibly never before had a commoner wielded such influence in the arena of high society; the triumph of celebrity over aristocracy was both novel and alarming, but, Jesse insists, "this is no fiction": he knew the lady.

The charge, both erotic and mercenary, was fueled by music and drink. Although alcohol was not served on the premises, many arrived late from the theater or elsewhere already quite drunk. Added to this nightclub atmosphere was the particular delight of people who believed they had gained entry to a gathering of an elite, which amounted to a frenzy, according to Lord Melbourne: "You, who know Almack's, know that this is one of the strongest, if not the very strongest passions of the human mind." Of the Regency mind, and Brummell's, Lord Melbourne's assertion would certainly hold.

Most nights the assemblies remained relatively staid, but on Wednesdays the dancing went on well into Thursday morning. Even so, no one was admitted after 11:00 P.M. The Duke of Wellington himself was once refused entry by Lady Jersey, "such that hereafter no one can complain of the application of the rule of exclusion." Perhaps because of the potential for "frenzy," the ladies attempted to control the dancing as they did the entry. Gentlemen who could dance well were shown particular favor in coming seasons and this was some of Brummell's appeal to the lady patronesses in the early years of his time in London. He danced for a few seasons, then took to scrutinizing from the sidelines, helping the patronesses adjudicate on those who could and could not dance. The latter might find themselves off the list. Captain Gronow tells of one Guards officer who found himself included and his wife excluded on those grounds and challenged Lady Jersey's husband to a duel on this account.

In this fraught but sexually heightened atmosphere, the latest dances were introduced into London society. The quadrille, a new French "square" dance that gained enormous popularity, was first seen at Almack's, but only after Lady Jersey had mastered it. The waltz, meanwhile—a continental prospect of almost as much imaginative erotic charge in London as Napoleon himself—was only accepted under the personal patronage of the much admired Countess Lieven.

For those not wishing to be seen waltzing at Almack's before sufficient rehearsal, the Duke of Devonshire allowed classes at Devonshire House. "No event ever produced so great a sensation in English Society as . . . the German waltz," wrote Thomas Raikes. "In London fashion is—or was then—*everything* [so] old and young returned to school, and the mornings which had been dedicated to lounging in the Parks, were now absorbed at home in . . . whirling a chair around a room to learn the step and measure of the German waltz." It is unclear if Brummell took to waltzing, though it is tempting to suggest there was some new exercise in his indolent lifestyle: the Berry Brothers' records show that he lost the weight he had gained in the early years of Watier's gastronomy club soon after the waltz craze hit London.

The same year, 1813, that brought the waltz also brought Parisian socialite and writer Madame de Staël to London, with her daughter in tow. They threw themselves into London society with gusto, made a beeline for Almack's and were sufficiently informed on all matters English to know that they should endeavor to make a good impression on Mr. Brummell. Byron observed them in action and was unsurprised when Brummell and Alvanley, among others, "took an invincible dislike to the de Staëls, both mother and daughter." "Despite all her talents and attractions," Captain Gronow claimed, London thought her "somewhat of a toady." Brummell, according to Byron, "was her aversion and she his . . . they [the dandies] persecuted and mystified Mme de Staël most damnably."

Germaine de Staël had got on the wrong side of many people she had determined to charm in the past, as Byron well knew. Napoleon went so far as to exile her from France. She was said to lack a sense of humor, which may well have been the worst trait in Brummell's mind, but in any event he and Alvanley played an elaborate practical joke on her and her pushy daughter, Albertine, whom Brummell nicknamed "Libertine," for the amusement of themselves and those in on the joke. Brummell whispered to Madame de Staël at Almack's that his friend Alvanley, the stocky bachelor, was worth a full £100,000, in want of a wife and more than usually vain about his looks (it was acknowledged generally that he had none). One of Alvanley's favorite stories for years afterward was how, dancing the new waltz with "Libertine" at Almack's, he saw Lord Jersey enter and said to Albertine, "What a handsome man Jersey is!" soliciting the response from his eager French escort, "He shall not be so pretty than you, milord."

Almack's was not the only club that threw balls in the evening. White's also did on occasions considered worthy of committee members' attentions. The Prince of Wales had come near to handing in his membership when White's threw a ball celebrating the recovery of his father from one of his bouts of illness, but when Napoleon was defeated in 1814, Brummell and the rest of the club were rightly convinced that the prince would approve of a grand celebration. King Louis XVIII of France visited London in May, and in June "Napoleon's Vanquishers" came to London: the Czar of Russia and the King of Prussia. Balls were thrown in their honor all through the summer and one of the earliest and grandest was organized by White's.

The club has kept details of the planning for the fete, held on June 21, 1814, for which Brummell was one of the committee. On April 25, 1814, it was "Resolved that the Club at Whites will give a ball in celebration of the late glorious events and that a subscription be opened for this purpose, not exceeding twenty guineas per member." By 1814 there were five hundred members, but even so they struggled to find the £10,000 cost of the ball they threw. The new Duke of Devonshire, Georgiana's son, lent them Burlington House for the occasion, which suffered a crush of nearly four thousand people, including the visiting Czar of Russia and King of Prussia. White's spent £800 on candles, £900 on wine and £2,575 on the dinner; £200 worth of china was broken.

Watier's was not to be outdone, and in the frenzied summer of festivities the club decided to throw a ball, which was set for the week following White's, on July 1. There had already been "illuminations and fireworks, a fair in Hyde Park, frigates on the Serpentine and going in State to the theatres and great dinners without end and great parties and balls for the great people." John Cam Hobhouse wrote that this round of celebrations left "no repose either of body or mind." So Brummell and his club members at Watier's set on reviving jaded socialites by adding a touch of sex to the metropolitan glamour. They invited everyone in masquerade, and along with their society lady friends, included the courtesans. Harriette Wilson left a long account in her memoirs. The demireps finally stormed the barricades of respectable society, dressing as boys and shepherdesses (Julia Johnstone and Harriette respectively) and waltzing with the czar of all the Russias. They queued in their carriages from "five in the afternoon as, by so doing, we should stand a chance of arriving between nine and ten o'clock." The men were either in full dress uniform or in fancy dress, but they were all masked. Only the members of Watier's were distinguishable, and dressed as light blue dominoes.

Dancing and socializing might command much of his time, but as his day in the high life wore into late evening, Brummell moved to the gaming tables. They provided both excitement and success for Brummell, who certainly had his fair share of thrilling wins. He was estimated one season to have won over £30,000 on horses and another £26,000 during one sitting at cards. Jesse claimed he once won £60,000, three times the amount of his original patrimony, but failed to put it into annuities and lost it all again within the week. Although his inheritance had furnished him with more ready cash than most men of fortune could expect in their early twenties, there was no land or investments to back up the style of high-stakes gambling that had become de rigueur at the London clubs. At night they were, as one commentator explained, little more than gambling dens:

How easy is [their] only rule!
Buy toys—make love, laugh eat and drink,
Not often sleep, and never think.
From joy to joy, unquestioned, ramble:
But chiefly, O my pupils, *gamble*.

Faro, or pharoah, had been popular in England in Stuart times, possibly introduced from France by Charles II's mistress Louise de Kerouaille. It was fitting then that her, and his, descendant, Charles James Fox, should help repopularize the game at Brooks's in the later eighteenth century. It made him a fortune, which he promptly lost again. It is a card game played between a dealer, who keeps the bank, and the rest of the company. Fox and his friend Richard Fitzpatrick kept the bank for Brooks's, and Fox later told George Selwyn, the writer and politician, that he had made £30,000 in the first year. "Charles and Richard's d . . . d faro bank," wrote Selwyn, "swallows up everybody's cash who comes into Brooks's." The game was still running when Brummell joined the club a generation later, with several families already ruined, but other fortunes secured for generations. Lord Robert Spencer, for instance, won £100,000 and never played again.

The point about faro was that it favored the house or bank, like roulette. Georgiana, Duchess of Devonshire, optimistically tried to set up her own faro bank as a means of making money to pay off previous gambling debts, and for every horror story there was one on whom Fate had more than smiled. "I never saw such a transition from distress to opulence," wrote Selwyn, about one of Fox's winning streaks, "from dirt to cleanliness. He is in high spirits and cash." Brummell hit a particularly purple patch after the false victories over Napoleon in 1814. Although Europe would be at war again within a year after Napoleon's escape from Elba, the brief peace saw London thronged with battle-weary officers whose brush with mortality had sharpened their optimism, if not their skills, at the gaming tables. In the true spirit of an addict, Brummell also found a good luck talisman, the loss of which he later blamed for his financial ruin. It was a crooked sixpence, a symbol of Christmas good fortune, that he picked up one dawn in Mayfair.

It was five o'clock one summer's morning [wrote Thomas Raikes], when Brummell was walking home with me through Berkeley Street and was bitterly lamenting his misfortune; he suddenly stopped on seeing something glittering in the [gutter]; he stopped down and picked up a crooked sixpence. His countenance immediately brightened. This, said he, is the harbinger of good luck. He took it home, and before he went to bed, drilled a hole in it and fastened it to his watch-chain. The spell was good (this was I think in 1813) during more than two years he was a constant winner at play or the turf, and I believe realized nearly £30,000.

The losses that might be sustained during a winning streak were more problematic for Brummell if they continued for any length of time as, by his mid-twenties, his capital was already dwindling. His response at first was histrionic, and he playacted a sort of fey desperation—as he might have done in the face of being made to ride in wet weather at the risk of splashing his white boot tops. When he lost a particularly large sum at table, for instance, he called for the waiter to fetch him some pistols so that he might shoot himself. At this, another club member, a Mr. Hythe, supposedly mad but not so mad as to miss the opportunity of a joke at Brummell's expense, offered him his own pistols with the words: "Mr Brummell, if you wish to put an end to your existence, I am extremely happy to offer you the means without troubling the waiter." Thomas Raikes recorded that the primary effect of this offer, after laughter, was alarm around the club that their maddest member should be in possession of loaded pistols.

Life as a professional gambler beckoned as Brummell moved into his thirties. Play was hard and fast at Watier's, and while he won there was sustenance from its sport. The main game here, unlike Brooks's or White's, was macao. This was a variant on twist or vingt-et-un—aka blackjack—which required only nerve and an ability to dissemble, qualities Brummell had acquired early in life.

Raikes recalled Brummell coming in one night to Watier's from the opera to find the tables crowded and the play particularly high. All places were taken, so he joined Tom Sheridan, his old friend from Donnington. Sheridan was ill, in debt and fighting a legal action in Scotland for "assault and trespass," i.e., adultery, served against him by his lover's husband. The "damages" were set at a thousand pounds.

Tom Sheridan was never in the habits of play but, having dined freely, had dropped into the club and was trying to catch the smiles of fortune by risking a few pounds which he could ill afford to lose . . . Brummell proposed to him to give up his place and go shares in his deal; and, adding to the £10 in counters which Tom had before him £200 himself, took the cards. He dealt with his usual success, and in less than ten minutes won £1,500. He then stopped, made a fair division and, giving £750 to Sheridan, said to him, "There, Tom, go home and give your wife and brats supper and never play again."

As Raikes said, the gesture was "characteristic of the times, the set, and of the spirit of liberality in Brummell which was shown towards an old friend in a way that left no pretext for refusal."

Brummell played with panache, nerve and great success but, like his much wealthier friend Georgiana, Duchess of Devonshire, he did not know when to stop. Either that, or his nihilistic gambling was symptomatic of a darker strain in his personality. Raikes claimed his glittering personality could turn black and morose and in this his gambling was both cause and effect.

The life which Brummell led at last plunged him into difficulties. He had lived constantly beyond his means, was deeply in debt, and the notorious usurers Howard and Gibbs refused further supplies unless furnished with the securities of friends. Here his popularity supplied a source which was fatal to the purse of many of our friends in the sequel. At this period Watier's Club, which had been originally established for harmonic meetings, became the resort of all the fine gentlemen of the day; the dinners were superlative and high play at macao was gradually introduced. The first effort of the beau was unsuccessful, and, as he was then addicted to games of chance, his depression became very great indeed.

Lord Byron, who knew Brummell well during his years as president of Watier's, was equivocal about the joys and horrors of gambling. For him, like Brummell, gambling was another sensory sport with which to distract attention from the world—indeed, Byron compared it explicitly to sex. He might have been describing Brummell on the precipice of his fall when he wrote:

I have a notion that Gamblers are as happy as most people, being always *excited*. Women, wine, fame, the table, even Ambition, *sate* now and then: but every turn of the card, and cast of the dice, keeps the Gamester alive: besides one can Game ten times longer than one can do anything else . . . I have thrown as many as fourteen *mains* running, and carried off all the cash upon the table occasionally: but I had no coolness or judgement or calculation. It was the *delight* of the thing that pleased me.

Brummell's notorious "coolness" allowed his early formidable success as a gambler. What, then, changed his fortune? Perhaps simply the roll of the dice: there is a certain providence in the fall of the cards that gamblers acknowledge means a true winner must know when to quit. It may be that Brummell found a new excitement, a new, desperate means of feeling alive in the luxuriant tedium of London society, by risking more than he knew he should. In this, he may also have been expressing the self-destructive impulse that was beginning to exhibit itself in his personal behavior. As Thomas de Quincey, "the English Opium Eater," observed, "the true impulse in obstinate incorrigible gamesters . . . is not faith, unconquerable faith, in their luck; it is the very opposite principle— a despair of their own luck; rage and hatred in consequence as at the blind enemy working in the dark."

When Brummell was in one of his winning patches he decided to throw a masked ball. Several other members of the Dandiacal

Body, Lord Alvanley, Henry Pierrepoint and Henry Mildmay, were also doing well at the tables, so the four set about hosting an evening at the Argyle Rooms, which, it was decided, should be another masquerade. It suited them well, perhaps especially the actor in Brummell, to produce an event of the innate theatricality of a masked ball. It also allowed them to include their wide circle of friends on both sides of the divide of social respectability. The Argyle, meanwhile, on what became Regent Street, was associated with parties "emanating from the leading ladies of the *demi-monde*," according to Lord William Pitt Lennox, where "balls and fancy-balls were constantly got up . . . where nothing could exceed the entertainment and the mirth was . . . uproarious." On Brummell's insistence, however, no invitation was sent to the prince regent. He and Brummell were in the middle of one of the periodic spats that appeared to be punctuating the decline in their mutual affection. They still moved in similar circles, but were not, that month, talking to each other. Whether Brummell would have maintained this unusual stance, of not inviting the prince, is unlikely. His interest in throwing a well-received party might have won out over his interest in piquing the prince. The regent, however, simply announced from Carlton House his intention of attending a much-talked-of party, so the dandies were obliged to send an invitation, signed by all four of them.

On the evening of the masquerade the hosts lined up at the doors of the Argyle Rooms to greet their guests. The masked guests came in full military regalia or fancy dress, the women in elaborate costumes. The hosts, however, dressed as bewigged footmen of the seventeenth century and greeted their guests holding multibranched candelabra.

The prince arrived, and bowed first to Henry Pierrepoint. Next in line was Brummell, but the prince ignored him and moved on to Alvanley, then on from him. Many witnessed the event: the four dandies and the guests both behind and in front of the royal party. There was a slight shocked silence at this "cut": Brummell was, after all, one of the hosts. Then Brummell's classically trained voice enunciated loudly to his neighbor: "Alvanley, who's your fat friend?"

Pierrepoint later wrote that in the eyes of London society, if not the prince in those days, "[Brummell] could do no wrong," and it must be assumed that Brummell thought his words would be taken—like so many other of his precisely wrought impertinences—as "a witty retort to a provocation, rather than an unmannerly insult." Those further into the room, however, could see the prince's face and were immediately aware that the remark, which has since gone down in the annals of British comedy, had "cut to the quick" the hefty heir to the throne "by the aptness of the satire."

Had Brummell lost his knack of the perfectly judged comic line? Or was his attack on his first protector another example of a man suffering a breakdown—financial, possibly physical and certainly, as it transpired, social?

It was not the end of the evening—which was accounted by many a great success—nor was it the end of Brummell's reign in London, as some writers later suggested. The remark, as with so many stories surrounding Brummell, was recounted frequently and with different supporting characters and locations (Lord Moira and St. James's Street, for instance). But the effect was the same, no matter the details of the incident, an effect more slowly corrosive than explosive. Brummell found himself finally, unintentionally perhaps, but decidedly and categorically *outside* the royal circle. This left him much more vulnerable to his creditors, who, as his gambling addiction worsened, turned into a clamorous horde.

II

NO MORE A-ROVING
SO LATE INTO THE NIGHT

So, we'll go no more a-roving
So late into the night
Though the heart be still as loving,
And the moon be still as bright
For the sword outwears its sheath,
And the soul wears out the breast,
And the heart must pause to breathe,
And love itself have rest.
                    Lord Byron, 1816

In Society, stay as long as you need to make an impression,
and as soon as you have made it, move on.
                    George Brummell

Late in his day in London, like so many promiscuous men of his
generation, Brummell contracted a sexually transmitted disease.
"Dates," as Harriette Wilson aptly put it, "make ladies nervous
and stories dry," and the exact occasion of Brummell's infection
can only be surmised by analysis of his later symptoms. He might
have noticed a tiny, painless chancre on or near the glans of his
penis about three weeks after the sexual act that passed on to him
the disease-carrying spirochetes. He might not. But five to twelve
weeks after the sexual encounter, he developed a severe fever, ac-

companied by a strange copper-colored rash, which would not have itched, on his soles and palms. For a fastidious man like Brummell, this would have been unsettling, yet not nearly so unsettling as what happened next. Small, lightly suppurating patches appeared on his mouth and gums, followed by a patchy loss of body hair, aching bones, loss of appetite, insomnia, a terribly sore throat and headaches that, cruelly and punctually, racked him at set times of the day. Brummell, a man of the world and former dragoon officer, a man who offered advice on sex to professional courtesans, cannot have been ignorant for long that he had contracted syphilis.

Like any dragoon officer or London rake, he knew exactly what to do. He went to an establishment like Mrs. Philip's Warehouse on Half Moon Street, "seven doors up from The Strand, on the left," which sold sheep-gut condoms—in three useful sizes—to the cognoscenti, but also mercury, arsenic and iodine pills, and soothing almond oils. In less than a fortnight, he would have hidden the symptoms of the pox—which abated after treatment with these strong poisons and unguents—and thought himself cured.

On the one hand it is hardly shocking to discover, quite simply written in Brummell's medical records in France, that he suffered for many years from syphilis—"the clap" or "pox," as he would have called it. (The two were thought to be differing stages of the same disease, and often gonorrhea, "the clap," and syphilis, "the pox," were indeed contracted at the same time.) Only a little later in the century, it was estimated that fifteen percent of the population of Paris and London had them both, but the proportion was higher in the circles in which Brummell moved. The fact of his syphilis, buried until now, puts much of Brummell's later life in a radically different context. It also colors an understanding of his sexuality and how he spent the end of his days in London's high society, as well as what compounded the trauma of his leaving it.

Theories on Brummell's sex life abound. The fascination originated in his personal attractiveness, noted by his contemporaries, that was, in part, sexual. It relates also to his place in the history of fashion, for vanity and style-consciousness in men have, for whatever reasons, traditionally been linked to the sexually proactive or deviant. Moreover, Brummell himself has been described by cultural historians as a symbol, not unlike Byron, of a sort of New Man, of "overstated manliness" and "unambigous masculinity," but who was also clearly in touch with his feminine side. This, in juxtaposition to his apparent indifference to sex, intrigued even the writers who knew him personally—Jesse, Raikes, Gronow and Wilson—who found that his sexuality presented some sort of enigma they felt drawn to address. These contemporaries, like the later biographers, covered all the possibilities and fall accordingly into four overlapping camps, arguing that Brummell was either asexual, homosexual, heterosexual or bisexual.

Brummell as an asexual has had particular appeal to the ascetically stylish, who hold that dandyism is incompatible with conventional sexuality. It was the position held, in effect, by Jesse: "The organ of love in his cranium was only faintly developed. Independently of his deficiency in warmth, he had too much *self-love* ever to be really *in love* . . . he was a thorough flirt but his love was as light and as elegant as everything about him." He reconciled Brummell's unmarried state to a sexual persona that was self-involved and emotionally unavailable. Even so, Jesse went on to catalogue a series of love letters written by Brummell and to entitle one passage of his book "The Beau in Love," as if to cover any accusation of effeminacy on Brummell's part but leave him untouched by sex.

Jesse's position on the subject of Brummell's sexuality is at best evasive and at worst deliberately obscurantist. His primary interest appeared to be to protect Brummell's name and, by extension, his own work. It would have been evident to many as a distinct possibility that a man with Brummell's later symptoms was dying of syphilis, but this would only have compounded a role Jesse knew Brummell was fulfilling in the early Victorian imagination: that of a justly ruined profligate. So textbook perfect were Brummell's later syphilitic symptoms that Jesse would have been at pains to whitewash his hero and put readers off the scent of sexual degeneracy.

Beyond this it should also be pointed out that the image of

Brummell as an asexual, utterly uninterested in sex, was also refuted by his school friends, some of them even in Jesse's own account. And then there is the undeniable evidence of his attending doctors in France, Dr. Edouard Vastel and Dr. John Kelly, who were in a position by 1840 to realize the clear link between Brummell's symptoms and an ancient syphilitic infection. This puts paid for good to the image of Brummell as the virgin saint of fashion.

Though in theory it is possible to catch syphilis from any sexual encounter and, in unlikely circumstances, by kissing, in practice syphilis was spread by armies on the move, by professional sex workers and by those who consorted frequently with either. Brummell may have been supremely unlucky, as he became at cards and dice, but it is unlikely that his syphilis points to anything other than a fairly active, though ill-considered, sex life.

By one particularly cruel twist of fate, the aftershock of the battles of the Napoleonic Wars may have had a double impact on Brummell's decline, with regard to both his gambling debts and his syphilis. The victorious British Army affected both. The rush to the tables of officers fresh from continental battles, playing hard and raising stakes, was a much-noted aspect of the years 1814–1816. Brummell was not the only man ruined financially (debts compounded Byron's need to leave England and necessitated Scrope Davies's flight). But those same officers imported a different fever from the continent, and rushed from the gaming tables to the brothels of the West End with a virulent new strain of syphilis that spread quickly through the officer classes, the bagnios and brothels of London and thence, in turn, to their other habitués. It was a common effect of troop movements at the time, as one later writer memorably warned: "there is a splendid [new] pox in town, as pure as the time of Francis I. The entire army has been laid up with it, boils are exploding in groins like shells, and purulent jets of clap vie with the fountains."

Asexuality therefore provides an unsatisfactory explanation of Brummell's sexually "cool" persona, which must have developed in response to a more complex sexual psyche. There is nothing in his syphilitic infection, however, to negate the theory that he was gay. The potential for his being homosexual may be inferred perhaps from the absence of heterosexual opportunism expressed by Thomas Raikes's "he was not a man of intrigue"; from Hester Stanhope's interrogator who asked about his "eccentricities"; and from countless writers since who have described him unjustly as "mincing," "camp" or even as a "bitchy queen." However tempting this conflation of the perceived style of the man and his apparent distance from women, the weight of opinion at the time, and the weight of evidence since, points strongly against his being exclusively homosexual. His school friends thought him strongly heterosexual—although admittedly this posture is not uncommon among adolescent boys regardless of their eventual sexual orientation. But those who wrote about him soon after his death were adamant in asserting his heterosexuality, as if rumors of something then considered "a monstrous sin against nature" had already been added to the catalogue of his sins that justified, in some popular morality tale, his demise in France.

Was Brummell, then, despite his apparently advanced feminine side, quite simply an emotionally unavailable heterosexual? It might seem the simplest answer, for all one would expect him in that case to have left in his wake, as that other celebrity dandy Lord Byron did, a trail of emotionally shortchanged women. His affairs, as compared to his passionate friendships, seem tepid, yet they yielded some finely wrought love letters from a man more used to high style than high romance: "It was scarcely possible," admitted Jesse, "for him to be constantly in the society of the most beautiful girls in Europe . . . without having a preference for one of them, or perhaps half a dozen: and this was the case." As evidence, Jesse cited the numerous letters Brummell had kept, containing "silken tresses and delicate distresses" that he destroyed later in life. Count d'Aurevilly concurred that "with such success, such command over society's opinion, such extreme youth to enhance his fame, and his air of charm and cruelty that women both revile and adore, there is no doubt that he inspired many conflicting passions." How serious

Brummell was in his conventionally romantic dalliances is a matter of conjecture, but it seems doubtful that they ever had his whole attention, let alone his heart. His appearance on the London stage as a young rake about town was a role he played to the hilt, with the expectation, like the hero of any stage or novel romance of the period, that closure would come with matrimony. Not only did he bet a friend that he would marry as early as the winter of 1799–1800, he also wrote long letters early in the new century to a woman whose identity remains a mystery. He was told, probably not for the first time, and in the time-honored fashion, that the lady would rather be friends than a lover, and it is unclear how seriously Brummell was pursuing the liaison. Young men of the period played a good deal at the game of love, with professional courtesans and actresses, as well as with women in their own social class to whom they might or might not intend marriage. Brummell's good nature, not to mention his stage-honed sensitivity to the verbosity of eighteenth-century sentiment and its potential for humor, rescued these letters from dullness, but give little evidence as to his true feelings or to the identity of the addressee(s). One of these letters makes it clear it was written in 1800, so he should also be allowed his youth: he was only twenty-two. Less easy to forgive than youthful dalliance, however, are Brummell's repeated "engagements" to young women in London, played as tricks for his own vanity, the amusement of his friends or out of a misplaced sense of courtesy. "He never attained any degree of intimacy with a pretty young woman that he did not make her an offer," wrote Jesse, meaning an offer of marriage, "not with the idea of being accepted, but because he thought it was paying the lady a compliment and procured her an unusual degree of *éclat* in the fashionable world." The ladies in question may have felt differently about the éclat of being proposed to and, in effect, jilted by London's most famous bachelor all within the space of an evening. "The most favourable opportunity that presented itself for [proposing] was at a ball in the neighbourhood of Grosvenor Square, but his measures on the occasion were so badly taken that he and the intended Mrs Brummell were caught in the corner of the next street, a servant having turned mother's evidence."

If this last point is true, it deserves more pause than Jesse gives it. Brummell was set to elope but was thwarted by a lady's maid on the corner of Grosvenor Square? It is the stuff of Lydia Languish's less improving bedside reading and scarcely attributable to Brummell, unless, of course, he had no intention of more than a play-acted elopement. It sounds as disingenuous as his intention to marry "Lady Mary," which didn't work out, he told a friend, because he discovered the lady in question "ate cabbage."

His "affairs" in adult life bear the same hallmarks as his early attempts at seduction as an Eton schoolboy, serenading the headmaster's daughter under her window. They were lighthearted dramas with Brummell casting himself as the juvenile lead; humorous, elegant and enacted as if with an audience in mind or in sight, a romantic suit to be tried on and discarded as ill-fitting. All of which would be understandable of a young man schooled in the ways of "Gentleman" Lewis, the romantic-comedy leading man at Drury Lane, and humorous in the context of a sixteen-year-old. But in the context of the harshly commercial Georgian marriage market, where the loss of a woman's reputation could cost her a lifetime of unhappiness, Brummell seems to have been carelessly cruel.

The other letter to which Jesse had access is also from the end of an affair, a little later in Brummell's adult London life.

The Lady Jane————, Harley Street
My Dear Lady Jane,
With the miniature it seems I am not to be trusted, even for two pitiful hours; my own memory must be, then, my only disconsolate expedient to obtain a resemblance.

As I am unwilling to merit the imputation of committing myself, by too flagrant a liberty, in retaining your glove, which you charitably sent at my head yesterday, as you would have extended an eleemosynary sixpence to the supplicating hat of a mendicant, I restore it to you; and allow me to assure you, that I have too much regard and respect for you, and too little practical vanity myself (whatever appearances may be against me) to have entertained, for one treacherous instant, the impertinent intention to defraud you of it.

    I am always

Your miserable slave

George Brummell

Again Brummell references his frenzy and the celestial provenance of the lady he addresses. He mixes liberally stage rhetoric, frivolity, mock theology and vague appeals for amicable forgiveness. In affairs of the heart, Brummell was infuriating. He presumes upon an affection sufficient to tease Lady Jane about the glove "which you charitably sent at my head yesterday," but he has been asked for an immediate return of the miniature—a significant token of regard at the time—which could only mean Jane was already fearful for her reputation. The inference is that Brummell might use the miniature as evidence of an attachment in which Lady Jane did not feel secure. His playacting at romance also presumed an audience, just as it had when he was a schoolboy of the men who later fed these stories around town and years later to Jesse.

Brummell played at affection, was adept at flattery, was evidently attractive and amusing and knew it, but in addition to this he chose deliberately to send out a differing signal. He was also unavailable. He had been "cut dead" by Miss X but only after she had been forced to get angry with him for "trespassing on consecrated ground" (the idea of marriage, or perhaps she was already engaged). He is desperate, in the conclusion of these amatory skirmishes, to be seen in the best light; to remain friends and to avoid hurt—but it is apparent that damage was done. Miss X and Lady Jane were left with eloquent and elegant letters (not so attached to them that they were unavailable to Jesse twenty years later: perhaps they had been sent back to Brummell, who then kept them), but little else.

Brummell's heart was with his older women friends, with

Princess Frederica in particular, and his character had been set quite early as a brittle confection. His dalliances, epistolary and we may assume actual, were flirtations with the idea of romance and marriage but little more. They were hurtful to the women involved, but they were never, as Brummell himself later confessed, "that un-affected and fervent homage which [is] a heart's life blood." He did not know what it was like to be in love until many years later and too late in the day to do anything about it.

His elusiveness in love and the offense it caused is also apparent in the number of times he was "called out" to duel. This was the only acceptable closure for a love affair in which the woman felt her honor, and by extension that of her family, was called into ques-tion: "If a gentleman detract from another gentleman, the resource that is prescribed . . . [is a duel]," wrote the authors of *The Laws of Honour and the Character of Gentleman,* stating that the most common grievance between gentlemen was their conduct vis-à-vis unmarried women. Brummell was challenged frequently to ac-count for his conduct, but opted to treat even this as a joke. When he was challenged to offer "satisfaction or an apology" by the pro-tector of one lady and given five minutes to make up his mind which he would choose, Brummell replied, "In five minutes, sir! In five seconds or less if you prefer!" He joked that he was "not natu-rally of an heroic turn" and turned the one duel he did fight, at Chalk Farm, into an extended self-deprecatory monologue casting himself as world-weary coward: " 'You have taken a load off my mind!' He said to his second [his opponent had failed to show up], 'Let us go *immediately*!' "

In respect of these letters and putative love affairs, there is a dif-ferent possibility of their context: they may not have been written to "respectable" women at all but to courtesans. Their playacted, stylized sentiment, and the emotional thrust and parry of gloves thrown and men "cut dead," is precisely the manner in which the professional courtesans and actresses traditionally negotiated the early stages of an affair. This is not the light in which Jesse presents them, but it is possible that Brummell was adhering to the family tradition of allying himself very closely with the demimonde, and even contemplating marriage with ladies who played a game he enjoyed.

~

If through fifteen years in the high life Brummell never formed a conventional sexual relationship or, despite the financial and societal pressures to marry, only once found himself in a half-hearted and aborted elopement, was he, perhaps, a closet homosexual? Or given his recorded affairs with women, was he bisexual?

The strongest case for a Brummell affair with another man is weak, but tempting to consider, as the other party in the story is the bisexual Lord Byron. Brummell kept two poems that Byron had given him in his album. One, quoted previously, was on the subject of fallen women in general, Lady Caroline Lamb and Julia Johnstone, seemingly, in particular. The other poem Byron gave directly to Brummell:

> To one who promised on a lock of hair
> By Lord Byron
>
> Vow not at all, but if thou must,
> Oh! Be it by some slender token;
> Since pious pledge, and plighted trust,
> And holiest ties, too oft are broken
> Then by this dearest trifle swear,
> And if thou lov'st as I would have thee,
> This votive ringlet's tenderest hair
> Will bind thy heart to that I gave thee.

The poem had its first publication, undated, in Jesse's *Life of George Brummell,* and was not published in Byron collections for over a century. It bears comparison with some of Byron's earliest known poems, "A Woman's Hair" and "To a Lady Who presented the Author with the Velvet Band which Bound Her Tresses" (both 1806) and has been dated by some Byron scholars to this period.

However, it is more likely, recent Byron scholars claim, to have been written in 1814, when Byron was twenty-six and Brummell thirty-six. It might have formed a "companion piece" to the other poem in Brummell's collection, which Byron wrote between 1812 and 1814. Both were shown to Lady Melbourne, but it seems Byron gave "To One who Promised" to Brummell. It is a winning piece, and "if thou lov'st as I would have thee" presses an urgent suit indeed if it is written by one bisexual young man to another. But there is nothing more. The letters Brummell had in his possession from Byron, which he claimed "would produce more than sufficient to pay my debts," he destroyed. It was the Age of Sentiment: it might have been another parlor game—the poem might even have been written about Lady Caroline Lamb and given to Brummell in some spirit of bonded machismo. Byron's sexual predilection seems to have been for late-adolescent boys, and having his mistresses, Caroline Lamb for one, dress as pages. There is no record of his sexual interest in any older man.

On the other hand, there was an ill-defined bond between Byron and Brummell, a mutual fascination that had more than a frisson of pure attraction. Byron, after all, had said he would rather be Brummell than Napoleon, and his personal style, his "Byronic" manner, was inspired in part by Brummell, as previously discussed. His poetry also became marked by the dandy pose, "the characteristic rapidity of movement from absurdity to seriousness," as one Byron scholar noted, that typifyies Brummell's letters, the move from sentiment to satire and the ability to encompass every tone "from the tender to the devastatingly dismissive which we associate with the best satiric poetry." In this sense, too, Brummell is closely caught up in the style that informed Byron's sexually athletic hero of *Don Juan*. The epic poem, published after Brummell and Byron's respective flights from London, tells the story of the mythic womanizer, but sets his tale in part in the world that both dandies knew well: London's high society. Brummell is mentioned by name, along with many other members of the *haut ton*, and Don Juan was taken largely, and rightly, as a Byronic self-portrait. Others were less sure, and in the 1819 *Don Juan Unmasked, Being a Key to the Mystery Attending That Remarkable Publication,* the author suggests the other personalities who have informed the poetic creation:

He abounds in sublime thought and love of humour, in dignified feeling and malignant passion, in elegant wit and obsolete conceit. [He] alternately presents us with the gaiety of the ballroom and the gloom of the scaffold, leading us among the airy pleasantries of fashionable assemblage and suddenly conducting us to haunts of depraved and disgusting sensuality . . . [he] turns decorum into jest, and bids defiance to the established decencies of life.

To those who knew any of the dandies, but especially Brummell, this amounted to an espousal of the entire dandy code. Don Juan turned the world upside down: the ridiculous was serious, passion was met with indifference, decorum was turned into jest. But Don Juan, like Byron, knew well the haunts of "disgusting sensuality." Did Brummell also bid defiance to the established decencies of life as Byron had? If he did not have an affair with Byron—and it is flimsy evidence on which to base the claim—is there evidence for his bisexuality anywhere else?

Jesse, again, was keen to put readers off the idea, which may be read as a clear signal that he knew or suspected more than he let on. Conversely it might have meant there was nothing to know. The very term "sexuality" dates from Brummell's period, and it is worth recalling that our modern nomenclature for sexual tastes would have bemused men of Brummell's generation, linguistically and practically. There had been no such thing as a "homosexual" in Brummell's school days, only people who committed "sodomitical acts"; neither in his adulthood was there general acceptance of the idea of bisexuality. People were as they practiced, and in Brummell's circle there was a wide-ranging definition of sexual morality. Any hint of sodomy as a sexual practice, however, between parties

of whichever sex and no matter whether consensual, was so abhor-
rent that the very possibility was enough to compound Byron's
need to flee the country.

Brummell's practice we cannot know, any more than Harriette
Wilson's—and she wrote about a lifetime as a professional courtesan yet mentioned only a single sexual act. Brummell's *personality*,
on the other hand, was considered deviant in sexual terms, through
his disinterest in attaching himself to one declared mistress and his
conspicuous "self-love" (homosexuality in the classical sense).
Moreover, although his school days and their period, in the late
eighteenth century, were typified by a laissez-faire attitude to acts
that today would be termed homosexual, attitudes in London were
shifting fast in his early adulthood toward the supposed moral high
ground of the Victorians. Although the age was yet to turn against
the rakish heterosexual behavior of Brummell's friends, it was already turning strongly against homosexuals. Economic turmoil
and the war played their parts doubtless, as did the shifting ideals
of masculinity in which Brummell had played a key role. If he was
bisexual, Brummell would have been wise to keep a mask over the
issue, as his later acolyte Jesse would over the whole area of his sex
life. As for his syphilis, if anything this may count slightly against
his being bisexual. At the time, it was widely held by many doctors
that syphilis could not be caught through acts "of sodomies and
bestialities." In strictly clinical terms they were wrong, but in early
nineteenth-century epidemiological terms the doctors knew what
they saw; syphilis was almost unheard of among Regency homosexual men. Dr. Swediaur, the leading authority at the time, wrote
of one particularly baffling case, "after a voyage of four months a
violent [syphilitic attack] broke out before [the man, an East India
Company official] went ashore, though he could have received no
infection during the voyage, *as there was not a woman onboard*
[emphasis mine]. It simply did not occur to doctor or patient that
syphilis could be caught other than by heterosexual sex. Clearly, in
this instance, en route to India, there were infected sailors who in-

fected others (and there were East India Company officials who were less than honest with their doctors), but homosexual infection was so rare as to be unthinkable to a physician like Dr. Swediaur after a lifetime's experience. Brummell's syphilis is inconclusive in absolute terms as it relates to his sexuality, but at the time—simply by virtue of experience and empiricism—it would have been taken as further evidence of his heterosexuality.

It must also be acknowledged that the apparent enigma of Brummell's sexuality was possibly itself a construct of a deliberately beguiling man. Brummell refused to be pinned down. Just as he refused to sit for a full-length portrait, he knew that he would be less powerful in society if his status was clearly attached to one person: wife, lover or courtesan. He knew, like Byron, that the lowliest "end of Fame" was merely "to have, when the original is dust/ A name, a wretched picture, and worse bust." His was the most famous image of Regency masculinity, and yet there is no adequate record of how he looked or dressed. He knew that an element of his renown needed to be ill-defined, uncaptured. To this extent, those who have argued that a true dandy can never marry are right.

One last speculation remains, bolstered by the likelihood that Brummell's syphilis developed before, possibly long before, he left England. By 1816 he was already exhibiting symptoms—reckless behavior, the self-loathing concomitant to gambling addiction, lethargy and sexual lassitude—that may be symptoms of a well-established syphilitic infection. No date, no person and no sex can be attached absolutely to his infection. However, the fact of his infection, in conjunction with his known circle in London, makes it likely that Brummell, though romantically elusive, was sexually active in the West End brothels that had been local fixtures for the Brummell family for several generations. He may have had a public persona of emotional unavailability and sexual ambiguity, but in private it appears likely he had sexual liaisons within the circle of the professional courtesans he knew so well. Recent scholars have achieved detailed resuscitations of the life of the demimondaine

Harriette Wilson, and it is in juxtaposition to her unconventional career trajectory, and that of Julia Johnstone, that Brummell, the syphilitic, is probably best understood.

After the opera, the theater or Carlton House, and invariably on a Saturday night, the place for men like Brummell to repair was the champagne supper hosted by the Three Graces—Harriette Wilson, Julia Johnstone and Harriette's sister Amy Dubochet—at York Place. Alcohol flowed freely, men vied for the attention of the few women there and there was food late into the night, dismissed airily by Harriette as "merely a tray-supper."

Under the pseudonym of Bernard Blackmantle, one habitué of these evenings later published a scandalous roman à clef, *The English Spy,* with a chapter and verses on life with the courtesans. The Cyprians, as the courtesans were invariably called, threw wild parties:

In the supper room . . . spread forth a banquet every way worthy of the occasion . . . the rich juice of the grape and the inviting richness of the dessert were only equalled by the voluptuous votaries who surrounded the repast . . . Ceremony and cold restraint of well regulated society was banished in the free circulation of the glass. The eye of love shone forth the electric flash which animated the heart of young desire, lip met lip and soft cheek of violet beauty pressed the stubble down of manliness. Then, while the snowy orbs of nature undisguised heaved like old ocean with a circling swell, the amorous lover palmed the melting fair, and led her forth to . . . penetrate the mysteries of Cytherea.

Frequently in her memoirs, Harriette mentions Brummell's presence at these soirees, and his conspiratorial affection for the courtesans is remarkable. Harriette ultimately said she found him "cold," but nevertheless sought his company and even his advice on how to deal with men who did not want to stay after sex: "The man does not want you to pass the night with him?" said Brummell, "so e'en put your head on the pillow and read Peter Pindar, or fancy yourself in the steam-boat, while they are pumping."

Brummell was a fairly constant presence in the lives of Harriette and Julia: he lived his late evenings in the demimonde as, in a sense, his family always had. He and Julia had a deeper and long-established understanding. They remet at the opera, more than a decade after the teenage fumblings in the corridors of Hampton Court Palace. He said they were "very old friends"; she said he had been "violently in love with her." Harriette inferred that they took up where they had left off, as lovers, which Julia denied, but Brummell, by virtue of being the subject of their argument, was tied ever more tightly to the courtesan world. Even Fanny, another of Harriette's sisters, informed Harriette that Brummell and Julia had been "making strong love lately. . . . Oh the shocking deceiver!" "Tell Julia," said Harriette, knowingly, "not to believe one word he says." The truth will never be known. It is unlikely Brummell ever slept with Harriette, who was a little too commercially inclined for all that they had an affinity of independent-mindedness. It is likely, however, he resumed his affair with Julia at some stage, but it should be noted that despite her notoriety she had slept with few men. Had anything else happened within their clique to explain how Brummell caught a virulent dose of the pox and put himself into a tailspin of nihilistic depression and reckless gambling?

One symptom of primary syphilis is a cruely erratic libido; one minute, the thought of sex is almost repugnant; the next, the sufferer is gripped with what Guy de Maupassant, another syphilitic, memorably described as "the majestic pox! Alleluia! I screw the street whores and trollops, and afterwards I say to them, 'I've got the pox,' and I just laugh." In the throes of his syphilitic euphoria he once coupled with six prostitutes within an hour (with witnesses). If Brummell was infected early with the pox, in his twenties even, it might have determined his whole adult sexual persona—"cool" alternating with a more desperate neediness, and the possibility of more reckless couplings. Of course, this does not explain his initial infection. It is likely, though, that he caught syphilis late in his day in London. For one thing, although it killed him, he lived as long in exile as he had in the high life. For another, his self-immolating behavior followed by a slow decline into physical disability and eventual madness expresses the full pathology of primary, secondary and tertiary syphilis played out over the years from around 1814.

There were specific ways, too, in which it is reasonable to speculate he may have become infected. Brummell was a central figure in a crowd of men who frequently courted as a group the attentions of a single woman—a leading lady in society like Princess Frederica or more often a courtesan. Harriette Wilson once admitted to being in a large gathering of men, all of whom she had known sexually. It was part of the demimonde scene that was also Brummell's. "The amorous beaux," wrote the author of *The English Spy*, "naturally inflame the ardour of each other's desires by their admiration for the general object of excitement [a courtesan or prostitute] until the possessing of such a treasure becomes a matter of heroism." Sexual conquest in this scenario becomes "a prize for which the young and gay will perform the most unaccountable prodigies, sacrifice health . . . and eventually life, to bear away in triumph the fair conqueror of hearts."

It could be argued that this behavior exhibits an extension of the "unnatural" world of public schools like Eton, where sexuality is first understood in the context of an all-male world. It must also be said that this particular style of promiscuity, reminiscent of the activities of modern sports teams or, for that matter, Russian ballet stars, where the esprit de corps of a group of men is expressed in competitive courting, or even group sexual activity with a single woman, speaks of a barely suppressed homosexual bond.

The Cyprians' balls were in a tradition of entertainment for men that had as its premise and ultimate goal a much more erotic intent than dancing. Perhaps the most famous was the Grand Bal de Mort, held by the courtesan Elizabeth Mitchell, but attended by many aristocratic ladies of fallen reputation. The invitees wore fig leaves, in the biblical tradition, but over their faces and were otherwise naked. The evening, inevitably, declined into an orgy. Masquerades, such as the one organized by Brummell in 1813 at the

Argyle Rooms, were barely concealed imitations of this Cyprian practice. Masqueraders could flirt without fear of recognition, but were also likely to be more aware of their body language. The theatricality of the Cyprian fetes went to its extremes for the reenactment, staged by Mrs. O'Kelley, of the "Tahitian Feast of Venus"— a spurious tribute to the anthropological researches of Captain Cook. The masqueraders were entertained by live sex acts performed by South Sea islanders (Mrs. O'Kelley's latest girls), "all spotless virgins," and "a dozen well-endowed athletic youths . . . each holding a dildo-shaped object wreathed in flowers." Twenty-three gentlemen "of the highest breeding," including five members of Parliament, turned up to watch and participate. The nature of the entertainment on offer at the Cyprians' balls was altogether more sedate, but the purpose was identical. The Cyprians found theatrical means to drum up support for their particular endeavor: Harriette, Julia and Amy sold sex.

The tight world of the Cyprians, where only gentlemen of the *ton* were admitted, expressed masculine exclusivity in terms Brummell would have well understood. Sex was part of the group experience. If Brummell's supposedly semihidden sexuality and projection of a "cool" sexual persona was symptomatic not of asexuality but of a highly sexual if troubled bisexuality—might such an experience after a Cyprians' fete explain his syphilis? Even his earliest encounters with Susan Heath, the headmaster's daughter, or Julia Johnstone, may be seen as setting a pattern that was continued, disastrously, in adult life. Brummell chased women in the company of men; his sexual development was arrested at this adolescent stage. In this he was far from atypical of his class, time and a means of sexual relation that has been described as homosocial. When the evidence is taken together, on the one hand his syphilitic condition and on the other the amount of time he spent in the company of courtesans—now understood as a wildly promiscuous rather than a merely scandalous world—a case can be made that he was most likely sexually involved with one or more of them, within the context, however intimate, of their shared "ownership" by his coterie of men. The picture of the Cyprians' ball in *The English Spy* and its description from Bernard Blackmantle make it clear that there were many more sexually available women present than just the Three Graces. One of these may well have been the sexual partner, shared with others present at different times, who passed on the infection to Brummell.

~

By 1816 it must have been obvious to Brummell, and to his friends, that he had syphilis. It was unlikely to have been talked about: gentlemen didn't. The advertisements for the cures that appeared at the time in French and English periodicals make it clear that this prevalent disease was dealt with quietly, privately and, to a surprising degree, effectively. Doctors were known to treat ladies infected by their husbands without either party within the marriage being aware of the diagnosis. The mercury administered as pills and as ointments did rid the patient of the more obvious symptoms of infection: the chancre disappeared; the rash subsided. But men like Brummell were tragically in error when they thought they were cured and could resume their lives and sexual practices. The horror that awaited many was not so much the return of the disease, but that their infection would be passed on, even to unborn children. And then there was the depression. Brummell wrote frequently about his "blue devils," which would have been exacerbated by his syphilis and by the mercury poisons. This, as much as the alternating effect on his libido by the disease, was what caused his growing isolation and his self-destructive behavior. The man, the disease and its effect were known well to Bulwer-Lytton when he created his fictionalized Brummell in *Pelham*:

It was a strange thing to see a man with costly taste, luxurious habits, great talents peculiarly calculated for display, courted by the highest members of the state, admired for his beauty and genius by half the women in London, yet living in the most ascetic seclusion from his kind, and indulging in the darkest and most morbid despondency. No female was seen to win even his momentary glance of admiration. All the senses appeared to have lost for him, their customary allurements.

Those who knew Brummell, and who recognized what was happening to him, had good cause to be anxious for his welfare and for the future.

THE END OF THE DAY

12

PLAY HAS BEEN
THE RUIN OF US ALL

"Play" he said "has been the ruin of all."
"Who do you include in your all?"
He told me there had been a rot, in White's Club.
Harriette Wilson quoting Beau Brummell

May 1816 was one of the bleakest on record. Unknown to Londoners, the Indonesian volcano of Tambora had erupted the previous year and sulphur clouds were playing havoc with the world's weather. The winter had been more than usually harsh in England, with a road opened down the frozen Thames and thousands dying of cold; the trees in Green Park, which Brummell had known since he was a boy, did not come into leaf until late in the spring. It became known as "the year without a summer."

It was also a year of unremitting gloom for Brummell. He was suffering the fitful depressions and physical malaise associated with syphilis and its mercury therapy, but to compound this he was also approaching financial crisis. From 1811 to 1815 he had bought into a series of annuity schemes allowing him to be advanced large cash sums by City bankers on the promise of long-term—indeed, lifetime—repayments. In so doing he had been obliged to find co-lenders of obviously aristocratic and monied backgrounds, with clear expectations of inheritance. He turned to his old friends Lords Robert and Charles Manners.

Brummell's own expectations of advancement were decreasing and moneylenders in the City made it their business to be aware of the rising and falling hopes of the *haut ton*. The ball at the Argyle Rooms had marked publicly the deterioration in his relationship with the regent. He was becoming less able to service his debts, and the acknowledgment of his credit unworthiness is evidenced in his need to borrow money from as far outside the City as Ripley in Yorkshire. The Manners brothers, like Brummell, were gambling heavily, but they had large allowances from their elder brother, the Duke of Rutland, and until 1813 they were presumed heirs to the dukedom. Their names stood well in Brummell's favor, and the cash, borrowed in the three names jointly, was nearly all for their impecunious friend.

The state of Brummell's financial affairs is best delineated in the Muniment Room at Belvoir Castle—the Duke of Rutland's family archive. It contains a number of detailed accounts of the debts Brummell accrued in collusion with Lords Charles and Robert Manners. Like any modern credit card abuser, Brummell and the Manners brothers went back time and again to different money-lenders to mine lines of credit that they had little prospect of repaying. There are two annuity covenants, as examples, from May 1811, one of which runs:

Covenant between George Bryan Brummell, Esq., and Lord Robert Manners and William Walker of South Lambeth, County of Surrey, for the purchase of an annuity of £100 during the lives of George Brummell and Lord Robert Manners for the sum of £600 to be paid by the said William Walker to George Brummell and Lord Robert Manners.

In other words, William Walker "invested" £600 for the satisfying return of £100 a year up to the death of the last of the two rakes. The second covenant from the same month was for a much larger sum, £1,080, paid by a Mr. George Jackson of Ripley against the annual repayment for life of £180, again by Brummell and Lord Robert. Three years later, in 1814, Brummell again sought cash with the Mannerses as co-guarantors, but this time with Lord Charles as signatory. The six annuities detailed in the Belvoir archive harvested total cash sums of £6,496 in the years 1811–1814, against a repayment of £1,024 due annually from the three of them for the term of their natural lives. There is every reason to believe that by 1816 Brummell had bought into more of these schemes elsewhere. Financially, it was madness. All three men were in their early thirties, and would pay off the whole sum within six years. If they lived and honored their debt, the annuitants—William Walker and George Jackson—stood to make a killing (somewhere between a present-day equivalent of $4.5 to $5 million would be repaid). Meanwhile the borrowers would have had to be very desperate indeed to secure cash on such terms.

Only the recklessness of gambling addicts or the self-destructive impulses associated with syphilitic or liminal crisis makes any sense of these actions. The Belvoir archive points to the crux of the issue for Brummell: his smaller debts could be ignored for years, but gambling debts needed immediate payment. Brummell could not maintain his position in society otherwise. In 1814 several annuities were bought on the same day: October 14th. Brummell had some desperate need for cash that could only have been a gambling debt. The hope, as with any gambler, was that Lady Luck would return, whereupon the annuities might be bought back—at great expense. But Brummell must have known that his financial redemption was falling below the horizon of possibility. He had sold his life into the hands of unscrupulous moneylenders and into an unsustainable future.

Then in early May 1816 Brummell joined Lord Alvanley and the Marquess of Worcester—Harriette Wilson's former lover—in raising yet another loan. Though not as badly in debt as Brummell, Alvanley had exhausted his regular lines of credit: after a lifetime of applying to Jewish moneylenders in the City, he joked with dinner guests in March 1815 that he needed to find the lost tribes of Israel, as he and Brummell had "exhausted the other two." Most likely a large proportion of the money was meant to cover Alvanley and Brummell's existing annuity payments. According to Julia Johnstone, this 1816 loan was for the sum of £3,000, but Harriette Wilson said she had heard—and she was in a better position to know—that it amounted to £30,000. If it was the latter figure, Brummell was probably hoping to buy back some of his more expensive annuities, but his good intentions did not last long. With the recklessness of a gambling addict and a depressive, Brummell took his share of the money straight to the card tables. He lost again, heavily. He had not even dared to show his face at Watier's but had gambled instead at a club with an even harsher house banker: Gordon's on Jermyn Street. He stayed on, late into the night, until he had lost over five thousand pounds. He went back to Watier's, found Worcester and confessed what he had done with the money. He would be unable to meet his share of the repayments on the loan secured to pay off previous ones. Worcester then did something foolish or angry or both: he told Richard Meyler, who was one of Brummell's many minor creditors. It was Meyler, armed with this information, who became known, in Harriette Wilson's much-quoted phrase, as "the dandykiller."

Richard Meyler had arrived later on the London scene with the dandies and courtesans who surrounded Brummell, and he had been regarded at first with some suspicion. He was an Etonian contemporary of Brummell's younger friend the Marquess of Worcester but was, like Brummell, an orphan who had come into an equivalently large inheritance (£30,000) before he was of age. They had therefore a certain amount in common and might perhaps have been friends, but Meyler developed a loathing for Brummell, a poisonous mix of envy, jealousy, disdain and class-consciousness. This might have been a result of Brummell's snobbery, which was reaching Gothic proportions—Meyler's money was new, from the Bristol sugar trade, and Alvanley referred to him as "that damned methodistical little grocer." The mutual disdain was more directly a result of Meyler's infatuation with Harriette Wilson and his suspicion—correct—that Brummell made fun of him to her from their opposing boxes at the King's Theatre. Meyler sat with his friend the Duchess of Beaufort, "who was known to encourage a very motherly kindness towards young men, particularly if they were well-looking," while Brummell sat, laughing, with Harriette. Harriette was considering moving on from her protector, the duchess's son, the Marquess of Worcester, who had been sent abroad by the family to cool his ardor. Harriette's warnings about Meyler, from Brummell among others, only made him more attractive to her. "No woman can do anything with [him]," she was told, "for Meyler really don't know what sentiments means . . . [He] is a mere animal, a very handsome one, it is true, and there is much natural shrewdness about him." He was considered a little unhinged, dangerous even, especially sexually: "His countenance is so peculiarly voluptuous that, when he looks at women, after dinner, though his manner is perfectly respectful, they are often observed to blush deeply, and hang down their heads, they really cannot tell why or wherefore."

This apparent animal magnetism, and Meyler's position as a sudden favorite with Worcester's mother, seems to have made him irresistible to Harriette. They began a passionate affair, conducted often at the home of Julia Johnstone, for fear, initially, of Worcester finding out. But when Worcester, Brummell and the rest of society became conscious of the affair, Meyler was painted as the wrong-doer much more than Harriette, and Harriette encouraged him to believe that Brummell had poisoned society against him. Harriette set up with Meyler as her protector—ironically in the same house that Worcester had rented for her at the height of their affair, on Lisson Grove near the new Regent's Park—and they began several years of violent disagreements followed by passionate reconciliations. She described him as "one of the worst tempered men in England"; he called her "a very tyrant . . . who neither esteemed nor trusted [me]." By 1816 the affair was over, and Meyler and Worcester, in the way of men who had Harriette in common, became friends. But Brummell's name was linked forever in Meyler's mind with the emotional stress of life with Harriette and the humiliations heaped upon him by Brummell's coterie at the outset of his liaison with her.

So when Worcester told Meyler that Brummell was comprehensively going to renege on a debt, Meyler decided to act. The next day, Wednesday, May 15, 1816, he went to the club he shared with Brummell on St. James's Street: White's.

Harriette Wilson soon heard the news, and her schadenfreude at the time can be guessed from the relish with which she later narrated the unfolding drama:

The story was this. Brummell, Alvanley and Worcester agreed to raise thirty thousand pounds, on their joint securities. Brummell, having made Worcester believe that he was, at least, competent to pay the interest of the debt, the money was raised, and the weight of the debt was expected to fall on the Duke of Beaufort [Worcester's father], who, after strict enquiry, partly ascertained that Brummell was deeply involved without even the most remote prospect of ever possessing a single guinea. When Meyler heard of this he became furious, both on Worcester's account, and his own, declaring that Brummell had borrowed £7000 from him which he had lent, in the fullest conviction that Brummell was a man of honour.

I asked Meyler how he could be so very stupid as to have been deceived even for an instant, about Brummell?

"I would forgive him the £7000 he has robbed me of," [said Meyler], "but on Worcester's account, I shall expose him tomorrow at White's."

"Why not let Worcester fight his own battles?"

"That is just what, for the Duchess of Beaufort's [his mother's] sake, I wish to prevent . . . Brummell, I will certainly expose: because he has basely obtained a sum of money . . . I hold it my duty, as an independent gentleman, never to give my countenance, nor society, to a man who has done a dishonourable action . . ."

[He] kept his promise of exposing Mr Brummell at White's Club, where he placed himself, the following morning, for the sole purpose of saying to every man, who entered, that Mr Brummell's late conduct, both towards the Marquess of Worcester and himself had been such as rendered him a disgrace to society and most unfit to remain a member of that club. Tom Raikes it was, I believe, who acquianted Brummell of this glowing panegyric on his character.

The impact of this on Brummell's position in London society cannot easily be overstated. Meyler was "asking him out," or threatening him to a duel, if he chose to defend his name. If he did not, if he accepted the truth of what was said and Meyler's right to say it, he would put himself outside society. Meyler was only stating what was widely known to be the case, but to state it drew a line under Brummell's career: his name as a gentleman had been impugned, and his options were fight, flight or pay up.

Brummell addressed a few lines to Meyler [Harriette continued] begging him to be informed if such had, really and truly been the expressions made use of? Meyler answered that, not only he had used the expression, but, that he further proposed returning to the club, on the following day, for the sole purpose of repeating them, between the hours of two and four, to any body who might happen to be present, and if Mr Brummell had any thing to say to him in return he would be sure to find him at White's during that particular time.

The inevitability of what was happening would not have lessened the gnawing ignominy of facing it. Brummell made no reply and spent the rest of the day alone. He made one insouciant purchase at his snuff purveyors, Fribourg and Treyer on the Haymarket, of a two-and-a-half-pound jar of Martinique, and went home. Harriette claimed he went around "about a dozen" of his acquaintances begging fifty-pound notes, but this was an unlikely preparation for the subterfuge that followed. He did, however, write to one friend, Scrope Davies, who happened to be at dinner with Lord Byron in Charles Street, Pall Mall. Captain Gronow recorded the letter and its reply partly for their distinct dandy panache in the face of tragedy, partly because Scrope's inability to help nailed Brummell's fate as surely as it pointed to his own.

Whilst [Byron] was dining with a few friends, a letter was delivered to Scrope Davies, which required an immediate answer. Scrope, after reading its contents, handed it to Byron. It was thus worded:—

> My dear Scrope,
> Lend me £500 for a few days; the funds are shut for the dividends, or I would not have made this request.
> G Brummell

The reply was:—

> My dear Brummell
> Tis very unfortunate, but all my money is locked up in the three per cents.
> Scrope Davies

The next day, Thursday, May 16, 1816, there was an air of celebration in London in what had otherwise been a dismal year. The heir to the throne, Princess Charlotte of Wales, had announced her engagement to Prince Leopold of Saxe-Coburg-Saalfeld and crowds gathered at the Queen's House—later remodeled as Buckingham Palace—to offer congratulations. There was such a crush that ladies' court trains were ripped and men lost their hats, only to recover them, somewhat dented, on tables lining the exit, and the cartoonist Cruikshank scored another commercial success caricaturing the ridiculous rich squeezing through a palace doorway.

For Brummell the day was no laughing matter. He stayed quietly at home and wrote some letters, made plans and dined alone on cold capon and a bottle of claret that he ordered in from Watier's.

Then he dressed. He wore his usual evening attire of sheer black pantaloons, black coat and waistcoat, white shirt and cravat. Nothing was unusual in his manner or appearance. It has always

been related that he attended the opera that night as usual to acknowledge a few acquaintances, but he cannot have done so. There
must have been a last-minute change of plan as *The Times* records
that the second benefit performance for the tenor Mr. Braham of
the opera *La Cosa Rara* at the King's Theatre was canceled at short
notice. Presumably Brummell went instead to Covent Garden, as
he was seen in public in a theater box, and saw the last act of a play
there. The title must have given him pause for thought: it was *Love,
Law and Physic*. There were acquaintances at Covent Garden to
whom he could nod recognition, but he slipped out before the curtain call into the warm spring night.

A coach was waiting for him, but not his own. It drove him
across old Westminster Bridge to Clapham Common, two miles
south of the river, where his own carriage was waiting in a place
where no one was likely to recognize it. He had slipped out of London as suddenly as he had arrived seventeen years before, and by
the time theatergoers were looking for him in the lobby of Covent
Garden, in the Great Subscription Room at Brooks's or the supper
parties of the courtesans, he was galloping through Kent heading
south to the coast. He traveled through the night the seventy turn-
pike miles via Dartford, Rochester, Sittingbourne and Canterbury
to Dover, where he chartered a small boat that slipped its moorings
before dawn to take him to France. He never set foot in England
again.

"He did quite right to be off," quipped his boon companion,
Lord Alvanley, who was one of the very few to know of the plan.
"It was Solomans's Judgement."

PART THREE

A MAN OF FASHION,
GONE TO THE CONTINENT
1816–1840

A Catalogue
Of
A very choice and valuable assemblage
Of
Specimens of the rare old Sèvres Porcelaine
Articles of Buhl Manufacture
Curiously chased Plate
Library of Books
Chiefly of French, Italian, and English Literature, the best
Editions and in fine Condition
The Admired Drawing of *The Angry Child,* and others
Exquisitely Finished by Holmes, Christall de Windt
and Stephanoff
Three capital double-barrelled Fowling Pieces
by Manton
Ten Dozen of capital Old Port, sixteen dozen of Claret (Beauvais)
Burgundy, Claret, and Still Champagne;
The whole of which have been nine years in bottle in the
Cellar of the Proprietor
also, an
Assortment of Table and Other Linen, and some Articles of
Neat Furniture
The genuine Property of
A MAN OF FASHION
Gone to the Continent
Which
by order of the Sheriff of Middlesex
will be Sold by Auction
by M. Christie
on the Premises, No 13 Chapel Street, Park Lane
on Wednesday, May 22nd and following Day.

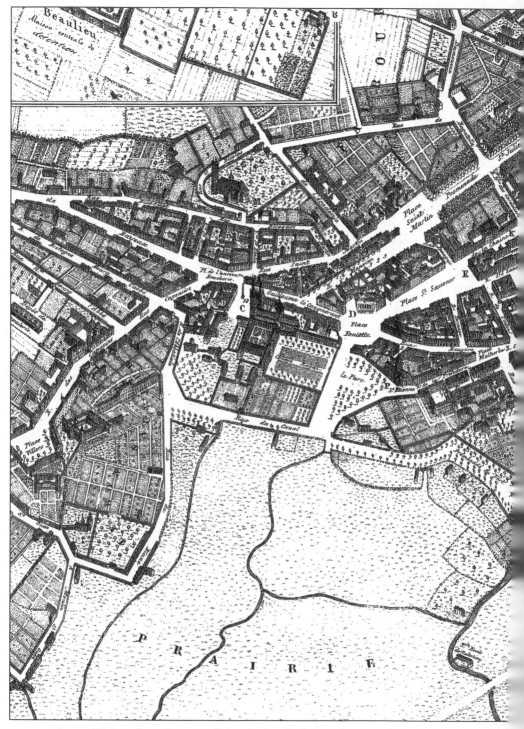

Caen, 1840, where Brummell lived after he left Calais unti his death
in the year this map was drawn. The prison is visible off the Place
Fontette and the asylum of Bon Sauveur is on the far left.

13

ROI DE CALAIS

1816–1821

Calais is peopled with English slight sinners and heavy
debtors, the needy and the greedy [it is] a sort of purgatory
for half-condemned souls.

Harriet "Harryo" Cavendish (later Lady Granville Leveson
Gower), daughter of Georgiana, Duchess of Devonshire

Early in the afternoon of Saturday, May 18, 1816, the boat Brummell had hired to take him across the channel docked in Calais. The ancient city presented a gray and unappealing prospect, being a semifortified staging post rather than a town such as Brummell had ever known before. But it represented freedom of a sort. Had Brummell stayed in England, he would have faced the censure of society but also the living death of debtors' prison without any realistic prospects of paying back the money he owed. Any of the dozens of London tradesmen to whom he owed money could, in theory, have had him incarcerated. In practice, the arrest warrants were expensive, so several would have had to club together to issue a writ for debt, but this was far from uncommon once word of ruin was out. When the stock market crashed in 1825, 101,000 writs for debt arrest were issued, and at any given time during the Regency there were upward of a thousand gentlemen imprisoned in London for debt—most often in the notorious King's Bench prison in Southwark.

The continent provided the only answer, and one that was, for men and women in Brummell's position, both traditional and commonplace. But debtors stayed in Calais if they had been forced to flee without preparation. An Englishman was beyond English law in Calais, but could only proceed farther into France with a passport, and a passport would not have been granted to anyone thought likely to be fleeing the law.

The place to stay in Calais for debtors on the run and English travelers was Dessin's Hotel just off the place des Armes. It was run by a Gascon family who had long profited from English gentry on the first or last leg of grand tours, and from distressed gentlefolk like George Brummell who beached themselves first, and often permanently, in Calais.

Dessin's—or Dessein's—Hotel offered guests a large courtyard and garden, "commodious baths," a small theater and even the novel concept of a "restaurant," unheard of in London in 1816. It was sufficiently regal—and suitably well-placed next to the Hôtel de Ville—for it to have been used by the returning Bourbon monarch three years earlier for his first address as King Louis XVIII on French soil. As a result it was known as *"L' Auberge des rois."* But Dessin's was almost as famous among the British for having been the home of Laurence Sterne, the author of *Tristram Shandy.* Brummell settled himself in, with his mind entirely on the English side of the channel, and began what would be a long and voluminous epistolary relationship with his former London friends.

His first letter—of apology appropriately enough—was to Robert and Charles Manners. They had been left to shoulder large debts without him, which they could only hope to cover by going cap in hand to their brother, the Duke of Rutland. Brummell wrote to them from Dessin's on the day he arrived.

Calais, May 18, 1816
Dear Lords Charles and Robert,
Persecuted to the worst extent by those to whom I was indebted, without resource or the hope to evade or protract the execution

of those menaces which, I was well assured, would have been instantly enforced against my personal liberty, I have been driven to the only alternative yet left me upon earth—that of quitting my country for ever. I am indeed most sensible, acutely so, of the heavy wrongs which such a step must inflict upon those who from their former friendly regard for me were induced to impose upon themselves a future charge for my immediate assistance . . . I have not extenuation to advance beyond the desire to retain the only blessing, if such it can be called, still within my reach, which is personal freedom and even that I would have voluntarily yielded could I have felt assured its surrender might in any way have exonerated you from the trust in which you have been involved on my account. The responsibility would still have existed the same on your parts had I forfeited myself to a gaol.

His characteristic interweaving of the self-dramatizing, the self-pitying and the truly heartfelt was only remarkable for the uncharacteristic absence of humor. There was little to joke about. Brummell's state of mind was, for him, fairly honestly exposed and his feelings of guilt were unguarded along with his desperate anxiety. His sensation of intense loneliness can only have been exacerbated by his strange new surroundings and the suddenness of the change. He had moved from the largest city in the world—where he had been a celebrated figure for fifteen years in a sociable, voluble and cosseted circle—to a provincial port with few social amenities surrounded by working people who spoke a language in which he was far from fluent. It is hardly surprising his mind was reflective and backward-looking. And there was much to repine.

The sale intended to recoup some of these debts for Brummell's creditors took place within days of his flight, on Wednesday, May 22. While Brummell sat scratching out apologetic letters in Dessin's Hotel in Calais, in Mayfair, 13 Chapel Street became choked with excited buyers—the curious-minded as well as bargain hunters—waiting for Mr. Christie to start the bidding. News had spread fast of Brummell's disappearance, and there were wild rumors about the money he owed, and about the amount he had run away with. One gossip reported inaccurately that "the fraternity of [the] high life is thrown into a state of extreme consternation by the disappearance of Beau Brummell . . . with £40,000, the whole of which he is said to have fraudulently obtained." A few days later the same scandalmonger repeated a story that "Brummell's private debts are very considerable . . . Lord Wellesley says he is in Picardy." On May 20, Sir Robert Peel wrote to Lord Whitworth that "Mr Brummell has decamped to the confusion of his collaterals and his creditors . . . and has conferred the benefit of his countenance upon the Continent . . . I believe some public good as far as the rising generation is concerned, will result from the downfall of such heroes as Mr Brummell." *The Times*, meanwhile, started running daily advertisements for the Christie's sale: "Rare old Sève [*sic*] Porcelain, Buhl, Cabinets, books, Drawings, Plate and Wines etc. Tomorrow and the following day, punctually at one. THE very elegant EFFECTS of a MAN of FASHION GONE to the CONTINENT, at his late residence, 13 Chapel Street, Park Lane." The sale was set for Wednesday and Thursday, but in the event, everything was sold within a few hours on Wednesday. The Duke and Duchess of York sent a representative, Lords Bessborough and Yarmouth were there to bid, with Lady Warburton and Sir Henry Smith. But also present was Brummell's creditor John Mills, in the company of one Colonel Cotton— Brummell's rival for the affections of Julia Johnstone twenty years before.

In France, Brummell may have lost his old knickknacks but was not for long without his friends. Dessin's was busy that summer. Prince Esterhazy stayed on his way back to London and was therefore one of the first of Brummell's many visitors in exile. Lord Glenbervie came a short while later. He had married one of the daughters of Lord North whom Brummell had known as a boy. Lord Glenbervie wrote to his son "how Brummell had changed since we saw him at Brighton on his first joining the Tenth Dragoons—handsome, ingenuous and clever . . . Brummell, who has now been twenty-two or twenty-three years on the town, and has been nicknamed [in Calais] The Dowager Dandy." But Dessin's Hotel proved either too expensive or too public for Brummell, or both. "The hotel," according to a contemporary travel writer, was "frequented by none but persons of rank and fashion, the charges, therefore, are proportionately high."

Brummell had left England not quite as destitute as he claimed to the Manners brothers, but even so, he claimed he had "means of subsistence" for just six months. Wisely he had remained in possession of his carriage. He had paid to load it onboard the boat that he had chartered at Dover (three guineas extra for haulage). One of his early practical actions in France was to sell it to the owner of Dessin's, Monsieur Quillac, which freed up some much-needed capital. Brummell had also managed to smuggle out of Chapel Street at least one trunk of precious clothes, and also some small items of Buhl furniture and even china. These he kept for the time being, and started looking for lodgings.

By law, Brummell could only consider accommodation within the ancient city walls of Calais. Fortunately there was plenty of rental accommodation on offer, and the rooms he chose were conveniently close to the entertainments of Dessin's, in a former hotel that had been converted into apartments and a bookstore. The former Hôtel d'Angleterre overlooked the rue Royale, which ran from the place des Armes to the rue Française, where Emma Hamilton had died in 1815. The artificial grandeur and high-ceilinged dimensions of a hotel once the haunt of traveling aristocrats was perfect for Brummell's idea of himself in exile. The building had been abandoned during the Revolution, then bought in the mid-1790s by a Monsieur Leleux, who had done well out of the years of the Terror. Listed as a joiner when he signed up to the revolutionary Garde Nationale in 1789, he had made so much money fighting in the Americas under General Miranda that he had returned to Calais, bought up the ransacked hotel and remodeled the ground floor as a bookshop, soon said to be the best in Calais. But the building was too large for his needs, so he let the upper floors to lodgers. At this grand but distressed building, under the blank ovals that had once framed busts of King George II and his consort, before their images were torn down by a revolutionary mob, Brummell set up home.

He had two large rooms overlooking the busy rue Royale—its name newly restored along with the Bourbon monarchy. He also had a small bedchamber at the rear, connected to the other two rooms by a corridor. His resilience of spirit was remarkable. He furnished the rooms with the few things he had brought from London, then set about spending the money from the sale of his carriage, buying the accoutrements he would need to set himself up as a gentleman of fashion, living elegantly, as Lord Stuart de Rothsay and Brummell himself later quipped, "between London and Paris."

For many months, cash appeared not to be a problem. Monsieur Leleux rented him a small garden under the ramparts of the old city walls, and granted him permission to redecorate his rooms, even to the extent of laying a checkered marble floor in an unused corridor and staircase that connected his apartments to the street, thus fashioning for Brummell a private entrance. The flooring was of the same design Brummell must have remembered from the entrance hall at Downing Street. Next he papered the dining room with expensive crimson wallpaper and ordered furniture from Paris, so much over the years, that Jesse heard the supplier had made thirty thousand francs' profit on the transactions. He re-created a London salon in the ruins of his former Calais hotel, with floor-to-ceiling prints and drawings, matching suites of Buhl and ormolu furniture in the Louis XIV style favored by the British regent, bronzes, japanned screens and "a large cabinet with brass wire doors" for his new collection of "extremely beautiful Sèvres china." For a man who claimed he was destitute, Brummell cut a regal figure around Calais. Where did all the money come from? One story went around that an anonymous benefactor had made a large deposit into a Calais bank in his name, another that the Duchess of York had bought an annuity scheme for him, which was paid until her death in 1820. It seems likely that both stories were true, as Brummell lived relatively well for several years, and it was widely allowed that Captain Samuel Marshall, Calais's British consul, was paying over sums to him. Brummell also knew that an appearance of wealth would extend credit to him when he needed it. And soon enough he did.

Meanwhile, he entertained in his apartments. The European peace—brokered at the Congress of Vienna in 1815 and after the Battle of Waterloo—meant that Calais was once again bustling with visitors on their way to or from Britain. The quayside was rebuilt, a lighthouse constructed for night crossings to England, and between 1816 and 1818 there were upwards of four hundred departures a month. Many of these were explained by continuing repatriations of British troops—twelve thousand men along with some three hundred horses per month in 1816. With them came many officers, some known to Brummell, and in their wake many more aristocratic visitors. Talleyrand's comrade in amours, Beau Montrond, passed by en route to London and gave Brummell a Siena marble ink blotter that had once been Napoleon's. The Dukes of Wellington, Richmond, Beaufort and Bedford all visited. Lord Yarmouth was back and forth, buying French art and antiques toward what would become the Wallace Collection. Lords Sefton, Jersey, Willoughby d'Eresby and Stuart de Rothsay all climbed the stairs from the checkered hallway to pay court—as if, as Harriette Wilson said, Brummell were some "lion at a zoo." "Every bird of passage from the fashionable world," wrote Prince Pückler-Muskau, "pays the former patriarch the tribute of a visit." Fellow Etonian Berkeley Craven was soon in exile, too, bringing news that their school friend Thomas Raikes would also visit on his way back from Paris. Brummell immediately wrote to Raikes asking him to buy snuff: "21b of Façon de Paris [best Paris snuff] . . . I have not a pinch remaining to befriend my sluggish evenings." It wasn't long also before Brummell saw Lord Alvanley again and Lady Granville wrote to her sister later that year of his exile to say,

"Mr Brummell is the happiest of men, lives chiefly with the natives and enters into all the little gossip and tittle-tattle of the place with exactly the same zest as he was wont to do in England."

Calais turned out to be an excellent venue for Brummell, a European crossroads where everyone was forced to wait for the tide, and pay court to the Beau in exile. When Harriette Wilson, en route to Paris, decided to pay a call, she noted immediately that nothing much had changed in the world since she had last seen Brummell carousing in Mayfair. She littered her description with dialogue, as ever, much of it in her eccentric rendition of French:

Curiosity induced me to enquire about him as I passed through Calais . . . I made the beau a hasty visit, just as the horses were being put to my carriage. My enquiry, *si Monsieur Brummell etoit visible?*[1] was answered, by his valet, just such a valet as one would have given the beau, in the acme of his glory, *bien poudre, bien ceremonieux, et bien mis, "que Monsieur fesoit sa barbe. Pardon,"*[2] added the valet, seeing me about to leave my card, *"mais Monsieur recoit, en fesant la barbe, toujours. Monsieur est à sa seconde toilette actuellement."*[3]

I found the beau en robe de chambre, "de Florence," and if one might judge from his increased embonpoint and freshness his disgrace had not seriously affected him. He touched lightly on this subject in the course of our conversation, *fesant toujours la barbe, avec une grace toute particuliere, et le moindre petit rasoir que je n'eut jamais vu.*[4]

"I have heard all about your late tricks, in London," said I. Brummell laughed, and told me that, in Calais, he sought only after French society, because it was his decided opinion that nothing could be more ridiculous than the idea of a man going to the Continent, whether from necessity or choice, merely to associate with Englishmen. I asked him if he did not find Calais a very melancholy residence?

"No," answered Brummell, "not at all. I draw, read, study and . . ."

[1] If Monsieur Brummell was seeing visitors.
[2] He was powdered, stuffy and ceremonial.
[3] "The Monsieur is shaving. Apologies."
[4] "Monsieur always receives visitors when he is shaving."

then turning to me [he said] "There are some very pretty French actresses . . . I had such a sweet, green shoe, here, just now. In short, I have never been, in any place, in my life, where I could not amuse myself."

There had, however, been one stunning change in Brummell's appearance. When he arrived in France he shaved off all his hair. This was noted without alarm by Harriette and others, and Brummell even mentioned it to his friend Tom Raikes, but to those in the know it was another sign that he was not well. The stress or a mismanagement of his mercury regime had led to the recurrence of a syphilitic symptom: alopecia. Undaunted, he shaved off the hair that remained, the better, it was acknowledged at the time, to apply the mercury unguents that kept the skin complaints at bay, and commissioned a smart brown wig that was, according to Harriette "nature itself," and passed himself off as twenty-five "at a little distance."

He wrote a defiant if melancholy missive to Thomas Raikes later in the summer:

As to the alteration in my looks, you will laugh when I tell you your own head of hair is but a scanty possession in comparison with that which now crowns my pristine baldness; a convenient, comely scalp, that has divested me of my former respectability of appearance (for what right have I now to such an outward sign?) and [with my new wig] I should certainly pass at a little distance for *five and twenty*. And so, let me whisper to you, seems to think Madame la Baronne de Borno the wife of a Russian officer who is now in England, and in his absence resident in this house [Leleux's]. Approving and inviting are her frequent smiles and she looks into my window from the garden-walk; but I have neither the spirits nor inclination to improve such flattering overtures.

Entertaining actresses in his Florentine dressing robe and smiling from his window at Madame la Baronne, Brummell wiled away his days, with no particular "spirits nor inclination" to take advantage of his position as a local celebrity to seduce anyone. His syphilis, intermittently, would have precluded such an idea. It was wrongly assumed at the time that syphilis was noncommunicable when the symptoms were in abeyance, and generally people preferred to believe themselves cured but, unsurprisingly, syphilis and its mercury treatment could cause impotence and general loss of libido.

He was further held back in his sociability by the poor standard of his spoken French and this he sought to rectify. He engaged a former abbé who charged him three francs an hour for French lessons—his first since leaving Eton. Scrope Davies cruelly joked to Byron that he had heard their old friend Brummell was struggling with French grammar, and had "been stopped, like Buonaparte in Russia, by the *elements.*" Byron stole the joke to use in his poem "Beppo":

> *Crushed was Napoleon . . .*
> *Stopped by the Elements—like a Whaler—or*
> *A blundering novice in new French grammar.*

The poet had the decency to acknowledge his plagiarism and said, with regard to Davies, that "fair exchange [is] no robbery" as Davies had "made his fortune" telling Byron stories at dinner. In any event, it was all an unfair joke at Brummell's expense. His written French had always been adequate—he had been reading letters from Princess Frederica in French all through their relationship—but in France it was the spoken word he struggled at first to master. Eventually his language master pronounced that he had *"un ton parfait,"* and expressed surprise that he had never learned to speak the French language in England.

Monsieur Leleux appreciated his efforts. He spoke of him with enormous admiration and affection several decades later, describing him as *"si amusant, si amusant qu'on ne pourrait rien lui refuser"!* [5] "Sir," he continued, "I would have kept him for nothing if he would have stayed: ah! He certainly was a very droll fellow." An ability to amuse suggests Brummell's lessons paid off, and he was

[5] "So amusing that we could refuse him nothing!"

41. Burlington Arcade.
The epicenter of the
new shopping economy
of London's West End.

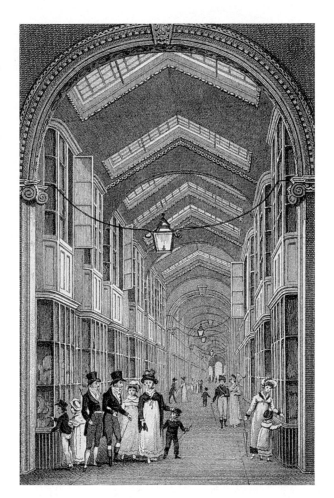

42. Hyde Park Corner.
The main route west
out of London, but
also the entrance to
Rotten Row (*Route du
Roi* or King's Road) in
Hyde Park, where
fashionable Londoners
rode and walked in the
afternoons.

43. Princess Frederica of Prussia, Duchess of York. Twelve years his senior, "Princess Fred" and Brummell formed a passionate and loyal friendship.

44. Georgiana, Duchess of Devonshire, the "Most Envied Woman of the Day." Forty-three years old when she met the seventeen-year-old Brummell, she later gave him several love poems.

45. "I was never what you call handsome, but brilliant." Lady Hester Stanhope, Downing Street hostess, traveler and eccentric. She called Brummell "an exceedingly clever man."

46. Elizabeth Howard, Duchess of Rutland. Their relationship cooled after Brummell publicly teased her about her dress sense.

47. "Julia and I are very old friends you know." Julia Johnstone was one of the most famous courtesans of the age, one of the Three Graces whose affairs and parties captivated Regency London.

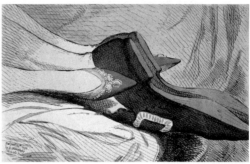

48. "Fashionable Contrasts, or the Duchess's little Shoe yielding to the Magnitude of the Duke's Foot." Princess Frederica set a fashion for small, tight shoes.

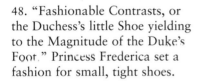

49. Brummell's friend Harriette Wilson, another of the Three Graces and the century's most infamous courtesan after the publication of her memoirs. Her lovers were given the opportunity to buy their way out of being mentioned, leading the Duke of Wellington, it was said, to tell Harriette to "publish and be damned."

50. Covent Garden, the foyer to the private boxes. The courtesans took boxes by the season to advertise themselves.

51. Admission was by subscription token, or recognition by a box keeper: an opera box for the season could cost over a thousand guineas. Seats could also be bought on the night—Brummell sent his valet Robinson to bag seats, so he could arrive fashionably late.

52. The King's Theatre on the Haymarket was larger and grander than La Scala in Milan. "The lighting is better adapted for being seen than for watching . . . The *Haut Ton* seemed to assemble only to see and be seen."

53. The Circular Room at Carlton House, the prince regent's palace on Pall Mall to which Brummell had privileged access in the years of his intimacy with the prince.

54. The Grand Entrance Hall, Carlton House (demolished in 1826). The Siena marble room was forty-four by twenty-nine feet and illuminated at night by gas lights behind the glass dome.

55. Above: "The first quadrille danced at Almack's." No new dance could be accepted in society until the lady patronesses of Almack's had given it their blessing.

56. Almack's Assembly Room, on King's Street, St. James's. "The Seventh Heaven of the Fashionable World." All the men were obliged to dress according to Brummell's preferred style of evening wear: the beginnings of white tie and tails.

57. Brummell preferred masquerades, which could be attended by courtesans as well as "respectable" society. He threw a masked ball in 1814 in honour of the Russian czar and the defeat of Napoleon. Only the hosts were unmasked.

58. "A Continental prospect of as much imaginative erotic charge in London as Napoleon . . . no event ever produced such a sensation in English Society as the waltz." The first (official) waltz in London took place at Almack's in 1813.

59. The Cyprians' Ball at the Argyle Rooms. The Regency Cyprians (courtesans) were sufficiently wealthy and confident to throw lavish parties. Harriette Wilson is on the far right, standing. Amy, the third of the Three Graces, is sitting below the cello. Julia, famed for her dancing, is likely to be on the dance floor. No respectable woman could attend.

60. A high-class brothel in St. James's—the last stop on a dandy's progress through the West End.

61. "I commune with my inveterate morning companions, the blue devils."
Brummell suffered depression for most of his life, but in their chronic later form
his "blue devils" were probably symptoms of his syphilis.

62-65. In Brummell's absence, London's dandy craze grew to ridiculous proportions, encouraging the sort of excess that would have appalled Brummell. Calf implants in stockings were not uncommon, corseting for men was encouraged, as well as cravats so tight and so stiffly starched that men could not see their feet.

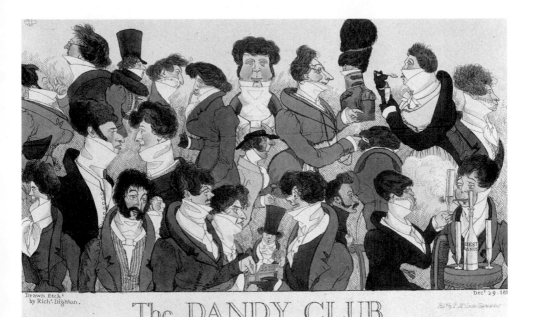

The DANDY CLUB.

Though
eminently
suitable for
satire, the
extremes of the
dandy movement
were eschewed
by most men.
Brummell's
simple, elegant
lines and
attention to
detail and to
tailoring evolved
quietly into the
Savile Row suit;
possibly Britain's
most enduring
contribution to
the art of dress.

The Dandies Coat of Arms.

66. The Dandy of Sixty. The prince regent became King George IV in 1820. Though he visited Calais, he failed to receive Brummell and the former friends never saw each other again.

This is THE MAN - all shaven and shorn,
All cover'd with Orders - and all forlorn;
THE DANDY OF SIXTY,
Who bows with a grace,
And has taste in wigs, collars, cuirasses and lace.

67. "If thou lov'st as I would have thee." Brummell's friend Lord Byron was forced to flee England almost at the same time as Brummell.

Me, miserable, which way shall I fly—
Infinite wrath, and infinite despair?
Which way I fly is Hell, myself am Hell;
And in the lowest depth, a lower deep
Still threatening to devour me, opens wide,
To which the Hell I suffer seems a Heaven.

"The Devil's in the Moon for mischief,
And yet she looks so modest all the while."

DON JUAN.

The LORD of the FAITHLESS.

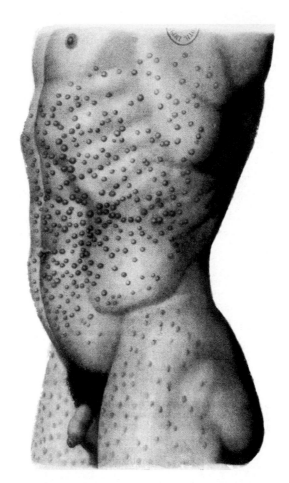

68. Roseolas —the rash that signifies the onset of secondary syphilis, depicted in a contemporary French medical textbook. Brummell's habit in later life of bathing in milk is explained by his syphilitic infection.

69. An advertisement from Brummell's time in France. There was a huge demand for discreet home remedies.

70. Caen, Normandy. The house of Madame Gueron de St.-Ursain and her daughter Aimable on the rue des Carmes, where Brummell lived from 1830 to 1832.

71. The Hôtel d'Angleterre, rue St. Jean, Caen, where Brummell lived (on the top floor) from 1832 to 1839.

72. The broken ~~Beau~~ Bow!
Brummell drew this for Aimable.
Cupid claws at his own flesh while
gazing pensively at his broken bow
and arrow. "The ridiculous words [of
the title] were written in a moment of
haste," Brummell said, "not to be
seen by others."

The broken Beau Bow!

73. Brummell in Caen outside
Armstrong's shop.

*Keen blows the wind, and piercing is
the cold
My pins are weak, and I am growing
old
[…] Alas! Alas! Which wind and rain
do beat
That great Beau Brummell should so
walk the street!*

very sincerely Yours
George Brummell.

74. Brummell, aged sixty. The
mercury treatments prescribed for
syphilis robbed him of his teeth
as well as all his hair, so he wore a
wig. Penury forced him to wear a
cheap black cravat.

75. and 76. The asylum of Bon Sauveur outside Caen where Brummell was admitted in 1839, suffering from "general paralysis of the insane" (tertiary syphilis) and where he died in 1840. The room as it was when he died (*above*). The derelict pavilion of the asylum as it is today (*below*).

able to communicate with his trademark panache, in French, within his first year in Calais. "We used to call him *le roi de Calais,*" the town tobacconist's wife recalled to Jesse, "he was a truly fine man, very elegant, and [to start with] he always paid his bills and was very good to the poor."

In order to maintain his lifestyle, he hoped to be appointed British consul in place of Captain Marshall. Unfortunately for him, consular positions in France were often held for life and Marshall was in conspicuously good health. To complicate matters, Brummell came to be on very friendly terms with Marshall and "all his family"; they even had a running schoolboy joke about their bad French. His alternative hope was that Marshall might be promoted to another post, and Brummell appointed as consul in his stead. This could only be effected at a fairly exalted level in the Foreign Office, so Brummell assiduously buttonholed his high-placed friends as they passed through Calais to lobby on his behalf. He lived his life as he always had: on expectations of future advancement and on his charm.

His life in Calais soon settled into a routine, punctuated by the arrival of the ships from England and the possibility of visitors. He described to Raikes how

"surprised [you would be] to find the sudden change and transfiguration . . . accomplished in my way of life and *propria persona.* I am punctually off the pillow at half past seven in the morning. My first object—melancholy it may be in its nature—is to walk to the pier head and take my distant look at England. This you may call weakness, but I am not yet sufficiently master of those feelings which may be called indigenous to resist the impulse. The rest of my day is filled up with strolling an hour or two round the ramparts of the dismal town, in reading, and the study of that language which must hereafter be my own, for never more shall I set foot in my own country.

He took to the French taste for café au lait, and read the *Morning Chronicle,* at Dessin's, dispatched from England. "I dine at five, and my evening [is] occupied in writing letters. The English I have seen here—and many of them known to me—I have cautiously avoided . . . Prince Esterhazy was here yesterday, and came into my room unexpectedly without my knowing he had arrived. So much for my life hitherto on this side of the water."

Brummell became so punctual in his routine that Calais workmen recalled to Jesse setting their lunch hour by his hour of dressing for the afternoon (they would see him move from his parlor overlooking the street to the back): *"Ah, voilà Monsieur Brummell; c'est midi."*

He contracted a valet, Sélègue, within weeks of arriving in Calais. Brummell's levees were soon open to visitors as they had always been: Harriette Wilson was specifically invited in at this hour. He was attended regularly, however, only by his dog, Vick, and by his parrot. The parrot was not housebroken, and was meant to live in a garden cage, but joined Brummell often to be fed on "wine and biscuit." It had, it was said, a marked similarity in feature, and in habit of repetition, to Byron's close friend John Cam Hobhouse, who visited Brummell soon after his arrival in Calais. "I could hardly believe [my] eyes," he said condescendingly, "seeing Brummell in a great coat drinking punch in [his] little room." As revenge, Brummell named his voluble parrot after Byron's companion and introduced it to all his visitors as "my Hobhouse."

Vick was a terrier bitch, who became so grossly obese on the diet of tidbits fed her by Brummell and his visitors that she slowed down the progress of her master's walks around the ramparts of Calais. After many months of this regime of overindulgence she died. "Brummell, in great distress standing at her side," said, in typically self-dramatizing vein, that he had "lost the only friend he had had in the world." Vick was buried in the gardens of Dessin's Hotel and Brummell refused to see visitors for three days.

As the months dragged on, Brummell's routine became ever more fixed, and his obsessive love of his dogs the more marked. Like Princess Frederica in her unofficial retirement at Oatlands, he settled into a prematurely aged pattern of life, but the burghers of

Calais thought of him as a harmless and amusing English eccentric, strolling with his dogs and talking to them as friends. He had a series of poodles after Vick, including one, Atous, who was trained by a soldier of the Calais garrison to take hot muffins from the fire and offer them around to Brummell's English tea guests. Whether they accepted them from the dog's mouth is unrecorded. "Like a true cynic," wrote Jesse, Brummell ceased to be affected by the stories brought to him by his friends from London of the sufferings or joys of people he had once known, "though a flood of tears was always ready when a dog died."

Brummell's afternoons were spent with his dogs and looking out to sea. He cut a melancholy figure. The cliffs of Dover were sometimes visible from the ramparts—and he was often visible to incoming vessels. At five he returned to Leleux's to dress for dinner, which he took, most every day, at Dessin's Hotel at 6:00. It was noted that he favored imported Dorchester ale to any of the French wines on offer, and although he took a box in the small theater attached to Dessin's, he just as often spent his evenings in the hotel garden. There, in the summer house where hotel guests were served tea, Brummell began to write his memoirs.

14

MALE AND FEMALE COSTUME AND OTHER WORKS

1821–1830

When we have made our love and gamed our gaming
Drest, voted, shone, and, maybe, something more
With dandies dined, heard Senators declaiming
There's little left but to be bored and bore . . .
                              Don Juan, Canto 15, xviii

Less than a year after Brummell had first fled to France a rumor spread that he was preparing to publish memoirs. Thomas Moore had recorded in his diary that John Murray, Byron's publishers, was offering Brummell "£5000 for The Memoirs." He added that he had heard "that the Regent had sent Brummell £6000 to suppress!" Scrope Davies also heard that Murray "really had some idea of going to Calais to treat with Brummell" and the Duke of Rutland was told that Brummell intended to "set everything at defiance [and] disclose to the world every anecdote he has heard, everything that has come to his knowledge in the intimacy of friendship. And those who have thrown him off he shall treat with utmost severity." London society was alarmed and excited at the prospect in about equal measure, and the publishers envisaged, especially after the runaway success of Harriette Wilson's *Memoirs by Herself,* that Brummell's might sell very well indeed.

In Calais, Brummell started to hint at what he might be writing.

He was often to be seen in the summer house in Dessin's gardens working at his memoirs. Or he would flick through the pages of his manuscript at his lodgings, telling visitors, "Here is a chapter on Carlton House; here one on Mrs Fitzherbert and the Prince, this is devoted to Lady Hertford." It was all deliberately tantalizing. Leleux told his tenant that he thought he would be foolish to turn down any offers of money for it. He was already aware that Brummell was struggling financially:

I frequently asked him why he did not accept [terms for publication], to this he usually made some frivolous excuse, but on one occasion, when I pressed hard for his real reason, he said this: "I [have now] promised the Duchess of York that I would not publish any notes of mine during the lifetime of [the Prince Regent] or his brothers; and I am under so many obligations to her, and have such deep respect for her generous and amiable conduct to me in our early friendship, and since, that I would rather go to gaol than forfeit my word. She is the only link that binds me in this matter."

Whether Princess Frederica was acting entirely from her own motives is unclear: the regent himself was informed of Brummell's plans to publish, and if he did not respond directly, he might well have put pressure on Frederica to use her influence on her friend. Brummell was not involved in anything so unseemly as blackmail, but there is a clear implication in one letter he wrote to his old friend from the Tenth Light Dragoons, Lord Petersham, that he wished the regent to feel his distress. Petersham had risen to be a lord of the bedchamber to the regent. The letter Brummell sent to him from Calais in 1818 is preserved not in the Stanhope papers, however, but in the Royal Archives in Windsor, thus indicating that it was probably shown to the prince.

I have been almost constantly occupied in writing a sort of history of my own time [wrote Brummell], confining myself to private life . . . it will be ready for publication early in the winter [1818–19]—You may perceive I

have not included the flattering side of representations in the many portraits that form my cabinet . . . Of one personage who professed to be
my earliest friend and patron I have endeavoured to speak with as much
becoming deference to his <u>public situation</u> as candour and the nature of
my record would allow . . . I have depicted what had come immediately
under my own cognition and forth it will go to the world with all its own
faults as well as those of others upon its shoulders for I cannot starve
from a punctilious principle of unrequited feeling even towards the <u>high-
est</u> among the Lords Ordained.

He then added just before his signature: "You need not make
this a <u>secret</u>." The implication was clear: he wanted the regent to
hear what he intended to do, from someone well placed to tell
him—one of his lords of the bedchamber and a friend, from happier days, to both Brummell and the prince. Brummell begged to
point out also that he "never intentionally offended [the prince]"
and was aware of the censure he risked from his former friends. "I
have not written to please their palates," he went on, "but to provide for my own. I have recorded nothing but the truth in my descriptions, and if the cap chases their temples [if the cap fits?], let
them remember their own desertion and abuse of me the moment
misfortune had compelled me to seek refuge in another country."
    The prince might have considered paying Brummell off, as
Thomas Moore had heard. But in the end he found a more expedient resource in his sister-in-law, Princess Frederica. Brummell had
not issued a direct threat, and the indirect response was more
courtly and, as it turned out, entirely efficient. Indeed, it seems
likely Brummell neither wished to publish, nor to put direct pressure on his former friend to pay for his memoirs' suppression.
Things went a roundabout route as Brummell might have intended.
Frederica and the prince had been on friendly terms for nearly
thirty years. Her letters to him are embroidered with some of the
same grandiloquent playfulness she uses with Brummell, though
they are a good deal less flirtatious. The prince had Frederica write

to Brummell, urgently supplicating him not to publish—and to destroy what he had written.

It is of deep regret to historians of the period that Brummell agreed. Beyond overcoming his financial embarrassment, he might simply have wanted an acknowledgment of his worth and of his former position. To be recognized had always been important to Brummell, and flaunting the possibility of memoirs may have been as tempting to him as to sell them.

Why Princess Frederica, among all others, should have been so anxious to suppress his writing, and be so beneficent toward him in his exile, exhibits an appealing loyalty to both Brummell and the prince. Allied with this was an interest in her own and the royal family's reputations. And then there was the issue of inheritance: Princess Frederica had failed in her singular duty to provide an heir to the Hanoverian dynasty, and this ancient regret pressed more painfully after the death of Princess Charlotte in 1817. The old business of a Hanoverian heir was one on which Brummell's memoirs might have been expected to throw an ugly light. Brummell was in contact in his exile with the intended husband of Mrs. Fitzherbert's "niece" Minney Seymour. It is possible that Princess Frederica, along with the entire legitimate royal house, was alarmed at the prospect of someone as well placed as Brummell speculating anew on the marriage between Mrs. Fitzherbert and the regent. More recent research has also thrown up compelling evidence that there were a large number of prospective "heirs" from this illegal union, including Minney, all born in the years when Brummell had shared close friendship with the prince, the Yorks and Mrs. Fitzherbert.

Above all this, Princess Frederica was motivated by genuine affection. She had loved Brummell, as a friend and quite possibly much more than that, and had a continuing desire to keep him from the ignominy of selling royal secrets. She gave Brummell money, tucked discreetly inside the handmade items that she made for him and sent to France. "A purse, a card-case, a note keeper; the work of her own fair hand" arrived for Brummell from Oatlands, and a glass-topped box framing a particularly fine piece of her own embroidery depicting two lovebirds drinking out of the same vase. She had an armchair expensively covered with green velvet and decorated with some of her own needlepoint, then shipped to France. It was delivered to Brummell in Calais, and was one of the few possessions he never gave up.

In return he began work on an appliqué collage screen to send to her. On one panel he stuck a picture of a poor boy outside a grand house on a "wretched night" singing the "insinuating line: 'I've lost my way, ma'am; do pray let me in.'"

This plea for sympathy from his royal supporter, if such it was, was never heard. The screen was never quite completed and never sent to Oatlands because, in August 1820, Brummell received word that Frederica had died.

On the back of a note from the princess that Brummell had kept, he scribbled that her death was met with the "deep regret of all the world." This was certainly an exaggeration, but the personal blow—they had been very close for more than fifteen years—was pressed home by a more urgent problem. She had been his primary financial support and her death put him into a still more perilous position.

He might have flirted again with publishing the memoirs. There is a theory that he came back to London, incognito, to negotiate with the publisher John Murray, or with Harriette Wilson's Joseph Stockdale, but this is based on a note in the weighing book at Berry Brothers. According to this much-thumbed almanac, Brummell came in for one last time on July 26, 1822. He weighed ten stone, thirteen pounds (153 pounds) in his boots. If it was him, he was a shadow of his former self (this is at odds with Harriette Wilson's description of his "increased embonpoint," but a symptom of secondary syphilis can be fluctuating weight). It seems scarcely credible that he should have been in London, least of all in the heart of St. James's where he owed money to dozens of tradesmen, including, most likely, the Berry Brothers themselves. Why would he choose to announce his presence in this way? Either he did it as one more reckless gamble—perhaps when he was on the point of getting into a coach back to Dover, to cock a snook at London one more time—or the entry is a red herring, perhaps the work of a prankster refusing to buy wine unless Berry Brothers put him in their records as Brummell.

What is certain, however, is that by the early 1820s Brummell was sinking fast in both spirits and finances. He had pinned some hopes, it would seem, on the succession to the throne of the prince regent, which finally took place on the death of George III in 1820. Although he had held the reins of monarchy since 1811, it was widely assumed that George IV's accession would mark a change in a wide range of policies and attitudes. It did not. And, specifically, it did not lead to any softening on the part of the new king toward his former friend in Calais.

The following September 1821, George IV arrived in Calais en route to Hanover. The mayor declared a holiday and, according to Macfarlane, Brummell accompanied him—the mayor was his wine merchant and also a friend—to the landing jetty that protruded from the city walls. Here they were due to meet the royal barge. "I was told that many of the English purposely made room for [Brummell], sharing his hope and expectation that His Majesty would at least recognize him with a gracious smile, which might have the effect of tranquilizing some of his Calais creditors." But Macfarlane related "that the King, who almost touched him as he passed up the pier, must have seen him; [but] turned his Royal head another way, and that Brummell turned as pale [as] a ghost."

"Falstaff," remarked Macfarlane in a literary vein, "was not so sad when turned off by 'sweet Prince Hal.' "

The encounter was hardly less dramatic in the version told by Leleux, the landlord. He said that Brummell had missed the arrival of the king's boat as he was out walking his dog on the ramparts. As the king and the French ambassador were making their way across the Place d'Armes to the rue Royale and Dessin's Hotel, Monsieur Leleux was an eyewitness to Brummell's plight:

I was standing at my shop door and saw Mr Brummell trying to make his way across the street to my house, but the crowd was so great that he could not succeed, and he was therefore obliged to remain on the opposite side. Of course all hats were taken off as the carriage approached, and when it was close to the hotel door, I heard the King say in a loud voice: "Good God, Brummell!"

The latter, who was uncovered at the time, now crossed over [the rue Royale] as pale as death, entered the house by [his] private door and retired to his room without addressing me.

Though differing slightly in geography, both stories paint Brummell as profoundly shocked by the encounter—or, rather, the missed encounter. He certainly appears to have been taken off-guard, as were his friends in Calais. They had assumed that the central figure in all Brummell's anecdotes would do more for his old friend. However, the discomfort, for both parties, was far from over.

A "sumptuous dinner" was given at Dessin's, within earshot of Brummell's lodgings, to which he was not invited. He lent his valet, Sélègue, to the hotel, as he spoke English and Brummell had trained him in the ways of English servants. He was to make a punch for the royal party. Brummell even remembered to send a bottle of maraschino, the king's favorite liqueur on which they had gotten drunk on the day of the royal wedding in 1796. He later claimed it was his best brandy: a thirty-year-old bottle. Still no invitation arrived. Later that evening the king found himself out of snuff, and asked someone near him, the mayor (or consul, according to Jesse), if he might borrow some. Word was sent to Brummell, who dispatched some of his own mix, "with all my heart," while remembering not to include his best snuff box, "for if the King saw it I should never have it again."

By the time the snuff arrived at Dessin's the royal party had moved on to the adjacent theater, which had organized an evening's musical entertainment, and the king was reported as saying to the person who offered him the snuff box: "Why sir, there is only one person I know who can mix snuff in this way; where did you get this?"

To which the answer came: "It is some of Mr Brummell's, Your Majesty."

"And here," Jesse records, "the conversation closed."

The next morning, despite all this, Brummell wrote his name in the visitor's book of the hotel—the equivalent of leaving his card— as further evidence that, from his point of view, the time had come for a reconciliation. If the king was made aware of it—it seems probable that he was not—he ignored it.

Brummell received other members of the royal retinue in his rooms at Leleux's, and Jesse reported that several tried to convince Brummell that he should ask for an audience with the king, either immediately or on the royal party's return from Hanover. Brummell pointed out that there had been no sign from the king thus far that such an overture would be favorably met and that he had done more than etiquette demanded of him already.

The king and his large retinue resumed their places in their carriages, ready to depart. The king sat opposite Sir Arthur Cassel, who had commanded the yacht that had brought them from England. As they pulled away from Dessin's, the king looked out of the window, according to Sir Arthur, and said, "I leave Calais, and have not seen Brummell." But he did not ask to stop, nor make plans to see him on his return via Calais in the months to come.

Although this sad missed opportunity was marked by many as the beginning of the end for Brummell, Brummell at first took it all in good part. He claimed, initially, that the king's comments in the coach, which were reported back to him, almost immediately expressed regret that they had not met, which proved that a reconciliation might still be possible. Yet when the king returned from Hanover a month later his carriage drove straight to the landing stage without stopping in Calais.

~

In a quite uncharacteristic fit of practicality, Brummell gave up on being rescued by the king from his penury and put his energies back into writing. As well as the potential financial benefit, it seems likely he needed a different validation, a new idea of self-worth if he was to accept that he was never again to be the prince's favorite or society's darling. The subject he chose to write about was the one dearest to his heart, once his friends and gossip had been put beyond the limit of his pen by his refusal to countenance the idea of selling his memoirs: fashion.

Male and Female Costume—a history and aesthetic study of Greek, Roman and British costume—became a work of exacting and slow pastiche, rather akin to the screen he had made for Princess Frederica. But unlike the screen, by 1822, *Male and Female Costume* was completed. *If* Brummell visited London in 1822, it might as easily have been in an attempt to sell his manuscript to a publisher. Not only did he use his time through 1821–1822 to rediscover a schoolboy love of ancient civilization—a third of the ensuing work was dedicated to the fashions of antiquity—he also decided his work should be illustrated and indicated to his unnamed publisher the pictures that would be needed and how they should be colored. He included a color diagram for the purpose. He cut out reproductions of classical dress from the works he used for consultation—ordered from Paris—and delicately shaded these with watercolors as text illustrations.

The work he produced is a detailed and at times amusing account, utterly of its moment. "The Athenians," he began, "to whom we owe whatever we know of the fine arts, ranked Costume as one of these. However varied its details may be, its principles are as fixed, and its means of producing effects, its power of expression, as definite, as those of the other arts." Brummell was schooled as a neoclassicist and his thesis on fashion was typical of the age. Rules of line and shape, simplicity and "truth of judgement," shaped and codified taste. "Did any men," he asked rhetorically, "ever look like Greeks and Romans? They were the handsomest, the noblest, the most unaffected, and the best dressing; in short, the most *gentlemanly* people that ever were or will be." His thoughts on the culture of the ancients are now debatable, but were widely accepted at the time.

On the subject of "modern" dress, he wrote, of course, from direct experience. He demolished those who criticized the fashionable and fashion-conscious as "paltry sophists," pointing out quite reasonably that "there is quite as much vanity and coxcombry in slovenliness as there is in the most extravagant opposite." Perhaps he was tilting gently at the cult of Byronic disarray when he went on to use as an example of this vanity of undress "the minor poet who goes into company with a dirty neckcloth and straggling locks . . . and anticipates the question 'Who is that?' " He was already aware that "dandy" had come to mean something altogether more romantically distressed than anything he had seen fit to wear in St. James's.

Brummell was at his most eloquent and scientific in *Male and Female Costume* on the subject of color. Because the aesthetic he espoused segued smoothly into the dark sobriety of Victorian male fashions, and the dawning of what has been termed more recently the age of men in black, it is assumed he had little knowledge of, or interest in, color. *Male and Female Costume* refutes this: his strict adherence to a limited palette of colors was based on sound color principles that he attempted to define. His ideas were meant to be applicable to the more colorful wardrobe of women, but it was based on a predominance-of-one-color ideology that was immediately recognizable as Brummell's, and as applicably masculine.

Male and Female Costume is a work without the easy humor of Brummell's recorded speech and letters and is undeniably pedantic, despite the occasional arresting aphorism. Nevertheless it would doubtless have sold in London simply by virtue of having his name on the frontispiece, particularly as the subject matter was so pertinent to his fame. It seems probable that he could not find a publisher who would meet his terms or that, having completed it, possibly in the frenzy of a syphilitic "manic" phase, he put it aside when the "blue devils" returned. It came to light in the early twentieth century, and received a limited edition publication in New York.

~

The death of the Duke of York in 1826 was a further blow to Brummell's prospects of financial redemption. Because he had been heir to the throne since the death of George IV's daughter Princess Charlotte in 1817, there had been reasonable prospects of advancement for Brummell in what had seemed the likely event of Frederick ascending the throne. On this assumption creditors had even extended money to the duke. He planned to demolish Oatlands and rebuild it with an eighty-two-foot ballroom, all financed on credit. Across the channel, Brummell had encouraged his bankers in the belief that even if George IV would not appoint him to some lucrative consulate, Frederick I certainly would. It was not to be.

Lord William Lennox visited Brummell shortly after the news of York's death and found him in low spirits. Lennox was accompanied by Adolphus FitzClarence, an illegitimate son of the Duke of Clarence (later William IV). Both FitzClarence and Lennox were in the traveling retinue of the Duchess of Gloucester. When the duchess decided to press on to Hanover, the two younger men decided to stay put and enjoy the regal rooms at Dessin's that had been booked in advance. Lennox later wrote:

[M]y companion and myself found that dinner had been ordered for eight persons and there were only [we] two left to partake of it [. . .] we . . . at once sent for Brummell to make up a third. [Brummell arrived looking] pale and emaciated; his still well-fitted clothes were what is usually termed "seedy"; his boots were not so brilliant as they used to be when he lounged up Bond Street in the days of the fashionable promenade; his hat, though carefully brushed, showed symptoms of decay, and the only remnants of dandyism left were the well-brushed hair, the snow-white linen, and an unexceptional tie . . . At first the ex-king of fashion was dull, but after few glasses of champagne he revived and kept us alive until a late hour, telling us anecdotes of his past career—his misunderstanding with the Prince Regent, his support for Mrs Fitzherbert.

There was a slight upturn in Brummell's mood and prospects in August 1827. George Canning, the prime minister, died and a cabinet reshuffle put Lord Dudley into the Foreign Office and Lord Goderich into 10 Downing Street. Dudley had known Brummell, from Harriette Wilson's Cyprians' parties and boxes at the opera, and Lord Alvanley persuaded the Duke of Wellington to lobby him on Brummell's behalf. Even so, nothing happened. Two years later Lord Dudley told Charles Greville, clerk to the Privy Council, why. At first Dudley had "objected [to lobbying the king for a consulate for Brummell] and at last owned that he was afraid the King [George IV] would not like it," and when he finally did approach him, Brummell's fat friend was as mercurial and petty as ever, "abusing Brummell—said he was a damned fellow and had behaved very ill to him—the old story, always himself, *moi moi moi.*"

Even so, after the king had "let out his tether of abuse," approval was apparently extracted. By late 1827, Mrs. Fitzherbert was writing to her adopted daughter that "George Brummell is to be made Consul at Calais. The King has given his consent." Unfortunately, the Goderich government collapsed, Dudley lost his post and the king's reluctant commands were left undone.

Once again, Brummell was left languishing and unclear about his financial future. His letters to England became increasingly anxious. He had managed to juggle his finances, paying the small shopkeepers whose services were vital, promising late payments to Leleux, and telling his bankers that all would be well. But it all came to a head in the summer of 1828. As time went by the prospect of a consulship receded, yet Brummell had treated every positive sign of attaining such a post as an excuse for immediate lavish expenditure. His larger creditors came to push much harder for repayment. Brummell was again forced to beg his English friends for help.

The young man he chose in 1828 as emissary for his round of

pleas was well placed in London for the task. Lieutenant Colonel the Honorable George Dawson was the younger son of an Irish peer, Lord Portarlington. However, he had bagged one of the great prizes on the Regency marriage market, erstwhile "niece" and the adopted "daughter" of Mrs. Fitzherbert, Minney Seymour, more than commonly good-looking and with investments worth over £40,000. Minney Seymour may also have been in possession of an uncommonly valuable secret: that she was the daughter, one of several children, born to Mrs. Fitzherbert and the prince regent. If this was the case, it was probably a secret known also to George Brummell.

Mrs. Fitzherbert had strongly disapproved of the match between Minney and Dawson, for while he had returned from Waterloo a hero—two horses had been shot from under him—he had few prospects, a reputation as a rake and, according to his prospective mother-in-law, had been spoiled as a child. In an attempt to separate the two, Mrs. Fitzherbert had removed her daughter to the continent and asked the Duke of York to have Dawson sent far away on military business. Through their travels, both Minney and Dawson came to know Brummell, probably through Alvanley, who was frequently in Paris and Calais and was instrumental in keeping the lovers in touch. Dawson had even mentioned favorably Brummell's attractive Calais apartments. Fortunately for the lovers, a solution straight out of a Jane Austen novel was duly arranged, whereby Dawson's standing was artificially raised by an old aunt, who gave him her estate in Dorset on condition he change his name to Dawson-Damer, and Minney straightaway did the same.

He was beholden to his adopted mother-in-law in matters financial and social, so it was canny that Brummell should write to him when he needed a favor. Dawson-Damer was a young man-about-town, but one with plenty of goodwill to earn in the royal circles he had joined. It may also, subtly, have reminded the well placed and well connected that George Brummell, too, had once been well placed and was still party to damaging secrets.

Calais, July 20, 1828
To Lieut Col the Hon George Dawson
c/o Mrs Fitzherbert, Tilney Street, Park Lane, London

My Dear Dawson,
Will you so far extend your usual kindness as to endeavour to be
of *instant* service to me. It is not to yourself particularly that
I take liberty to address myself, for you must be very much
changed, if you have any money at command; but to three or four
of those former friends who you may think willing to stretch a
point in my favour at the moment. I am in a serious scrape from
my utter inability to provide for a rascally bill which had been
long due . . . —the amount is £73.

. . .

I am, as you may have heard, expecting employment [a con-
sular post] through the interference of that best of friends, [the
Duke of] Wellington, but before such expectation may be realised
I am sadly alarmed lest some overwhelming disaster should fall
upon me.
Ever sincerely yrs
George Brummell

Mrs. Fitzherbert was clearly meant to learn of Brummell's distress. He could not, for form's sake, directly approach a lady, but
she was known to be wealthy, had also suffered from the inconstancy of George IV and still had influence. The "overwhelming
disaster" Brummell spoke of was the threat of being rendered
homeless if Leveux, his banker, refused him further credit and
Leleux, his landlord, demanded his overdue rent. Dawson wrote
back with excuses for his and everyone else's delay. He pleaded illness and being bedridden. Brummell's friends, he claimed, continued to be away from London. He advised Brummell to continue
pushing for any consular appointment, and to try to smooth the
exit of the incumbent in Calais, Captain Marshall, by keeping

his ear to the ground for appointments elsewhere. Alvanley, meanwhile, sent him fifty pounds via Drummonds, the bankers, so Brummell, yet again, was rescued at the last minute.

A picture of Brummell as he entered his fifty-first year is provided by the travel writer Major Chambre, who stayed in Calais in 1829 on the first leg of a continental tour.

I found him, on the contrary, [to] the common and received idea of him in England . . . of a consummate dandy . . . a quiet, gentlemanlike man, without pretension, apparently about fifty years of age, and exceedingly agreeable.

Chambre stayed in Calais longer than he had intended, simply to enjoy the company and stories of his new friend, Beau Brummell, and these provided him with a whole chapter of his subsequent travelogue. Brummell told him about the prince regent, about the visit to Calais when he "quite forgot his kingly bearing" and declined to acknowledge Brummell. He told Chambre the story of his lucky sixpence and how to prepare the best snuff: "moistened with cold green tea." He also told stories at the expense of the local burghers of Calais, including how he charmed people into inviting him to dinner and found ways to recycle the small gifts of pâté he brought as a gift to his hosts. Less amusing, as the weeks wore on, was Chambre's realization that Brummell was in dire straits financially and that his delaying tactics were working less and less well:

Whenever any one of my creditors calls upon me [explained Brummell], I commence an amusing conversation, and tell him anecdotes that I think will interest him. This has hitherto succeeded very well, for I divert their attention from the subject that brings them to me. We shake hands, and part on good terms; but my stock in trade is exhausted, and I am now completely used up. I have nothing left to tell them, and what to do I know not.

Evidently Chambre was won over by Brummell's candor, and offered some small practical assistance, as he saw it, without realizing that Brummell's financial incontinence was all but incurable. He suggested selling some of Brummell's collection of antiques. He had noticed in their evenings together that Brummell not only had a fine collection of furniture, but also many less practical items that he had accumulated over the years in exile, as gifts or as small purchases for himself, "curious snuff-boxes, articles of *vertu*." Brummell "jumped at the idea." Chambre, true to his word, spoke to an auctioneer friend of his back in London—the son of William Crockford, the club owner—who duly decided it was worth his while to come over to Calais. He gave Brummell a good price for a large part of his collection and shipped it back to England. Brummell had bought wisely and with taste over the years. It was a good time to be buying in France; much had come onto the market in the years after Napoleon's fall. At auction one tea set owned by Brummell went for two hundred guineas, and a pair of vases for three hundred pounds; Brummell's Sèvres was described as "the finest and purest ever imported into England."

Still no news came from England. The Duke of Wellington seemed unable to elicit a definite answer from the ailing George IV, even though Dudley had already gained acceptance in principle for Brummell to receive a consulship. It seemed as if the obese old king—though half-crazed on laudanum and looking like "a featherbed"—would go on forever.

It was a tough winter. Visitors were less frequent, creditors more pressing. Still Brummell remained, erratically, buoyant. In the spring, Charles Greville found himself stuck in Calais for the afternoon, between the arrival of *Rob Roy*, the new steam packet, and the departure of his coach for Paris. He spent the time with Brummell. "Just as gay as ever. I found him in his old lodging, dressing; some pretty pieces of old furniture in the room, an entire Toilet of Silver and a large green Macaw perched on the back of a tattered silk chair with faded gilding, full of gaiety, impudence and misery."

The old chair was the gift from Princess Frederica. The bird was the aging Hobhouse. The silver shaving set was Brummell's pride and joy: one of the few important things he had not sold on to Crockford's. Greville took the trouble to write immediately to the Duke of Wellington, insisting Brummell have some immediate placement to a consulate. Finally, it was done. Brummell received notification that he would receive a position.

It was generally assumed that Brummell achieved his long-held ambition of a consulship only on the accession of the Duke of Clarence to the throne in 1830, and that the enmity that George IV had held against his former friend lasted to the end. But this was not quite the case.

At a little before 3:00 A.M. on June 26, 1830, George IV died and his brother the Duke of Clarence, with no heirs but ten illegitimate FitzClarences by the actress Mrs. Jordan, moved out of Chesterfield Street and became King William IV. But the papers appointing Brummell as His Britannic Majesty's Consul—to the vacant post of a small but important coastal town, Caen in lower Normandy—were already signed. George IV had relented as one of his dying acts.

Brummell was appointed before March 20, 1830—probably as a result of Greville's letter to Wellington, now lost. He did not take up his post in Caen, however, until September 25. This should not be interpreted, as it was at the time, as evidence that he was appointed only after the accession of William IV. It was because his creditors in Calais, who had finally seen Brummell's ship come in, would not let him go.

Principal among them were his banker, Leveux, and his valet, Sélègue. Jesse took down details from the records he found in France. As even Brummell's meals at Dessin's Hotel had been paid for on account by Leveux, it makes for a comprehensive overview of his living expenses in exile. He could hardly be said to have learned much about economy after thirteen years "vegetating":

Leveux's Bill	Francs
To his valet, François Sélègue, for house expenses and etcs	6,162
Bill at Dessin's for dinners	3,488
Lefevre, hatter	54
Lamotte, Pion, } tailors	373
Baudron, Samson, } chemists	176
Lafond Bressell, Bonvarlet, Lemoine, } upholsterers	75
Parque Waillier, draper	309
Ducastel, decorator of ceilings	24
Desjardins, Boissard, } jewellers	35
Fasquel, bootmaker	150
Piedfort, perruquier [wigmaker and restorer]	8
Washerwoman	100
Fille de chambre	50
Isaac Pecquet, banker	500
Cr: 0	Dr: 11,504

The linen, washing and even wig-maintenance bills are understandable. But Brummell was also still spending a fair amount on clothes: the tailors' and draper's bills together total 682 francs. The greatest claim on him was from the long-suffering Sélègue, who was substantially out of pocket. It shows a touching loyalty, or an insider's confidence in Brummell's future prospects, that Sélègue should work for nothing for so long, and actually support his master out of his own pocket. He did not, however, opt to follow Brummell when he left Calais, but set up a hotel in Boulogne, then prospered greatly as the man who had been trained in service by Beau Brummell. The large chemist's bill Jesse tried to explain away as a consequence of Brummell's excessive use of cold cream, due to "the extravagant character of his ordinary habits in dress." The truth, of course, was that Brummell needed regular doses of expensive mercury pills and ointments to keep his syphilis symptoms at bay.

Only the so-called heavy metals of the day, mercury, bismuth and arsenic, were thought able to attack the spirochetes that caused syphilis deep in the tissue. There was empirical evidence that this could work and, in fact, early-nineteenth-century doctors understood much of what was going on with the progress of syphilis. Their drastic therapies, up to a point, were effective. Brummell seems to have been on a regime of old-fashioned *unguentum saracenium,* an ancient mercury ointment that was rubbed into the skin and genitals. This was used in conjunction with sweet mercury or calomel and white precipitate (mercuric nitrate) usually in blue pills called *Hydrargyrum cuim creta,* made of mercury and chalk. It was rendered palatable by the addition of rosewater and licorice, which also hid the halitosis associated with mercury treatment.

The ointments were generally preferred to the pills and used in the dormant stage of the disease, now referred to as "secondary syphilis." This was because oral intake of mercury, even in conjunction with chalk, almost invariably caused diarrhea.

The therapy—whether as pill or ointment—was taken to the point of salivation, in other words, until the mouth began to moisten excessively. This was unsightly, but within the precepts of a time that understood health in terms of "humours" and approved sweating out a sickness. One pill, four times a day, was sufficient to clear up a secondary chancre. Ironically, Brummell's own regiment had been subjected to medical experiments during the Peninsular Campaign of 1808–1814 to improve the treatment of syphilis. It was noted that the Portuguese seemed to recover from the rampant syphilitic infections within the armies of the time much more quickly than the British, but without mercury treatment. Further experiments were performed on infected Coldstream Guards, and published in 1817. But in a backwater like Calais, Brummell would have been stuck on mercury, as indeed were the majority of syphilitics well into the nineteenth century.

The money owed to Leveux and to Sélègue amounted to over a thousand pounds at the exchange rate of the day. Jesse claimed Brummell owed twelve thousand francs and had a further twelve-thousand-franc overdraft. He had already spent the money he had made from Crockford's auctioneers in servicing his previous debts. Brummell sold more of his "Fine Old Furniture," but this brought in only five hundred pounds—half of what he needed.

On March 20, therefore (which proves he already had the expectation of the consular appointment *before* the old king died), he signed over power of attorney and, as before with the Manners brothers, he sold his future to refinance his past. The monies due to him by the Foreign Office for his services as British consul in Caen—£400 a year—were to be paid over to James and Lewis Hertslet of the Foreign Office, who in turn had arranged with Leveux to pay £320 a year to the Calais bank to redeem Brummell's debts. It is unclear when this arrangement was to end. It seems likely that Brummell had been forced to enter into another annuity arrangement where his debt would cost him proportionately vast amounts as the years went by. More to the point, in the short term, he would be obliged to put up in Caen on an income of eighty pounds a year—the sort of money he would once have spent on a coat.

Nevertheless, and remarkably, Brummell saw the appointment in Caen as the rescue he had longed for. He could turn over a new leaf, leave behind the tedium of Calais, establish himself in a town known for its elegant streets and educated inhabitants. And, for the first time in decades, he was briefly out of debt.

He responded with blithe amusement to his friend Marshall, the British consul, after a request to contribute to a new Anglican church for the English residents in Calais and an invitation to dinner with a passing bishop:

My Dear Marshall

You must excuse me not having the pleasure to dine with you and the Trustees of the Church establishment this day. I do not feel myself sufficiently in spirit to meet a bishop, or in pocket to encounter the plate after dinner; moreover I should be a fish out of water in such a convocation.

Truly Yours,

GB

[P.S.]

Really I am very sorry that you did not call last week, for it was only yesterday that I became a Catholic. But never mind, put my name down for a hundred francs.

Even once he was released from Calais, and had made his farewells to Leleux and Leveux, Captain Marshall and Sélègue, he did not proceed straight to his appointment. Instead he decided to visit his old friend Lord Stuart de Rothsay at the British Embassy on the rue Faubourg St.-Honoré. He had spent thirteen years in France but had not had a passport, or the opportunity, to go to Paris.

He did not even have to pay for his journey. Captain Marshall arranged for him to travel with a king's messenger carrying diplomatic papers. Brummell slept all the way to Paris. The king's messenger later avowed that the celebrated Mr. Brummell "snored very much like a gentleman."

15

HIS BRITANNIC MAJESTY'S CONSUL

1830–1832

During those years that I have vegetated upon the barren moor of my later life, I have sedulously avoided running my crazy head into what may be termed inconsequent distractions [but] now, in spite of all my theoretical circumspection . . . all considerate reason has . . . utterly abandoned me and I find myself over head and ears, heart and soul, in love with you. I cannot, for the life of me, help telling you so. I shall put myself into a strait waistcoat, and be chained to the bed-post.

Consul Brummell, Caen, 1831

Brummell spent a week in Paris. It was like old times. He stayed at the palatial British Embassy on the rue Fauboug St.-Honoré as a guest of Lord Stuart de Rothsay, and his host took advantage of having a celebrated houseguest and invited a series of the great and not so good of Parisian society. The dazzlingly duplicitous Charles Maurice Talleyrand—Prince de Benevento, thanks to Napoleon, but no longer using the title—was a fellow guest on several nights. So, too, was Talleyrand's friend Beau Montrond. Brummell also sat next to the Princess Bagration, the notorious *bel ange nu*, a celebrated Parisian hostess, gourmet and *grande horizontale*. The kitchens of the British Embassy must have been put into something of a spin over these events, as Talleyrand and Princess Bagration were two of the city's most famous gourmets.

Brummell ate very well, and he sang for his supper. He entertained the ambassador's guests with tales of life with the British regent and the mock horrors of the bourgeois captivity from which he had just been released. If it was a shock to his increasingly fragile system to be dining with the richest gourmets in France, and in a Faubourg St.-Honoré palace, when only a few months previously he had narrowly escaped bankruptcy, he took it all in his stride. On his first morning in Paris he strolled along the rue de la Paix. It was one of the capital's more fashionable new streets. He left an order at Dabert's, the jeweler, for a snuff box in celebration of his freedom. It was to be gold and enamel and was to cost 2,500 francs. He had no way of paying for it, but that had never hindered him in the past.

Eventually Brummell had to drag himself away from Paris. On September 25, 1830 he left the British Embassy in a carriage and four—most likely paid for by Lord de Rothsay as a last act of official beneficence—and traveled through the day to Caen.

It was late by the time the carriage wheels hit the hard cobbles of the old Pont de Vaucelles. The bridge over the river Orne marked the city boundary. The carriage drove up the slightly kinked rue St. Jean and past the distinctly kinked tower of the Church of St. Jean—most of central Caen was built on a marshy island and several of the larger buildings leaned precipitously. It then spun into the courtyard of the old Hôtel de la Victoire, just by the castle gates. Brummell jumped out and beckoned to the first person he saw, who happened to be the hotel's cook. He addressed him, in English, with words remembered from his days in St. James's: "The best rooms, the best dinner," he said, "and the best Lafitte."

For Brummell, Caen in 1830 presented a very different prospect than Calais had. Although less of a thoroughfare or port, it still had its fair share of travelers, boarding ships to set sail down the Orne and out to sea. It had a long-standing connection with England, from Norman times; its university had been founded by the same medieval English king who had founded Brummell's old school, Eton. Caen even looked a little English. Its houses were built of soft cream sandstone and its Norman and Perpendicular churches would not have looked out of place in the Cotswolds. There was also a long-established English-speaking community, and Caen had been a stronghold of French Protestantism since the seventeenth century. So far as British consular positions were concerned, Caen was a welcoming port.

Brummell did not stay long at the Hôtel de la Victoire. He dubbed it the "worst hotel in Europe," but the truth was that they had almost certainly heard of his reputation, and asked for payment in advance, in cash. He moved out after a week.

He found lodgings on the rue des Carmes, a few doors nearer the rue St. Jean than the British Consulate, right at the center of Caen. He liked it so much he signed a twelve-month lease on his rooms for 1,200 francs a year. From there, a few weeks later, he wrote to his friend Marshall in Calais:

October 25th 1830
rue des Carmes, Caen
My Dear Marshall,
Good fortune at length [has] led my steps to an admirable lodging, half a house, the property of a most cleanly, devout old lady . . . excellently furnished with a delightful garden, two Angola cats, and a parrot that I have already thrown into apoplectic fits with sugar . . . The two leading *Amphytrions de nos compatriots* established in Caen are Messrs. Villiers and Burton, two very good men of independent fortune, with numerous families. Their houses, and without exaggeration, are Devonshire House or the Embassy in Paris . . . I am doing all that I can to make all parties satisfied with me. I condole with the outs, and agree with the ins; as to my own nation, I have upon all who are worthy of such a compliment. I shake hands and gossip with the fathers and

mothers, and pat all their dirty-nosed children upon the head, and tell them that they are beautiful. What can I do more with my scanty means?

I foresee that little or nothing is to be made of my department; *n'importe*. I shall try something in the spring to better it. I am perfectly contented with my *Chancellor* Haytner, who is well versed in his business, and from my investigation, I believe to be an honourable adjoint. Prostrate my remembrances at the feet of Mrs Marshall, and of all your family. Scribble me what is going on in *your little fishing-town* of Calais, for I shall always bear an interest towards it; and if there is nothing better to record, tell me whether it makes fine or bad weather.

Very truly yours

George Brummell

Brummell's "Chancellor" was the vice consul, Benjamin Haytner, a naval lieutenant on half pay and a married man with six children and every reason to accept Brummell's offer that he stay on in his post and run the consulate. His "cleanly devout" landlady was Madame Aimable-Angle Gueron de St.-Ursain, a well-connected widow. She had one daughter, also called Aimable, who was just sixteen and *"une jolie blonde"* when Brummell became their lodger.

Number 47 rue des Carmes no longer stands, but there are photographs of it in the Caen archives and Jesse provides a description of the interior as he had, characteristically, insisted on a tour. It was a large, solid house opening straight onto the busy little street. There was a walled garden at the back, facing onto the gardens of the rue de l'Engannerie. A kitchen and two large rooms were on the ground floor; there were two large rooms and one small one on the first floor, and the same again above that. Madame de St.-Ursain, her daughter and the cook, Marie Godard, and maid, Marie Vantier, lived at the top. Brummell had two rooms on the first floor, and one for his new valet, Isidore Lébaudy, who replaced Sélègue. It was a crowded household and, for Brummell, notably feminine.

Even the cats, as he pointed out and whom he befriended, were female.

The business of the consulate, on the corner of rue des Carmes and the quayside, was minimal and conducted largely by Haytner. There were British ships coming and going, cargos of iron and coal for the new foundry over the river and imports from British colonial possessions in the West Indies: coffee, sugar and spices. Brummell was occasionally asked for his signature on official documents—one remains in the Caen archive—but his intention was to fulfill some less-defined diplomatic role as an exemplar of British manners.

To begin with the people of Caen took to him rather well. There had been excited expectation before his (delayed) arrival, and his letters of introduction from Paris to the gentry of the town impressed all. Not only had he been, by repute, an intimate of the past and present kings of England, he was also on friendly terms with Count Molé and the Corsican Minister of War General Sebastiani. Both these dinner guests at the British Embassy had furnished Brummell with introductions. So although he lodged in somewhat bourgeois conditions on the rue des Carmes, he had invitations from the Marquise de Séran, "a genuine marquise of the ancient régime," who lived at 42 rue des Carmes, and from Pommeraye, the local deputy who had ridden as escort to King Charles X.

Several wealthy British lived outside the old city walls in a street of large new houses called the rue des Chanoines, including William Cooke, a gentleman of private means, and William Cox, a retired colonel. There were also two doctors who administered to the British community, a Dr. James Woodman and a Dr. John Kelly. It was Kelly whom Brummell took aside, in the way a gentleman did, to explain, as the Prince of Wales had once termed it, about "his old business."

On his perambulations, introducing himself to the British and the natives of Caen, Brummell also walked into the bay-windowed shop of Charles Armstrong, an English grocer and supplier of goods to the British community. It was at 133 rue St. Jean, between the leaning tower of the parish church and the turning for the rue des Carmes. Armstrong became Brummell's counsel and support, and ultimately his most loyal friend. To begin with, however, it seems likely Brummell went in to inquire after the availability of snuff.

The rhythms of his life followed their familiar course, but Brummell was more settled, and definitely happier, than he had been in Calais. He ordered new clothes, walked daily on the Cours Caffarelli—a promenade of trees on the far side of the quay—and he attended the Salon Littéraire on the rue de l'Engannerie. He even went to the inauguration of a Caen Philharmonic in the little theater on the Champ de Foire. He fell in with the "Legitimist" or "Carlist" set, who opposed the new regime of Louis Philippe, the Bourbon prince who had seized the throne from Charles X in the July Revolution of 1828. But his politics, as ever, were social rather than heartfelt: he refused to fly the union flag outside his residence on Louis Philippe's official birthday, for fear of offending his Carlist landlady Madame de St.-Ursain. But he and Haytner flew it outside the British Consulate to stay friends with the authorities.

The person he came closest to in Caen was Aimable, his landlady's teenage daughter. Mademoiselle Aimable de St.-Ursain was in her late teens when Brummell arrived in Caen, but she was mature for her age. Her mother, who had aristocratic pretensions and connections for all she was a landlady, had high hopes for her daughter's future. For reasons of social advancement, both within Caen or with a view to travel, Madame de St.-Ursain wanted her daughter to learn English. She asked Brummell if he would consent to be her tutor. Aimable already spoke Italian. Brummell accepted, possibly with a view to a future reduction in rent. Aimable and Brummell had lessons together, but also, happily, they wrote, sometimes several times a day, as a way to improve her written English. Many of these letters came into Jesse's hands via "a relative of the lady" and it soon became apparent why

Aimable had kept her famous tutor's letters. Swiftly, hopelessly—
and certainly dangerously—Brummell had fallen in love. Aimable
was seventeen. He was fifty-three.

Tuesday

Millions of thanks to you for [the novel] *Ayesha*. I have not quite
finished with her, for I cannot now read, nor write, nor do anything in a methodical way; therefore I return her to you, with
every expression of admiration at your mutual excellences; with
Ayesha, indeed, I have only made a transitory acquaintance—*you*
I know already by heart.

    Why, in the name of common prudence and my own tranquil-
ity, could I not have been contented to restrict my knowledge of
you to the worldly etiquette of taking off my hat to you when we
casually met? During those years that I have vegetated upon the
barren moor of my later life, I have sedulously avoided running
my crazy head into what may be termed, inconsequent distractions; and now, in spite of all my theoretical circumspection and
security, I find myself over head and ears, heart and soul, in love
with you. I cannot for the life of me help telling you so; but, as all
considerate reason has not at times utterly abandoned me, I shall
put myself into a strait waistcoat, and be chained to the bed-post.

How Aimable responded to this letter is unknown. She seems to
have been remarkably cool and self-possessed, which may have
been part of her attraction for Brummell. But it seems likely she did
not tell Madame de St.-Ursain what was going on. They continued
to discuss books and the seaside, almost as if nothing had been said
of Brummell's feelings. Eventually Aimable responded in some way
Brummell found pleasing. He had always been mortified at the idea
of offending anyone accidentally (deliberately was another matter).
Having declared his love, he seems to have spent as much emotional energy pulling back again for fear of losing the friendship he
would have known could never be more than that.

~

At the same time that the middle-aged British consul was sending sketches and love letters to his landlady's daughter, a separate drama was unfolding. All the while, a young army officer on leave from India was recording Brummell's sayings and doings, largely unaware at the time of the love affair but sensing the separate issues of Brummell's crumbling physicality and finances. The army officer was William Jesse, who would go on to write extensively on Brummell. He was only twenty-five at the time.

He and Brummell met first at one of Mrs. Burton's soirees on the rue des Chanoines. Jesse immediately recognized Brummell from descriptions he had read of him, as far away as India. "I felt he could be no other than the exiled Beau." He was struck by his elegance, of dress and manner, and his eyes followed him around the room as he made a series of bows and smiled acknowledgments to the company.

His dress on the evening in question consisted of a blue coat with a velvet collar, and the consular button, a buff waistcoat, black trowsers and boots . . . the only articles of jewellery that I observed about him were a plain ring, and a massive chain of Venetian ducat gold, which served as a guard to his watch. Only two links of it were to be seen. The ring was dug up on the Field of the Cloth of Gold by a labourer, who sold it to Brummell when he was in Calais.

Jesse and Brummell were introduced, and came to be on friendly terms relatively quickly, as had happened with Major Chambre when he was passing through Calais. Brummell was often lonely, and happy to be visited at his lodgings. His elaborate dressing and exfoliating regime is recorded by Jesse, along with details of his daywear and manner. He wrote that Brummell still took elaborate pains in shaving and rubbed himself all over with a pig-bristle brush till he shone like a "scarlet fever" victim. He was able to record all this as he watched the aging dandy through a half-open door as they carried on their conversation. The skin regime was almost certainly an attempt on Brummell's part to keep the more obvious symptoms of his syphilis at bay. He was likely to have worked out, by 1832, a fairly reliable regime of mercury ointment "inunction" that would immediately depress the rashes and secondary chancres that must have been developing by this stage of the disease.

The other issue impinging on Brummell's romantic frame of mind was his finances. Within less than a year of his arrival in Caen, he had been forced to write to his banker back in Calais. He wrote in French:

> À Monsieur Jacques Leveux,
> Banquier, Calais
> I scarcely expected [when I left Calais] to find myself once more reduced to the extremity of having recourse to your kindness. I have relied too much, as you know, on my friends' promises, they have done nothing for me and it may be another wretched age of four or five months before they choose to rescue me from the situation with which I have recently been trying to cope. This situation has finally become most threatening—I am not concerned at being deprived of the luxuries and amenities of life, for I have long been forced to learn to do without them, but at the moment my honour is at stake, my reputation and all my present and future interests since I have reason to fear that the total lack of means to provide for the official expenditure which is daily demanded of me by my consular office and the ignominy of being continually harried for the small debts that I have necessarily contracted in this town, may shortly be the cause of my losing my place here.

This was a clever argument to Leveux in Calais, because the Calais debts could never be recouped if Brummell lost his job in Caen. By the same token, Leveux knew that Brummell's professional outgoings were negligible: it was the cost of being Beau Brummell that was forcing him back toward bankruptcy.

I therefore beg you to consider the difficulties of my situation in your own interests, which I vow are more sacred to me than my own; I beg you to reflect on them and to make every endeavour to provide for my pressing need. Be influenced only by those sentiments of liberality and friendship which you have shown towards me for fifteen years, and which I shall never abuse. Pay no heed to the unworthy counsel of those (I know them but shall not name them) who, to satisfy their unjust and miserly claims against me, will seek to injure me in your esteem.

Avec la plus parfaite consideration
Je suis, mon cher Monsieur
Votre tres-fidèle et obeisant serviteur

Leveux did not respond. Brummell wrote again a month later "pushed to the last extremity . . . I have only the shirt on my back left," and Leveux relented and cashed a check for him in order that he might pay his most pressing new debts in Caen. He must have known that Brummell could not survive on the small portion of his consular salary that reached him. Like everyone else, the Calais banker had been impressed into believing that Brummell's rich London friends would continue to bail him out, and they did—but the money took longer to arrive, the amounts became smaller and Brummell's debts continued to rise. The London friends, meanwhile, were surprised to find their long-standing generosity was still to be called upon. They had assumed that Brummell's appointment was the end of his, and their, worries.

Brummell wrote to his old acquaintance from Harriette Wilson's parties, Lord Palmerston, now at the Foreign Office, to request a brief leave. He needed to make a rendezvous in Le Havre with an attorney. Seemingly this was with regard to his ancient annuities, or monies that had been arranged for him by Princess Frederica. Either that, or he was finally in negotiation to sell his memoirs. Whatever it was, it required a meeting at a midpoint between London and Caen as the mysterious stranger "cannot be away from London for more than five days" (the round trip to Caen took more than a week). In requesting a few days' absence, Brummell took the opportunity of addressing Palmerston on his own future prospects. He still had his eye on the more lucrative consulship at Calais, or a post in Italy, ideally at Leghorn, as the Tuscan port of Livorno was then known. "I will take the liberty of availing myself of this occasion in most humbly soliciting Your Lordship's consideration of me, should a vacancy occur in the Consular establishments of any of the other Ports of [France], and particularly that of Calais." To strengthen his case for promotion, Brummell next took a big political gamble. He decided to tell Palmerston that the Caen consulship should be abolished:

I may represent to Your Lordship that which might be prejudicial to my own individual interest, but, with every zealous anxiety to make myself of use in preserving Your Lordship's protection and the only means which enable me to exist, I will beg unreservedly to sate the almost total inutility of the appointment of a Consul at this place, and that the situation might be abolished altogether without any probable detriment to His Majesty's Service.

Brummell was granted his few days' leave—unnecessarily as it turned out, as his attorney could not get away—and there was no immediate response to his bold suggestions. But in time there would be.

As he waited, Brummell began to lean on the locals financially, rather than rely solely on his friends back in England, and in particular on George Armstrong, the grocer. Armstrong was known and trusted by the whole British community and did far more for them than dispense tea and snuff. He sold tickets for the steam packet, he was a wine merchant, lodgings agent and, in the absence of anyone better qualified for the posts, he acted as American vice consul and minor banker, insofar as he cashed checks. It was in this last capacity that he came to play a central role in Brummell's life in Caen. The English wrote checks to him for Brummell, and he provided money. Eventually he extended credit to Consul Brummell. Brummell could arrange credit for most of the necessities of life; he had a lifetime's experience of living in that way. But servants required wages, and he had not found, in Isidore, as compliant a manservant as Sélègue had been in Calais. He was soon forced to go cap in hand to Armstrong:

> À Monsieur Armstrong.
> Rue St Jean.
> That [damned] ungrateful brute, Isidore, persecutes me at every instant: the fellow says he is going to Paris on Thursday, and will not depart without being paid, in money or by bill, and I believe him capable of employing a *huissier* [bailiff]
>
> I am wretchedly bedevilled, and out of spirits, and hate going out of the house.

Things became worse fairly rapidly. Word got out, almost certainly from Isidore, that the consul was struggling to meet his obligations. Other creditors pressed Brummell for payment, and he could think of no one other than Armstrong to turn to for ready money. He wanted to sell or pawn some of his possessions but was afraid of causing more alarm in town if he was seen doing so.

Then Brummell received a letter from England bearing diplomatic seals. He must have thought he had been saved again at the eleventh hour. His letter to Palmerston had been taken seriously, much more seriously than he could have thought—but not in the way he wanted. He was not offered a consulate in Italy or elsewhere in France. In March 1832, he found that Palmerston had taken his advice and was abolishing the post of consul at Caen. He did not offer Brummell any other post in its place.

March 21 1832

Sir,

His Majesty's Government having had under their consideration the present Consular Establishment of the country with a view to effect therein every practicable reduction, they have come to the conclusion that the Post of British Consul at Caen may be abolished without prejudice to the public service.

In acquainting you with the determination of His Majesty's Govt. to abolish the office of Consul at Caen, I have the satisfaction to express to you my approval of your conduct during the period in which you have executed the Duties of that Office.

Your Consular Functions being at an end, your Salary will cease on the 31 May—and you are at liberty to quit Caen as soon after the receipt of this Despatch as may suit your convenience.

Brummell was out of a job, and immediately deeply out of favor with his various creditors. It should not have been known that he was due to leave, but, with impressive selflessness, one of his first thoughts when he had read Palmerston's letter had been for Haytner, the vice consul, and his six children. Brummell wrote to the Foreign Office, recommending Haytner's "assiduity, skill and accuracy," and suggesting he at least be retained. Haytner's wife, ungraciously but with understandable annoyance at Brummell for the letter he had written, let the cat out of the bag. Within hours all Caen had heard that Brummell had been dismissed as consul. His creditors came straight to get their money.

Bailiffs arrived at the door of number 47, early in May 1832, and Brummell was forced to hide in Madame de St.-Ursain's bedroom (bailiffs were forbidden to enter a lady's bedroom under French law). The full force of the civil law had been set on him by Longuet, the restaurateur on the rue St. Jean: Brummell owed him 1,200 francs for meals and wine. Such was Brummell's social popularity in Caen, however, among those to whom he did not owe money, that a delegation of regular Longuet diners was got up to persuade the restaurateur to cease persecuting the now ex-consul, and, briefly, he staved off the bailiffs.

He wrote frantically to Armstrong: "Send me seventy-five francs to pay my washerwoman: I cannot get a shirt from her, and she is really starving on my account. I have not actually money to pay my physician, or for my letters to and from England."

It was touching that, on the verge of bankruptcy yet again, Brummell was worrying about the washerwoman "starving on my account." Meanwhile his health was suffering under the strain. His body needed all its defenses, as well as the chemical toxins to slow down the attack of the syphilis, and emotional strain would be followed by a new attack. Armstrong, possibly under guidance from Dr. Kelly, was persuaded to let Brummell's friends in London know that things were again reaching an impasse. Many already knew Armstrong's name and his sound reputation. They also knew he cared for Brummell. Armstrong agreed to visit London on Brummell's behalf. While he was gone, Brummell busied himself trying to retrieve expenses from the Foreign Office, and simultaneously lobbying them to reinstate Haytner as a vice consul. Haytner also wrote to Palmerston, saying he was willing to work for nothing if he could retain the fees he collected (he was in a position to know that they could amount to more than a Foreign Office stipend anyway). He estimated this income to be forty pounds per annum, but explained that he had a "large family of very young children" to support. By 1832 the Haytners had had their seventh child.

Brummell found himself, at fifty-four, broke and beset by the manifold ailments of secondary syphilis. He ached constantly, and the pain woke him at night. He suffered headaches and acute sensitivity to heat and cold. All this he alluded to in his letters, but he was also suffering most likely from the intestinal ailments associated with the disease. Then on a particularly drab and cold evening, late in the summer of 1832, he suffered a new sort of attack. Aimable kept the letter he had been writing to her when he collapsed:

Oh this uncomfortable weather! I am freezing . . . I cannot shake off its gloomy influence. I should like to retire to my bed, and, if it was possible, to sleep till the spring, or till nature would beneficially animate my dejected thoughts as she regenerates the leaves and flowers and the earth. I am at the instant subdued by chillness and blue devils, and feel as if I was in my grave, forsaken and forgotten by all those who were once so dear to me. *le plus grand des malheurs est celui de ne tenir à rien, et d'etre isolé.*[1] I am sick of the world and of existence.

You must perceive, that is, if you have the patience to read these vague saturnine jeremiads, that

At this point Brummell's pen fell from his hand and he slumped in his chair.

Someone heard the noise, went to check on him and found him paralyzed down his right side, unable to speak.

Dr. Kelly was sent for. He administered leeches and blisters, but would have known that the paralysis was the worst possible sign: the syphilis was attacking Brummell's brain. Tabetic neurosyphilis arose from a treponemal attack on the substance of the spinal cord: a progressive wasting away that was characterized by sudden crises of intense pain, incoordination, peculiar sensations, loss of reflexes and sudden, violent functional disturbances. Sudden paralysis was a classic symptom. Its effects were identical to those of a stroke except that recovery was relatively swift. Brummell carried on having intense headaches for the next several days, but he recovered control of his facial muscles and regained his speech.

Perhaps it was the half-finished letter that gave the game away for Brummell and Aimable. Perhaps Madame de St.-Ursain had guessed all along that something more than a teacher-pupil relationship had developed between them. But within days of the attack, Brummell had left 47 rue des Carmes. He made a relatively swift recovery from this first attack of paralysis, "and those excru-

[1] The greatest unhappiness is to be held to no one and to be alone.

ciating spasms," but it signaled for him the desperate hopelessness of his infatuation. It was a distressing time for everyone. Brummell had been intended to further Aimable's entree into society—in Caen, Paris, maybe even London—but Madame de St.-Ursain had not counted on him falling in love with her daughter, and she was not pleased. He owed her rent. The rooms were no longer necessary or affordable without the consular position. He left without saying good-bye—he later said he would willingly have done so, "but I was in tears."

16

HÔTEL D'ANGLETERRE

1832–1835

My papers are the only things I possess to which I attach particular value, they are of no use to any one else, but to me they are treasure.

George Brummell, on his arrest

The Hôtel d'Angleterre was on the east side of the busy rue St. Jean between the rue de la Poste and the rue de l'Engannerie. It was only yards from Caen's Salon Littéraire and only a few minutes' walk from Madame de St.-Ursain's on the rue des Carmes. Brummell took a set of rooms on the third floor, facing the street. There were other long-term residents: a Mrs. Emma Harris and her five children, and Mr. and Mrs. George Morton with their two. At that time a hotel in France would not have expected guests to move on swiftly, and offered competitive rates compared to private rented apartments and lodgings. Hoteliers like Monsieur and Madame Fichet at the Angleterre made their money instead from their restaurant, and guests were expected to eat in at the table d'hôte. Brummell had full bed and board for sixty pounds a year, which marked quite a saving on his outgoings at Madame de St.-Ursain's, not that he had been up to date with his rent there.

Although Brummell's health continued to be an anxiety, there was soon good news from England and from Armstrong. He had collected money in London from Alvanley, Worcester (Meyler had clearly been wrong all along in thinking Brummell had offended Worcester), Lord Pembroke, Charles Standish and Lord Burlington, among others. There was enough money to pay off Brummell's Caen debts—Longuet, the restaurateur, in particular—and the promise of regular contributions to support Brummell in his ailing retirement, to the tune of £120 a year.

Brummell's "blue devils," his sudden depressions, were often upon him, along with more physical pains associated with his illness. These were sometimes so severe that he prayed they "would put an end to my sufferings in this world." But on his good days, he felt, as he always had, that he could perform some service to the world if he could amuse it, and he continued to wave to other walkers on the Cours Cafarelli and to write letters to Aimable that were remarkable for their blithe disregard of his illness and his situation in life.

Madame de St.-Ursain had other plans for her daughter than that she should languish in Caen with an aging London dandy. Aimable was twenty in 1834, and her mother thought her firm command of English, along with the connections she could forge via her illustrious tutor, warranted a trip to England. It seems possible that this idea was first placed in her mind and Aimable's by Brummell. It certainly grew under his tutelage, as well it might, when their letters, and presumably conversations, were so taken up with English literature, history and the attractions of London. Brummell grafted onto Aimable his own metropolitan conceit that Caen was essentially a backwater from which people left for adventure. It was inevitable that she would go. He gave her his entire album, filled with verses by him and Sheridan, Georgiana, Duchess of Devonshire, and Charles James Fox. She had seen it often before, and used its contents for study. He gave it to her as a parting gift.

In early 1834, Haytner, who had worked as vice consul, left Caen. He had tried to increase his salary from forty to a hundred pounds but been refused, so with a mixture of pique and expediency (he had by now eight children), he decided to emigrate to the wide-open spaces of Canada. Charles Armstrong, the grocer and honorary American vice consul, applied to replace him, and asked for Brummell's support. Brummell pitched himself into campaigning, writing letters to Palmerston and Alvanley and hosting a testimonial dinner at the Hôtel d'Angleterre at which guests put their name to the application to be sent to Le Havre (the local consulate after the abolition of the Caen office) and to London.

~

Near the end of April 1834, Brummell's health deteriorated suddenly. The first symptom began at dinner. He went down as he did every day to dine in the hotel restaurant. It started, as meals perforce did in France in the 1830s, with soup. As he raised the spoon to his mouth, he had the sudden sensation of the most ghastly over-salivation, exactly the fear of social embarrassment faced by any syphilitic on a mercury regime. He took the napkin to his mouth, as he must have done many times in the past, but realized as he returned it to his lap that it was not oversalivation this time, but soup that had been running down his chin. He stood up, the napkin shielding his mouth, and retired to the empty salon where there was a mirror.

One side of his face was pulled upward in an unmoving rictus, like half of a masquerade mask. He had suffered another neurosyphilitic stroke. He went up to his room and sent for Dr. Kelly.

This time his recovery was slower. Dr. Kelly almost certainly increased the dosage of mercury, and might have added the more fashionable arsenic and iodide treatments that were now being alternated with mercury cures. Potassium iodides made from burned fresh sponge and seaweed were taken in suspension or as pills, and had proved successful in Paris and Dublin as alternative or complementary additions to the traditional mercury cures. Dr. Kelly must have been beginning to realize that Brummell was going to need increasingly expensive treatment, and was unlikely to be able to meet his bills. Although there was both ignorance and anxiety among patients and doctors on the issue of neurological disorders, the most pressing concern with syphilitics tended to be an abatement of the gross physical signifiers: the chancres, rashes, tumors and mouth ulcers. If these could be treated, and generally they could, it was wrongly believed that the disease would progress more slowly to the central nervous system. By 1834, Armstrong must also have been aware of Brummell's illness, if only as his medicines were such a regular item of his expenditure.

Jesse's descriptions of Brummell's skin regime suggests he was forced to apply mercury as ointment. This would have had its own unpleasant effects, in the medical language of the time: inunctions caused "scattered inflammatory oozing, crusted and infiltrated patches and plaques of wide distribution . . . Purpuric manifestations are occasionally seen and a follicular popular eruption is recognised." Brummell dressed as carefully as he always had, but with a slightly differing motive as the years went by: he needed to cover painful and unsightly blemishes. He continued to lose teeth and hair, and was plagued by chest pains, a symptom of the neuro-syphilis, quite possibly a syphilitic tumor on his lungs. His eyesight was failing, and he missed colors as a result of the iritis that accompanied the syphilis. To add to his torments, Dr. Kelly was a firm believer in cupping and blistering, the favored method of the age for drawing evil "humours," especially from the head. The last vestige of his hair, at the nape of his neck, was shaved at Kelly's insistence, to provide a new site for blistering.

"I am unwell," Brummell confessed laconically. "I flattered myself that I was progressing towards my ancient regular health; and now those who look after me professionally will insist upon it that my lungs are seriously affected, and pester me with all the alarming hyperbole of their vocation, upon my malady. They are weaving a shroud about me; still, I trust I shall escape."

Within a few weeks he attempted to go down to the hotel restaurant for dinner, only to have to return to his room. Perhaps he was still struggling with his mouth muscles, but more likely— as it seems he was asked to leave by Monsieur Fichet, the hotel owner—he was oversalivating to a distressing degree and fellow diners, whether or not they recognized the symptom, would have been understandably upset. He improved, mercury dosage was regulated at a new level and finally he was well enough by the summer of 1834 to accept an invitation to Luc-sur-Mer.

While Brummell recuperated by the sea, probably at the house of his wealthy friend Monsieur de Chazot, in Delivrande, Armstrong was again in London. In part he was on official business as vice consul, but he traveled with a letter from Brummell to Alvanley and also a copy of Brummell's Caen accounts, to demonstrate to his friends his reduced circumstances:

[August] 1834
My Dear Alvanley,
I have examined Armstrong's account of expenditure and receipts for me during the last twelve months, and I find it in every respect accurate and just. I have delivered to him the . . . Bank of England notes; but alas! My dear fellow, this will provide but in a very trifling degree for the liquidation of that I owe for my humble support during the last year [he owed six months' board and lodging to Fichet at the Hôtel d' Angleterre and was overdrawn with Armstrong by nearly two thousand francs]. I am suffering from a most severe and apparently fixed rheumatism in my leg, and I am in dread lest I should be compelled to have recourse to crutches for the rest of the ill-starred days.

My old friend, King Allen, promised, at least so it was represented to me, to send to me some habiliments for my body, denuded like a newborn infant—and what a Beau I once was!

Alvanley said he would send a check, and was true to his word, enclosing a note to Armstrong: "I beg that you will protect and assist poor Brummell, and rely on my making it good to you."

The money trickled in—enough to support Brummell, but not to service his debt to Leveux's bank in Calais. He chose to ignore the issue. By the winter of 1834–1835, he seemed largely recovered from his second stroke. He reentered the Caen winter season of dinner and musical soirees at which he had become a fixture, and some of his easy good humor resurfaced. He seemed resigned to a sedate but lonely old age, relieved only by the minimal diversions of the pretty little town he now knew as home.

~

Then on May 4, 1835, just after dawn, the Hôtel d'Angleterre was surrounded by *gens d'armes* and entered by a *juge-de-paix*. The justice had a warrant, issued by Leveux, the banker in Calais, for the arrest of George Brummell, debtor. A "jack booted gentleman" entered room 29 while Brummell was still asleep, woke him and issued him with the writ for fifteen thousand francs. Brummell was informed he could either pay, or go immediately to prison.

Leveux was entirely within his rights to issue the writ. It followed years of prevarication by Brummell over the Calais debt, and specifically his inability to carry on paying over the £320 per annum from his consular salary, which had ceased in 1832. But Leveux was also moved to action by the knowledge that Brummell still had rich friends, who might make good the debt in such dramatic circumstances. On May 5, with all of the clatter and brouhaha that the local police could muster, Brummell was ordered to dress, and his request to do so in private was refused. He was told, indeed, to get a move on and that he was "under the necessity of dressing in a hurry."

Monsieur Fichet, meanwhile, had dispatched one of the hotel workers, possibly his son Hippolyte, to acquaint Armstrong of what was happening.

By now all of the other guests were awake, and doubtless much of the immediate area, too. The hotel had been surrounded, quite unnecessarily, but to prevent escape of the intended prisoner, by enough *gens d'armes* for the locals to comment they had never seen a debtor "so handsomely arrested." Brummell nervously entrusted his papers to Madame Fichet.

He was bundled into the waiting fiacre (hackney coach), which clattered through the gathering market crowds of the rue St. Jean, attracted by the drama of a big arrest and by news of an ice ship, newly arrived from Norway. It drove at speed past the exhibition of flowers at the pavilion, and left on the rue St. Pierre to the place Fontette.

Just in front of the old Protestant cemetery of the city, in the area known as the Quartier St. Martin, was the place Fontette, with its forbidding courthouse and more forbidding jail: La Prison Royale. The fiacre took only ten minutes to get there from the hotel. Brummell was taken through the courthouse and locked into a stone room, with three other new felons. Probably they were the others listed as arrested that week: Gaudron, Farine and Jean Besnard, all charged with vagabondage. There were three trundle beds only, all of them already occupied. Brummell stood in a corner by the door, until a jailer brought in a chair.

17

PRISON

1835–1839

In Prison 5 May 1835 I still breathe, though I am not of the living—the state of utter abstraction in which I have been during the last thirty hours yet clouds my every sense.

Beau Brummell

"I have just received your note," Brummell wrote to Mrs. Burton, the wife of his rich Caen friend, Francis Burton, who had been made instantly aware of his arrest. "May heaven bless you all for your good devotedness in remembering me at such a moment. I have been the victim of a villain, who had closed upon me, without giving me the remotest intimation of his designs."

In truth, Brummell had been given every intimation of what was likely to happen. One day, he must have been aware, Leveux would press for repayment. But Brummell had never treated debts seriously, nor learned to fit his expenditure to his income. His life had been punctuated by sudden deluges of money rather than anything approximating a steady income. His inheritance, his winnings from cards and dice, the kindness of his benefactors set him on a pattern of overly optimistic financial management. There had never been in his world a concept of money earned or saved, or ever any reason to assume that tomorrow might not bring good fortune as equally as bad.

He could also justify his actions to himself, in relation to Leveux, as those of a gentleman. He had made over his consular salary to his banker in all good faith at the time. If he had subsequently lost the post on which the deal was predicated, and through a selfless act of impartial advice to an ungrateful government, he was not to be blamed for being unable to service the debt.

Leveux, on the other hand, was simply acting in the best interests of his bank.

Brummell gave himself up to utter self-pity in the traumatic first days of imprisonment and "sobbed like a child." He "threw himself into the arms" of his first sympathetic visitor, saying, "I am surrounded by the greatest villains ... imagine a position more wretched than mine." Less sympathetic to the modern ear was what he added next: he complained bitterly about the poor quality of the food and then added that he had been "put with all the *common* people."

Brummell's French and English friends in Caen were unsurprised by his attitude and by what had happened. But if they could not do much to alleviate his debt, they could at least help with his last two concerns: the food and his immediate company. Debtors' prison, in France as in England, was a legal limbo of dubious practical benefit. It precluded the guilty from making amends for their crime, but it persuaded, in the case of Brummell, his friends to make amends on his behalf. Brummell was able to have visitors and to have his own food sent in. He was also moved, at the suggestion of his influential Caen friends and a note from Dr. Kelly, to a semiprivate sleeping space. He did not have his own room, so much as the end of a corridor, no wider than his bed. He slept there on a straw mattress, but during the day he was allowed to spend time with the jail's most illustrious prisoner, Charles Godefroi.

The Prison Royale had many political detainees. The government of the "revolutionary" Orléans prince Louis Philippe, the so-called July Monarchy, proved litigious and oppressive. Godefroi was the editor of the L'*Ami de la Verité,* a Legitimist—i.e., anti–Louis Philippe—newspaper. It came out in Caen on every Sunday,

Wednesday and Friday, and was doing well; in 1835, it started publishing in tabloid form; yellowing copies of its later editions are kept in the municipal archives in Caen. With its innocuous advertisements for local lodgings and musical events—and for live swans, "applications should be made in person to the office"—it seems at first glance an unlikely basis for the political imprisonment of its editor. But it also ran a column of news on press freedom called Liberté de la Presse, which had led to Godefroi's arrest. *L'Ami de la Verité* loyally printed, week by week, the number of days Godefroi had been in prison. It struggled on, in the end for several years, without him. From his prison cell, as if to goad his political enemies, Godefroi mounted a running campaign of letters to his and others' papers, so much that Brummell worried he would "probably prolong his detention here [by] ten years."

But Godefroi had the largest room in the prison, the *chambre des prisonniers civils,* with what was considered one of the finer views: over the old Protestant cemetery, but also over the yard in which the women prisoners exercised. On the negative side, it was next door to the cell reserved for condemned men, and those awaiting deportation or sentences of hard labor. There was a communicating fireplace with a grille. It was to the accompaniment of "lawless and riotous neighbours," and surrounded by the desperate graffiti of previous prisoners, that Brummell and Godefroi spent their days, telling each other stories and talking politics. Even in early summer, Brummell suffered from the cold and huddled by the large open fire, near the grille that separated him from the condemned. A feature of his declining health was persistent bone pain, which could be alleviated to some extent by heat, but he seemed to be losing any accurate sense of temperature, yet another symptom of the syphilis.

To begin with, he held out hope that his friends in Caen would arrange for him to be sent to the hospital in the Abbaye des Dames. He wrote optimistically to Mrs. Burton on the Sunday after his arrest:

11 May. [1835] In Prison. The kindness of every human being within the sphere of this town had by degrees restored me to equanimity. How shall I be able to repay you for this benevolence? . . . I am I believe this evening to be transferred from my present den of thieves to the towers of Matilda and to the sainted arms of *les Soeurs de Charité*. There I shall again breathe fresh air and be comparatively at peace. I cannot describe to you what I have suffered here.

Though he worried that the anxiety of his experience might make him "relapse into my recent imbecilities," he ended the letter with a typical piece of Brummell whimsy: worrying about using a prison wafer instead of wax to seal his letter: "You will perceive the extremities to which I am reduced—I am about to seal to you with a wafer! Do not even whisper this indecorum, for perhaps I may again frequent the world."

He did not frequent the world nearly as soon as he wished, and he did not transfer to the hospital. Leveux wanted him kept in the jail until the debt was paid, and the money could only realistically come from England. The banker instructed his lawyer to fight any attempt by Brummell for a transfer or release.

Armstrong, therefore, as well as planning a visit to London on Brummell's behalf also contracted the Hôtel d'Angleterre to send Brummell's meals to him in prison and make sure that Brummell's medical supplies arrived when they should. With both pharmacy and hotel bills still awaiting payment, the slow response from both businesses was perhaps understandable. Within the week, Brummell was complaining, especially about the poor quality of the food he was being sent. Armstrong talked to the Fichets and the chef at the Hôtel d'Angleterre and met with some success. Soon Brummell was writing back within days to arrange for the safekeeping of his things at the hotel. But it was evident that there would be no quick release, and Brummell's thoughts turned to how he would maintain his strict regime of cleanliness and skin treatments in prison. He asked for towels to be sent, but Godefroi was impressed with every aspect of his grooming regime. It is thanks to Godefroi, and Jesse's trouble in interviewing him a decade later, that we learn Brummell arranged to have his large wash basin brought to the prison, and a daily delivery of twelve to fifteen liters of clean water with—to the astonishment of all—two liters of milk. With this, to equal astonishment on Godefroi's part, Brummell "actually washed and shaved himself every day, and made a complete ablution of *every part of his body.*" Godefroi likewise noted Brummell's use of a "dressing case full of vials of medicines and ointments," which doubtless included Dr. Kelly's preparations against syphilitic eruptions. The use of milk, dismissed by Jesse as "an absurd caprice," was almost certainly to counterbalance the toxic effect of the mercury ointments and soothe Brummell's skin.

To carry all this water and milk and to run small errands for Brummell, another prisoner, Paul Lépine, was contracted to act as valet, for a few sous a day, paid by Armstrong. Lépine was a former army drummer, recently returned from Africa, who was serving three months for a "civil" offense.

At 7:00 each morning Brummell was woken by a prison guard, who unlocked the end of the passage where he slept and rattled a "bouquet of keys" in his face. The latrines in the prison were public and open air. They were in the far corners of the prison yards, Brummell's being in the distant apex of the Cours des Civils beyond the Cours du Geôlier. It was, he said, a particular horror to have to use it—he had once insisted, after all, on traveling with his own commode—and there was no door. The other prisoners sensed his "bashfulness" and offered him catcalls and hisses before he scurried back to the *chambre des prisonniers civils* he shared with Godefroi.

As the spring of 1835 moved toward summer, there was still no sign of any money from England. Armstrong, still unable to leave his vice consular post in Caen, organized a whip-round of the local inhabitants. But this was always likely to prove inadequate. The ambassador in Paris—by then Leveson Gower, Lord Granville, the son-in-law of Georgiana, Duchess of Devonshire—heard of Brummell's plight and opened a fund to help. His wife, Lady Granville, who had traded sonnets and sketches with Brummell in happier times, appealed to her brother, the Duke of Devonshire, who evidently responded positively, as her next letter makes clear: "A thousand thanks for poor Mr Brummell. There never was such an act of charity. I am in good heart about the subscription." But the Paris subscription fund did not amount to the £800 that Armstrong had calculated was needed to cover Brummell's Caen and Calais debts, which would secure his release from prison.

He read constantly during the day with Godefroi—there was insufficient light to read where he slept as his eyesight was failing. He even began a conversation with Godefroi about Byron, whose *Life* he had been sent, only to fall away into a sad reflection when he admitted "this poet, this great man, he used to be my friend." (By 1835, Byron had been dead for a decade.) But still, no news came from England.

Armstrong was able eventually to leave Caen on July 7, two months after Brummell's arrest, the delay explained by his need to contact the British Foreign Office to ask for a leave of absence from his post as unpaid vice consul. He traveled via Calais, where he met with Leveux to ascertain the exact terms on which he would consent to Brummell's release, which, under French law, lay in his gift. Armed with this intelligence he proceeded to London.

Armstrong returned with good news. He had secured the £800, and a promise of more. Although Thomas Raikes had feared that such a sum could not be raised "after the endless applications that have been made by [Brummell] to his old friends since he left England," Armstrong set about his task "as a man of business . . . unembarrassed by any feelings of delicacy." This direct and brutally honest approach worked. Lord Alvanley and Worcester naturally subscribed more money. But so, too, did the king, William IV, who was approached by General Upton and Sir Herbert Taylor after Armstrong had come knocking. General Upton had been the lover of Amy Dubochet, Harriette Wilson's sister, when they had all danced together at the Argyle Rooms. The Duke of Devonshire, Lord Sefton, General Grosvenor, Colonel Howard, Colonel Dawson-Damer, Mr. Greville, Mr. Chester and Mr. Standish, former dandies to a man, all contributed. Lord Palmerston, once a member of the circle himself, was presented with a draft of a letter that would give official compensation from the government to Brummell for loss of the consulship:

> July 1835
> My Lords,
> On a Revision of the Consular Establishment in the early past the year 1832, I found that the British Consulate at Caen in Normandy might be abolished without prejudice to the Service; and that the salary of £400 a year, assigned to that Post, might be saved to the Publick [sic].
>
> This reduction was accordingly carried into effect and Consul Brummell's salary ceased on the 31st May 1832. Subsequently to that Period I have received various representations [via Lord Alvanley and Charles Armstrong among others] from Mr Brummell stating the pecuniary difficulties into which he was plunged by the suddenness of the abolition of his consulship—the stopping of his Salary; and requesting that some sort of pecuniary assistance might be granted to enable him to effect his Release from Prison.

Palmerston deleted "to enable him to effect his Release from Prison" and wrote instead simply "him." It was the gentlemanly thing to do.

Mr Brummell's case appearing to be one of great hardship, I venture to recommend to your Lordship's favourable consideration the grant of a Gratuity, equal to Half a year's salary [i.e., £200] as Compensation to Mr Brummell on the Abolition of his Office as HM's Consul at Caen, which he had held upwards of two years.

Palmerston changed the last words to "nearly three," then initialed the draft to be written up and submitted. Armstrong was able to add the £200 to his fund, paid by the treasury.

On the morning of July 21, 1835, Monsieur Youf, an attorney who worked in the courthouse next door, entered the room Brummell shared with Godefroi and another prisoner named Bresnily each day, notified Brummell that Leveux's debt had been cleared and that he was free to go. Brummell took the news calmly, showing not "the slightest surprise or joy, or indeed any emotion whatever." He spent the afternoon packing his few things and at five o'clock walked out onto the *terrasse* of the prison overlooking the Place Fontette, a free man. Godefroi had said good-bye to him back in the *chambre des prisonniers civils,* Lépine showed him to the *guichets* (gate). Despite his complaints about the food sent to prison by the Hôtel d'Angleterre, he nevertheless returned to room 29, the third-floor suite. His bill had been paid, and Armstrong had pointed out to Monsieur Fichet the potentially beneficial attraction to English tourists of the hotel's celebrated guest.

Brummell immediately changed for dinner. There was a large soiree that evening at General Corbet's home, and he decided to make an entrance back into Caen society with as much panache as he could muster. Because his release had been so sudden, his appearance made a distinct impact. He strode to the center of Corbet's salon as all the company stood and applauded. With "an air of nonchalance," as he might have adopted in his King's Theatre box, he thanked the company for their good wishes and said, "Today is the happiest day of my life; because I have been released from prison," then added, "and because we have salmon for dinner."

In Caen as in London, it was felt that after Brummell's prison experience he was never quite the same again. If they had not realized it already, his London friends now accepted that they would have to support him for the rest of his life, and only hoped he would find ways to economize. The British community in Caen, and the many French with whom Brummell socialized, were more aware of his continuing physical deterioration, and that imprisonment seemed to have "shaken his intellect." The reappraisal of Brummell's image in contemporaries' minds was compounded by a sketch he had made that was shown around Caen, much to Brummell's embarrassment. It was one of the many sentimental drawings he sent with letters to friends, Aimable in particular. It depicted Cupid, a frequent motif in Brummell's artwork, having apparently discarded a broken arrow. Brummell titled it "The broken ~~Beau~~ Bow!"

Though it may have been given to Ellen Villiers, the Villiers's daughter, it seems more likely that the recipient again was Aimable—as it was offered to "your album" in the letter that accompanied it. Brummell was mortified that others were allowed to see it. Fresh from the dishonor of prison, he did not want to be an object of pity, and the piece may have had more particular meaning. The "ridiculous words [of the title] were written in a moment of haste," he said, "and with no other idea than being laughed at by *you* . . . not to be seen by others." But the "ridiculous" title was only part of the embarrassment: the picture held other meanings. It is a finely and delicately wrought piece by an accomplished copyist (Jesse even used it as a frontispiece to his chronicle of Brummell's life and letters). So it can be no accident that Cupid's hands are drawn as claws. The mythic messenger of desire claws at his own soft chest flesh while gazing pensively at his broken bow and arrow. Aimable had every right to feel a little shocked and embarrassed.

The gift of the "broken Beau" sketch and the letters that accompanied it are among the last Brummell seems to have written to Aimable after her return from England. Her extended family had largely left Caen, and it seemed likely that her life would take her elsewhere, too. Brummell gave her more sketches for her collection—as the last of the many gifts he had bestowed on her.

Brummell was fifty-seven, but looked much older. He had been bald for years, and may well have lost his eyebrows to the syphilitic alopecia. Another drawing of the period, most likely by Jesse himself and signed by Brummell, shows him as an old man, with a tidy top hat but a shaggy overcoat. He appears to be toothless. He had begun to shuffle when he was out walking. At first this was taken as a sign of his fastidiousness: an attempt to avoid the dirt of the street as he had so few clothes and a restricted laundry budget. He instructed friends to walk a few paces away from him, to avoid splashes. But the condition grew worse, and the man who had once had the "best figure in England" began to stoop.

"*Tabes dorsalis*" was the term given to the wasting damage to the nerves in the spinal cord caused by syphilis. It took many years from the initial syphilitic infection to reach the spinal nerves, and even then the effect was slow. There is a slight loss of position sense and progressive inability to coordinate bodily movements; almost invariably it affects gait. The sense of having unusual sensations haunted "tabetics." Stiffness of gait progressed to a wide-based stumbling, zigzag pattern of walking, sometimes with the dragging of a foot. Symptoms also included joint pains that could only be alleviated with heat, and incorrect perception of temperature changes. Brummell, who had spent his prison months huddled up to Godefroi's fire claiming he was cold, now had syphilis attacking the nerves of his lower limbs and back.

In 1836, a Cambridge undergraduate happened to be staying at the Hôtel d'Angleterre, where Brummell was pointed out to him in the dining room. He could not believe what he was being told. "The very quiet, very refined elderly gentleman to whom some of the guests and all of the servants of the house seemed to pay unusual attention" was the great Beau Brummell. He looked, wrote the student, "poor indeed."

After the first few months out of prison his old spending habits began to creep back. He had agreed with Armstrong and his English benefactors to adhere to strict economy, and "brought himself down to one complete change of linen [only]" per day. But he still ordered fresh primrose yellow kid gloves regularly and expensive macassar oil for his wig, and shoe blacking.

Armstrong began to insist on the most severe economy. He

made it known around Caen that he would pay bills on Brummell's behalf only if he had agreed to the expenditure in the first place. He limited Brummell's shirt linens and laundry expenses, and after this it was said that "a great change took place in his personal appearance": Brummell ceased to wear his trademark white cravat. In mourning for his lost fortune and fashionability, he took to wearing black. Though much commented on in Caen, this was in truth Brummell's acceptance that fashion had moved on. Black stocks and cravats were eminently practical—especially, it was said, for snuff takers—and the preformed black stock would become accepted city wear throughout Europe and America by the middle of the century.

The rest of his wardrobe was deteriorating, and it gave Brummell as much pain as it aroused comment from those who saw him. He appealed to Armstrong on this point, but was met with practical, rather than dandy solutions. When Armstrong sent him a new winter dressing gown not made of shawl, as was considered gentlemanly, but of toweling cotton, Brummell threw it from his third-floor window at the Hôtel d'Angleterre. It nearly caused an accident on the rue St. Jean.

Armstrong, the Burtons and the Marquise de Séran all noted his continuing deterioration. At first it was small things. He repeated himself. He would tell anecdotes everyone knew already, "drawling with prolixity." He frequently forgot who he was speaking to, which sometimes caused embarrassment though equally sometimes led to comedy. While he was still on the side of confusion that is called eccentricity, he was happily suffered by his Caen hosts. He told the anxious mother of a teenage girl not to worry about her daughter as she was "too plain for anyone to run off with her." He commented loudly, and in unflattering terms, about the menu at a dinner party, thinking he was at the table d'hôte of the hotel. The hostess burst into tears, but the guests thought it was funny. He was asked not to attend the philharmonic as he moved his jaw constantly, and not in time to the music. Mrs. Burton was asked why she continued to invite "the old driveller." "He is never in our way," she explained, "and though it is true he is no longer the amusing character he used to be, I like to see him take his seat before my fire." But the invitations around town, inevitably, dried up.

In July 1837, General Corbet asked him for dinner, but only because Brummell's old friend Tom Moore was in town, along with his grown son. "The poor Beau's head's gone," wrote Moore, "and his whole looks so changed that I never should have recognised him. Got wandering in his conversation more than once at dinner."

He went out less, and his social contact narrowed, which accelerated his mental deterioration. Without the necessity to dress, he would sometimes stay all day in the hotel in his dressing gown. And when his trousers needed mending, he was forced to stay indoors, as by 1837 he had only one pair. The tailor, to whom Brummell had given much business when he first came as consul, took in his clothes and "mended them for nothing." "I was ashamed," the tailor explained in French to Jesse, "to see so famous and distinguished a man, who had created a place for himself in history, in so unhappy a state." It was slightly easier for Brummell in winter. His long fur-topped overcoat had survived well and covered everything else, and in this, he could more easily venture out.

Like his old friend George IV, he took more and more to the sweet comfort of maraschino brandy, a luxury, of course, denied him by Armstrong. He begged it anyway from Madame Magdelaine, who kept the café on the rue St. Jean opposite the Hôtel d'Angleterre. She gave him every day at 2:00 P.M. a single glass of maraschino, and a *biscuit de Rheims* to dip into it. Brummell would sit watching the traffic over the Pont Vaucelles and waving to strangers with a little movement of his fingers "like Charles X." Monsieur Magdelaine eventually noticed what was going on, and asked Brummell to pay up. He was forced to pawn some of the valuables Armstrong had saved for him: his vases and his gold watch. But Brummell's maraschino habit kept up, and Magdelaine ended up with Brummell's gold ring, his gold watch chain and his last silver snuff box.

Brummell was again a sight on the streets as he had been in

Mayfair, stared at and pointed out, but for all the wrong reasons. An English schoolboy on holiday in the town wrote a cruel ditty that somehow found its way into Jesse's collection:

> Keen blows the wind, and piercing is the cold,
> My pins are weak, and I am growing old.
> Alas! Alas! Which wind and rain do beat.
> That great Beau Brummell should so walk the
>   street!

Brummell continued to solicit better care and attention from Armstrong, which meant, in effect, more money. Armstrong said he could not continue to act on Brummell's behalf if Brummell kept up his habit of also writing direct appeals to London. It became an issue of control as much as money. Elsewhere in France, Brummell's old friend Scrope Davies had been worrying about his own deteriorating condition. He knew from his doctor that his depression was likely to be "a precursor of . . . [syphilitic] derangement." "Lethargic days and sleepless nights," he wrote, "have reduced me to a state of nervous irritability . . . At present I must visit nobody and strictly follow the advice which [my doctor] gave me . . . Of all uncertainties, the uncertain continuance of reason is the most dreadful."

Similarly Brummell, while arranging practicalities with Armstrong, was intermittently aware that something was terribly wrong. In public he continued to blame prison, which he likened to a "knock on the head." In the semiprivacy of the hotel, he must have been aware that his mind was deteriorating. He was behaving very strangely. His confusion was inconsistent and alternated with extreme mania, when he would order staff around, and frantically obsess about his clothes. Then he would realize, quite suddenly, where he was and what was going on: that he was not in Mayfair, and no longer a dandy.

Tabes dorsalis had been the precursor with Brummell of something more alarming and psychologically bizarre. Just before the onset of full-blown tertiary syphilis and the dementia that attends it, something exotic was observed to happen to the mind:

Right before madness [writes one authority on the disease] the syphilitic was often rewarded in a kind of Faustian bargain for enduring the pain and despair, by episodes of creative euphoria; electrified, joyous energy . . . dazzling insights and almost mystical insights . . . mood shifts become more extreme as euphoria, electric excitement, bursts of creative energy, and grandiose self-reflections alternate with severe, often suicidal depression. Delusions of grandeur, paranoia, exaltation, irritability, rages and irrational, antisocial behaviour define the progress to insanity. The patient may suddenly begin to . . . imagine owning vast riches. A calm person becomes emotional, a neat person sloppy . . . Here the condition is often misdiagnosed as paranoid persecutory psychosis or schizophrenia.

For all these reasons, the detailed descriptions of Brummell's last months at the Hôtel d'Angleterre, given to Jesse and Count d'Aurevilly by the hotel staff, can be read now as textbook examples of incipient general paresis: syphilitic dementia.

While instruction was still clear and possible and Brummell appeared to be in command of his faculties, he began to hold soirees at the Hôtel d'Angleterre. At first Fichet and his staff were bemused, as they knew his social circle had shrunk, but they accepted orders for candles and flowers for Brummell's room. "On these gala evenings," Jesse was informed by hotel staff, "some strange fancy would seize him." He would rearrange the furniture and even set out a whist table.

Suddenly, and as if divided into two, he announced in a loud voice the Prince of Wales, then Lady Conyngham, then Lord Yarmouth, then all the high personages of England for whom he had been the living law; and imagining them to appear as he announced them, and changing his voice, he went to the doors to receive them; the open double doors of the empty salon through which, alas, no one was to pass on this or any other evening. And he saluted these chimeras of his imagination, offered his arm to the women of this company of phantoms he had called up and who would certainly not have cared to leave their tombs for one instant to attend the fallen Dandy's rout.

Later he trained the Fichet family to announce these phantom guests for him. They were, naturally enough, appalled but fascinated. Fichet would announce carriages at 10:00, and so end the macabre pantomime. On other occasions, the party ended earlier, when Brummell realized that his mind and memory had played a cruel trick on him. The contrast between nostalgic fantasy and present reality would reduce him to tears: "Finally, when the room was full of these ghosts and when all the company had arrived from the other world, reason suddenly re-asserted itself, and the unhappy creature perceived his illusion and madness. And then he would fall stricken into one of the solitary chairs, and would be discovered weeping."

The Fichets coped with the phantom galas. So long as Brummell's declining mental health stayed within the bounds they thought acceptable, his life could continue at the hotel, and on balance they were remarkably accommodating. But then Brummell had a series of falls that meant he required constant supervision. These seem to have taken place very late in 1837. He collapsed once in the street, on his way back from the chemist, and once in his room. At first an old woman was posted to keep an eye on him in room 29, but Brummell took an immense dislike to her—even in his confusion—and she was replaced by a former army corporal called François, who was strict with him, "but kindly."

Jesse was told by François that, by the summer of 1838, "Brummell's imbecility was complete." He sat obsessively combing his wig, he raged incoherently at times and at others was quiet for hours at a time. He destroyed a great number of letters and effects "from royal personages" and billets "[enclosing] silken tresses." He had a raging appetite, but was refused a place at the *table d'hôte* in the hotel's restaurant as he was considered "injurious to himself" and in a "deplorable state of person."

Late in the summer of 1838, Brummell became doubly incontinent, the effect of the advanced tabetic attack on his spinal nerves. He was aware of what was happening, and tried to blame the mess, and the smell in his room, on the hotel's dog, a pointer called Stop. In October, the Fichets told Armstrong they could not cope any longer. In November, Armstrong wrote to London, probably to Alvanley:

I have deferred writing for some time, hoping to be able to inform you that I had succeeded in getting Mr Brummell into one of the public institutions . . . They will not keep him at the hotel, and what to do I know not: I should think that some of his old friends in England would be able to get him into some hospital, where he could be taken care of for the rest of his days.

Still nothing happened through the Christmas season of 1838–1839. François seems to have left the employ of the hotel, and Brummell, other than occasional visits from the Anglican curate, was left lying on a soiled straw mattress in the corner of room 29. "His linen," Jesse was informed, "was changed once a month."

~

In January 1839, Armstrong and Fichet came together to room 29. They found Brummell sitting in his dressing gown, with his wig on his lap. Rather than tending it with oil, as was his usual obsession, he had worked up a lather in a shaving bowl, and was painting the foam onto it.

"*Bonjour, Monsieur!*" said Fichet

"*Laissez moi tranquille!*" replied Brummell.

Jesse continues his record of the scene, from Fichet's memory of it, in English: "But I have ordered a carriage for you to take a drive with me. You promised that you would go, and the carriage is now at the door."

Brummell said he was not well and did not wish to go.

Armstrong and Fichet then said what a lovely day it was for a ride. Brummell still refused. Fichet lost his temper, grabbed the wig, which had fixed Brummell's attention, and threw it across the room. The scene degenerated into a brawl. Armstrong and Fichet, possibly with the help of Fichet's son and others, bundled Brummell down the three flights to the rue St. Jean. "He kicked and fought as violently as his swollen legs and reduced strength would permit; screaming and shouting at the top of his voice, 'You are taking me to prison—I have done nothing.' " And then, according to Fichet, "a shriek followed that was heard at the end of the court."

Within minutes of being in the carriage, somewhere at the top of the rue St. Jean where it turns into the rue St. Pierre, Brummell suddenly calmed. He saw an acquaintance he recognized, but explained to Armstrong, "I did not bow to him, for I am not fit to be seen in such a dishabille as this."

His mood changed just as swiftly as the large iron doors of Bon Sauveur asylum shut behind him, and he "wept bitterly, muttering, 'A prison, a prison,' " but a nun took him by the hand and somewhere his old courtly manners came to his rescue: *"Vous êtes bien une jolie femme,"* he said, and she led him into his new room.

18

ASYLUM

1839–1840

It's like being bound hand and foot in the bottom of a deep dark well. Fear. White moss in the mouth. Sweet thick hair falls to the floor, gleaming patches of scalp in the candlelight. Salve: mercury mixed with rosewater, honey, liquorice, conserve of rose petals, lard. I rub it everywhere . . . I smell like fried potato . . . Tongue like an ox . . . Saliva gushes like a river, teeth rattle, and rot, penis the colour of slate.

> Portrait of a nineteenth-century syphilitic

Babylon in all its desolation is a sight not so awful as that of the human mind in ruins. It is a firmament without a sun, a temple without a God. I have survived most of my friends; Heaven forbid I should survive myself . . . The dead are less to be deplored than the insane.

> Scrope Davies to Thomas Raikes

The Abbé Jamet had been receiving lunatics into the former Capuchin convent at l'Hôpital du Bon Sauveur since 1818. He was considered fashionably progressive in his treatments of the insane, and Bon Sauveur was expanding to meet the growing demand in early-nineteenth-century France for secular treatments for the disabled and the mentally ill.

Founded originally in 1723 at St. Lô by an aristocratic nun called Anne Leroy and intended for deranged and fallen women, the convent had been suppressed during the Revolution and not re-founded until 1804. In 1806 it had again begun to admit patients: fifteen women. They were to be cared for by twenty-one Sisters of Charity, some lay workers and Abbé Pierre-François Jamet. From 1820, the new Bon Sauveur accepted men.

Abbé Jamet had an amateur interest in the new sciences of the mind and body, and in hydrotherapy. He was also considered a "financial gymnast" and secured for the convent an eighteen-hectare site on the outskirts of Caen, surrounding the original Capuchin convent, which happened to have a tributary of the Orne River flowing through it. Bon Sauveur, with its sympathetic regime and modish water therapies, attracted patients from all over Normandy and even beyond. It specialized in the treatment of the deaf and dumb, as well as all those who were, in the terminology of the time, classed *"aliené"*: "deranged."

By modern standards the huge site was bleakly institutional, but to a town like Caen—which only a generation before had kept lunatics in dungeons, and fed them with scraps thrown down by passers-by—Bon Sauveur looked paradisiacal. It was dominated by a cathedral-like chapel and fifty-foot bell tower, and many of the elegant pavilions had four stories. The windows, however, were all barred.

Bon Sauveur had continued over the years to take in "fallen" women—often pregnant, unmarried girls—as well as the blind, deaf, disabled and disturbed, and together they tended vegetable and flower beds. When Brummell entered, there were between six and seven hundred inmates. Bon Sauveur had grown in the twenty years it had been accepting both sexes to be the third-largest asylum in France. But there was still only one doctor. According to Brummell's surviving medical records—kept in the institution that operates as an asylum to this day—he was seen once every two months by Dr. Vastel.

The Sisters of Charity who ran Bon Sauveur had a reputation for kindliness. The grounds were enormous and the scale of the new site, which the mother superior had described in 1818 as "salubrious and well aired," had encouraged an ambitious building program. Bon Sauveur boasted that none of its inmates were in dormitories, but "each madman has his own cell . . . [being] quieter and cleaner in isolated rooms." Bourienne, previously Napoleon's secretary, had found benign sanctuary at Bon Sauveur in the closing years of his life, and Destouches, who inspired Count d'Aurevilly's most famous novel, *Le Chevalier des Touches,* was also incarcerated there.

All classes were represented at the asylum, but on the whole they did not mix. The sexes were separated, and so, too, were broad classes of inmates, defined socially as well as medically; those considered *"tranquilles"* were separated from the *"semi-tranquilles"* and *"épileptiques"* from *"les malpropres, les gâteux et les agités"*— the unclean, depraved and disturbed. Because of Brummell's incontinence and erratic behavior, Armstrong had feared he would be placed with the common incurables in the notorious *cachets* and *cabanons,* or chained and isolated cells. But a little extra money, as well as Brummell's local celebrity, found him a room of his own, with a view—one of the finest in the asylum. Brummell was unaware that the locked chamber in which he was placed—just off the gardens in the Pavilion St. Joseph—was the one in which Bourienne had died a few years before. Here he was attended almost constantly, and remained, mainly, calm.

Surprisingly, quite a lot is known about the daily routine for inmates. An unusual statement of intent written at the asylum has survived from just before the law of 1838, which gives an indication of the regime Brummell faced at Bon Sauveur. Though some items are missing, it is stated that the means of treatment should be ordered accordingly:

1. A total "rupture" from normality and the acceptance of the necessity of obedience . . . is the first means of treatment . . . isolation is one way.
2. [missing]

3. Warm baths, not daily except to begin with, but always frequent—the head being refreshed with light showering, constitutes the principal and greatest means of treatment, with very rare exceptions.

4. Manual occupations like gardening, the care of the [Bon Sauveur] farm, laundry, help given to the wardens, can be of very great aid in the treatment of the working classes.

5. Walking and carriage riding, excursions to the countryside, billiards and music will replace manual work for those of our inmates whose social position or infirmity makes such exercise unsalutary.

6. [missing]

7. [missing]

8. We have no special medication for the treatment of insanity. The drug we use most often however is valerian water [a sedative] which despite its unpleasant odour is quite happily accepted by our inmates.

9. Moral care; kindness and distraction; the example of a religious and regulated life.

Brummell, suffering tertiary syphilis, would undoubtedly have had some of his more distressing physical symptoms alleviated by Bon Sauveur's water treatments. He was in no physical state to join the flower bed–digging detachments, but in any case his class precluded this: Armstrong had made it clear in signing him over to the Bon Sauveur authorities that *"Brummell, Georges, célibataire"* was *"ex Consul de Sa Majesté Britannique."*

Life in the asylum was run with strict discipline. Even in 1839, it was, in theory, controlled by the doctor, Edouard Vastel, who was not answerable to Abbé Jamet or the mother superior, and it was under his supervision that the nuns and lay workers structured the daily lives of inmates.

Brummell was woken each day at 5:30. He was allowed an extra half hour in bed through the winter of 1839–1840. One of the Sisters of Charity would check his bed linen in case it had been soiled during the night, and then he would be encouraged, with the help of a nun, to make his own bed.

He had the right to a weekly shave by the asylum barber, but had brought his dressing case with him: Armstrong knew what was important to Brummell even in his confusion.

A half hour after the inmates were woken, breakfast was served in one of the large refectories—there was one for each social class. It was considered important to get them out of their rooms, and in this time the lay staff had the unpleasant task of emptying chamber pots and commodes.

A prayer was "said in full voice" before each meal—a return to school for Brummell—and the nuns served café au lait and bread.

At 7:00 there was Mass, but it was not obligatory, and it is highly unlikely Brummell attended.

The only palliative Bon Sauveur could offer syphilitics was water treatment. Recent studies at the Hôpital des Vénériens in Paris under Dr. Philip Ricord had recommended frequent alkaline and mercurial baths for cases like Brummell's. These involved adding to a "tubful of warm water . . . two pounds of glue . . . two pounds of subcarbonate of potash and half an ounce of corrosive sublimate." He also recommended turpentine, lead plaster, lavender oil, hyssop and wormwood, followed by bathing.

Dr. Vastel at Bon Sauveur recognized in Brummell the symptoms of meningeal syphilis, which presented with headaches, nausea, vomiting, cranial nerve palsies and seizures, as well as personality changes and memory loss. Brummell's was a classic case. Meningovascular syphilis, specifically, from which Brummell was clearly suffering, begins with headaches, insomnia and psychological abnormalities. Facial strokes are a key signifier. The catalogue of symptoms explained to Vastel by Dr. Kelly would have alerted him to this diagnosis in Brummell, and for this reason—there was no test possible—he recorded after his examination on February 2, 1839 that Brummell was suffering "dementia and general paralysis." He was not paralyzed in the physical sense: the term was used to express the wider effect of the syphilis attacking the meninges, the membranous wrappings about the brain and spinal cord. General paralysis, or general paresis, the terms used interchangeably at this time in France as in England, was believed—correctly, as it turned out—to be the final stage of a syphilitic infection. Once the disease attacked the central nervous system, the mercury therapies were regarded as ineffectual. There was no cure, and Vastel would have known that the signs of infection in the brain meant that Brummell's decline would be fast and devastating, both physically and psychologically.

The insane gentlefolk were expected to sit in the ornamental gardens and sew or sketch. Brummell had little ability left to do either. His iritis was well advanced now, and it is unlikely that he could distinguish colors at all. Some would even have been painful for him to gaze upon.

He was wheeled up and down the graveled walkways of the gardens in an "easy chair." The nuns and staff whom Jesse interviewed gave the best possible impression of Brummell's mood and his time in the asylum, as well they might, and said he was rarely left alone. When he was visited by a Caen friend—possibly Mr. or Mrs. Burton—he claimed that "this excellent nurse of mine [one of the nuns] is so kind to me that she refuses me nothing; I have all I wish to eat and such a large fire; I was never so comfortable in my life."

On the whole and for many of the inmates, including Brummell, Bon Sauveur offered balm to tortured minds and bodies. But the asylum archives make it evident that not everyone was compliant all the time, and it is unlikely, given the advanced state of his dementia, that Brummell was always the "docile patient" the nuns later spoke of.

Jesse and d'Aurevilly both allude to degradations so awful that even mention of them would be unpalatable, and it is likely that both writers knew of the advanced state of Brummell's syphilis in Bon Sauveur, and the more extreme remedial treatments he suffered.

Bon Sauveur straitjacketed three percent of its inmates at any given time, and had force-feeding implements for those no longer able or willing to partake of its famously nutritious soups. It also had a row of isolation cells, "cabanons," which were the first mentioned item on the statute of remedies for the noncompliant. These were reserved for the "violent, mutinous, chronically deranged and those who used profane invective or were sexually exhibitionist." They were much used at night, though it was barely possible to lie down. There was straw on the floor and an open latrine hole in one corner.

As the disease took its final hold on Brummell's brain and body, the symptoms became increasingly distressing. Syphilitics who survived well into the tertiary phase, as Brummell did, suffered facial paralysis and quivering, as well as loss of bladder and bowel control. Their teeth fell out, if they had not already, as did their nails. Eventually Brummell's tongue would have swollen, turned black and cracked and this stage was accompanied almost invariably in male cases by large testicular tumors and scrotal ulcers. All the mucous membranes of Brummell's body would then have ulcerated: his throat, tonsils, gums and nostrils. Doctors spoke of the particular smell associated with tertiary syphilis: a sweet smell of decay, not unlike the mercury and rosewater ointments that had previously held the disease at bay, or like "fried potatoes." The bones ached unremittingly, which was often misattributed as rheumatism, as it was with Brummell. At night the deep bone pains were excruciating. The brain itself shrank away from the insides of the skull and granulated. "Gummy tumours" (now called gummas) developed in the legs and large unbleeding buboes—or swollen glands—opened spontaneously on the limbs. Sufferers of advanced tertiary syphilis like Brummell could survive many months like this, with the syphilitic pallida well advanced in the brain and flowering as weeping thymus ulcers in every sensitive part of the body.

The indignities and horrors of which Jesse and d'Aurevilly spoke were the final stages of tertiary syphilis, when Brummell, alternately raving and quivering like a lost soul, and most likely covered in sores, was hosed down in *cabanon* when the staff could no longer bear to touch him. Sufferers like Brummell remained intermittently conscious: their confusion alternated with recurrent patches of complete lucidity, clarity and an awareness of their pain and what was happening to them, which was, in a sense, the cruelest thing of all.

The summer and autumn of 1839 passed with some less bad days in the midst of these horrors. There were moments of relative calm. Brummell was visited by some of his Caen friends, though he did not recognize them. Just once he realized who Fichet was and immediately ordered a place at dinner for that evening: *"Table d'hôte toujours à cinq heures? Très bien, très bien, je descendrai."* His condition stabilized a little through the winter, but he declined steeply through the early months of 1840. Dr. Vastel noted that he was "sinking further and further." Armstrong and the Burtons visited and, in his professional capacity, the Anglican pastor. Jesse does not name him, but the local records make it clear that this was the Reverend Martin Rollin. Brummell seems not to have attended the "Temple Protestant" in Caen, but Rollin had taken to visiting him in the final months he spent at the Hôtel d'Angleterre, finding that Brummell, like the character in *Granby,* "thought religion was a good thing, and ought to be kept up, and that, like cheap soup, it was excellent for the poor." Rollin was unsympathetic to Brummell's plight, and frustrated in his attempts to persuade Brummell to repent for past sins:

Mr Brummell was in an imbecile state . . . incapable of remembering any occurrence five minutes together; but occasionally recalling some anecdote of days long since passed. Mr Brummell appeared quite incapable of conversing on religious subjects. I failed in every attempt to lead his mind—if he can be said to have retained any power of mind—to their consideration. I never, in all the course of my attendance upon the sick, aged and dying, came in contact with so painful an exhibition of human vanity and apparent ignorance, and thoughtlessness, of and respecting a future state; for I have before visited persons whose mental powers were equally shattered, but still it was possible to touch some chord connected with religion . . . with him there was some response, when sounded on worldly subjects; none on religious—until a few hours before he died, when in reply to my repeated entreaties that he would try and pray, he said, "I do try," but he added something which made me doubt whether he understood me.

The dying man was granted almost permanent supervision. The epilepsy-like seizures had become more frequent. When they came, he needed restraint. He shook almost constantly.

On Monday, March 30, 1840, the weather changed suddenly for the better: it had rained almost daily since January, but the sun shone, and Brummell was taken out into the garden. Just after the hour when he should have been sleeping, the nun in attendance noticed something in his manner she had not seen before:

The debility having become extreme [she told Jesse], I observed him assume an appearance of intense anxiety and fear, and he fixed his eyes upon me, with an expression of entreaty, raising his hands towards me, as he lay in the bed, and as though asking for assistance *(ayant l'air d'implorer que je vienne à son secours)* but saying nothing. Upon this, I requested him to repeat after me the *acte de contrition* of the Roman ritual, as in our prayer books. He immediately consented, and repeated after me in an earnest manner *(un air pénétré)* that form of prayer. He then became more composed, and laid down his head on one side; but this tranquility was interrupted, about an hour after, by his turning himself over, and uttering a cry, at the same time appearing to be in pain; he soon, however, turned himself back, with his face laid on the pillow towards the wall, so as to be hidden from us who were on the side. After this he never moved, dying imperceptibly.

It was a quarter past nine in the evening. Brummell was not yet sixty-two years of age.

∼

The records of the Protestant cemetery in Caen do not relate who paid for Brummell to be buried. His funeral and the small plot, two square meters only, conceded to his body in perpetuity, cost a hundred francs. The space allowed only six feet in length, which was inadequate for Brummell and may have been the reason an extra fifty francs was paid without the usual guarantee of having a stone tended for twenty years. It is likely, but unproved, that Armstrong and the local lodge of Masons put up the money for the coffin and cemetery plot. The local undertaker had frequent requests for lead coffins to repatriate bodies to England, but this was not suggested for Brummell. Armstrong went to record Brummell's death at the Hôtel de Ville, as both friend and vice consul, but did not go to the burial, which, it is related, was attended only by Rollin. As the body passed by without mourners, a girl on the rue St. Pierre asked: *"Qui est-ce? Un pauvre fou?"*

"Un pauvre fou," replied her mother. *"Un certain Brummell."*

Notes on Sources

Full publishing details of the items cited or quoted are provided in the bibliography. Translations are the author's own unless otherwise stated. The rare 1844 first edition of Captain Jesse's *A Life of George Bryan Brummell, Esq.* has been cited whenever possible. Some letters and some of Jesse's own interpolations are quoted from the 1854, 1886 and from the 1927 Navarre Society editions, and the references alter accordingly. The following abbreviations are used in the notes:

ADCC   Archives Départementales du Calvados, Caen
AMC   Archives Municipales de Caen
BL   British Library
DNB   *Dictionary of National Biography*
MLCC   Museum of London Costume Collection
OED   *Oxford English Dictionary*
PRO   National Archives (Kew), Public Records Office
RA   Royal Archives, Windsor Castle

FRONTMATTER EPIGRAPH

vii   "Much more than the cult of": Camus, A., *L'Homme Révolté*; "Bien plus que le culte de l'individu, le romantisme inaugure le culte du personage."

PROLOGUE

xiii   "Nothing was lacking. Lustres, candelabra": J. B. d'Aurevilly, trans. D. B. Wyndham Lewis, *The Anatomy of Dandyism*, p. 60n.

xiv   "Room 29 was at the top": AMC, *Extrait du Plan de l'Hôtel d'Angleterre, Troisième Étage*. The front rooms of the hotel were numbers 29–33 in a plan that may postdate Brummell's era at the hotel: it is possible, therefore, that the room numbers had changed over the years. However, room 29 was, in effect, the only suite of two rooms on the third floor, which tallies with Kathleen Campbell's description from the later 1930s, before the hotel was destroyed. "They still show the room with pride. It seems painfully small and dark, and the tiny dressing room will hold no more than a chest of drawers," K. Campbell, *Beau Brummell*, p. 172.

xiv "Babylon in all its desolation": T. Raikes, *A Portion of his Journal from 1831–1847*, vol. 2, pp. 113ff. Letter from Scrope Davies, Monday, May 25, 1835: Davies appears to be writing about his own impending symptoms of tertiary syphilis, as diagnosed by Sir George Tuthill.

xv "The Frenchman would then blow out the candles": Details of Brummell's last soirée are taken from a note in d'Aurevilly's *Du Dandysme*, as well as from Jesse's *Life*. D'Aurevilly appears to be deploying an anecdote he collected in Caen from the staff of the Hôtel d'Angleterre that he had intended for use in a biography of Brummell; the note spills over three pages of the text. D'Aurevilly, trans. D. B. Wyndham Lewis, *The Anatomy of Dandyism*, pp. 59–61n; Jesse, *A Life of George Brummell, Esq.*, 1927, vol. 2, pp. 244–5.

INTRODUCTION

3 "If the world is so silly": D. Castronovo, *The English Gentleman*, p. 98.

3 "If three things sum up": J. B. d'Aurevilly, trans. G. Walden, *Who's a Dandy?*, pp. 15–16.

4 "But long before our time . . . *in his person*": d'Aurevilly, trans. D. B. Wyndham Lewis, *The Anatomy of Dandyism*, p. 32 (my italics).

4 "cold, heartless and satirical": H. Wilson, *Memoirs*, 1831, vol. 1, p. 100.

4 "the most admired man": W. Jesse, *A Life of George Brummell Esq.*, 1844, vol. 1, pp. 141ff.

5 "If John Bull [Everyman] turns around": H. Wilson, *Memoirs of Harriette Wilson*, 1831, vol. I, p. 100.

13 "satellite to the great": Lord William Pitt Lennox, *Celebrities I Have Known*, vol. 2, pp. 92–4.

14 More than a third of the 1844: L. Melville, *Beau Brummell*, p. xi. The original letters were in the possession of Mr. J. Preston Beecher, vice consul in Le Havre in the 1920s. Brummell's *Male and Female Costume*, dated 1822, was owned by Messrs. E. Parsons and Sons, 43 Brompton Road, London, in the 1920s, but sold and published in New York in the 1930s.

15 It forms an invaluable foundation: G. Brummell, *Male and Female Costume*. "In the fall of 1924 I bought an old manuscript, Male and Female Costume . . . It was listed as an original, unpublished manuscript by G. B. Brummell. It is bound in two volumes and dated 1822": Eleanor Parker in the preface to the 1931 edition. Lewis Melville had noted the existence of the treatise and been allowed access to it by Messr. E. Parsons for his *Beau Brummell*.

17 "that Frivolity could show": J. B. d'Aurevilly, trans. G. Walden, *Who's a Dandy?*, p. 95.

Part I: Ascendancy, 1778–1799

I: BLESSED ARE THE PLACEMAKERS, 1778–1786

24 "number 10 or number 11 Downing Street": BL Add Manuscripts 41335 380m. The records of the Brummell boys' baptisms, kept at Westminster Abbey but from the register of St. Margaret's, Westminster, give no place of birth. The records do not contain reference to Maria, or to the Brummell parents' wedding. Although, by 1786, the Brummells seem to have had an address on Abingdon Street, Westminster, they are referred to as living on Downing Street at late as 1780. The likelihood therefore remains that George was born in Downing Street, not Abingdon Street as is sometimes stated. On his certificate of admission to the Masonic Lodge in Caen, his place of birth is cited as "Witchall, cité de Westminster" (Whitehall).

26 "Their mother visited the studio on March 22": D. Mannings and M. Postle, *Sir Joshua Reynolds. A Complete Catalogue of His Paintings,* Cat. 269.

26 "These two paintings": J. Bryan, *Kenwood,* Cats. 48 and 83.

27 "Mary Robinson, known to history": P. Byrne, *Perdita,* pp. 184ff.

28 built only twenty years before: N. Pevsner, *The Buildings of England,* pp. 128–9; *Country Life,* 124 (September 18, 1958), pp. 588–91 (September 25, 1958), pp. 654–7 (October 2, 1958), pp. 714–17. The house may have been built as early as 1759, but a date of 1763 seems more likely.

29 realigning the old Bagnor and Lambourn: *History of Newbury,* 1839, p. 171.

29 "Chippendale Gothic": N. Pevsner, *The Buildings of England,* pp. 128–9.

29 "wit and humour": W. Smyth, *Memoir of Mr Sheridan,* p. 65.

30 There was shooting and riding: Recent archaeological digs as a result of the Newbury bypass (A34) and for English Heritage have uncovered a wealth of musket shot from the period, but also livery buttons predating their mass production in the later nineteenth century. Archaeological reports held at Donnington Grove, pp. 9 and 11. English Heritage, Register of Parks and Gardens, PG1516 30/11/1986.

30 Donnington Priory, had children of the same age: It was also the childhood home of Thomas Hughes, author of *Tom Brown's Schooldays.*

30 There were only eight principal bedrooms: Mrs. Brita Elmes, who still lives on the estate, recalls the private parties held there by her relative, Mrs. Daisy Fellowes. Despite additions of many servants' rooms since Brummell's time, house parties rarely numbered more than a dozen.

30 Captain George Blackshaw of a local family: George Blackshaw of the Rifle Brigade was painted by Sir Thomas Lawrence (1769–1830) sometime before 1806. Honolulu Academy of Arts.

30 Maria's move from London: Maria seems to have been unwilling, as much as unable, to contribute to the collections made to help her brother in his later penury, although she wrote to him. Her two daughters married well although, tellingly, abroad: such was the scandal their uncle had brought upon the family. Mary

Blackshaw became Baroness de Maltzhan and Fanny Blackshaw Countess Linowska.

31 the flint hermitage by the weir: Inappropriately for a "hermitage," the flint folly at Donnington is close to the busy small bridge by which visitors arrive. News from London, if the boys were playing at the hermitage, might be delivered there before guests reached the house.

2: THESE ARE NOT CHILDISH THINGS: ETON, 1786–1793

34 "Spence's tooth powder": BL MSS Loan 70, vol. 1, Scrope Davies Eton Accounts.

34 The masters had it shut down: The freehold of the land on which it stood was swapped with the Crown for lands Eton owned—including Primrose Hill.

35 *le vice anglais:* J. Peakman, *Lascivious Bodies,* pp. 240ff.

35 A boatman cad who had found himself: W. Jesse, *A Life,* vol. 1, pp. 32–3.

36 "My dear fellows, don't": ibid., p. 32.

36 "All these three most happy years": ibid., vol. 1, p. 35.

36 Dr Goodall: Dr. Joseph Goodall, headmaster 1802–1809, succeeded Dr. Heath.

36 scoring zero out and twelve runs: F. Ashley-Cooper, *Eton and Harrow at the Wicket,* p. 18. (Ashley-Cooper is further convinced that Brummell became an early member of the MCC, but no records survive before 1833.)

37 "roughed about among boys": Maria Edgeworth, in N. Vance, *The Sinews of the Spirit,* p. 11.

37 "whether some miscarriages": V. Knox, *Liberal Education,* p. 354.

37 "from hardy sports": speech by the Chancellor of Cambridge University, 1811, in M. Cohen, "The Construction of the Gentleman," in Gobel, Schabio and Windisch, *Engendering Images of Man in the Long Eighteenth Century,* p. 226.

38 The "Captain of Montem," a "blooming youth": Eton College Archive, "On the Montem," in *A New Copy of Verses,* composed by Herbertus Stockhore, 1793. This poem places George Brummell at the 1793 Montem, as it states Harris as the captain:

   Next the Capt Harris, a blooming youth, I'm told

The Montem Lists, also in the Eton College Archive, clearly have Brummell as a musician poleman in the same Montem that Harris is captain, even though this Montem is assigned the date, in pencil, 1790.

38 Young "Captain" Dyson spent £205: Eton College Archives, Montem Lists.

39 Captain Harris netted £1,000: ibid.

39 a triennial event: ibid. Brummell is recorded in the Montem Lists of 1787, 1790 and 1793.

39 "Eton uniform": There was no school uniform at Eton until much later in the nineteenth century. The black uniform in use today is often said to have originated as mourning for George III, but there is no record of this being true.

40 "This first time I saw him": W. Jesse, *A Life,* 1844, vol. 2, p. 382.

42 "George," said I, "what's the matter?": W. Jesse, *A Life,* 1854, vol. 1, p. 27.

3: THE WORLD IS VERY UNCHARITABLE, 1793–1794

43 [A young man] may commit an hundred: J. Johnstone, *Confessions of Julia Johnstone,* pp. 52–3.

43 Julia Johnstone, née Storer: The name "Mrs Johnstone" was taken by Julia in her later life with Colonel Cotton. She was never married and there was never a Mr. Johnstone.

44 "What a fortune is my mother's!": J. Johnstone, *Confessions,* p. 10.

45 "I was handed out of the carriage": ibid., p. 12.

45 Julia, like George, first saw the modish uniform: The barracks at Hampton Court Palace, on the approach to the main gate from Hampton Bridge, remain the oldest continuously inhabited barracks in the country.

46 "The Brummell family had moved from suite 17": Suite 17 was given to Thomas Tickell, brother-in-law of R. B. Sheridan; he either fell or jumped from it in 1793.

46 Each grace-and-favor apartment found a way to improvise: The original Tudor kitchens have recently been restored and are used again as kitchens. The Georgian kitchens, built away from the palace at the end of Tennis Court Lane, remain a separate residence.

47 "He is an old flame of mine": H. Wilson, *Memoirs of Harriette Wilson,* vol. 1, p. 86.

47 "a little Eau de Portugal": ibid., p. 103. Like eau de cologne, "eau de Portugal" was a light aftershave.

48 "For never handsome gypsy drew in": H. Luttrell, *Advice to Julia,* p. 2.

49 "I never had the honour to refuse": J. Johnstone, *Confessions,* p. 64.

49 "Julia and I . . . are very old friends": H. Wilson, *Memoirs,* vol. 1, p. 227.

49 "Unhappy child of indiscretion": This poem, written in Brummell's hand in his album, is also attributed to Georgiana, Duchess of Devonshire. The sexes reversed in the fourth stanza, she sent the poem as a comment on her illegitimate child (born in 1792) at a later date. Of Brummell and Georgiana, who was the originator and who the copyist is a matter for conjecture. Attributed to Georgiana, Duchess of Devonshire: A. Foreman, *Georgiana,* p. 267; to Brummell, W. Jesse, *A Life of George Bryan Brummell Esq.,* 1844, vol. 1, pp 190–1.

50 "A hussar's cap and feather": J. Johnstone, *Confessions,* p. 11.

50 In early March 1793: Westminster City Archives, St. Martin-in-the-Fields, Register of Burials, vol. 115, March 1793.

51 "a year and a day exactly": ibid., March 1794.

52 In May 1794, after the Easter holidays: Oriel College Archives, 1768–1809, S II K 14, Easter Term 1794. "William Brummell. Mr White, 6 Lincolns Inn, Commoner, May 27. George Brummell. Commoner. May 27." These two entries are

consecutive in the register, which may explain why there are no contact details for parents or guardians in George's entry.

52 "I spent fourteen months at Magdalen": R. Porter, *Edward Gibbon, Making History*, p. 35.

53 "the discipline of the university": J. Harris, *Diaries and Correspondence of James Harris, First Lord Malmesbury*, vol. 1, p. ix.

54 *The Angry Child: The Times*, May 21 and 22, 1816. Christie's advertisement for the sale of Brummell's possessions: ". . . and in fine condition, the much-admired original drawing, *The Angry Child*, and others by Holmes, Christal, Dewindt and Stephanoff . . ."

4: THE PRINCE'S OWN, 1794–1799

55 "You all no doubt have heard": *The Hussars, a New Song, attributed to a Field Officer of The Marines the Accompaniment for the Piano Forte by the Band of the Tenth*, London, c. 1825.

56 "every kind of uniform": W. Thackeray, *The Four Georges*, p. 92.

56 "Bastille of Whalebone": MLCC A27042. Donated by A. T. Barber in 1924. The prince's waist expanded eventually to over fifty inches (125 centimeters).

56 "the compleat uniforms, accoutrements": A. Aspinall, ed., *The Correspondence of King George IV, 1812–1830*, vol. 4, p. 298.

57 "My husband understands how a shoe": V. Cumming, "Pantomime and Pageantry," in C. Fox, ed., *London*, p. 40.

57 "I have no option but to lead": Aspinall, ed., *Correspondence of George IV*, vol. 3, pp. 38 and 47.

58 cornetcy—the first rank of commissioned officer: The rank was abolished in 1871, but until then it was a cornet who held the regimental banner.

59 "soon as he began to mix in society": R. Gronow, *Captain Gronow's Last Recollections*, p. 59.

59 "acquitted himself to the Prince's satisfaction": W. Jesse, *A Life of George Bryan Brummell Esq.*, 1844, p. 40.

59 "He . . . displayed there all that the Prince of Wales": J. B. d'Aurevilly, trans. D. B. Wyndham Lewis, *The Anatomy of Dandyism*, p. 21.

60 Sir John Macpherson, a close associate: A. Aspinall, ed., *The Correspondence of George Prince of Wales, 1770–1812*, vol. 2, p. 24. "PS 20 July I am now with our friend Mr Brommell [sic] at Donington [sic] Grove near Newbury on my way to Bath." Sir John Macpherson to Captain J. W. Payne, Letter 463.

60 to buy a cornetcy in the Tenth Light Dragoons: A.P.C. Bruce, *The Purchase System in the British Army, 1660–1871*, p. 41ff. The money was held by the government against an officer's good behavior. The purchase system of ranks in the British Army was not abolished until 1871. The prices were first fixed and published in 1720. By 1854 the average entry commission—cornet or ensign—stood at over £1,000.

60 It would cost him £735: C. Oman, *Wellington's Army, 1809–1814*, pp. 198–201, "General Regulations for the Army, 12 August 1811." The prices were later changed, but had been standard for many years.

61 " 'Tarleton' helmet": P. Byrne, *Perdita*, p. 180. Tarleton and Mary Robinson were lovers. They met in Joshua Reynolds's studio on the same day that Mary Robinson met three-year-old George Brummell.

62 They made all the prince's uniforms: RA GEO/29408, 29410, 29417, 29419. The prince bought Tenth Light Dragoons outfits from Schweitzer and Davidson in the 1790s and into the 1800s, but switched his allegiance to Jonathan Meyers, possibly at Brummell's instigation, and even occasionally ordered uniforms from John Weston, RA GEO/29431.

62 single uniform bill of £399 7s. 6d.: W. Carman, *British Military Uniforms*, p. 121.

62 and the prince's uniforms . . . over £344 each: RA GEO/29457, J. Meyer 1807: complete Hussar uniform.

62 It was the most expensive part: RA/GEO 29337, Schweitzer and Davidson accounts, 1803.

62 "Extra superfine blue cloth Polony": RA GEO/29408, J. Meyer.

63 "the White Horse cellar": C. Harper, *The Brighton Road*, p. 4. The site is now occupied by the Ritz Hotel.

63 Only four passengers could ride inside: ibid., pp. 4 and 23ff.

64 "men of Fashion": J. Mollo, *The Prince's Dolls*, p. 16.

64 "The officers of those days": U. Macnamara, *The British Army*, pp. 38ff.

64 "The reputation of being . . . left the table": ibid.

65 "the life and soul of the mess": W. Jesse, *A Life*, 1886, vol. 1, p. 39.

65 "powers of mimicry were so extraordinary": C. Hibbert, *George IV*, p. 63.

65 "all more or less distinguished": G. and P. Wharton, in L. Melville, *Beau Brummell*, p. 32.

66 "Tik nuttis!!": H. Wilson, *Memoirs of Harriette Wilson*, 1929, p. 331. "Take notice! The word 'draw' is only a caution! At the word 'swords' you draws them out, taking a firm and positive grip on the hilt. At the same time, throwing the sheath smartly backwards, thus: 'DRAW, SWORDS!' "

66 "to teach their Subalterns their duty": J. Houlding, *Fit for Service: The Training of the British Army 1715–1795*, pp. 272ff.

67 "WHOSE HORSE IS THAT?": Slade MSS. Notes on the life and career of Sir John Slade, compiled by his son Wyndham Slade, c. 1916 (Col. Mitford Slade, 1972).

68 "a transparent painting of His Royal Highness's": *Public Advertiser*, July 1794.

69 "No, Your Highness, for alas, His Grace": J. Munson, *Maria Fitzherbert*, p. 253.

70 "If, as seems most probable, he contracted a venereal disease": *Lancet*, 1846, vol. I, p. 703; vol. II, p. 369. The *Lancet* claimed that 25 percent of military recruits were already infected with venereal disease, but that a full third of the merchant navy was infected, causing particular concern to garrisons in close contact with ports and sea traffic.

71 "are the fertile hotbeds": G. Dartnell, "On the Prevalence and Severity of Syphilis in the British Army," *British Medical Journal,* April 28, 1860.

71 This marriage was illegal: The 1772 Royal Marriages Act forbade marriage by members of the royal family, under the age of twenty-six, without the consent of the king and Privy Council, and marriages to Roman Catholics were illegal for the House of Hanover after the 1701 Act of Settlement.

71 "treated as a queen": J. Croker, *The Correspondence and Diaries of the late John Wilson Croker,* p. 125.

71 She also attended with them the race meetings: J. Munson, *Maria Fitzherbert,* p. 253.

72 To complicate matters, Mrs. Fitzherbert: J. and P. Foord-Kelcey, *Mrs Fitzherbert and Sons,* pp. 48ff.

72 "In a scurrilous rating of the attributes": "Countess of Jersey Beauty: 11, Figure: 6, Elegance: 1, Wit: 2, Sense: 0, Grace: 11, Expression: 12, Sensibility: 5, Principles: 0' scored out of 20." "Scale of the Bon Ton," in *Morning Post,* July 1776.

72 In London society she was known as "Lucretia": R. Edgcumbe, ed., *The Diary of Frances, Lady Shelley 1787–1817,* p. 37.

73 "in which she was to have an important situation": recollections of Lord Stourton, in J. Munson, *Maria Fitzherbert,* p. 259.

73 "the union between this fashionable pair": *Bon Ton Magazine,* July 1794, p. 194.

74 "indelicate manners, indifferent character": Wellington to Lady Salisbury, F. Fraser, *The Unruly Queen,* p. 43.

75 "Does the prince always behave like this?": Harris, *Correspondence of First Lord Malmesbury,* vol. 3, p. 218.

75 "whose virtues no less": *Bon Ton Magazine,* April 1795, p. 39.

76 "passed the greatest part of his bridal night": Lady Charlotte Bury, in S. David, *Prince of Pleasures,* p. 168; Thackeray, *Four Georges,* p. 111; Fraser, *The Unruly Queen,* p. 62.

76 "constantly drunk, sleeping": Caroline, Princess of Wales, as reported by Lord Minto; A. Aspinall, ed., *Correspondence of George Prince of Wales,* vol. 2, p. 460.

78 On returning, they found that the two officers: R. Grant, *The Brighton Garrisons, 1793–1900,* p. 15.

79 "the square thing"; "Just the thing": His catchphrase, according to Harriette Wilson.

79 "keep up [repair] his expensive uniform and horse appointments": A. Bruce, *Purchase System in the British Army,* p. 73.

80 "The fact is, Your Royal Highness": W. Jesse, *A Life,* 1844, vol. 1, p. 46. Jesse includes the note: " 'This conversation about Manchester,' observes Brummell's friend Jack Robinson, 'is utterly unworthy of him and impossible; he was incapable of it.' All I [Jesse] can say is that Brummell told this anecdote to my friend

Wells and other persons at Caen. But it is possible his [true] reason for leaving the 10th was that the expense exceeded his means, and that he wanted the money with which he purchased his commissions."

81 "Hussar dress—outlandish, outrageous": J. Mollo, *The Prince's Dolls*, p. 33.

82 "The future George IV": J. B. d'Aurevilly, trans. D. B. Wyndham Lewis, *The Anatomy of Dandyism*, p. 21.

82 "violent intimacy": T. Raikes, *Reminiscences*, p. 270.

82 Indeed, one biographer of the prince regent: S. David, *Prince of Pleasures*, pp. 283–4. "The obvious inference is that Brummell was homosexual. He certainly enjoyed displaying his naked body to morning callers (including the Prince)."

83 "He was liberal, friendly . . . always living": Raikes, *Reminiscences*, p. 278.

Part II: A Day in the High Life, 1799–1816

85 "I will attempt to sketch the day": C. Goede, *A Stranger in England*, vol. 1, pp. 88–9.

5: DANDIACAL BODY

91 "A Dandy is heroically consecrated": T. Carlyle, *Sartor Resartus*, p. 279.

91 "Amongst the curious freaks of fortune": R. Gronow, *Reminiscences of Captain Gronow*, 1862, p. 56.

91 £20,000 . . . a middle figure of £30,000: W. Jesse, *A Life of George Bryan Brummell Esq.*, 1844, vol. 1, p. 51; Jesse claimed that the money had "accumulated during his minority [and] amounted to thirty thousand pounds."

91 "His brother William": William Brummell married Miss Anne Daniell, daughter of James Daniell of the East India Company, in 1800.

92 "The house he moved into in 1799": For an examination of 4 Chesterfield Street before major renovations in 2004–5, I am indebted to Her Grace the Dowager Duchess of Devonshire, and also Mrs. Iris Armitage and Strutt & Parker Estate Agents. The house belonged to Anthony Eden until 1952, then to the 11th Duke of Devonshire until it was sold in 2004.

92 (since demolished): Devonshire House was pulled down in 1925. The site was redeveloped but includes the current north entrance of Green Park Underground station.

92 "enclose[d] more intelligence": George Selwyn, quoted in R. Tannahill, *Regency England*, p. 36.

93 a fine Arab stallion named Stiletto: "Stiletto": a short dagger considered in eighteenth century a Moorish weapon (OED), i.e., probably an Arab stallion. See Lady Hester Stanhope to George Bryan Brummell, Chapter 7.

94 "Make it two hundred guineas": £150 a year was a reasonable but not exorbitant

wage for a valet: the Royal Archives show that many of the royal household's valets earned less, although they had substantial perks on pitch-and-platter days (anniversaries of royal events). R. Gronow, *Reminiscences*, 1862, p. 222.

94 "the best works of the best authors": ibid., p. 62.

94 Among the books were "some good historical works": W. Jesse, *A Life*, 1844, vol. 1, p. 348.

94 a bet that he would be married: "Mr Brummell bets Mr Osborne twenty guineas that (Mr B) is married before him (Mr O)": "Paid" is recorded against Brummell's name. White's Betting Record, 1798–1800, White's Club, St. James's Street (London Metropolitan Archives).

95 "and every part of his body": This last observation is from Caen jail, so may relate to Brummell's regime to keep the symptoms of his syphilis at bay—but he bathed religiously from an early age. W. Jesse, *A Life*, 1844, vol. 2, p. 203.

95 "trinkets or gew-gaws": W. Pitt Lennox, in L. Melville, *Beau Brummell*, p. 46.

96 He exfoliated his body all over: Both the exfoliation and the milk regime may have been added to Brummell's elaborate toilette only after he had suffered an initial skin outbreak associated with his syphilis. W. Jesse, *A Life*, 1844, vol. 2, p. 60.

96 "Kings by birth were shaved by others": S. Rogers, *Recollections*, p. 274.

96 The Dandiacal Body bought cakes: BL MSS Loan 70, vol. 4, Spike 3, 200.

96 "was the first who revived and improved": W. Jesse, *A Life*, 1844, vol. 1, p. 61.

96 "test their fitness for use": ibid.

97 The collars on Brummell's shirts: MLCC 77.97, 2 1052.

97 "The first *coup d'archet*": W. Jesse, *A Life*, 1844, vol. 1, p. 60.

97 "The [neckcloth] oft bespeaks the man": *Necklothitania*, 1818, p. 3.

98 "More tellingly, the arrangement of 4 Chesterfield Street": There was a small servants' staircase behind the main grand staircase in an area now utilized by a dumbwaiter and a series of cupboards and wardrobes.

98 "My neckcloth, of course, forms my principal care": L. Melville, *Beau Brummell*, p. 47.

98 Lord Byron was an assiduous disciple: D. Langley Moore, "Byronic Dress," in *Costume*, pp. 1–4.

99 half a nail: A "nail" was two and a quarter inches, or a sixteenth of a yard. Its use denoted an expensive, often embroidered, fabric.

99 (finest Irish muslin or cambric): MLCC 77.97 and 2 1052: shirts made for George IV, some dating from his regency or before. The shirts have pleated fine Irish muslin over the chest.

99 Lord Byron also required six nightcaps: D. Langley Moore, *Lord Byron, Accounts Rendered*, p. 485.

99 Thomas Jefferson . . . Thomas Coutts: MLCC and Monticello Collection, University of Virginia, Charlottesville, VA, USA.

100 once irredeemably sweat-stained: MLCC 77.97 and 2 1052. One white waist-

coat belonging to the regent from 1817 also has underarm crescents: 38.294/4.3 and 2.

100   Even so, it was an expensive business: BL MSS Loan 70, vols. 3 and 4, tailor bills: 111 and 245.

100   "The character of the classical body": C. Char, in G. Perry and M. Rossington, eds., *Femininity and Masculinity in Eighteenth Century Art and Culture*, p. 154.

100   "He was tall, well made": T. Raikes, *Reminiscences*, p. 277.

101   "He was about the same height": W. Jesse, *A Life*, 1844, vol. 1, p. 52.

101   [the Apollo Belvedere]: Named after its location, the Belvedere Courtyard (now part of the Pio-Clementine Museum at the Vatican), the statue was placed there by Pope Julius II in 1503. It is seven feet (over two meters) tall, but appears of perfect proportion and "lifesize." *Vatican Museum Guide*, 2002.

102   "Dressed form became an abstraction of nude form": A. Hollander, *Sex and Suits*, p. 89.

103   "I have heard sensible people say that a man": L. Temple, *A Short Ramble*, p. 36.

104   Thanks to the descriptions of Brummell: if it is taken as a principle that the Apollo Belvedere might also fit contemporary models of ideal proportion.

104   After four years of almost constant riding: Berry Brothers' Great Scales Ledger, no. 3, St. James's Street, London. George Brummell, Esq.: 38 entries from January 23, 1798 to July 6, 1815. His brother William is also recorded, but only twice. William was not as large as George, weighing only nine stone nine (135 pounds or 63 kilograms) in his shoes in 1812.

104   the currently accepted scale of ideal weight: height/weight tables, G. G. Harrison, *Annals of Internal Medicine*, 1985, no. 103, pp. 489–94.

104   a full six inches (fifteen centimeters) taller than the average: Average height for males in late-eighteenth-century London was around five foot six (or 168 cm— Brummell stood around 183 cm). A. Werner, *London Bodies*, p. 86.

105   "having well-fashioned the character of a gentleman": H. Wilson, *Memoirs*, 1825, vol. 1, p. 101.

105   surviving tailors' bills: MLCC. Silk jersey breeches, A9243, 1800; buff leather breeches, A 15048, 1805; coats: 53.101/23 1810, 33.119 1800, A 9244 (Sir Gilbert Heathcoat) 1795.

106   The prince became a devotee: G. Cruikshank, *His Most Gracious Majesty King George IV*, British Museum Prints and Drawings.

106   "The Father of Modern Costume": Max Beerbohm, in E. Moers, *The Dandy*, p. 33.

106   "the man who is rich and idle": C. Baudelaire, *The Painter of Modern Life and Other Essays*, pp. 26–7.

107   "that bright morning": M. Beerbohm, "Dandies and Dandies," in S. C. Roberts (ed.), *The Incomparable Max*, pp. 12–13.

107   "He was envied and admired": Lady Hester Stanhope, in W. Jesse, *A Life*, 1844, vol. 1, p. 143.

107 "struck by the misapplication of this title": Rev. G. Crabbe, in Jesse, *A Life*, 1844, vol. 1, p. 68.

6: *SIC ITUR AD ASTRA:* SHOPPING IN LONDON

109 "Turning the corner of a lane": T. Carlyle, *Sartor Resartus*, p. 297.

109 the umbrella being a novelty: J. Macdonald, *Memoirs of an 18th Century Footman*, p. 236.

110 And single-handedly he began the decimation: R. Grant, *Ghost Riders: Travels with American Nomads*, London, 2003, pp. 112ff. "Brummell popularised a new style of beaver felt hat, which spread from London to Paris, Vienna, St Petersburg, New York, and all over the civilised world, which decimated beaver populations in Europe and raised the price of beaver pelts, and so enabled the Rocky Mountain fur trade."

110 Not only might it bring the Prince of Wales: Approximately £35,000 in today's money. RA GEO/29331-29347.

111 Glasshouse Street: Glasshouse Street, west of Regent Street, is now Vigo Street and Burlington Gardens.

111 Mr. Sheridan had set up home there: The house is now the headquarters of the couturier Hardy Amies. An internal window is preserved on the central staircase, from which Sheridan would spy approaching visitors and claim to be out if they were creditors.

111 "The Prince wears superfine": "Sir John . . . a good-humoured baronet and brother Etonian . . ." related this story to Jesse: W. Jesse, *A Life*, 1844, vol. 1, p. 48.

112 "a-shopping": N. Waugh, *The Cut of Men's Clothes, 1600–1900*, p. 117.

112 "it was a gentleman's world": Savile Row tailor Tom Gilby, in R. Walker, *The Savile Row Story*, p. 65.

112 The first, Schweitzer and Davidson: Savile Row, before the creation of Regent Street in the early nineteenth century, had more the feel of one of Soho's small alleyways. It was a dead end until, with the redevelopment of the area, Regent Street cut through to the east.

113 He bought his hats on St. James's Street: Westminster City Archives, rate books, Fribourg and Treyer ledgers, Lock's Hatters, St. James's Street, ledgers.

114 "[This] tailor was of course a foreigner": T. Hook, *Sayings and Doings*, 2nd series: *The Sutherlands, The Man of Many Friends, Doubts and Fears, Passion and Principle*, p. 194.

114 "a small fortune invested": A. Adburgham, *Silver Fork Society*, p. 130.

114 £100,000: ibid., p. 131. Stultz the tailor was rumored to have retired on this sum.

114 "When he stopped to be measured": T. Surr, *A Winter in London*, vol. 2, pp. 82–3.

115 Soft domette: a soft plain cloth in which the warp is cotton and the weft wool.

115 lappet cloth: or lappet hair, now called "lapthair" on Savile Row. Modern lapthair is still made with horsehair but also synthetic fibers that allow it to bend in only one direction. It is unclear if this effect was possible in the early nineteenth century.

115 "baiste," "baisters," "baiste fittings" remain a commonplace element of Savile Row bespoke suit making, but the term is unknown to the OED, although "baisters" and "baisting" are acknowledged as early-nineteenth-century terms in buttonhole making and finishing.

115 "Pockets were relegated": MLCC 33.119.

115 "you might almost say the body thought": W. Jesse, *A Life*, 1844, vol. 1, p. 70.

115 "The shape of the coat": W. Pitt Lennox, *Fifty Years' Biographical Reminiscences*, vol. 1, p. 74.

116 "Though the cut is fuller": MLCC. Coat made by John Weston, Old Bond Street, 1803.

117 "Good morning Sir; happy to see you": E. Bulwer-Lytton, *Pelham*, p. 113–14.

118 forty-two and a half inches from nape: *c.* 73 inch = total height. Seven eighths of 73 = *c.* 64, two-thirds of 64 = *c.* 42 and a half.

119 "pantaloons": pantaloons, originally "connected breeches and stockings in the same stuff," took their name from the Italian Commedia del'Arte character, Pantalone. Modern American usage of "pants" may have descended from this, or via the French *"pantalon."* Trousers were initially taken to mean wide-cut trousers in imitation of naval, military and boys' wear, but by the early nineteenth century the terms were becoming interchangeable.

120 "I found my very constant and steady admirer": H. Wilson, *Memoirs of Harriette Wilson*, 1831, vol. 1, p. 223.

121 Recent fashion theorists: A. Ribiero, *The Art of Dress*, pp. 105ff.

121 "immodest and unflattering to the figure": M. Khan, *A Persian at the Court of King George IV, 1809–10, The Journal of Mizra Abul Hassan Khan*, p. 137.

121 "extremely handsome and very fit": Anon., *Essay Philosophical and Medical Concerning Modern Clothing*, p. 45. A French doctor, L. J. Clairian, meanwhile opined that trousers (pantaloons) that were too tight would be prejudicial to men's health, but that conversely complete lack of support could be harmful: *Recherches et considérations médicales sur les vêtements des hommes*, 1803.

121 "one could always tell what a young man": F. Chenoune, *The History of Men's Fashion*, 1993, p. 30.

122 ruthlessly starched: MLCC 38.294/4 and 38.294/3, waistcoats, c. 1815.

123 "You can tell a Stultz coat anywhere": E. Bulwer-Lytton, *Pelham*, in A. Adburgham, *Shopping in Style*, p. 129.

123 "scorned to share his fame with his tailor": T. H. Lister, *Granby*, vol. 1, p. 108.

124 "ride in ladies' gloves, particularly," he said: H. Wilson, *Memoirs*, 1831, vol. 1, p. 100.

124 "the polished ease": T. Lister, *Granby*, vol. 1, p. 109.

125 "It is folly that is the making of me": George Brummell to Lady Hester Stanhope, in W. Jesse, *A Life*, vol. 1, 1844, p. 148.

125 "Eccentricity [is the] fruit of English soil": J. B. d'Aurevilly, trans. D. B. Wyndham Lewis, *The Anatomy of Dandyism*, p. 10.

125 "Dandyism . . . is the force of English originality": ibid., p. 3.

125 Joseph Lock, Brummell's hatter: Lock's Hatters, St. James's Street. Sales ledger, 1808: Friday, December 9, 1808, "Mr Brummell paid Mr Lock . . . 2 Round hats." The wording on the ledger "Paid Mr Lock" strongly suggests that James Lock II served Brummell.

7: THE LADIES WHO RIDE

130 "almost as often as each session of Parliament": Chateaubriand, *Mémoires d'Outre-Tombe*, vol. 3, p. 210.

130 In the afternoon, especially in good weather: Henry VIII had originally appropriated the land for hunting after the dissolution of the monasteries.

130 Rotten Row: "Rotten Row" is thought to be a corruption of *Route de Roi*, and may be the original King's Road, west from the capital.

130 "Where the fashionable fair": Byron, *Don Juan*, Canto II, lxv.

130 "In the art of cutting": T. Lister, *Granby*, vol. 1, p. 108.

130 "Have you ever endured so poor a summer": R. Gronow, *Reminiscences*, 1863, p. 72.

131 "None view it awestruck or surprised": H. Luttrell, *Advice to Julia*, p. 41.

131 " 'Robinson,' he said, turning to his valet": W. Jesse, *A Life*, 1844, vol. 1, p. 118.

132 Apsley Gate: Hyde Park Corner.

132 "Is there a more gay and graceful": Disraeli, in E. Moers, *The Dandy*, p. 65.

132 "of rank and fashion": R. Gronow, *Reminiscences*, 1863, p. 73.

133 "Never was there such a man": T. Raikes, *Reminiscences,* pp. 268–9.

134 "Little G. (Georgiana)": Lady Georgiana Cavendish (1783–1858) married the brother of Brummell's other great love, Elizabeth, Duchess of Rutland, George Howard, 6th Earl of Carlisle.

136 "I've Known all the Blessings of Sight": by Georgiana, Duchess of Devonshire, in Brummell's Album, in L. Melville, *Beau Brummell*, pp. 277ff.

137 "These additional stanzas": V. Foster, ed., *The Two Duchesses: Family Correspondence of Georgiana, Duchess of Devonshire and Elizabeth, Duchess of Devonshire*, p. 131.

138 "generous natures": Letter from G. B. Brummell "To a Lady," in L. Melville, *Beau Brummell*, p. 144.

138 "Here in the bower of beauty": by Georgiana, Duchess of Devonshire, in Brummell's album, in ibid., pp. 278ff.

139 "It is related of [Brummell] that he came": W. Jesse, *A Life*, 1844, vol. 1, p. 125. It is impossible to attribute this anecdote precisely to any one occasion or affair:

the 1844 version refers to an earl and "your countess," some later versions have "noble friend" and "your duchess." It seems likely, given Brummell's known relationships with three duchesses—Devonshire, York and Rutland—and no noted countesses, that Jesse deliberately obfuscated by changing the title. If it is a countess, the most likely candidate is the Countess of Bessborough, Georgiana's sister.

140 "The Butterfly's Ball": *The Butterfly's Ball and the Grasshopper's Feast,* by W. Roscoe for his children, was set to music by order of George III and Queen Charlotte for Princess Mary, later Duchess of Gloucester. W. Jesse, *A Life,* 1844, vol. 1, p. 241.

140 "The Butterfly's Funeral": ibid., pp. 240ff.

141 "John Wallis, went on to sell more": ibid., p. 240.

141 "Mr Brummell keeps us waiting rather than wishing for him": *Se fait plutot attendre que desirer.*

142 "He sketched for her": In 1844 this painting was in Jesse's possession but has subsequently been lost; Jesse, *A Life,* 1844, vol. 2, p. 95.

143 "Princess Frederica Charlotte Ulrica Catherine": Princess Frederica, Duchess of York, born May 7, 1767, eldest daughter of King William II of Prussia, married HRH Prince Frederick, Duke of York and Albany and Bishop of Osnabruck, Berlin, September 29, 1791 in Berlin. Died, Oatlands Park, Surrey, August 6, 1820.

143 "Frederique": RA GEO/44527–44558, letters of the Duchess of York to Prince Regent and Duchess of Cambridge.

143 "The Duchess [of York] was very partial": R. H. Stoddard, ed., *Personal Reminiscences,* pp. 270–1.

144 "The Duchess resides entirely at Oatlands": *Bon Ton Magazine,* April 1793.

144 "Mein Gott, dey are so dependent": Matthew "Monk" Lewis, in L. Melville, *Beau Brummell,* p. 151.

145 "she pays her tradesmen's bills": *Bon Ton Magazine,* August 1792, p. 234.

145 "These were enclosed with her trademark pink": RA GEO/44527–44558, letters of the Duchess of York to Prince Regent and Duchess of Cambridge. RA GEO/ 44558 deep pink. RA GEO/Add 50/103, Duchess of York to Charles Culling Smith.

145 "It has been mentioned": Anon., *An Address to Her Royal Highness the Dutchess* [sic] *of York Against the Use of Sugar, Nihil humani a me alienum puto,* p. 10.

145 inspired a fashion for tiny, tight shoes: The Duchess's feet were a subject of great curiosity after her husband ordered shoes for his bride-to-be. See illustrations.

145 "a very superior mind," T. Raikes, in W. Jesse, *A Life,* 1844, vol. 2, p. 2.

146 "the most unvarying steadfast affection": Letter from George IV to the Duke of York on the occasion of the death of his wife, 1825, in C. Hibbert, *George IV,* p. 711.

146 "I will never forget the tender moments": Duchess of York to G. Brummell, in L. Melville, *Beau Brummell,* p. 83.

146 "They once bought a lottery ticket together": W. Jesse, *A Life*, 1927, vol. 1, p. 219.

146 "Please accept my most sincere thanks": ibid., pp. 220–1.

147 It was one of the more expensive items: RA GEO/Add 50/99–100.

8: THE DANDY CLUBS

149 White's and Brooks's ... in 1799: *Memorials of Brooks's MDCCLXIV–MCM*, "Mr Brummell. Proposer and Seconder Mr Fawkener. Date of Election 2 April 1799."

149 "To be admitted a member of that body": W. Fraser, *Words on Wellington*, p. 202.

150 The rules also stipulated that: After 1813 membership rose to five hundred.

150 a little later a bay window was added: in 1811.

150 "mustered in force": R. Gronow, *Reminiscences of Captain Gronow*, 1863, p. 46.

150 "an ordinary frequenter of White's": C. Gore, "Sketches of English Character," in E. Moers, *The Dandy*, p. 43.

151 "The conversation upon the topics": W. Pitt Lennox, *Celebrities I Have Known*, vol. 1, p. 295.

151 " 'My dear fellow,' said Brummell": Grantley Berkeley, in L. Melville, *Beau Brummell*, pp. 40ff.

152 "Damn the fellows ... they're upstarts": Colonel Sebright, in A. Lejeune, *White's, The First Three Hundred Years*, p. 89.

152 "White's Window would not permit it": W. Fraser, *Words on Wellington*, pp. 202–3.

152 "the most famous political club": Trevelyan, in P. Ziegler and D. Seward (eds.), *Brooks's*, p. 27.

153 "Whig Party at Dinner": ibid., p. 42.

153 "the Whigs kept the best company": recorded by John Cam Hobhouse, from a conversation between Brummell, Scrope Davies and himself in Calais, July 1817, in T. A. J. Burnett, *Rise and Fall of a Regency Dandy*, p. 145.

153 "having won only £12,000": P. Ziegler and D. Seward, *Brooks's*, p. 26.

155 "Mr Brummell bets Mr Irby": London Metropolitan Archives, White's betting book, 1743–1878, 1811: "Mr Brummell bets Mr Blackford thirty guineas to twenty-five that Mr William Jones beats Mr Darston for the Country of Gloucester now contesting between them, February 1811."

156 "cold meats, oysters etc": J. Timbs, *Clubs and Club Life in London from the Seventeenth Century to the Present Times*, p. 96, quoting White's rules, 1797.

156 "cold fowl, fruit, bisquits [*sic*]": C. Ray, "Table Talk," in P. Ziegler and D. Seward, Brooks's, p. 166.

156 One of the earliest uses of the word: OED, Gibbon's *Journal*, November 24, 1762.

157 "the eternal joints, or beef-steaks": R. Gronow, *Reminiscences*, 1863, p. 79.

157 "Labourie's dinners": C. Ray, "Table Talk," in P. Ziegler and D. Seward, *Brooks's*, p. 165.

157 "the dinners were so recherché": T. Raikes, in L. Melville, *Beau Brummell*, p. 70.

158 Watier's: The spelling of Watier's, like Brooks's, varies in the period: Wattier's, Brook's, Brookes's, etc. The modern spelling is Brooks's. Watier's club no longer exists, but the favored spelling stuck with the chef's name and one t.

158 Brummell bought snuff for the prince as early as 1799: Fribourg and Treyer ledgers, Westminster City Archives.

159 White's accounts concur: P. Colson, *White's*, p. 95.

159 Brummell bought Martinique: Fribourg and Treyer ledgers, Westminster City Archives. The last of Fribourg and Treyer's own blend of Macouba can still be bought at the snuff shop G. Smith's on Charing Cross Road.

159 "Sniff . . . with precision, with both nostrils": U. Bourne, *Snuff*, p. 7.

160 "My Lord! Allow me to observe": H. Cole, *Beau Brummell*, p. 93.

160 "The hogshead was duly opened": W. Jesse, *A Life*, 1844, vol. 1, p. 102.

9: THEATRE ROYAL

165 "Many a beau turned his head": H. Wilson, *Memoirs of Harriette Wilson* 1831, vol. 3, p. 76, and vol. 1, p. 100.

165 "Fred Bentinck": Younger son of the immensely wealthy Duke of Portland, Lord Fred Bentinck was an inner member of the dandy circle and frequenter of Harriette Wilson's; "Lord Fred," Harriette wrote, "always makes me merry."

165 "Lord Fife": James Duff, 4th Earl of Fife (1776–1857). Had a long-standing affair with London's prima ballerina La Mercandotti, who became the toast of the town at age fifteen; he lost her to the nouveau riche dandy Golden Ball Hughes—the subject of a ditty at Fife's expense:

> The fair damsel is gone and no wonder at all
> That bred to the dance she has gone to the Ball.

165 "the Duc de Berri": Charles Ferdinand de Bourbon, Duc de Berri (1778–1820). A French prince of the blood, son of the Comte d'Artois, later Charles X of France, he spent many years in London during the First Empire. He fought against Napoleon and entered Paris in 1814 with the Victorious Allies. A famous womanizer, his few legitimate children all predeceased him, but one posthumous child (the duc was assassinated at the Paris opera in 1820) became Henry V of France.

165 The King's Theatre: The four previous theaters on the site of today's Her Majesty's Theatre, Haymarket, included the King's Theatre, or Italian Opera House, known to Brummell. It became widely known as Her Majesty's after the accession of Queen Victoria in 1837 so that is the term used by Gronow, writing in the 1860s; it had originally been the Queen's Theatre, or Her Majesty's, in the days of Queen Anne (1704, as designed by Sir John Vanbrugh). Today's Theatre

Royal, Haymarket, is opposite, and dates from 1821. It is the oldest West End theater still in use. The Little Theatre stood on the same side of Haymarket, slightly nearer to Piccadilly Circus.

165 Between them, by the beginning of the nineteenth century: F. O'Toole, *A Traitor's Kiss,* p. 114.

166 "my friend Sherry": W. Jesse, *A Life of George Bryan Brummell Esq.,* 1844, vol. 1, p. 246.

166 grander than La Scala: E. Burford, *Royal St James's,* p. 238.

166 it was suggested that a Persian: Montesquieu, in F. O'Toole, *A Traitor's Kiss,* p. 116.

166 "to furnish out a part of the entertainment": O. Goldsmith, *The Citizen of the World,* p. 75.

166 "to assemble only to see and be seen": C. A. G. Goede, *A Stranger in England,* vol. 2, pp. 106ff.

167 Sheridan for one employed: F. O'Toole, *A Traitor's Kiss,* p. 119.

168 "the King's Theatre auditorium": In 1799 the interior of the Opera House (King's Theatre) was remodeled by Marinari, the principal scenery painter at Drury Lane. Jane Austen writes sympathetically to her sister when she is unable to see inside (D. Le Faye, ed., *Jane Austen's Letters,* Oxford, 1995, p. 71); see also P. Byrne, *Jane Austen and the Theatre,* London and New York, 2002, pp. 61–2.

168 The ensuing riot: A. Bank, ed., *The Drama: Its History, Literature and Influence on Civilisation,* vol. 15, pp. 101–2.

168 This was probably an exaggeration: MLCC A9243. Silk jersey breeches; either court or formal evening wear, c. 1810.

168 The theatre was not ticketed: W. Pitt Lennox, *My Recollections from 1806 to 1873,* p. 226.

168 The Duke of Bedford, for instance: ibid., p. 222.

168 "I make it a rule never to lend my box": Duke of Bedford to G. Brummell, in W. Jesse, *A Life,* 1844, vol. 1, p. 84.

168 "all fitted up with crimson velvet": Jane Austen to Cassandra Austen, in P. Byrne, *Jane Austen and the Theatre,* p. 51.

168 "in front of every box": E. M. Butler, ed., *A Regency Visitor,* p. 178.

169 "ran up three times to the opera": H. Wilson, *Memoirs,* 1929, p. 206.

169 "seated in the box nearest the stage": E. Bulwer-Lytton, *Pelham,* p. 162.

169 "one half come to prosecute their debaucheries": J. Brewer, *The Pleasures of the Imagination,* p. 348.

170 "The celebrated beau, George Brummell": H. Wilson, *Memoirs,* 1831, vol. 3, p. 76.

170 "when the performance had concluded": ibid., vol. 1, p. 100.

170 "happy was she in whose opera box": T. Raikes, *Reminiscences,* p. 268.

171 "were meant for no more than six": W. Pitt Lennox, *My Recollections,* p. 226.

171 Opera boxes could cost from a hundred: F. Wilson, *The Courtesan's Revenge,* p. 67.

171 "The opera may be called the exclusive property": C. A. G. Goede, *A Stranger in England,* vol. 2, pp. 106ff.

172 "Let the theatre be got up upon the same": "Dramatic Taste," *Fraser's Magazine,* February 1830.

172 "in full court dress": R. Gronow, *Reminiscences of Captain Gronow,* 1863, p. 49.

172 "stamped with aristocratic elegance": ibid., p. 49.

172 "circular vestibule, almost lined": F. Wilson, *The Courtesan's Revenge,* p. 68.

173 *Sketches from the Round Room:* ibid., p. 68.

173 "cold, heartless and satirical": H. Wilson, *Memoirs,* 1831, vol. 1, p. 100.

174 From under Holland's Ionic columns: The columns now grace the portico of the National Gallery on the north side of Trafalgar Square. Other smaller internal fixtures of the house were salvaged for use at Buckingham Palace.

174 "see over the gates": W. Jesse, *A Life,* 1844, vol. 1, p. 271.

174 Big Ben Caunt: Big Ben Caunt, born Newstead, Nottinghamshire (1814), champion of All England 1841–5. The famous bell and its clock tower may equally have been nicknamed Big Ben after Sir Benjamin Hall, the commissioner of works appointed to rebuild the Palace of Westminster after the fire of 1834. Nevertheless, the earliest record of the nickname in common use, beyond the portals of Carlton House, is its attachment to Ben Caunt the boxer.

176 "Mr Brummell, the place for your box": R. Gronow, *Captain Gronow's Last Recollections,* p. 57.

176 "It was this more than anything else": ibid., pp. 57ff.

177 "Neither have I resentments": W. Jesse, *A Life,* 1844, vol. 1, p. 273.

177 Three thousand guests were invited: M. Evans, ed., *Princes as Patrons,* p. 109.

177 "Nothing was ever half so magnificent": W. Dowden, ed., *The Letters of Thomas Moore,* vol. 1, pp. 152–3.

10: SEVENTH HEAVEN OF THE FASHIONABLE WORLD

180 "happy was the young lady": W. Pitt Lennox, *Celebrities I Have Known,* vol. 1, p. 318.

180 "most magnificent suite of rooms": E. Chancellor, *The Memorials of St James's Street Together with the Annals of Almack's,* p. 197.

180 "solemn proclamation": R. Gronow, *Reminiscences of Captain Gronow,* 1863, p. 44.

180 "silk stockings, thin shoes, and white neckcloths": Major Chambre, *Recollections of West End Life,* vol. 1, p. 241.

181 "Into this sanctum sanctorum": Lady Clementia Davies, in E. Chancellor, *Memorials,* p. 210.

181 "not more than half a dozen": R. Gronow, *Reminiscences,* 1863, pp. 43ff.

181 "Lady Louisa Lennox": *Burke's Peerage,* vols. 1 and 2; "Lady Louisa Lennox d. 1843. Dau. Duke of Richmond and Gordon, Duc d'Aubigny etc of Goodwood Park." Captain Jesse is evasive about the lady in question, and he could equally be referring to one of the other Lady Louisas in the extended Lennox family at the time, or even Lady Louisa, daughter of the Duke of Beaufort, who were all presented at court in the early nineteenth century.

181 "He is now speaking to Lord": W. Jesse, *A Life,* 1844, vol. 1, pp. 99–100.

182 "this is no fiction": ibid., vol. 1, p. 100.

182 "You, who know Almack's": E. Moers, *The Dandy,* p. 45.

182 "such that hereafter no one": G. S. Hillard, ed., *Life, Letters and Journals of George Ticknor,* vol. 1, pp. 296–7.

183 "No event ever produced so great a sensation": T. Raikes, in A. Adburgham, *Shopping in Style,* p. 8.

183 "Despite all her talents and attractions": R. Gronow, *Captain Gronow's Last Recollections,* p. 120.

184 "He shall not be so pretty than you": H. Cole, *Beau Brummell,* pp. 107–8, quoting variously Lord Byron, Lord Alvanley and Captain Gronow.

184 £800 on candles: P. Colson, *White's,* pp. 68–9.

185 "illuminations and fireworks": Lady Emma Sophia Brownlow, *The Eve of Victorianism,* p. 54.

185 "no repose either of body or mind": J. C. Hobhouse, *Recollections,* vol. 1, p. 73.

185 "five in the afternoon as, by so doing": H. Wilson, *Memoirs of Harriette Wilson,* 1831, vol. 4, p. 159.

186 "How easy is [their] only rule!": H. Luttrell, *Advice to Julia,* p. 83.

186 pharoah: this is the older spelling, from the original French cards that had a picture of an Egyptian pharaoh in place of the king.

186 "I never saw such a transition": A. Lejeune, *White's,* pp. 83–4.

187 "It was five o'clock one summer's morning": T. Raikes, *Reminiscences,* p. 272.

187 "Mr Brummell, if you wish to put an end": Lejeune, *White's,* p. 94.

188 "Tom Sheridan was never in the habits": T. Raikes, *Journals,* vol. 3, pp. 85–6.

188 "The life which Brummell led at last": T. Raikes, *Journals,* vol. 2, p. 210.

189 "I have a notion": T. Moore, *Lord Byron, Letters and Journals,* vol. 9, *Detached Thoughts,* No. 33.

189 "the true impulse in obstinate incorrigible gamesters": T. de Quincy, *The English Opium Eater,* vol. 1, p. 173.

190 "emanating from the leading ladies": W. Pitt Lennox, *My Recollections from 1806 to 1873,* vol. 2, p. 228.

II: NO MORE A-ROVING SO LATE INTO THE NIGHT

192 "So, we'll go no more a-roving": G. G. Byron, *Complete Poetical Works,* 1970, p. 101.

192 "In Society, stay as long as you need": J. B. d'Aurevilly, trans. G. Walden, *What's a Dandy?*, p. 103.

192 "Dates make ladies nervous": H. Wilson, *Harriette Wilson's Memoirs of Herself and Others*, 1929, p. 26.

193 advice on sex to professional courtesans: H. Wilson, *Memoirs of Harriette Wilson*, 1831, vol. 5, p. 334.

193 Mrs. Philip's Warehouse: Wellcome Institute, Images Collection L0022456. Advertisement for Mrs. Philip's Warehouse on Half Moon Street: "Seven doors up from The Strand, on the left."

 None in our wares e're found a flaw/Self-preservation's nature's law . . .

193 that he suffered for many years from syphilis: Dr. Edouard Vastel and John Kelly, MD, served the Caen asylum and the British community in Caen respectively in the 1830s. They attended Brummell, signed the medical certificates and attested to cause of death, recorded and kept in the Bon Sauveur asylum, Caen, where Brummell died. Professor Pierre Morel, former director of l'Hôpital Psychiatrique Départementale du Bon Sauveur, Caen, has copies of the original medical files kept at Bon Sauveur, which record the "general paralysis of the insane [*démence et paralysie générale*]," i.e., tertiary syphilis, from which Brummell died in 1840. The originals are in disputed ownership between the asylum and the Archives Départementales du Calvados, also at Caen.

193 fifteen percent of the population: D. Hayden, *Pox*, pp. 44ff.

194 "overstated manliness" . . . "unambiguous masculinity": D. Wahrman, *The Making of the Modern Self*, pp. 62–4.

194 "The organ of love in his cranium": W. Jesse, *A Life*, 1844, vol. 1, p. 126.

195 "there is a splendid [new] pox in town": Théophile Gautier, in C. Quetel, *History of Syphilis*, pp. 118ff.

195 Francis I: King of France (1494–1547). Not only did his reign see the arrival of syphilis in France, from the Americas, but his incessant warring helped spread the disease across European borders. He was also famously a sufferer himself; one nineteenth-century hagiographical reference noted *"l'abus des plaisirs lui avait causé des apostumes* [self-indulgent pleasure seeking had caused him physical corruption]," *Nouvelle Biographie Universelle*, Paris, 1861, p. 530.

196 "mincing": E. Tweedie, *Hyde Park*, p. 69.

196 "bitchy queen": S. Parissien, *George IV*, p. 113.

196 "a monstrous sin against nature": J. Peakman, *Lascivious Bodies*, p. 148.

196 "silken tresses and delicate": W. Jesse, *A Life*, 1844, vol. 2, p. 267.

196 "with such success, such command": J. B. d'Aurevilly, trans. G. Walden, *What's a Dandy?*, p. 103.

197 "He never attained any degree of intimacy": W. Jesse, *A Life*, 1844, vol. 1, pp. 124–5.

197 "The most favourable opportunity": ibid., pp. 125–6.

198 "eleemosynary": of or pertaining to almshouses and alms giving, OED.

200 "that unaffected and fervent homage": W. Jesse, *A Life,* 1844, vol. 1, p. 132.

200 "If a gentleman detract from another": *The British Code of Duel, A reference to The Laws of Honour and the Character of Gentlemen,* p. 14.

200 "You have taken a load off my mind": W. Jesse, *A Life,* 1844, vol. 1, pp. 298ff.

201 "Vow not at all, but if thou must": First published in W. Jesse, *A Life,* 1844, vol. 1, p. 288. J. McGann, ed., *Lord Byron: The Complete Poetical Works,* vol. 3, pp. 458–9: "Commentary Note 230: MS A copy in an unknown hand [possibly Brummell's] with "Byron" written at end (MS T location: Texas). Uncollected. First published in Capt. Jesse's *Life of George Brummell* (1844) 1, p. 288, from a copy in Brummell's (now lost) album book of verses; MS T printed in *Pratt* 128 where a date of 1806 is conjectured . . . In 1812 Byron had sent at least one stanza of "To [Lady Caroline Lamb]" to Lady Melbourne, and it is probable that Brummell had both poems from her, though Byron could have given them to Brummell himself (Byron's close acquaintance with Brummell in fact began only a few weeks after his April 25 letter to Lady Melbourne; see BLJ, iv, 117)."

201 "A Woman's Hair": ibid., pp. 6–7.

202 The letters Brummell had in his possession: W. Jesse, *A Life,* 1886, preface, p. xvi.

202 "from the tender to the devastatingly dismissive": J. D. Jump, ed., *Byron, A Symposium,* p. 113.

203 "He abounds in sublime": Anon., *Don John or Don Juan Unmasked,* p. 8.

203 There had been no such thing as a "homosexual": The terms "homosexual," "bisexual" and "heterosexual" all postdate Brummell, but that is not to say there was no sense of a homosexual community in London in the eighteenth and nineteenth centuries; it has been argued that some men saw themselves as part of a "sodomitical group." See J. Peakman, *Lascivious Bodies;* C. Craft, *Another Kind of Love;* C. White, ed., *Nineteenth Century Writings on Homosexuality.*

204 "of sodomies and bestialities": F. Swediaur, *Practical Observations on Venereal Complaints,* p. 314.

204 "after a voyage of four months": ibid., p. 4.

205 "to have, when the original is dust": Byron, *Don Juan,* London, 1819, Canto 1, ccxviii.

205 His was the most famous image: There are two color miniatures, neither of absolutely certain attribution. One was owned by the late Major Daniell, OBE, the other came onto the market in the late twentieth century, sold at auction at Bonham's, London. National Portrait Gallery Records, London, G. B. Brummell.

206 "In the supper room": B. Blackmantle, *The English Spy,* vol. 2, pp. 61ff. The Mysteries of Cytherea = sex.

206 "The man does not want you to pass": H. Wilson, *Memoirs,* vol. 5, p. 334.

207 "making strong love": H. Wilson, *Memoirs,* 1831, vol. 1, p. 220.

207 "the majestic pox!" March 2, 1877. Guy de Maupassant was twenty-seven. His euphoric response to a diagnosis of syphilis was in the context of a history of sex-

ual athleticism. However, the sexual fever of the early syphilitic is widely recorded. C. Quetel, *History of Syphilis,* p. 128.

209 "all spotless virgins": E. Burford, *Royal St. James's,* p. 228.

209 sexual relation that has been described as homosocial: E. Kosofsky-Sedgwick, *Between Men,* pp. 1ff.

210 "It was a strange thing to see a man": E. Bulwer-Lytton, *Pelham,* p. 150.

12: PLAY HAS BEEN THE RUIN OF US ALL

215 "Play . . . has been the ruin of all": H. Wilson, *Memoirs of Harriette Wilson,* 1831, vol. 4, pp. 207ff.

216 presumed heirs to the dukedom: Until the birth of the Marquess of Granby in 1813—fourteen years after the Rutlands' marriage—his younger brothers had been the duke's heirs.

216 "Covenant between George Bryan Brummell": Belvoir Castle Muniments Room, MSS, in Campbell, pp. 118–19 and reproduced by permission of His Grace the Duke of Rutland.

216 "to the death of the last of the two rakes": In signing joint annuities it was expected, in the place of modern life insurance cover, that each co-lender would bequeath assets to the others to cover the continuing debt.

218 "exhausted the other two": J. C. Hobhouse, *Recollections,* vol. 1, pp. 86–7.

218 "the dandykiller": H. Wilson, *Memoirs,* 1831, vol. 4, p. 196.

219 Meyler sat with his friend the Duchess of Beaufort: L. Blanch, ed., *Harriette Wilson's Memoirs,* 2003, p. 313.

219 Brummell sat, laughing, with Harriette: At this time Harriette had a box at the opera, bought by her lover the Marquess of Worcester, in which Brummell was a regular: Meyler, meanwhile, was a guest often in the Beauforts' box, directly opposite.

219 "His countenance is so peculiarly voluptuous": H. Wilson, *Harriette Wilson's Memoirs,* 2003, p. 314.

219 "a very tyrant": F. Wilson, *The Courtesan's Revenge,* pp. 138–40.

220 "The story was this . . . that particular time": H. Wilson, *Memoirs,* 1831, vol. 4, pp. 192ff.

221 Fribourg and Treyer: Final entries, Brummell account: April 15, 1816 and December 17, 1818. Total of £14. 8s. 0d. It seems likely that this latter date was when the account was wound up, and the purchase of a 2.5 pound jar of Martinique relates to the earlier date. Fribourg and Treyer ledgers, 1816, 1817, 1818, Westminster City Archive.

222 "My Dear Scrope": R. Gronow, *Reminiscences of Captain Gronow,* 1863, p. 211.

223 *La Cosa Rara:* (now more usually *Una Cosa Rara*) by Vicente Martin, 1776. Often cited as the first occasion at which a waltz was heard onstage.

223 *Love, Law and Physic: The Times,* May 16–20. *La Cosa Rara* was advertised as

Mr. Braham's benefit night for Thursday, May 16—"Tickets and boxes sold at The King's Theatre and from No 3, Tavistock Square." The second performance is listed as Saturday, May 18. There was no opera playing at the King's on the night Brummell left London, Friday, May 17. *Love, Law and Physic,* a farce in two acts by James Kenny, played at Covent Garden. The lead role, Flexible, required of its actor "a ready assurance, a glib tongue and strong powers of mimicry."

223 "It was Solomans's Judgement": Solomans's were Jewish moneylenders. E. Chancellor, *The Memorials of St James's,* p. 248.

Part III: A Man of Fashion, Gone to the Continent, 1816–1840

225 "A Catalogue of A very choice": frontispiece of Christie's Sale Catalogue, No. 13 Chapel Street, Park Lane, May 22 and 23, 1816, reproduced in W. Jesse, *A Life of George Bryan Brummell Esq.,* 1844, vol. 1, pp. 275–6 and also in *The Times,* May 21 and 22, 1816, which carried an advertisement with the same wording as the catalogue title page, but with the painting titled *The Refractory School Boy* referred to by its other name, *The Angry Child,* in the catalogue itself.

13: ROI DE CALAIS, 1816–1821

229 most often in the notorious King's Bench prison: W. Pitt Lennox, *My Recollections from 1806 to 1873,* vol. 2, pp. 3–4.

230 An Englishman was beyond English law: F. Coghlan, *A Guide to France, or, Travellers, Their Own Commissioners,* p. 5.

230 "commodious baths": ibid., p. 16.

230 "L' Auberge des rois": C. Borde, *Calais et la Mer 1814–1914,* pp. 36ff.

230 "Dear Lords Charles and Robert": Belvoir Castle MSS, Muniments Room, G. B. Brummell to Lords C. and R. Manners, May 18, 1816.

232 "Brummell's private debts are very considerable": *The Diary of a Diplomatist,* May 21 and 24, 1816, entries reprinted in *Monthly Magazine,* November 1846.

232 "Mr Brummell has decamped to the confusion": Sir Robert Peel, chief secretary for Ireland, to Lord Whitworth, May 20, 1816.

232 "Rare old Sève [*sic*] Porcelain, Buhl": *The Times,* May 21 and 22, 1816.

232 "how Brummell had changed since we saw him at Brighton": F. Bickley, ed., *The Glenbervie Journals,* Lord Glenbervie to his son Frederick, MP for Banbury. He exaggerates the number of years since Brummell was in the Tenth Light Dragoons by five years: Brummell left in 1798; Lord Glenbervie was writing in 1816. Vol. 2, pp. 193–4.

233 "The hotel . . . was frequented by none but": F. Coghlan, *A Guide to France,* p. 16.

233 "three guineas extra": ibid., p. 11.

233 "Listed as a joiner": L.-N. Berthe, P. Bougard, D. Canlier, et al., eds., *Villes et Villages du Pas-de-Calais en 1790*, pp. 502–3. 1790 *"Questionnaire" "Leleu . . . menuisier."* Garde Nationale, formed August 21, 1789; 545 names, p. 502.

234 "between London and Paris": T. Raikes, *Reminiscences*, p. 275; also, Pückler-Muskau quotes Brummell as describing himself as *"le ci-devant jeune homme qui passe sa vie entre Paris et Londres,"* in L. Melville, *Beau Brummell*, p. 165.

234 "Next he papered": W. Jesse, *A Life*, 1844, vol. 1, p. 350.

234 "a large cabinet with brass wire doors": ibid.

235 The quayside was rebuilt: C. Borde, *Calais et la Mer 1814–1914*, p. 37; 442 crossings between mid-October and mid-November 1818.

235 The Dukes of Wellington, Richmond, Beaufort: W. Jesse, *A Life*, 1844, vol. 1, p. 109.

235 "pays the former patriarch": Prince Pückler-Muskau, in L. Melville, *Beau Brummell*, p. 165.

235 "2lb of Façon de Paris": K. Campbell, *Beau Brummell*, p. 126.

236 "Mr Brummell is the happiest of men": ibid., p. 133.

236 "I have heard all about your late tricks": H. Wilson, *Memoirs of Harriette Wilson*, 1831, vol. 4, pp. 207ff.

237 "nature itself . . . at a little distance": R. H. Stoddard, ed., *Personal Reminiscences*, p. 274. Raikes dated the letter May 22, 1816, only two days after Brummell's arrival, which seems dubious given Brummell's obvious familiarity with Calais.

237 "As to the alteration in my looks": ibid., pp. 272–4.

237 It was wrongly assumed at the time: D. Hayden, *Pox*, pp. 58ff.

238 and expressed surprise that he had never learned to speak: *"que c'etoit aussi etonnat qu'heureux qu'il n'eut jamais appris à parler François en Angleterre [sic],"* H. Wilson, *Memoirs*, vol. 4, pp. 207ff.

238 "I would have kept him for nothing": W. Jesse, *A Life*, 1844, vol. 1, p. 344.

239 "We used to call him *le roi de Calais*": ibid., vol. 2, pp. 13–14.

239 running schoolboy joke about their bad French: "Prostrate my remembrances at the feet of Mrs Marshall and all your family . . . tell me whether it *makes* fine or bad weather," letter, G. Brummell to Captain Marshall, W. Jesse, *A Life*, 1844, vol. 2, p. 37.

239 "surprised [you would be] to find the sudden": R. H. Stoddard, ed., *Personal Reminiscences*, pp. 272–3.

239 "I dine at five, and my evening": ibid., pp. 272–4.

240 *"Ah, voilà Monsieur Brummell"*: W. Jesse, *A Life*, 1844, vol. 1, p. 337.

240 "I could hardly believe [my] eyes": Hobhouse visited Brummell in July 1817 in the company of Scrope Davies. T. A. J. Burnett, *The Rise and Fall of a Regency Dandy*, p. 121.

240 "Brummell, in great distress standing at her side": W. Jesse, *A Life*, 1844, vol. 1, p. 363.

241 "Like a true cynic": ibid., p. 364.

14: *MALE AND FEMALE COSTUME* AND OTHER WORKS, 1821–1830

242 "£5000 for The Memoirs . . . going to Calais to treat with Brummell": J. B. Priestley, ed., *Tom Moore's Diary*, p. 19.

242 "set everything at defiance": L. Melville, *Beau Brummell*, p. 140.

242 *Memoirs by Herself*: 1825, but rumoured for some years beforehand.

243 "I [have now] promised the Duchess": T. Raikes, *Journals*, vol. I, pp. 146ff.

243 "I have been almost constantly occupied . . .": RA/GEO 22219-20. Letter from G. Brummell to Lord Petersham, Calais, October 18, 1818.

245 all born in the years when Brummell had shared: J. and P. Foord-Kelcey, *Mrs Fitzherbert and Sons*, pp. 48ff, pp. 72–3 and 112ff.

245 "A purse, a card-case, a note keeper": W. Jesse, *A Life*, 1844, vol. 1, p. 108.

246 "I've lost my way, ma'am": W. Jesse, *A Life*, 1844, vol. 1, pp. 359ff.

246 "deep regret of all the world": ibid., vol. 2, p. 6. Back of "The Petition for a New-foundland Dog," given to the Duchess of York in 1815 and passed on to Brummell (the petition, not the dog).

246 He weighed ten stone, thirteen pounds: Berry Brothers' weighing books, "George Brummell, Esq 1822. July 26 10, 13 Boots."

247 "Falstaff . . . was not so sad": ibid.

248 "I was standing at my shop door": W. Jesse, *A Life*, 1844, vol. 2, pp. 7–8.

248 He later claimed it was his best brandy: Major Chambre, *Recollections of West End Life*, p. 285.

249 "And here . . . the conversation closed": W. Jesse, *A Life*, 1844, vol. 2, pp. 10–11.

250 *Male and Female Costume*: *Male and Female Costume, Grecian and Roman Costume, British Costume from the Roman Invasion until 1822* was lost for many years. It came on the market first in 1856, and was owned in the early 1920s by Messrs. E. Parsons and Sons, antiquarian booksellers on London's Brompton Road. An enterprising New Yorker, Eleanor Parker, bought it from Bretano's Antiquarian Books in Manhattan, which, presumably, had it from Parsons. It was published in America in 1932 and reissued in 1972.

250 "Did any men . . . ever look like Greeks": G. Brummell, *Male and Female Costume*, p. 123.

251 "there is quite as much vanity": ibid., p. 122.

251 "the minor poet who goes into company": ibid.

251 the age of men in black: J. Harvey, *Men in Black*.

252 "[M]y companion and myself found that dinner": W. Pitt Lennox, *Celebrities I Have Known*, vol. 1, p. 298.

252 "pale and emaciated; his still well-fitted": ibid., pp. 298ff.

253 "abusing Brummell—said he was a damned fellow": Charles Greville, *Letters*, in H. Cole, *Beau Brummell*, p. 155.

254 investments worth over £40,000: O. Munson, *Maria Fitzherbert*, p. 339.

254 one of several children: J. and P. Foord-Kelcey, *Mrs Fitzherbert and Sons*, pp. 48ff and 72–3.

254 according to his prospective mother-in-law: Bodleian Library, North Family MSS d 30 and 31: letter, Mrs. Fitzherbert to Lady Guildford, not dated but c. July 24, 1822.

255 "To Lieut Col the Hon George Dawson": MSS owned by Earl Fortescue in 1924, in L. Melville, *Beau Brummell*, p. 167.

256 Calais in 1829: ibid., p. 168.

256 "moistened with cold green tea": Major Chambre, *Recollections*, vol. 1, p. 286.

256 "Whenever any one of my creditors calls upon me": ibid., p. 292.

257 "curious snuff-boxes": ibid., pp. 292–3.

257 At auction one tea set: Cole, *Beau Brummell*, p. 161.

257 "Just as gay as ever": C. Greville, *Memoirs*, vol. 1, pp. 282–3.

259 Leveux's Bill: W. Jesse, *A Life*, 1844, vol. 2, pp. 24ff.

260 One pill, four times a day: J. Oriel, *The Scars of Venus*, p. 83.

260 Further experiments were performed on infected Coldstream: T. Rose, *Observations on the treatment of syphilis with an account of several cases of that disease in which a cure was effected without mercury*, 1817, Med-Chir. Trans 8:550.

261 as indeed were the majority of syphilitics well into: J. Oriel, *The Scars of Venus*, pp. 81ff.

262 "My Dear Marshall": L. Melville, *Beau Brummell.*, pp. 159ff.

262 "in spirit to meet a bishop": Dr. Michael Henry Thornhill Luscombe, later chaplain to the British Embassy in Paris and bishop of the Episcopalian Church. He came to later fame as the cleric who officiated at W. M. Thackeray's wedding in Paris in April 1836.

262 The king's messenger later avowed: W. Jesse, *A Life*, 1844, vol. 2, p. 28.

15: HIS BRITANNIC MAJESTY'S CONSUL, 1830–1832

264 It was to be gold and enamel: W. Jesse, *A Life of George Bryan Brummell Esq.*, 1844, vol. 2, p. 30.

264 "The best rooms, the best dinner": ibid.

265 founded by the same medieval English king: King Henry VI.

265 "October 25th 1830, rue des Carmes": W. Jesse, *A Life*, 1844, vol. 2, pp. 33ff.

265 "*Amphytrions de nos compatriots*": Amphytrion, a gourmet and food lover; from the eponymous hero of the Molière comedy but very current in Brummell's France as a term for fine hosts with superior tables, after the success of the *Manuel des Amphytrions*, a guide to gastronomy and the best places to eat in Paris.

269 "Tuesday. Millions of thanks:" W. Jesse, *A Life*, 1844, vol. 2, pp. 122–5.

269 "*Ayesha*": *The Maid of Kars*, a novel by James Justinian Morier, 1832.

270 "His dress on the evening in question": W. Jesse, *A Life,* 1844, vol. 2, pp. 76–7.

272 "I therefore beg you to consider": ibid., pp. 60–1.

273 "I may represent to Your Lordship": G. Brummell to Viscount Palmerston, May 19, 1831, Foreign Officer Papers, National Archives; H. Cole, *Beau Brummell,* p. 174.

274 "A Monsieur Armstrong": W. Jesse, *A Life,* 1927, vol. 2, p. 49.

275 "March 21 1832. Sir": PRO Foreign Office Papers. H. Cole, *Beau Brummell,* p. 182.

276 "Send me seventy-five francs to pay": W. Jesse, *A Life,* 1844, vol. 2, p. 107.

277 "Oh this uncomfortable weather!": W. Jesse, *A Life,* 1844, vol. 2, p. 109–10.

277 Tabetic neurosyphilis . . . Sudden paralysis was a classic symptom": S. M. Brooks, *The VD Story,* pp. 34ff.

277 "and those excruciating spasms": W. Jesse, *A Life,* 1844, vol. 2, p. 111.

16: HÔTEL D'ANGLETERRE, 1832–1835

279 "My papers are the only things": W. Jesse, *A Life of George Bryan Brummell Esq.,* 1844, vol. 2, pp. 182–4.

280 "would put an end to my sufferings in this world": W. Jesse, *A Life,* 1844, vol. 2, p. 111.

280 He gave her his entire album: Cole is of the opinion that the recipient of Brummell's later letters was not Aimable de St.-Ursain but Ellen Villiers, daughter of one of the English families. Jesse does distinguish between the earlier and later letters, but there is much to link them: Jesse introduces the recipient of the later letters as "Brummell's favourite correspondent" and she clearly has French, English and Italian, like Aimable. Jesse was trying to protect the reputation of Mademoiselle St.-Ursain, whose family he knew.

281 in Paris and Dublin as alternative or complementary: J. Oriel, *The Scars of Venus,* pp. 87ff.

282 "scattered inflammatory oozing": C. Drysdale, *On the Treatment of Syphilis and Other Diseases* and evidence from after the Peninsular Wars quoted in J. Stokes, et al., eds., *Modern Clinical Syphilology,* p. 217.

282 The last vestige of his hair: W. Jesse, *A Life,* 1844, vol. 2, p. 153.

282 "I am unwell": ibid., p. 156.

283 "[August] 1834. My Dear Alvanley": ibid., pp. 168–9.

284 By now all of the other guests were awake: ibid., pp. 182–4.

285 exhibition of flowers: *L'Ami de la Verité,* April 27, 1835, Archives Municipales de Caen.

285 all charged with vagabondage: ibid., May 8, 1835, Archives Municipales de Caen.

17: PRISON, 1835–1839

286 "I still breathe, though I am not of the living": W. Jesse, *A Life of George Bryan Brummell Esq.*, 1927, vol. 2, p. 142.

287 "put with all the *common* people": Jesse, *A Life*, 1844, vol. 2, p. 186.

288 "applications should be made in person": *L'Ami de la Verité*, April 17, 1835, Archives Municipales de Caen.

288 It struggled on . . . for several years, without him: *L'Ami de la Verité*, Archives Municipales de Caen. Godefroi was released in 1839. He accompanied Jesse on a tour of the prison in 1843. The prison was demolished in 1906 to make way for an exit road from the place Fontette.

288 "probably prolong his detention": W. Jesse, *A Life*, 1927, vol. 2, p. 164.

288 There was a communicating fireplace: *Plan Général au rez de chaussée de Prisons Royales de la Ville de Caen*, ADCC.

289 "11 May. [1835]": Jesse, *A Life*, 1927, vol. 2, p. 149.

289 "towers of Matilda": The Abbaye des Dames was founded by Queen Matilda, consort of King William I.

289 "You will perceive the extremities": Jesse, *A Life*, 1844, vol. 2, pp. 194–5.

290 "actually washed and shaved": Jesse, *A Life*, 1927, vol. 2, p. 156 (my italics).

290 *"chambre des prisonniers civils"*: *Plan Général au rez de chaussée de Prisons Royales de la Ville de Caen*, ADCC.

291 "this poet, this great man": Jesse, *A Life*, 1927, vol. 2, p. 167, *"ce poète, ce grand homme, fut mon ami."*

291 "as a man of business": ibid., pp. 256–7.

292 "July 1835. My Lords": Draft letter, July 27, 1835. (This money followed that which secured Brummell's immediate release.) Foreign Office MSS, in H. Cole, *Beau Brummell*, pp. 213–214.

293 "the slightest surprise or joy": W. Jesse, *A Life*, 1844, vol. 2, p. 263.

293 "an air of nonchalance": ibid., p. 264.

294 "shaken his intellect": ibid., p. 303.

294 "your album": W. Jesse, *A Life*, 1927, vol. 2, pp. 213–14.

295 *"Tabes dorsalis"*: D. Hayden, *Pox*, p. 58.

295 "brought himself down to one": W. Jesse, *A Life*, 1844, vol. 2, p. 296.

296 "a great change . . . in his personal appearance": W. Jesse, *A Life*, 1844, vol. 2, p. 300.

296 When Armstrong sent him a new winter: ibid., vol. 2, p. 303.

296 "drawling with prolixity": W. Jesse, *A Life*, 1844, vol. 2, p. 304.

297 "The poor Beau's head's gone": W. Dowden, ed., *The Journal of Thomas Moore*, vol. 5, pp. 1892–3; diary entry, July 1837. *Letters* cited in bibliog. Also *Tom Moore's Diary*, ed., J. B. Priestley.

297 "I was ashamed . . . to see so famous and distinguished": *"J'avais honte de voir*

un homme si celebre et si distinguée et qui s'etait crée une place dans l'histoire dans un état si malheureux." W. Jesse, *A Life,* 1844, vol. 2, p. 308.

298 "Keen blows the wind, and piercing is the cold": ibid., p. 312.

298 "a precursor of": Letter from Scrope Davies, Monday, May 25, 1835; T. Raikes, *A Portion of his Journal from 1831–1847,* vol. 2, pp. 113ff.

299 "Right before madness": D. Haydn, *Pox,* p. 56.

299 "Suddenly, and as if divided into two": J. B. d'Aurevilly, trans. D. B. Wyndham Lewis, *The Anatomy of Dandyism,* pp. 59–61.

300 "Finally, when the room was full": ibid.

300 "but kindly": W. Jesse, *A Life,* 1844, vol. 2, pp. 319–20.

300 "from royal personages": ibid., p. 322.

301 "I have deferred writing for some time": W. Jesse, *A Life,* 1927, vol. 2, pp. 251–2.

301 "His linen . . . was changed once a month": W. Jesse, *A Life,* 1844, vol. 2, p. 331.

301 In January 1839: Jesse claimed Brummell was not moved to Bon Sauveur until May, but the asylum records place his date of entry as January 17 and his first proper examination by Dr. Vastel as February 2. Archives de l'Hôpital Psychiatrique du Bon Sauveur, Caen, January 1839.

301 *"Bonjour, Monsieur!"* said Fichet: W. Jesse, *A Life,* 1844, vol. 2, pp. 346ff.

18: ASYLUM, 1839–1840

303 "It's like being bound hand and foot": D. Haydn, *Pox,* pp. xiff.

303 "Babylon in all its desolation": T. Raikes, *A Portion of his Journal,* vol. 2, pp. 113ff. Letter from Scrope Davies, Monday, May 25, 1835. Davies appears to be writing about his own impending symptoms of tertiary syphilis, as diagnosed by Sir George Tuthill. He is advised "on such occasions [as an outbreak, to] avoid all possible excitement, or the consequences must be most lamentable."

305 "salubrious and well aired": P. Morel and C. Quetel, *Du Bon Sauveur au CHS,* p. 26.

305 "each madman has his own cell": ibid. p. 26. "Mère Supérieure en 1818, "chaque insense à sa cellule . . . ils sont plus tranquilles et plus sainement dans des chambres isolée."

305 "1. A total 'rupture' from normality": ibid., pp. 48–9.

306 *"Brummell, Georges, célibataire":* AMC MSS, "Age et domicile du malade, Brummell, Georges. 17 Janvier 1839," Archive de l'Hôpital Psychiatrique du Bon Sauveur

307 A half hour after the inmates were woken: P. Morel and C. Quetel, *Du Bon Sauveur,* pp. 55–6.

307 "tubful of warm water": P. Ricord, *Illustrations of Syphilitic Disease,* pp. 71–3.

307 general paresis, the terms used interchangeably: Alexander Morison of Bethlem Hospital (Bedlam) gave a good description of general paresis in 1840 and observed that Esquirol (1814 and 1838) and Palmeil (1826) had previously termed the condition "general paralysis of the insane." "The possible relation of syphilis

to general paresis was commented upon by Esmarch and Jesser as early as 1857, while Kjelberg of Uppsala in 1863 expressed the definitive opinion that syphilitic infection was invariably the cause of general paresis or general paralysis. Not until 1913 were Moore and Noguchi able to demonstrate the presence of Spirochaete pallida in the brains of general paretics." C. Worster-Drought, *Neurosyphilis*, p. 118.

308 "this excellent nurse of mine": W. Jesse, *A Life*, 1927, vol. 2, p. 266.

309 "violent, mutinous, chronically deranged": P. Morel and C. Quetel, *Du Bon Sauveur*, p. 60.

309 All the mucous membranes of Brummell's body: J. Beaney, *Constitutional Syphilis . . . in its Secondary and Tertiary Phases*.

309 "Gummy tumours": P. Ricord, *Illustrations of Syphilitic Disease*, pp. 327ff.

309 unbleeding buboes: J. Bacot, *A Treatise on Syphilis*, pp. 223ff.

310 *"Table d'hôte toujours"*: W. Jesse, *A Life*, 1844, vol. 2, p. 348.

310 "sinking further and further": AMC, Archives du Bon Sauveur, G. Brummell, 1839–40. "Le malade s'affaisse de plus en plus, fevrier 1840, idem mars—il est mort le 30 mars 1840."

310 "but the local records": ADCC, MSS 80F7.

310 "Mr Brummell was in an imbecile state": W. Jesse, *A Life*, 1844, vol. 2, pp. 349–50.

311 "it had rained almost daily since January": *The Times*, April 5, 1840, reporting the newly arrived French papers.

311 *"ayant l'air d'implorer"*: Jesse uses her original French in his report.

311 "an extra fifty francs was paid": ADCC, 80F44, no. 49 in the cemetery Register of Concessions.

312 *"Qui est-ce?"*: "Les Dix Ans de la vie caennais du 'dandy.' " *Caen Hebdo*, April 21, 1971, quoting local story.

Bibliography

Manuscripts

ROYAL ARCHIVES
RA GEO/29210–29427 (Accounts, 1783–1830; Wardrobe, Swords, Spurs, Regimental Colours)
RA GEO/29428–29643 (Accounts, 1783–1830; Wardrobe, Swords, Spurs, Regimental Colours)
RA GEO/22219–20 (Letter from G. B. Brummell to Lord Petersham)
RA GEO/44527–44558 (Letters of the Duchess of York to Prince Regent and Duchess of Cambridge)
RA GEO/Add 50/98–105 (Letters of the Duchess of York to Charles Culling Smith)

BRITISH MUSEUM
Scrope Davies Papers—MSS Loan 70
Whitefoord Papers—Add MSS 36 595 No. 295, No. 305
Sir Robert Wilson Select English Letters—Add MSS 30 115
Add MSS 41335 380m—Masonic Initiation Certificate
L'An de la V L 58 32 le 19ème jour du 2ème mois (February 19, 1832)
Add MSS 36 593, 38233, 38307

NATIONAL ARCHIVES (PUBLIC RECORDS OFFICE, KEW)
FO 27/419, 435, 453, 455, 491, 493, 510
PRO 30/29/417 Prob 11/958, 1242

LONDON METROPOLITAN ARCHIVES
Brooks's and White's betting books
Memorials of Brooks's MDCCLXIV–MCM April 2, 1799
White's betting book 1743–1878. 1811

WESTMINSTER ABBEY ARCHIVE
St. Margaret's, Westminster: baptismal, marriage and burial records

WESTMINSTER CITY ARCHIVES
Baptismal, marriage and burial records, St. James's Piccadilly and St.-Martin-in-the-
Fields
Rate books: Bond Street, Piccadilly, Bury Street
Account ledgers: Fribourg and Treyer

BELVOIR CASTLE MUNIMENTS ROOM
Letter from G. B. Brummell to Lords Charles and Robert Manners, 1816
Annuities, Lords Charles and Robert Manners

BERRY BROS. & RUDD, ST. JAMES'S STREET, LONDON
Weighing books

JAMES LOCK & CO., HATTERS, ST. JAMES'S STREET, LONDON
Ledgers, 1798–1815

MEYER & MORTIMER, TAILORS, SACKVILLE STREET, LONDON
Ledger, 1809–1817
Waterloo tailor's notebook

BODLEIAN LIBRARY
north family mss

ETON COLLEGE ARCHIVES
Musae Etonenses, Nugae Etonenses
School lists, Montem lists, boardinghouse appendices
On the Montem, composed by Herbertus Stockhore, 1793
Eton College Register 1753–1790
Preces Quotidianae in usum Scholae Collegii Regalis apud Etonam, Eton College Daily
Prayer Book, 1793
*Etoniana Ancient and Modern, Being the Notes of the History and Traditions of Eton
College,* republished from *Blackwood's Magazine* with additions, 1865

ORIEL COLLEGE, OXFORD
Archives, 1768–1809, Easter term, 1794 [ref. S II K 14]
Buttery books, 1793–1795

ARCHIVES DE L'HÔPITAL PSYCHIATRIQUE
DU BON SAUVEUR, CAEN
Admissions and Inmates: *G. B. Brummell, ex Consul de Sa Majesté Britannique,*
1839–1840

ARCHIVES DÉPARTEMENTALES DU CALVADOS
M 220 Nomination d'un Consul Étranger, 1830
Archives du Cimetière Protestant
Register of Concessions
MSS 80F44—Archives Départementales du Calvados

ARCHIVES MUNICIPALES DE CAEN
Plan de l'Hôtel d'Angleterre, Troisième Etage, 79–81 rue St. Jean, Caen, Calvados, avant guerre 1939–1945
Plan Général au rez de chaussée de Prisons Royales de la Ville de Caen, 1788. Archives Municipales du Calvados

Costume Collections

The Museum of London, Collection of Dress and Textiles
The National Museum of Costume, Bath
The Victoria and Albert Museum
Cosprop Costumiers, London

Contemporary Periodicals

Alfred and Westminster Evening Gazette
Annual Register
Bon Ton Magazine, or Microscope of Fashion and Folly
Covent Garden Journal
Crim-Con Gazette
Fraser's Magazine
Gentleman's Magazine
Harris's Lists of the Ladies of Covent Garden
Journal de la Normandie
Lady's Magazine
L'Ami de la Verité, Caen
Lancet
Monthly Magazine
Morning Chronicle
Morning Post
Public Advertiser
Punch
Ramblers' Magazine

Revue de Paris
Spectator
St James's Chronicle
Tatler
The Times

Other Primary Material

MEMOIRS, DIARIES AND LETTERS

Anon., *Picture of London for 1805 Being a Correct Guide to All the Curiosities, Amusements, Exhibitions, Public Establishments, and Remarkable Objects In and Near London with a Collection of Appropriate Tables.* London, 1805.

Aspinall, A., ed. *Correspondence of King George IV, 1812–1830.* Cambridge: Cambridge University Press, 1938.

———. *Correspondence of George, Prince of Wales, 1770–1812.* London: Cassell, 1963.

Bentley, Richard, ed. *Anecdotes of the Upper Ten Thousand: their legends and their lives* by Grantley F. Berkeley. 2 vols. London: 1867.

Bickley, Francis, ed. *The Glenbervie Journals.* London: Constable, 1928.

Brownlow, Lady Emma Sophia. *The Eve of Victorianism, Reminiscences of the Years 1802–34.* London, 1840.

Butler, E. M., ed. *A Regency Visitor; The English Tour of Prince Pückler-Muskau described in his letters 1826–1828.* Trans. Sarah Austen. London: Collins, 1957.

Cave, Kathryn, Garlick, Kenneth and Macintyre, Angus, eds. *The Diary of Joseph Farington (the years 1793–1821).* New York: Yale University Press, 1998.

Chambre, Major. *Recollections of West End Life with Sketches of Society in Paris, India Etc.* 2 vols. London, 1858.

Chateaubriand, François-René. *Mémoires d'Outre-Tombe.* Paris: Flammarion, 1950.

Creasy, Edward Shepherd. *Memoirs of Eminent Etonians: with notices of the early history of Eton College.* London, 1850.

Croker, John Wilson. *The Correspondence and Diaries of the late Rt Hon. John Wilson Croker.* 3 vols. London: John Murray, 1884.

d'Aurevilly, Jules Barbey. *Du Dandysme et de George Brummel* [sic]. 3ème édition. Paris, 1876.

———. *Du Dandysme et de George Brummel* [sic]. Trans. D. B. Wyndham Lewis, *The Anatomy of Dandyism.* London, 1928.

———. *Du Dandysme et de George Brummell,* 1844. Trans. George Walden, *Who's a Dandy?* London: Gibson Square Books, 2002.

Dowden, Wilfred ed. *The Letters of Thomas Moore.* 2 vols. Oxford: Clarendon Press, 1964.

Edgcumbe, Richard (Earl Edgcumbe). *Musical Reminiscences of an Old Amateur Chiefly respecting Italian Opera in England, 1773–1823*. London, 1827.

———, ed. *The Diary of Frances, Lady Shelley 1787–1817*. London, 1912.

Foster, V., ed. *The Two Duchesses: Family Correspondence of Georgiana, Duchess of Devonshire and Elizabeth, Duchess of Devonshire*. Bath, 1898.

Fraser, William Augustus. *Words on Wellington*. London, 1889.

Goede, C. A. G. *A Stranger in England; or, Travels in Great Britain*. London, 1807.

Graham, Peter W., ed. *Letters of John Cam Hobhouse to Lord Byron, "Byron's Bulldog."* Columbus: Ohio State University Press, 1966.

Grenville, Richard Plantagenet Temple Nugent Brydges Chandos. *Memoirs of the Court of George IV . . . From original family documents*. 2 vols. London, 1859.

Greville, Charles. *The Greville Memoirs*. 3 vols. London, 1875.

Gronow, Captain Rees-Howell. *Reminiscences of Captain Gronow Formerly of the Grenadier Guards and M.P. for Stafford being Anecdotes of the Camp, The Court and The Clubs at the close of the last war with France, related by Himself*. 1st edition. London, 1862; 2nd edition, London, 1863.

———. *Captain Gronow's Last Recollections being the Fourth and Final Series of his Reminiscences and Anecdotes*. London, 1866.

Hairby, James. *Rambles in Normandy*. London, 1846.

Harris, James. *Diaries and Correspondence of James Harris, First Lord Malmesbury*. London, 1844.

Hillard, G. S., ed. *Life, Letters, and Journals of George Ticknor*. Boston, 1876.

Hobhouse, John Cam. *The Substance of Some Letters Written from Paris during the Last Reign of the Emperor Napoleon and addressed principally to The Rt Hon Lord Byron*. London, 1817.

———. *Recollections of a Long Life, In Five Volumes*. London, 1865.

Hook, Theodore. *Sayings and Doings*, second series: *The Sutherlands, The Man of Many Friends, Doubts and Fears, Passion and Principle*. London, 1825.

Jerrold, Walter, ed. *Bon-Mots of Samuel Foote and Theodore Hook*. London, 1894.

Jesse, Captain William. *A Life of George Brummell, Esq., Commonly Known as Beau Brummell*. 2 vols. London, 1844; with additions and illustrations, 1854, 1886; new edition, London: Navarre Society, 1927.

Johnson, Samuel. *Prefaces, Biographical and Critical, to the Works of the English Poets*. London, 1781.

Johnstone, Julia. *Confessions of Julia Johnstone, written by herself in contradiction to the fables of Harriette Wilson*. London, 1825.

Khan, Mizra Abul Hassan. *A Persian at the Court of King George IV, 1809–10, The Journal of Mizra Abul Hassan Khan*. Trans. M. M. Cloake. London, 1988.

Lennox, William Pitt (Lord). *The Story of My Life*. 3 vols. London, 1857.

———. *Fifty Years' Biographical Reminiscences*. 2 vols. London, 1863.

———. *The Adventures of a Man of Family*. 3 vols. London, 1864.

———. *My Recollections from 1806 to 1873.* 2 vols. London, 1874.

———. *Celebrities I Have Known, with Episodes, Political, Social, Sporting and The-atrical.* First series, 2 vols. London, 1876; second series, 2 vols. London, 1877.

Leveson Gower, Sir G., ed. *Hary-O: the Letters of Lady Harriet Cavendish, 1796–1809.* London: John Murray, 1940.

Lieven, Dorothea. *The Private letters of Princess Lieven to Prince Metternich 1820–1826.* London, 1937.

Macdonald, John. *Memoirs of an 18th Century Footman.* London: Century, 1985.

Macnamara, Ulysses. *The British Army: Condition at the Close of the Eighteenth Century, Compared with its Present State and Prospects.* London, 1839.

MacQueen, John, ed. *The Court of England under George IV: The Diary of a Lady-in-Waiting* [Lady Charlotte Bury]. London, 1896.

Meryon, Dr. C. L., ed. *Memoirs of Lady Hester Stanhope, as related by Herself to her Physician, Comprising her opinions and Anecdotes of Some of the Most Remarkable Persons of her Time.* 3 vols. London, 1845.

Moore, Thomas, ed. [Byron (George G.), 6th Baron,] *The Works of Lord Byron; with his Letters and Journals.* London: John Murray, 1832–3.

Moreland, Olivia. *The Charms of Dandyism, or, living in style. By Olivia Moreland, chief of the female dandies, and edited by Captain Ashe.* 3 vols. London, 1819.

Owenson, Sydney (Lady Morgan). *La France; par Lady Morgan. Par l'auteur de Quinze Jours et de Six Mois à Londres.* Trans. P. A. Lebrun des Charmettes. Paris, 1817.

———. *The Book of the Boudoir.* London, 1829.

Priestley, J. B., ed. *Tom Moore's Diary.* Cambridge: Cambridge University Press, 1925.

Pückler-Muskau, Prince. *Die Ruckkehr. Vom Verfasser der Briefe eines Verstorbenen.* Berlin, 1846.

Raikes, Thomas. *France since 1830.* 2 vols. London, 1841.

———. *A Portion of his Journal from 1831–1847.* Vols. I-IV. London, 1856.

———. *Reminiscences of Social and Political Life in London and Paris.* London, 1856.

Reynolds, F. *The Life and Times of Frederic Reynolds.* Vol. 1. London, 1826.

Smyth, William. *Memoir of Mr Sheridan.* Leeds, 1840.

Stoddard, R. H., ed. "Recollections of Thomas Raikes" in *Personal Reminiscences.* New York: Armstrong & Company, 1875.

Tattershall, John F., ed. *Reminiscences of a Literary Life, Charles Macfarlane 1799–1858, Author and Traveller.* From two quarto manuscript volumes. London, 1917.

Vermont, de (Marquis). *London and Paris, or Comparative Sketches.* London, 1823.

Walpole, Horace, and Wright, John, ed. *Letters.* London, 1840–46.

Watkins, John. *A Biographical Memoir of His Late Royal Highness, Frederick, Duke of York and Albany.* London, 1827.

Wilson, Harriette. *Memoirs of Harriette Wilson, Written by herself in Eight Volumes.* London: Peter Davies, 1929.

FASHION

Anon. *Dandymania, Just published Price One Shilling. Embellished with a coloured likeness of a well-known Dandy*. London, 1819.

———. *Essay Philosophical and Medical Concerning Modern Clothing*. London, 1792.

———. *Indispensable Requisites for Dandies of Both Sexes, by A Lady*. Dublin, 1820.

———. *Necklothitania or Tietania, Being an Essay on Starchers, by One of the Cloth*. London, 1818.

———. *Taylor's Complete Guide*. London, 1796.

———. *The Art of Tying the Cravat*. London, 1829.

———. *The Tailor's Masterpiece*. London, c. 1829.

———. *The Whole Art of Dress, by a Cavalry Officer*. London, 1830.

Brummell, George Bryan. *Male and Female Costume, Grecian and Roman Costume, British Costume from the Roman Invasion until 1822 and the Principles of Costume applied to the Improved Dress of the Present Day (1822)*. New York: Doubleday, Doran & Company, 1932.

Carlyle, Thomas. *Sartor Resartus (Fraser's Magazine 1833–4)*. London: Canongate Classics, 2002.

Compaing, C., and de Vere, Louis. *The Tailor's Guide*. London 1856.

de Vere, Louis. *The Handbook of Practical Cutting*. London, 1866.

Le Blanc, H. *The History of the Cravat*. London, c. 1825.

———. *The Art of Tying the Cravat Demonstrated in Sixteen Lessons including Thirty Two Different Styles forming a Pocket Manual*. London, 1828.

———. *The Art of Tying the Cravat, Preceded by a History of the Cravat*. London, 1829.

SEX AND SYPHILIS

Adams, Joseph. *Observations on morbid poisons, phagedœna, and cancer: containing a comparative view of the theories of Dr. Swediaur, John Hunter, Messrs. Foot, Moore, and Bell, on the laws of the venereal virus*. London, 1795.

Bacot, John. *A Treatise on Syphilis; in which the history, symptoms, and method of treating every form of that disease, are fully considered*. London: Longman, Rees, Orme, Brown, and Green, 1829.

Beaney, James George. *Constitutional syphilis: being a practical illustration of the disease in its secondary and tertiary phases*. 3rd edition. Melbourne, 1878.

Davies, David, Hunter, R., and Manchee, T. J. *An essay on mercury; wherein are presented formulae for some preparations of this metal . . . Being the result of long experience and diligent observation*. London and Bristol, 1820.

Drysdale, Charles R., M.D. *On the Treatment of Syphilis and Other Diseases without Mercury being a collection of evidence to prove that mercury is a cause of disease, not a remedy*. Royal College of Physicians, London, 1863.

Lagneau, L. V. *Exposé des diverses methods de traiter la Maladie Vénérienne*. Paris, 1803.

Marten, Dr. John. *A Treatise of all the Degrees and Symptoms of the Venereal Disease.* London, 1704.

Parker, Langston. *The modern treatment of syphilitic diseases, both primary and secondary. Comprising an account of the new remedies, with numerous formulae for their preparation, and mode of administration.* London, 1839.

Plenck, Joseph James. *A new and easy method of giving mercury, to those affected with the venereal disease* [also known as *Methodus nova et facilis argentum vivum aegris venerea labe infectis exhibendi.*]. Trans. William Saunders. Edinburgh, 1772.

Ricord, Philip. *Illustrations of Syphilitic Disease with the addition of a History of Syphilis.* Trans. Thomas Betton, M.D. Philadelphia, 1851.

Swediaur, F., M.D. *Practical Observations on Venereal Complaints, To which were added an Account of the New Venereal Disease which has lately appeared in Canada.* 3rd edition. Edinburgh, 1788.

———. *Traité complet sur les symptomes, les effets, la nature et le traitement des maladies syphilitiques.* 4th edition. Paris, 1801.

Wallace, William. *A treatise of the venereal disease and its varities.* London-Renshaw, 1838.

Welbank, Richard. *Practical commentaries on the present knowledge and treatment of syphilis: with coloured illustrations of some ordinary forms of that disease.* London: Longman, Hurst, Rees, Orme, Browne and Green, 1825.

MISCELLANEOUS

Anon. *An Address to Her Royal Highness the Dutchess [sic] of York Against the Use of Sugar.* London, 1792.

———. *Don John or Don Juan Unmasked being a key to the mystery attending that remarkable publication.* 3rd edition. London, 1819.

———. *Picture of London for 1805 Being a Correct Guide to All the Curiosities, Amusements, Exhibitions, Public Establishments, and Remarkable Objects In and Near London with a Collection of Appropriate Tables.* London, 1805.

———. *The British Code of Duel; A reference to The Laws of Honour and the Character of Gentlemen, An appendix in which is strictly examined the case between the Tenth Hussars and Mr Battier; Cpt Calla'n, Mr Finch, &c noted.* London, 1824.

Barrow, William. *An Essay on Education.* 2 vols. London, 1802.

Byron, George Gordon (Lord). *Don Juan.* London, 1819.

Carlyle, Thomas. *Sartor Resartus, Fraser's Magazine.* London, 1833–4.

Coghlan, Francis. *A Guide to France, or, Travellers, Their Own Commissioners, explaining every form and expense from London to Paris.* London, 1829.

Goldsmith, Oliver. *The Citizen of the World.* London, 1837.

Knox, Vicesimus. *Liberal Education.* Dublin, 1781.

Luttrell, Henry. *Advice to Julia, A Letter in Rhyme.* London, 1820.

———. *Letters to Julia in Rhyme to which are added Lines Written at Ampthill-Park.* London, 1822.

McGann, Jerome J., ed. *Lord Byron: The Complete Poetical Works*. 7 vols. Oxford: Clarendon Press, 1980.

Moncrieff, William Thomas. *Tom and Jerry; or, Life in London; an operatic extravaganza, in three acts and in prose, with songs*. 2nd edition. London, 1828.

Moore, John. *View of Society and Manners in Italy*. 2 vols., 2nd edition. London, 1781.

Pyne, W. H. *The Royal Residences of England; Windsor Castle, Hampton Court, St James's Palace, Carlton House, Buckingham House*. Vol. II. London, 1819.

Roque, J. *An Accurate Survey of Speen Manor . . . belonging to the Duke of Chandos, 1730s–1740s*. (Newbury Museum), Map of Berkshire, 1761.

Temple, Lancelot. *A Short Ramble Through Some Parts of Italy and France*. London, 1751.

Secondary Material

Anon. *A Most Humoursome and Laughable Description of those Modern Would-be Ring-tail Cocked-up Dandies, etc*. Belfast, c. 1820.

———. *Etoniana Ancient and Modern being notes of the history and traditions of Eton College*. London: William Blackwood & Sons, 1865.

———. *La Vie Caennaise du Consulat au Second Empire racontée par un bourgeois et un homme du peuple*. Caen, 1927.

Adams, James Eli. *Dandies and Desert Saints; Styles of Victorian Masculinity*. Ithaca: Cornell University Press, 1995.

Adburgham, Alison. *Shopping in Style: London from the Restoration to Edwardian Elegance*. London: Thames & Hudson, 1979.

———. *Silver Fork Society: Fashionable Life and Literature 1814–1840*. London: Constable, 1983.

Allen, Peter Lewis. *The Wages of Sin: Sex and Disease, Past and Present*. Chicago: University of Chicago Press, 2000.

Arnold, Dana, ed. "Lecture 6. Scandal and Society by Lindsay Boynton" in *Squanderous and Lavish Profusion, George IV and his Image and Patronage of the Arts*. London: Georgian Group, 1995.

Ashley-Cooper, F. S. *Eton and Harrow at the Wicket*. London, 1922.

Auty, Susan G. *The Comic Spirit of Eighteenth-century Novels*. London: Kennikat Press, 1975.

Bank, Alfred, ed. *The Drama: Its History, Literature and Influence on Civilisation*. Vol. 15. London, 1906.

Barrow, William. *An Essay on Education*. 2 vols. London, 1802.

Barthes, Roland. *Le Dandysme et la Mode*. Paris: Editions du Seuil, 1971.

Baudelaire, Charles. *The Painter of Modern Life and Other Essays*. Trans. and ed. by J. Mayne. London: Phaidon Press, 1963.

Beaney, James George. *Constitutional Syphilis; being a practical illustration of the disease in its secondary and tertiary phases.* Melbourne: F. F. Ballière, 1878.

Becker, S. William, and Obermayer, Maximilian E. *Modern Dermatology and Syphilology.* London: J. B. Lippincott, 1943.

Beerbohm, Max. *Dandies and Dandies,* 1896, in S. C. Roberts, ed., *The Incomparable Max.* London: Heinemann, 1962.

Berthe, Léon-Noël, Bougard, Pierre, Canlier, Danielle, Decelle, Jean-Michel and Jessenne, Jean-Pierre. *Villes et Villages du Pas-de-Calais en 1790, Vol. II, Districts de Béthune, de Boulogne et de Calais.* Arras: Mémoires de la Commission Départementale d'Histoire et d'Archéologie du Pas-de-Calais, 1992.

Blanch, Lesley, ed. *Harriette Wilson's Memoirs: The Greatest Courtesan of her Age.* London: Phoenix, 2003.

Borde, Christian. *Calais et la Mer, 1814–1914.* Paris: Presses Universitaires du Septentrion, 1997.

Boulenger, Jacques. *Sous Louis-Philippe; Les Dandys.* Paris: Libraires Paul Ollendorff, 1907.

Bourne, Ursula. *Snuff.* Princes Risborough. London: Shire Publications, 1990.

Boutet de Monvel, Roger. *George Brummell et George IV.* Paris, 1906.

———. *Beau Brummell and His Times.* London, 1908.

Brereton, Austin. *A Walk down Bond Street. The centenary souvenir of the house of Ashton and Mitchell, 1820–1920.* London: Selwyn & Blount, 1920.

Breward, Christopher. *Fashioning London: Clothing and the Modern Metropolis.* London: Berg, 2004.

Brewer, John. *The Pleasures of the Imagination: English Culture in the Eighteenth Century.* HarperCollins: London, 1997.

Brooks, Stewart M. *The VD Story.* New York: Littlefield, Adams & Co., 1973.

Bruce, A.P.C. *The Purchase System in the British Army, 1660–1871.* London: Royal Historical Society, 1980.

Bryant, Julius. *Kenwood, The Iveagh Bequest.* London and New Haven: Yale University Press, 2003.

Budd, Michael Anton. *The Sculpture Machine; Physical Culture and Body Politics in the Age of Empire.* New York: New York University Press, 1997.

Burford, E. J. *Royal St James's, Being a Story of Kings, Clubmen and Courtesans.* London: Robert Hale, 1988.

———. *Wits, Wenches and Wantons: London's Low Life: Covent Garden in the Eighteenth Century.* London: Robert Hale, 1990.

———, and Wotton, Joy. *Private Vices, Public Virtues: Bawdry in London.* London: Robert Hale, 1995.

Burnett, T.A.J. *The Rise and Fall of a Regency Dandy: the Life and Times of Scrope Berdmore Davies.* London: John Murray, 1981.

Byrne, Paula. *Jane Austen and the Theatre.* London: Hambledon, 2002.

———. *Perdita; The Life of Mary Robinson.* London, HarperCollins, 2005.

Calloway, Stephen, and Colvin, David. *The Exquisite Life of Oscar Wilde*. London: Orion Books, 1997.

Campbell, Kathleen. *Beau Brummell*. London: Hammond, Hammond & Co., 1948.

Camus, A. *L'Homme Revolté*. Trans. Anthony Bower, *The Dandy's Rebellion*. London: Penguin, 2000.

Carassus, Emilien, ed. *Le Dandysme et la Mode*. Paris: A. Colin, 1971.

Card, Tim. *Eton Established: a history from 1440 to 1860*. London: John Murray, 2001.

Carman, W. *British Military Uniforms*. Feltham: Spring Books, 1968.

Castronovo, David. *The English Gentleman: Images and Ideals in Literature and Society*. New York: Ungar, 1987.

Chancellor, E. Beresford. *The Memorials of St James's Street Together with the Annals of Almack's*. London: Grant Richards, 1922.

Chandos, John. *Boys Together: English public schools 1800–1864*. London: Hutchinson, 1984.

Chenoune, Faid. *The History of Men's Fashion*. Trans. Deke Dusinberre. Paris: Flammarion, 1993.

Clark, Andrew, ed. *The Colleges of Oxford: their history and traditions. XXI chapters contributed by members of the colleges*. London, 1891.

Coblence, Françoise. *Le Dandysme: obligation d'incertitude*. Paris: PUF, 1988.

Cochrane, Alexander Dundas Ross. *In the Days of the Dandies*. London: W. Blackwood & Sons, 1890.

Cohen, Michèle. "The Construction of the Gentleman," in Gobel, Walter, Schabio, Saskia and Windisch, Martin, eds., *Engendering Images of Man in the Long Eighteenth Century*. Trier: Wissenschaftlicher Verlag, 1987.

———. *Fashioning Masculinity: National Identity and Language in the Eighteenth Century*. London: Routledge, 1996.

Cole, Hubert. *Beau Brummell*, London: Granada, 1976.

Colson, Percy. *White's 1693–1950*. London: Heinemann, 1951.

Connelly, Willard. *The Reign of Beau Brummell*. London: Cassell, 1940.

———. *Count d'Orsay; the Dandy of Dandies*. London, 1952.

Craft, Christopher. *Another Kind of Love: Male Homosexual Desire in English Discourse*. Los Angeles: University of California Press, 1994.

Cumming, Valerie. "Pantomime and Pageantry: the Coronation of George IV," in Fox, Celina, ed., *London—World City*. London and New Haven: Yale University Press and Museum of London, 1992.

Daudet, Alphonse. *In the Land of Pain*. Trans. and ed. by Julian Barnes. Jonathan Cape: London, 2002.

d'Aurevilly, Jules Barbey. *Oeuvres Complètes: Le Rideau cramsoisi*. Paris: Gallimard, 1970.

David, Saul. *The Prince of Pleasure: The Prince of Wales and the Making of the Regency*. London: Little, Brown, 1998.

Day, Roger W. *Decline to Glory: A Reassessment of the Life and Times of Lady Hester Stanhope*. Salzburg: Salzburg University Studies in English Literature, Romantic Reassessment and Portland, Oregon: International Specialised Book Services, 1997.

de Balzac, Honoré. *"Traité de la vie Elegante," Oeuvres Complètes*, 1830–35. Vol. 2. Paris: Louis Conard, 1938.

de Contades, G. "La Fin d'un dandy. George Brummell à Caen," in *Bulletin de la Société des antiquaries de Normandie*. Caen, 1954.

de Langlade, Jacques. *Brummel ou le Prince des Dandys*. Paris: Presse de la Renaissance, 1984.

Delbourg-Delphis, Marylène. *Masculin singulier; le dandyisme et son histoire*. Paris: Hachette, 1985.

Deschamps, Colette. *Sur les pas de Brummell à Caen*. Caen, 1996.

Donelan, Charles. "Romanticism and Male Fantasy in Byron's Don Juan," in *A Marketable Vice*. London: Macmillan, 2000.

Dumont, E. *La vie caennasie du Consulat au Second Empire*. Caen: Jouan & Bigot, 1929.

Ellmann, Richard. *Oscar Wilde*. London: Penguin, 1987.

Evans, Mark, ed. *Princes as Patrons, The Art Collections of the Princes of Wales*. London: Merrell Holberton, National Museums and the Royal Collection, 1998.

Feldman, Jessica R. *Gender on the Divide: The Dandy in Modernist Literature*. Ithaca: Cornell University Press, 1989.

Felstiner, John, and Gollancz, Victor. *The Art of Lies: Max Beerbohm's Parody and Caricature*. London: Gollancz, 1973.

Feschott, Jacques. *Sur la tombe de Brummell*. Caen: Société d'Impression de Basse-Normandie, 1932.

Figes, Orlando. *Natasha's Dance: A Cultural History of Russia*. London: Allen Lane, 2002.

Fillin-Yeh, Susan, ed. *Dandies: Fashion and Finesse in Art and Culture*. New York: New York University Press, 2001.

Fitzmaurice, Edmund George Petty. *Life of William, Earl of Shelburne, afterwards first Marquess of Lansdowne. With extracts from his papers and correspondence*. London, 1875.

Foord-Kelcey, Jim and Philippa. *Mrs Fitzherbert and Sons*. Sussex: The Book Guild, 1991.

Foreman, Amanda. *Georgiana, Duchess of Devonshire*. London: HarperCollins, 1999.

Foulkes, Nick. *The Last of the Dandies, A life of Count Alfred d'Orsay: Passion and Celebrity in the Nineteenth Century*. London: Little, Brown, 2003.

Fox, Wilfrid S. *Syphilis and Its Treatment: with special reference to syphilis of the skin*. London: H. K. Lewis, 1920.

Franzero, Carlo Maria. *The Life and Times of Beau Brummell*. London: Alvin Redman, 1958.

Fraser, Flora. *The Unruly Queen*. London: Macmillan, 1996.

Garelick, Rhonda K. *Rising Star, Dandyism, Gender and Performance in the Fin de Siècle*. Princeton: Princeton University Press, 1998.

Gathorne-Hardy, Jonathan. *The Public School Phenomenon, 697–1977*, London: Hodder & Stoughton, 1977.

George, Laura. "Byron, Brummell and the Fashionable Figure," in *Byron Journal*. London: The Byron Society, 1996.

Girault, Jean-Marie. *Mon été 44; Les ruins de l'adolescence*. Caen: Editions du Mémorial de Caen, 2004.

Gloag, John Edwards. *Georgian Grace. A social history of design, 1660–1830*. London: Adam & Charles Black, 1956.

Gordon, A. G. *Diagnosis of Oscar Wilde. Lancet*, vol. 357, no. 9263, April 14, 2001.

Grant, R. C. *The Brighton Garrisons, 1793–1900*. Worthing, CPO Print, 1997.

Hague, William. *William Pitt the Younger*. London: HarperCollins, 2004.

Halstead, Ivor. *Bond Street*. Falmouth: Barcliff Advertising & Publishing, 1952.

Hamel, Frank. *Lady Hester Lucy Stanhope: a new light on her life and love affairs*. London: Cassell, 1913.

Harper, Charles G. *The Brighton Road: old times and new on a classic highway*. London: Chatto & Windus, 1892.

Harvey, A. *Sex in Georgian England: Attitudes and Prejudices from the 1720s to the 1820s*. London: Duckworth, 1994.

Harvey, John. *Men in Black*. London: Reaktion Books, 1997.

Hayden, Deborah. *Pox. Genius, Madness and the Mysteries of Syphilis*. New York: Basic Books, 2003.

Hazlitt, William. *The Complete Works of William Hazlitt*. London: J. M. Dent, 1932.

Hetenyi, G. "The terminal illness of Franz Schubert and the treatment of syphilis in Vienna in the eighteen hundred and twenties," in *Canadian Bulletin of Medical History*. vol. 3, pp. 51–65, 1986.

Hibbert, Christopher. *George IV*. London: Penguin, 1972.

Hickman, Katie. *Courtesans*. London: HarperPerennial, 2003.

Hobhouse, Christopher. *Fox*. London: Constable, 1934.

Holland, Vyvyan, Holland, Merlin and Hart-Davis, Rupert, eds. *Complete Letters of Oscar Wilde*. London: Henry Holt, 2000.

Hollander, Anne. *Sex and Suits*. New York: Knopf, 1994.

Horne, Alistair. *The Age of Napoleon*. London: Modern Library Edition, 2004.

Houlding, J. A. *Fit for Service: The Training of the British Army 1715–1795*. Oxford: Clarendon Press, 1981.

Howells, Bernard, ed. *Baudelaire: Individualism, Dandyism and the Philosophy of History*. Oxford: Oxford University Press, 1996.

Jenkin, H. C. Fleeming. *Mrs Siddons as Lady Macbeth and as Queen Katherine*. New York: Dramatic Museum of Columbia University, 1915.

Jerrold, Clare. *The Beaux and the Dandies: Nash, Brummell, and D'Orsay, with their courts.* London, 1910.

Jones, Christopher. *No. 10 Downing Street: the story of a house.* London: BBC Books, 1985.

Jump, John D., ed. *Byron, A Symposium.* London: Macmillan, 1975.

Kempf, Roger. *Sur le Dandysme, Vie de George Brummell, Balzac, Baudelaire, Barbey d'Aurevilly.* Paris: Union Générale d'Éditions, 1971.

Kosofsky-Sedgwick, Eve. *Between Men: English Literature and Male Homosocial Desire.* New York: Columbia University Press, 1985.

Langley Moore, Doris. "Byronic Dress," *Costume, the Journal of the Costume Society.* London: V&A Society, 1971.

————. *Lord Byron: Accounts Rendered.* London: John Murray, 1974.

Law, Ernest. *The History of Hampton Court Palace.* London, 1897.

Lejeune, Anthony. *White's, The First Three Hundred Years.* London: A. & C. Black, 1993.

Levillain, Henriette. *L'Esprit Dandy de Brummell à Baudelaire.* Paris: Librairie José Corti, 1991.

MacCarthy, Fiona. *Byron, Life and Legend.* London: Faber, 2002.

McDowell, Colin. *The Man of Fashion: Peacock Males and Perfect Gentlemen.* London: Thames & Hudson, 1997.

MacKie, Erin Skye. *Market à la Mode: Fashion Commodity and Gender in "The Tatler" and "The Spectator."* Baltimore and London: Johns Hopkins University Press, 1997.

mac Liammóir, Micheál. *The Importance of Being Oscar.* Dublin: Dolmen Press, 1963.

Mannings, D., and Postle, M. *Sir Joshua Reynolds. A Complete Catalogue of His Paintings.* London, 2000.

Marchand, Leslie A. *Byron, A Portrait.* London: The Cresset Library, 1970.

Maxwell-Lyte, H. C., KCB. *A History of Eton College, 1440–1884.* London: Macmillan & Co., 1899; 4th edition, 1911.

Melville, Lewis. *The Beaux of the Regency.* London: Hutchinson, 1908.

————. *Beau Brummell, His Life and Letters.* London, 1924.

Melvin, John. *Eton Observed: An Architectural Guide to the Buildings of Eton.* Burford: Wysdom, 1998.

Millar, Oliver. *Later Georgian Pictures.* London: Phaidon, 1969.

Miltoun, Francis. *Rambles in Normandy.* London: Duckworth, 1909.

Moers, Ellen. *The Dandy. From Brummell to Beerbohm.* London: Secker & Warburg, 1960.

Mollo, John. *The Prince's Dolls.* London: Leo Cooper, 1997.

Morel, P., and Quetel, C. *Du Bon Sauveur au CHS: Deux Siècles et Demi de Psychiatre Caennaise.* Paris: Editions du Luy, 1992.

Muir, Edward, and Ruggiero, Guido. *Sex and Gender in Historical Perspective.* Trans.

Margaret A. Gallucci with Mary M. Gallucci and Carole C. Gallucci. Baltimore: Johns Hopkins University Press, 1990.

Munson, James. *Maria Fitzherbert: The Secret Wife of George IV.* London: Constable, 2001.

Murray, Venetia. *High Society in the Regency Period.* London: Penguin, 1998.

Northcoate, James. *Conversations with James Northcoate, RA, with James Ward on art and artists.* Ed., E. Fletcher. London, 1901.

Ollard, Richard. *An English Education: A Perspective of Eton.* London: Collins, 1982.

Oman, C. *Wellington's Army, 1809–14.* London: Edward Arnold, 1912.

Oriel, J. D. *The Scars of Venus, A History of Venereology.* London: Springer-Verlag, 1994.

O'Toole, Fintan. *A Traitor's Kiss: The Life of Richard Brinsley Sheridan.* London: Granta, 1997.

Page, Frederick, ed. *Byron, Complete Poetical Works.* Oxford: Oxford University Press, 1970.

Parissien, Steven. *George IV, The Grand Entertainment.* London: John Murray, 2001.

Peakman, Julie. *Lascivious Bodies, A Sexual History of the 18th Century.* London: Atlantic Books, 2004.

Perry, Gill, and Rossington, Michael, eds. *Femininity and Masculinity in Eighteenth Century Art and Culture.* London: Manchester University Press, 1994.

Pevsner, Nicolaus. *The Buildings of England: Berkshire.* London: Penguin, 1966.

Pine, Richard. *The Dandy and the Herald: Manners, Mind and Morals from Brummell to Durrell.* London: Macmillan Press, 1988.

Poole, Stanley Lane. *The Life of the Right Hon. Stratford Canning, Viscount Stratford de Redcliffe.* London: Longmans, 1888.

Porter, Roy. *Mind-Forg'd Manacles: A History of Madness in England from the Restoration to the Regency.* London: Athlone Press, 1987.

———. *Edward Gibbon, Making History.* London: Weidenfeld and Nicolson, 1988.

———. *Flesh in the Age of Reason.* London: Penguin, 2003.

———. *London, A Social History.* London: Harnish Hamilton, 1994.

Price, Curtis, Milhous, Judith and Hume, Robert D. *Italian Opera in Late Eighteenth-century London:* Oxford: Clarendon Press, 1995.

Pushkin, Alexander. *Eugene Onegin.* Trans. J. Falen. Oxford: Oxford University Press, 1995.

Quennell, Peter. *The Singular Preference, Portraits and Essays.* Washington: Kennikat Press, 1953.

———, ed. *Genius in the Drawing Room, the Literary Salon in the Nineteenth Century.* London: Weidenfeld & Nicolson, 1980.

Quetel, Claude. *History of Syphilis.* Trans. Judith Braddock and Brian Pike. London: Polity Press, 1990.

Rappaport, Erika Diane. *Shopping for Pleasure: Women in the Making of London's West End*. Princeton: Princeton University Press, 2000.

Renard, Maurice Charles. *Brummell et son ombre, Caen, 1830–1840*. Paris, 1944.

Ribiero, Aileen. *The Art of Dress: Fashion in England and France 1750–1820*. New Haven: Yale University Press, 1995.

Roe, Frederic Gordon. *The Georgian Child*. London: Phoenix, 1961.

Rogers, Samuel. *Recollections of the Table Talk of Samuel Rogers To Which is Added Porsoniana*. London, 1856.

Ross, C. J. *Old Bond Street As a Centre of Fashion 1686–1906; A Souvenir of the inauguration of the Business of J & G Ross, 32 Old Bond Street*. London, 1906.

Sampson, Geraldine. *The Uncrowned Queen: the story of Maria Fitzherbert*. Brighton, 1971.

Schoene-Harwood, Berthold. *Writing Men: Literary Masculinities from Frankenstein to the New Man*. Edinburgh: Edinburgh University Press, 2000.

Shiroff, Homai J. *The Eighteenth Century Novel: The Idea of the Gentleman*. London: Edward Arnold, 1978.

Simon, Chanoine G. A. *Le Bon Sauveur de Caen*. Caen: Ozanne, 1955.

Sitwell, Edith. *The English Eccentrics*. London: Faber, 1933.

Société historique du 6e Arrondissement (eds.). *Splendeurs et Misères du Dandysme*. Paris: Mairie du 6ème Arrondissement de Paris, 1986.

Sontag, Susan. *Susan Sontag Reader*. New York: Farrar, Straus Giroux, 1982.

Stokes, John H., Beerman, Herman and Ingraham Jr., Norman R. *Modern Clinical Syphilology; diagnosis, treatment, case study*. 3rd edition. London: W. B. Saunders, 1944.

Stone, Lawrence. *The Family, Sex and Marriage in England, 1500–1800*. London: Penguin, 1977.

Tannahill, Reay. *Regency England*. London: Folio Society, 1964.

Tenenbaum, Samuel. *The Incredible Beau Brummell*. London and New York: Thomas Yoseloff, 1967.

Thackeray, William Makepeace. *The Four Georges*. London: Smith Elder, 1879.

Timbs, John. *Clubs and Club Life in London from the Seventeenth Century to the Present Times*. London, 1872.

Tweedie, Ethel. *Hyde Park, Its History*. London: Besant, 1930.

Vance, Norman. *The Sinews of the Spirit, The Ideal of Christian Manliness in Victorian Literature and Religious Thought*. Cambridge: Cambridge University Press, 1985.

Vincent, Leon H. *Dandies and Men of Letters*. London: Duckworth, 1914.

Wagner, Peter. *Eros Revived; Erotica of the Enlightenment in England and America*. London: Secker & Warburg, 1988.

Wahrman, Dror. *The Making of the Modern Self: Identity and Culture in Eighteenth Century England*. New Haven: Yale University Press, 2004.

Walden, Sarah. *Whistler and His Mother: Secrets of an American Masterpiece*. London: Gibson Square Books, 2003.

Walker, Richard. *The Savile Row Story.* London: Prion, 1988.

Wardroper, John. *The Caricatures of George Cruikshank.* London: Gordon Fraser, 1977.

Waugh, Nora. *The Cut of Men's Clothes, 1600–1900.* New York: Theatre Arts Books, 1964.

Werner, Alex. *London Bodies: The Changing Shape of Londoners.* London: Museum of London, 1998.

Wharton, Grace and Philip. *The Wits and Beaux of Society.* London, 1860.

Wheatley, H. *A Short History of Bond Street Old and New . . . Also lists of the inhabitants in 1811, 1840 and 1911.* London: Fine Arts Society, 1911.

White, Chris, ed. *Nineteenth Century Writings on Homosexuality, A Sourcebook.* London: Routledge, 1999.

Whitwell, J. R. *Syphilis in Earlier Days.* London: H. K. Lewis, 1940.

Williams, Andrew P., ed. *The Image of Manhood in Early Modern Literature; Viewing the Male.* London: Greenwood Press, 1999.

Wilson, A. N. *London: A Short History.* London: Weidenfeld & Nicolson, 2004.

Wilson, Frances. *The Courtesan's Revenge: Harriette Wilson, the Woman who blackmailed the King.* London: Faber, 2003.

Woodfield, Ian. *Opera and Drama in Eighteenth Century London: The King's Theatre, Garrick and the Business of Performance.* Cambridge: Cambridge University Press, 2001.

Woolf, Virginia. *Beau Brummell.* New York: Rimington & Hooper, 1930.

Worster-Drought, C. *Neurosyphilis: syphilis of the nervous system.* London: John Bale, 1940.

Ziegler, Philip, and Seward, David, eds. *Brooks's: A Social History.* London: Constable, 1991.

Novels and Plays

NOVELS

Humphry Clinker, Tobias Smollett. 1771.

Evelina, Fanny Burney. 1778.

Cecilia, or Memoirs of an Heiress, Fanny Burney. 1782.

Belinda, Maria Edgeworth. 1801.

A Winter in London, T. S. Surr. 1806.

Tales of Fashionable Life, Maria Edgeworth. 1809–1812.

Sense and Sensibility, Jane Austen. 1811.

Pride and Prejudice, Jane Austen. 1813.

Patronage, Maria Edgeworth. 1814.

Mansfield Park, Jane Austen. 1814.

Beppo in London, A Metropolitan Story (satire on Byron's *Beppo*), Anonymous. 1819.

The Charms of Dandyism or Living in Style, Olivia Moreland. 1820.
The English Spy, Bernard Blackmantle. Charles Westmacott, 1825.
Granby, T. H. Lister. 1826.
Vivian Gray, Benjamin Disraeli. 1826.
Pelham, The Adventures of a Gentleman, Lord E. Bulwer-Lytton. 1828.
The Exclusives, Lady Charlotte Campbell Bury. 1830.
Arlington, A Novel, T. H. Lister. 1832.
Godolphin, Lord E. Bulwer-Lytton. 1833.
Cecil, or the Adventures of a Coxcomb, Catherine Gore. 1841.

PLAYS
The School for Scandal, R. B. Sheridan.
The Rivals, R. B. Sheridan.
The Heir-at-Law, George Coleman the Younger.
The Clandestine Marriage, George Coleman the Elder.
Love, Law and Physic, James Kenny.
The Poor Gentleman, George Coleman the Younger.
A Cure for the Heartache, Thomas Moreton.
The Wags of Windsor, George Coleman the Younger.
Life in London: The true history of Tom and Jerry, Pierce Egan.
A Busy Day, Fanny Burney.
Love and Fashion, Fanny Burney.
The Modern Theatre, a Collection of Successful Modern Plays, as Acted at the Theatre Royal, London, 10 vols., London, 1811.
Beau Brummell, [sic] *A Play in 4 Acts,* Clyde Fitch. New York, 1908.
The Beau, Ron Hutchinson. 2001.

Appendix: Chapter Title Illustrations

The chapter title illustrations and the explanations below are taken from *Necklothitania or Tietania, Being an Essay on Starchers by One of the Cloth,* printed for J. J. Stockdale, 41 Pall Mall, London, in 1818 and the slightly later *The Art of Tying the Cravat* by H. Le Blanc.

Prologue, Introduction, Chapters 1 and 2: The Art of Putting on the Cravat; The Gordian Knot

In the first place the cravat for this tie must be of ample size and properly starched, ironed and folded. It will then be necessary to meditate deeply and seriously on the five following directions:

1. When you have decided on the cravat, it must be placed on the back of the neck, and the ends left hanging.
2. You must take the point K, pass it on the inside of point Z and raise it.
3. You lower the point K on the tie, now half-formed O.
4. Then, without leaving the point K, you bend it inside and draw it between the point Z which you repass to the left, Y; in the tie now formed, Y, O, you thus accomplish the formation of the desired knot.
5. And last, after having tightened the knot, and flattened it with the thumb and fore-finger, or more properly with the iron, you lower the points K, Z, cross them, and place a pin at the point of junction H, and at once solve the problem of the Gordian Knot. He who is perfectly conversant with the theory and practice of this tie, may truly boast that he possesses the key to all the others, which are, in fact, derived from this alone. A Cravat that has once been worn in this way, can only be used afterwards *en négligée,* as it will be so much tumbled by the intricate arrangement.

Chapter 3: Mathematical Tie

There are three creases in the Mathematical or Triangular Tie. On coming down from under each ear, till it meets the bow of the neck-cloth, and a third, in an horizontal direction, stretching from one of the side indentures to the other. The colour best suited to it, is that called *couleur de la cuisse d'une nymphe emue* [trembling nymph's thigh].

Chapter 4: Tie Collier de Cheval

This style greatly resembles the Oriental, from which it is evidently derived. It has been greatly admired by the fair sex, who have praised it to their husbands, their lovers, and even to their relations, and have thus promoted its adoption by every means in their power. The ends are fastened at the back of the neck, or are concealed in the folds; a whalebone stiffener is requisite, but starch is unnecessary.

Chapter 5: Oriental Tie

The Oriental Tie (not City dandies but owes its appellation to the Gentlemen of the East India College) is made with very stiff and rigid cloth so that there cannot be the least danger of its yielding or bending to the exertions and sudden twists of the head and neck. Care should be taken, that not a single indenture or crease should be visible in this tie: it must present a round, smooth and even surface—the least deviation from this rule will prevent its being so named.

This neck-cloth ought not to be attempted, unless full confidence and reliance can be placed in its stiffness. It must not be made with coloured neck-cloths but of the brilliant white.

Chapter 6: Sentimental Tie

The name alone of this cravat is sufficient to explain that it is not alike suitable to all faces. Be assured that if your physiognomy does not inspire sensations of love and passion, and you should adopt the *Cravat Sentimentale* . . . It is for the juvenile only, and there should be something boyish in the general appearance of the wearer. It may be worn from the age of seventeen to twenty-seven; but after that age it cannot. It is more fashionable in the country than in town. Cambric is generally preferred.

Chapter 7: Horse Collar Tie

The Horse Collar has become, from some unaccountable reason, very universal. I can only attribute it to the inability of its wearers to make any other. It is certainly the worst and most vulgar, and I should not have given it a place in these pages, were it not for the purpose of cautioning my readers, from ever wearing it. It has the appearance of a great half-moon, or horse-collar. I sincerely hope it will soon be dropped entirely—*nam super omnes vitandum est.*

Chapter 8: Tie à l'Américaine or à la Washington

The shape of the *Cravate à l'Américaine* is extremely pretty and easily formed, provided the handkerchief is well starched. When it is correctly formed it presents the appearance of a column destined to support a Corinthian capital. This style has many admirers here, and also among our friends the fashionable of New York, who pride themselves on its name, which they call "Independence"; this title may, to a certain point, be disputed, as the neck is fixed in a kind of vise, which entirely prohibits any very free movements. It requires a whalebone stiffener, and is commenced in the same way as the Gordian Knot, the ends are brought in front and lowered and fastened to the shirt bosom, like the *Cravat en Cascade.*

Chapter 9: Maharatta Tie

The Maharatta, or Nabob Tie, is very cool, as it is always made with fine muslin neck-cloths. It is first placed on the back of the neck, the ends are then brought forward, and joined as a chain-link, the remainder is then turned back, and fastened behind. Its colour: *Eau d'Ispahan.*

Chapter 10: Ball Room Tie

The Ball Room Tie when well put on, is quite delicious. It unites the qualities of the Mathematical and Irish, having two collateral dents and two horizontal ones, the one above as in the former, the other below as in the latter. It has no knot, but is fastened as the Napoleon. This should never of course be made with colours, but with the purest and most brilliant *blanc d'innocence virginale.*

Chapter 11: Trone d'Amour Tie

So called for its resemblance to the Seat of Love. The trone d'amour is the most austere after the Oriental Tie—it must be extremely well stiffened with starch. It is formed by one single horizontal dent in the middle. Colour: *Yeux de fille en extase.*

Chapter 12: The Gordian Knot

Or *Noeud Gordien*—see Chapters 1 and 2.

Chapter 13: Osbaldstone Tie

This neck-cloth is first laid on the back of the neck, the ends are then brought forward, and tied in a large knot, the breadth of which must be at least four inches, and two inches deep. This tie is very well adapted for summer; because instead of going round the neck twice, it confines itself to once. The best colour is ethereal azure.

Chapter 14: Irish Tie

This cravat very closely resembles the Mathematical, and differs only in the arrangement of the ends, which in the Irish are joined in the front and twine round each other—each end is then brought back to the side it comes from, and is fastened at the back of the neck. A whalebone stiffener is necessary.

Chapter 15: Hunting Tie

The Hunting or Diana Tie (not that I suppose Diana ever did wear a Tie) is formed by two collateral dents on each side, and meeting in the middle, without any horizontal ones. It is generally accompanied by a crossing of the ends, as in the Ball Room and Napoleon.

Chapter 16: Tie en Coquille

The tie of this cravat should resemble a shell; it is very pleasing, and easily formed; it consists of a double or triple knot, and the ends are fastened at the back of the neck. It does not require starch.

Chapter 17: Napoleon Tie

I have heard it said that Napoleon wore one of this sort on his return from Elba, and on board the *Northumberland*. It is first laid on the back of the neck, the ends being brought forwards and crossed, without tying, and then fastened to the braces or carried under the arms and tied on the back. It has a very pretty appearance, giving the wearer a languishingly amorous look. The violet colour, and *la couleur des lèvres d'amour* are the best suited for it.

Chapter 18: Tie à la Talma

This style is worn in mourning only. It is placed on the neck in the same way as the Byron.

Neck-cloths should always (except those worn in the evening, and even then they may be worn, if the ribs or cheques are not too visible) be made of ribbed or chequed materials, as it makes far better ties than when the stuff is plain. Muslin makes beautiful ties, especially for evenings.

Independently of all these numerous advantages—what an apparent superiority does not a starcher give to a man? It gives him a look of *hauteur* and greatness, which can scarcely be acquired otherwise. This is produced solely by the austere rigidity of the cravat, which so far from yielding to the natural motions of the head, forms a strong support to the cheeks. It pushes them up, and gives a rotundity of appearance on the whole face thereby unquestionably giving a man the air of being puffed up with pride, vanity, and conceit (very necessary, nay, indispensable qualifications for a man of fashion) and appearing as quite towering over the rest of mankind.

Picture Acknowledgments

Ashmolean Museum University of Oxford: 23 portrait miniature by Henry Bone photo Bridgeman Art Library, 44 portrait miniature by Jeremiah Meyer photo Bridgeman Art Library. The Art Archive: 52 photo Eileen Tweedy, 53 photo Dagli Orti. F. J. Bertuch *Journal des Luxus und der Moden,* 1788: 38. Bibliothèque des Arts Décoratifs Paris: 50 photo Dagli Orti/The Art Archive, 57 photo Bridgeman Art Library. Bibliothèque Nationale Paris: 58 photo Bridgeman Art Library, 68, 69. Bridgeman Art Library: 48 caricature by James Gilray.

Bernard Blackmantle (pseudonym of Charles Molloy Westmacott), *The English Spy,* 1825, vols. I & II, illustrations by Robert Cruikshank: 10, 13, 16, 17, 24, 37, 42, 56, 59. Courtesy Bonhams, London: 18. Roger Boutet de Monvel *Beau Brummell and his Times,* 1908: 19. The British Library: 8, 24, 55, 56, 59.

The British Museum, Department of Prints and Drawings: 49 caricature by H. H. Heath, 62 artist unknown, caricatures by George Cruikshank 60, 63 and 65. The Committee of Brooks's, London: 3, 20, 36. Kathleen Campbell *Beau Brummell,* 1948: 74. Christie's Images, London: 14 painting by Francis Alleyne photo Corbis. Corbis: 61 caricature by George Cruikshank. Corporation of London, Guildhall Library Print Room: 41. George Cruikshank: 66 from *The Political House That Jack Built,* 1819, 67 from *The Men in the Moon,* 1820.

Richard Dighton *Characters from the West End of Town,* 1818–1820: 32, 33, 34, 35, 64. English Heritage Photographic Library: 1. Reproduced by permission of the Provost and Fellows of Eton College: 15. Getty Images/Hulton Archive: 7, 10, 42, 45, 54. Historical Picture Library/Corbis: 26, 27. Rees Howell Gronow *Reminiscences and Recollections of Captain Gronow 1810–1860:* 55.

Hermitage St. Petersburg Russia: 4 portrait by John Hoppner/photo Bridgeman Art Library. Captain Jesse *The Life of George Brummell Esq.,* 1844, vols. I & II: 72, 73. Julia Johnstone *Confessions of Julia Johnstone,* 1825: 47. Claire Davies-Kelly: 76.

Lady Lever Art Gallery, Port Sunlight, Merseyside: 46 detail of portrait by John Hoppner/photo Bridgeman Art Library. Reproduced by permission of James Lock & Co., London: 30, 31. Lewis Melville *Beau Brummell His Life and Letters,* 1924: 70 photo J. Preston Beecher. Reproduced by permission of Meyer & Mortimer Ltd., London: 28. Museum of London: 29, 32, 33, 34, 35, 51, 64. National Portrait Gallery, London: 5 portrait by Nathanial Dance. Private Collections: 2, 6, 9, 11, 12, 21, 25, 39, 40, 66, 67, 71, 75. The Royal Collection © 2005, Her Majesty Queen Elizabeth II: 22 *Soldiers of the Tenth Light Dragoons* (detail) by George Stubbs, 43 portrait miniature by Cosway. Stapleton Collection/Corbis: 16, 17.

Acknowledgments

This biography was mainly written in the Rare Books Room of the British Library, and in the London Library in St. James's Square—yards from Brummell's family home, his clubs and several shops he knew and frequented. I am enormously grateful for all the friendly assistance of the staff in both libraries, especially in the Rare Books and Manuscripts Rooms at the British Library, and to the London Library for trusting me with the long-term loan of a great number of first-edition memoirs written by Brummell's contemporaries. I would also wish to thank the staff of the Royal Archive at Windsor Castle, especially Allison Derrett, and of the Museum of London Archive, the Wellcome Institute, the Westminster City Archive, the National Portrait Gallery, the Guildhall Library, the London Metropolitan Archives, the New York Public Library and the Bibliothèque Nationale in Paris. Of the many small and private archives relevant to Brummell's life, I am particularly grateful for the assistance of Rob Petre at Oriel College, Oxford; Tony Trowles at the Westminster Abbey Library; Penny Hatfield at the Eton College Library; J. R. Webster at the Muniments Room Archive, Belvoir Castle; and Charles Noble and Hannah Obee at Chatsworth House, Derbyshire. Madame Geneviève Mouchel and Madame Dordron at the Archives Municipales de Caen were particularly kind and informative, and at the archives of the Hôpital Psychiatrique Départementale du Bon Sauveur de Caen, my researches were met with the dedicated interest of Professor Pierre Morel, who not only uncovered and guarded Brummell's medical records but also took the trouble to explain them to me, give me an "insider's" tour of the asylum buildings and shared his insights into the Bon Sauveur regime in Brummell's day and the psychological aspects of syphilis and its treatment. Without him this story would have been greatly impoverished.

~

For permissions to consult and quote manuscripts in the Royal Archive, I wish to acknowledge the gracious permission of Her Majesty Queen Elizabeth II, and with regard to other private collections, the kind permissions, access and help given by His Grace the Duke of Rutland, His Grace the Duke of Devonshire, Her Grace the Dowager Duchess of Devonshire, the provost and fellows of Eton College, the dean of Westminster Abbey and the provost and fellows of Oriel College, Oxford. All efforts have been made to ask relevant permissions, but I apologize here if anyone has been missed: full amends will be made wherever possible.

~

I have worked in the shadow of many writers on this project. There have been several previous biographies of George Brummell and I am particularly indebted to the research provided by Hubert Cole, and by Kathleen Campbell in the 1930s—an insider at the Foreign Office—in tracing Brummell's consular correspondence and Brummell family documents, and also to Maurice-Charles Renard, Jacques de Langlade and to Lewis Melville for their further insights into Brummell's time in France and with regard to Brummell's own writing. The monumental work of Captain Jesse, *A Life of George Bryan Brummell,* is the main source for any writing on Brummell. Any subsequent work on Brummell is in his debt and shadow. However, I should acknowledge also the inspiration of Jules Barbey d'Aurevilly's essay on Brummell, which I first read in the vibrant translation provided by George Walden, as well as key secondary texts that have allowed me fast access to the detail in the wide panorama of Brummell's life: the works of Ellen Moers, Roy Porter, Frances Wilson, Deborah Hayden, Christopher Breward and Anne Hollander, to name but a few, have all informed the style and substance of this book. I hope they would approve. Of those who have read early drafts of the text, and added greatly with suggestions based on their deep knowledge of the period, I would like to thank

Paula Byrne, Julie Peakman, Steven Parissien, Sarah Parker, Stephen Calloway and Victoria Kortes Papp, who also provided many insights into Brummell's possible mental state in her other capacity as a practicing psychoanalyst. My editors Rupert Lancaster at Hodder & Stoughton, London, and Leslie Meredith at Simon & Schuster, New York, have taught me the pleasure of being edited: I would like to acknowledge here my profound gratitude for their skill, support, patience and friendship. And special thanks are due to my dandy agent, Ivan Mulcahy, who first encouraged me to pursue the elusive figure of George Brummell.

$\sim$

I have endeavored, wherever possible, to walk in the footsteps of Brummell, so must thank many people for physical guidance: first, those at Donnington Grove, Berkshire, James Gladstone, Chio Gladstone and Brita Elmes, and also Karen Hutt of Donnington Grove Country Club; at 4, Chesterfield Street, Mayfair, and Chatsworth, Her Grace the Dowager Duchess of Devonshire, Helen Marchant and especially Iris Armitage, and at Oatlands Park, Susan E. Barber and Karam Dhala; at Hampton Court Palace, Sarah Parker, Mark Meltonville and Richard Fitch; in St. James's Street, Simon Berry, Carol Tyrrell and Julian Stevens, of Berry Brothers & Rudd Wine Merchants, and Anthony Lejeune at White's Club, and Mrs. Sheila Markham, Miss Elizabeth Goodman and Mr. Graham Snell at Brooks's Club; on Charing Cross Road, the staff of the Snuff Shop and especially James Clapham; on Jermyn Street, Christopher Fenwick and the Jermyn Street Association, John Gaze of the Carlton Club, Richard Briers and Lucy Briers have all guided me toward important information. At St. Margaret's, Westminster, and St. James's Church, Piccadilly, I would like to thank the staff and clergy and especially Mr. Wai Tsang, and at St.-Martin-in-the-Fields, Mrs. Sheila Fletcher. I would also like to thank Sir Martin and Lady Nourse of Dullingham House, and especially Gay and Martin Slater of Stradishall Manor, Newmarket.

In France, I was greatly assisted by the staff of the Archives Municipales de Calais, and Calais Syndicat d'Initiative, and in Caen by Direction Régionale des Affaires Culturelles de Basse-Normandie, and CH du BS Centre Hôpitalier Specialisé du Bon Sauveur—now housed in some of the asylum pavilions Brummell would have known. The staff of the Archives Départementale du Calvados, also at Caen, and the Caen Memorial were particularly welcoming, and my thanks are due especially to Madame Denise Vogt of the Temple Église Reformée de France in Caen for her help in tracing the church and cemetery archives via the Société d'Histoire du Protestantisme en Normandie. At Luc-sur-Mer, Monsieur Lamy Pascal and the owners of Le Grand Orient on rue Charcot were very helpful, and my thanks and acknowledgment for support also to Brittany Ferries, Ross Williams at Brighter PR, Andrew Bamford at Les Fontaines, Barbery, Calvados and Valentina Harris at Le Touvent.

~

I have been guided toward the manifold pleasures of fashion, clothing, fabric and decorative arts by Stephen Calloway at the Victoria and Albert Museum and Christopher Breward, and at the Bath Museum of Costume by Elly Summers. I am particularly indebted to Juliet Brightmore at Hodder for her keen eye, and to Edwina Ehrman, curator of Dress, Textiles and Decorative Arts at the Museum of London Collections, and Oriole Cullen, her assistant curator, for their generosity with time, advice and in allowing me to see and touch fabrics and clothes of the period. In terms of an education in the ongoing legacy of Brummell, I would like to thank Gieves & Hawkes, Hugh Holland, Lara Mingay and John McCabe at Kilgours, Savile Row and also Campbell Carey and Michael Smith, the last bespoke breeches maker in London. Brian Lewis and Paul Laverty of the military tailors Meyer & Mortimer Ltd., 6 Sackville Street—direct descendants of Brummell's own tailors, Jonathan Meyers—were also very helpful, as was Janet Taylor at Brummell's hatters, James Lock and Company of St. James's Street. Tom Ford, Oswald Boeteng, Dan Crowe and Lauren Goldstein have all offered ideas, advice and enthusiasm. Thanks are due to Joanna Morgan, Gabriella Ingram and Charlotte Sewell for their help in tracing the tailors and costumiers Alan Selzer, Clare Christie and Tony Angel. And the late Chris Prins at Cosprop Costumiers in London, whose intimate knowledge of Regency undergarments and details of nineteenth-century men's tailoring was probably unsurpassed, lent his usual good humor, taste and eye for detail to this project, as well as allowing me to try on original early-nineteenth-century menswear from the Cosprop collection. You are greatly missed.

On the subject of the Georgian underworld, syphilis, its treatment and history, I am enormously in the debt of Julie Peakman at the Wellcome Trust, Natasha McEnroe of Dr. Johnson's House and to Hallie Rubenhold and Jonathan Meades. My thanks also to Simon Chaplin at the Hunterian Institute and family members in the medical and scientific worlds: Mr. Andrew Kelly, Professor Donald Kelly and Dr. Kate Gurney.

For their thoughts on dandyism, I am indebted to George and Sarah Walden, Philip Hoare, Ron Hutchinson and Caroline Hunt, and on Russian dandyism in general and Pushkin in particular, I am grateful for the advice and translations of Tobin Auber in St. Petersburg. On the subject of Brummell in opera and drama, I am grateful to Patrick O'Connell of BBC Radio 3. With regard to Brummell's time in the Tenth Light Dragoons I am grateful for the help and advice of Richard Adlington, military historian, Major Tim Guthrie-Harrison and the staff of the National Army Museum.

For help with translations I am grateful for the kind assistance of Boe Paschall and Zacharias Rogkotis, language and classics lecturers at Davies, Laing and Dick College, London, and my brother David Kelly. I have borrowed frequently from the translations of Captain Jesse, Kathleen Campbell and d'Aurevilly's various adapters, but especially George Walden and D. B. Wyndham Lewis.

On a more personal note, I would like to thank Joe Guthrie-Harrison, Isabel Pollen and Hugo Wilkinson for technical assistance and special thanks are due to Hazel Orme, whose skill in close-detail copyediting is both fearsome and inspiring. Heartfelt thanks are also due to those many friends and family members who have extended hospitality, or, vitally, donated their time in helping out with child care. First among them must be my mother and father, but also Mo Guthrie-Harrison, Andrew and Kate Kelly, Brigit and Jerry Gurney, Andrew and Blanche Sibbald, Lindsay Clay and Matthew White, Neneh Jalloh and Dawn Mayne. For hospitality and help in the early months of this project and for their subsequent detective work toward finding Brummell's *Male and Female Costume*, I would like to thank Arthur and Ellen Wagner in New York and also Simon Green, Jason Morell, Deborah Shaw, Peter Tear, Elysabeth Kleinhans and all the staff at 59e59 Theatre in Manhattan. And for invaluable and friendly counsel in the British Library tea rooms and elsewhere, I would like to thank my friends Mark Ashurst, Philip Hoare, Ingrid Waasenaar, Kate Chisholm and, as always, Erica Wagner.

Lastly, but loudly, I owe thanks beyond measure for the forbearance, inspiration and patient interest shown over many months by Claire, who, like my son, Oscar, has simultaneously suffered my absences for months of late nights in libraries. I owe you both many bath times.

Index

About the Author

Ian Kelly is an actor and writer. He lives in London with his wife Claire and son Oscar. His first book, *Cooking for Kings: The Life of Antonin Carême, the First Celebrity Chef,* was published in 2003.